PRIMITIVE TRIBES (PVTGs) OF CENTRAL INDIA

By the Same Author

- Aadivasi Gramo Mein Tikkao Vikas Ka Yatharth
- Aadivasi Vikas: Uplabthiya Avom Chunotia (Part 1)
- Agricultural Modernization and Social Change in Indian Villages
- Dalit Agenda and Grazing Land to Scheduled Castes and Scheduled Tribes
- Dalit and Tribal Leadership in Panchayats
- Human Rights and Poverty in India: Theoretical Issues and Empirical Evidences (in 5 Volumes)
- Tribal Developments Since Independence
- Tribal Education: Implications for Development

About the Editor

Dr. S.N. Chaudhary, Professor of Sociology and Former Dean, Faculty of Social Sciences is also Rajiv Gandhi Chair Professor at Barkatullah University, Bhopal. He has been a fellow of the A.N. Sinha Institute of Social Studies, Patna, Indian Institute of Advance Studies, Shimla and SMH, Paris. He has conducted field work among Red Indians in British Columbia (Canada). Dr. Chaudhary has completed 28 research projects and has published over 31 books and 63 research papers. Currently, he is working on Social Status of Scheduled Castes and Scheduled Tribes, Tribal Youth, Tribal Senior Citizens, Persons with Disabilities among Tribes and Tribal Livelihood.

PRIMITIVE TRIBES (PVTGs) OF CENTRAL INDIA
Then and Now

Edited By

S.N. Chaudhary

CONCEPT PUBLISHING COMPANY PVT. LTD.
NEW DELHI - 110 059

ISBN-13: 978-93-5125-245-0

First Published 2016

Published and Printed by

Concept Since 1974

Concept Publishing Company Pvt. Ltd.
A/15-16, Commercial Block, Mohan Garden
New Delhi-110059 (India)
T: 25351460, 25351794, *F*: 091-11-25357109
E: publishing@conceptpub.com, W: www.conceptpub.com
Editorial Office: H-13, Bali Nagar, New Delhi-110 015, India.

Cataloging in Publication Data--Courtesy: D.K. Agencies (P) Ltd. <docinfo@dkagencies.com>

Primitive tribes (PVTGs) of Central India : then and now / edited by S.N. Chaudhary.
pages cm
Papers presented at a national seminar organized by RG Chair in collaboration with Anthropological Survey of India (ASI), Kolkata, Indian Council of Social Science Research (ICSSR), New Delhi during May 29-30, 2015.
Includes bibliographical references and index.
ISBN 9789351252450

1. Central India--Scheduled tribes--Social conditions--Congresses. 2. Central India--Scheduled tribes--Economic conditions--Congresses. 3. Central India--Scheduled tribes--Government policy--Congresses. I. Chaudhary, S. N. (Shyam Nandan), 1954- author. II. Rajiv Gandhi Chair in Contemporary Studies (Barkatullah University), organizer. III. Anthropological Survey of India, organizer. IV. Indian Council of Social Science Research, organizer.

GN635.I4P75 2016 DDC 306.0954 23

FOREWORD

This edited volume has huge contemporary relevance in understanding the tribal situation of Central India with reference to PVTG who spread across the regional boundaries of India. In fact, Prof. Surajit Sinha and B.D. Sharma's seminal book titled *Primitive Tribes: The First Step* published by Government of India in 1977, has brought this segment of Indian tribes into focus leading to state's special intervention through tribal development policy which is perceived as Tribal Sub-Plan (TSP) which became effective since Fifth Five Year Plan. Since then there are multiple publications dealing with the PTGs which was reframed as PVTG in order to shade off the conceptual negativity which was embedded within the word 'Primitive'. This precious volume with seventeen contributions is the latest addition for understanding as well as examining the existing status of such vulnerable tribes by engaging anthropologist, sociologist and other social scientists. This volume deserves special appreciation as the contributors collectively focussed on various crucial issues like education, health, economy or livelihood patterns which may provide much deeper insights to our policy-makers and various agencies to reassess the impact of developmental initiatives on this marginalised segment of Indian tribes who also deserves equal rights or privileges which our Constitution enshrined while formulating tribal development policy in post-colonial era. Of course, a few cases studies are incorporated from eastern India to reflect on some crucial domains leading to some sociological constraints which need urgent attention so that the PVTG can also lead a sustainable livelihood pattern which our nation must ensure.

Prof. Sarit K. Chaudhuri
Director
Indira Gandhi RashtriyaManav Sangrahalaya
Bhopal

PREFACE

Adivasis constitutionally known as Scheduled Tribes constitute slightly more than 8.2 per cent population in the country. It is claimed that their social and economic condition is not upto the mark. Historically, inspite of various efforts significant number of tribes have moved towards insecurity and deprivation zone. But the condition of primitive tribes, now known as Particularly Vulnerable Tribal Groups (PVTGs) is more pitiable and vulnerable. After identifying some objective parameters these groups were termed as primitive tribes. There are seventy-five tribes across the country who are PVTGs. Various efforts have been made to improve their quality of life and standard of living. But inspite of these initiatives they are still at the critical stage. Why it is so? What are the factors and conditions, both local and outside, which works as inhibiting factors for their development? Why it is so that even civil societies are not fruitful and functional for them upto the desired level? What effort needs to be taken for their holistic development in a sustainable manner? These are some of the pertinent issues which need introspection for academic and policy perspective. For this purpose in mind RG Chair organized a national seminar during May 29-30, 2015 in collaboration with Anthropological Survey of India (ASI), Kolkata. Indian Council of Social Science Research (ICSSR), New Delhi also provided partial financial support to organize the seminar.

Present volume is an outcome of the above seminar. Several papers were re-submitted after needful revision, but logistically only 16 papers are included in this volume.

I am extremely thankful to ASI, Kolkata and ICSSR, New Delhi for their kind support and needful help. I am also obliged and thankful to university administration particularly Vice-Chancellor Dr. M.D. Tiwari for his guidance and cooperation at all levels.

Prof. Jagannath Dash and Prof. S.N. Ratha delivered Rajiv Gandhi Memorial Lecture. Revised version of their presentation is published in this volume. We are obliged and thankful to Prof. Dash and Prof. Ratha. Prof. M.N. Karna delivered keynote address and Prof. K.G. Iyer delivered valedictory address. Presentation of Prof. Karna could not be included in this volume. We are also thankful and obliged to Prof. Karna and

Prof. Iyer. I am extremely thankful to all the scholars who participated in the seminar, particularly those who responded to our request and provided their articles in time after needful revision for its inclusion in the present volume. Paper of Sajal Samadder although deals with PVTG of outside Central India, but it has been incorporated in the volume to get an idea about the quality of life of PVTG elsewhere for comparative comprehension.

I am also obliged and thankful to Professor Sarit K. Chaudhari, who inspite of his busy schedule kindly wrote foreword of this volume.

Last but not the least, all the academic staffs of RG Chair needs appreciation and acknowledgement for their help and hard work in both organization of the seminar as well as preparation of this volume for its publication.

S.N. Chaudhary

CONTENTS

LIST OF TABLES

LIST OF FIGURES

CONTRIBUTORS

Prof. Abhik Ghosh, Professor, Department of Anthropology, Punjab University, Chandigarh.

Prof. Debashis Debnath, Associate Professor, Indian Institute of Forest Management, Bhopal.

Prof. Jagannath Dash, Professor of Anthropology (Retd.), Utkal University, Bhubneshwar.

Prof. K. Gopal Iyer, Formerly Professor in Sociology, Punjab University, Chandigarh.

Prof. Manish Mishra, RA, Faculty area of Forestry, Indian Institute of Forest Management, Bhopal.

Prof. Neelu Rawat, Assistant Professor in Sociology, Dr. H.S. Gour Central University, Sagar, M.P.

Prof. Prodyut Bhattacharya, Professor and Dean of University School of Environment Management, Guru Gobind Singh Indraprastha University, New Delhi.

Prof. R.K. Mohanty, Associate Professor, BPSPA, Odisha.

Prof. S.N. Ratha, Former Professor, of Sociology, Sambalpur University, Sambalpur.

Prof. S.N. Tripathy, Professor of Economics, Gokhale Institute of Politics and Economics, Deccan Gymkhana, Pune.

Prof. S.P. Sinha, Professor, Department of Anthropology, Ranchi University, Ranchi.

Prof. Sajal Samadder, Visual Anthropologist and Filmmaker, (Free Lance Journalist) Kolkata.

Prof. Sunil Kumar Yadav, Junior Research Fellow, R.G. Chair, Barkatullah University, Bhopal.

Prof. Swapan Kumar Kolay, Associate Professor and Head, School of Anthropology and Tribal Studies, Bastar University, Jagdalpur.

Prof. Tapas Kumar Dalapati, Assistant Professor, M.P. Institute of Social Science Research, Ujjain.

Prof. V.K. Srivastava, Director (Retd.), Government of India, SC and ST Commission, Bhopal.

Prof. Y.G. Joshi, Professor Emeritus, M.P. Institute of Social Science Research, Ujjain.

Prof. Yatindra Singh Sisodia, Director and Professor, M.P. Institute of Social Science Research, Ujjain.

1

Introduction

S.N. Chaudhary

I

No society can be claimed to be homogeneous. However, its rate and magnitude differs from society to society or within the same society at different points of time. Those societies and communities which are relatively more exposed to the outside world, including forces of modernization, the speed of heterogenization is relatively fast incomparison to communities and societies with having relatively insignificant and *ad-hoc* acculturation. And the process of acculturation is slow primarily due to extreme special and geographical isolation since long coupled with near absence of push factors because of match between aspiration and achievement. Low population pressure contributes to isolation. This state of affair refers to the stage of self-sufficiency. But at the same time it also refers to under-development from modern sense of the term. Today we have so-called modern and objective indices of development and if we examine social groups in the light of these indices we see that groups and communities with having least exposure to outside world are found to be more underdeveloped. However, to some extent they are more self-sufficient. But even if there is self-sufficiency, there is always possibility of its erosion primarily because of culture contact not induced by the locals themselves rather by the outside forces. And as the outside intervention increases, there is a possibility of (a) heterogeneity within the so-called homogenous domain, (b) erosion of century old nature gifted support base, and (c) trend of increasing dependence of locals on non-locals, both people and policies/ Schemes. Particularly Vulnerable Tribal Groups (PVTGs) known as Primitive Tribe upto 2006 are the best example of this process.

So far as PVTGs are concerned they are going through the processes mentioned above. And constantly the speed of the process is increasing. During the Fifth Five Year Plan on the basis of certain parameters, viz. *pre-agricultural level of technology, very low level of literacy, subsistence level of economy*, and *relatively stable level of population growth*, it was realized that significant number of tribes are still at the bottom of the development and there is a wide socio-economic gap between them and rest of the tribal population. Dhebar Commission (1960) did not use the term as primitive tribe in its report but listed 50 tribes (p. 3) which he termed as extremely underdeveloped. However, Report of the Working Group (1980-85) quoted Dhebar Commission by saying that there are four layers of tribals vertically on the basis of their livelihood and economic status. And at the bottom there are 50 tribes which he termed as "extremely underdeveloped". But report of the Working Group of Tribal Development (1980: pp. 165-66) identified 50 tribes as Primitive Tribe. Today the country has 75 tribes who are known as primitive tribe. Making comments on socio-economic status of these tribes Shilu Ao team (1969) said that such backward tribes are extremely backward and some of them are still in the primitive food gathering stage. This team also raised question about criteria of backwardness. It also recommended tribe-wise study of primitive tribes to know their status, so that, tribe-wise steps may be taken for their development. In the light of recommendations and suggestions of different committees special steps were documented in the first tribal sub-plan prepared by the Planning Commission. It recommended four following steps:

(a) Special attention should be given to areas and groups facing special problems including primitive tribal groups in backward pockets, shifting cultivators and tribals affected by major projects.

(b) For the purpose, these communities and groups should be identified adopting well-defined criteria.

(c) The tribal sub-Plan must attempt, in broad terms, answers for the main issues facing the tribal communities in these areas and problems of special groups.

(d) Special assistance be provided for such groups or communities against a basic policy frame which could vary from the general approach in the sectoral programmes, unfettered by the existing formal, procedural or legal frame. The final course could be defined only after fully examining the impact of all the factors.

In the light of the above suggestions to study and prepare tribe-wise status report of 52 tribes upto the end of 1980, 25 reports were prepared. On the basis of these reports following recommendations were made.

(i) High priority should be given to the programme of primitive groups in the current Plan.
(ii) Identification of primitive tribal groups in accordance with the guidelines already issued should be expedited.
(iii) Project reports for the primitive tribal groups should be finalized during 1980-81.
(iv) The project reports should *inter alia* incorporate the following essential features —

   (a) There should be a unique programme for each group;
   (b) The programme must specially take into consideration the eco-system;
   (c) The first phase of development should aim at conservation and reorganization of the traditional skills of the group; and
   (d) The second phase should spell out the development programme.

Report of the Working Group on development of the scheduled tribes during Seventh Five Year Plan (1985) also recommended number of steps for the development of primitive tribes. These steps are holistic in nature, but it has been given in isolation from socio-political undercurrent.

Hence, to bridge gap between the two and to improve life chances of tribes at the bottom not only they were termed as "Primitive Tribes" hundred per cent grants were made available by the Central Government and during 2002-03 to 2007-08 total ₹ 40 crore were sanctioned for their development (Annual Report: 2007-08), but also special steps were taken by the State to improve their social and economic status. Non-Governmental Organizations were also encouraged to provide inputs. Attempts were made to depute Government functionaries with number of special benefits and concession in the areas inhabited by Primitive Tribes.

To what extent above parameters of primitiveness were relevant then and now? What is the nature and dynamics of relationship between these parameters? Why forest based parameters were ignored? Why health question was not addressed? Making comments on these parameters Working Group on the development of scheduled tribes during Seventh Five Year Plan (1985-90) observed that it is difficult to lay down quantitative guideline for application of these criteria. There are tribal groups which fulfill the above three criteria but there are also other tribes which contain two criteria but such tribes are numerically superior like Baiga. Therefore, the report warned that while using criteria circumspection needs to be taken into consideration. Socio-ecological environment and its quality should also be taken into account (p. 87).

The above Working Group (1984) suggested a number of steps to be taken by all the stakeholders for comprehensive development of primitive tribes. Some of the important suggestions are as under:

1. There is need to carry out ecological study on all the primitive tribes to know their socio-economic and ecological status;
2. Special steps needs to be taken for improvement in their health status;
3. There are some primitive tribes who are victims of ecological crisis and degradation. Rehabilitation measure may be taken for them;
4. Project report with the help of all stakeholders should be prepared within the given time frame;
5. Working Group cautioned that there is need to careful identification and introduction of economic development schemes for them;
6. Population size of some of the primitive tribes are decreasing day-by-day. To stop this process besides socio-economic steps, genetical study of each of such tribes is need of the hour for curative step;
7. For their overall development both institutional and voluntary steps needs to be taken;
8. Instead of community wise steps there is need to take family-wise economic development measure for their development;
9. There should be complete ban on purchase and settlement of land and other property with outsiders; and
10. In all the development measures leaders and functionaries of traditional and tribal institutions must be actively involved at formation, implementation, field visit and review stages.

How and to what extent these suggestions were translated into action by change agents? What are the nature and background of institutional and voluntary intervention? How effectively the local culture has helped primitive tribes to challenge usual and extra-ordinary problems? How the forces of modernization and globalization is influencing them and their traditional support base? What efforts are required to meet their basic requirements relating to education, health, nutrition and disease, economic support base and so on? How they may be empowered in a sustainable manner? What are the inhibiting factors responsible for their backwardness inspite of the presence of number of enabling factors and conditions? How their problems may be mitigated and their status may be improved, so that, they may come out of the trauma of primitiveness and backwardness? These are some of the broad issues which were debated in the national seminar. The seminar also attempted to prepare agenda for their development which may be actualized by all the concerned.

Broad Objectives

Broad objectives of the seminar were the following:

1. *PVTGs:* Conceptual, Cultural and Constitutional Dimensions;
2. Socio-Economic and Health Status of PVTGs in relation to other tribal groups;
3. Institutional intervention and development of PVTGs: Status and Challenges;
4. Role of Civil Societies, local culture and tradition in their development;
5. Globalization, Social Movement and the future of PVTGs;
6. Factors and conditions responsible for their underdevelopment and backwardness; and
7. *PVTGs:* Agenda for their Sustainable Development.

Themes and Sub-themes

Some of the specific themes and sub-themes of the seminar around which deliberations revolved are as under:

1. Institutional and voluntary efforts for overall development of PVTGs and its developmental implications: Historical overview;
2. Approaches for economic development of PVTGs;
3. Approaches for educational development of PVTGs;
4. Approaches for health and nutritional development and diseases management;
5. Basic requirements and development related concerns of Sahariya, Baiga and Bharia PVTGs of M.P.;
6. Social and cultural practices of PVTGs and its developmental implications;

7. Factors and conditions responsible for development/ underdevelopment; and
8. *Holistic development of PVTGs:* Agenda for Action. There are Sixteen articles included in this volume. Most of them are emprical and field based. Attempts have been made by the authors to cover all these issues in their respective chapter.

II

Jagannath Dash raised two methodological questions in his chapter. He said that a single tribe living in four states are treated four times while preparing the list of primitive tribes, for example *Birhor* is a primitive tribe in four states and instead of counting it as one primitive tribe, it has been enumerated as four tribes in total number of primitive tribes of the country. Similarly, *Kamar* is a primitive tribe in Madhya Pradesh and Chhattisgarh, but the same tribe has been denoted as a scheduled caste in Odisha with a new name '*Paharia*'. Similarly, there are three names to refer to Birhor in Odisha such as '*Birhor*', '*Mankidia*' and '*Mankirdia*'. Instead of counting as one tribe, it has been classified as three primitive tribes in the state. Dash located several loop holes in the classification and enumeration of primitive tribes. To him this needs to be corrected particularly for their development. He also made recommendations for their comprehensive development.

K. Gopal Iyer examines process of deterioration in socio-economic status of primitive tribes of Madhya Pradesh, Chhattisgarh, Jharkhand and Odisha in the historical perspective. To him unregulated variety of acculturation of tribes of these states with outside greed centric forces and their capitalistic culture is primarily responsible for poor status of primitive tribes. The chapter also examines different forms of resistance against exploitative acculturation since, the British days and its consequences. Attempts have also been made to underline impact of Forest Rights Act 2006 in their life. Towards the ends Iyer has raised major issues which are food for thought from academic and policy perspective. The chapter is based on both primary and secondary source information.

S.N. Rath made an attempt to map development status of *Lanjia Saora* primitive tribe of Rayagada district of Odisha state. He examined some of the major schemes launched by the State for welfare of *Lanjia Saora* over the time. His work is an attempt to underline glorious ecological and cultural past of this tribe. The chapter highlights that of course some of them have improved their quality of life due to state initiatives but majority of them have experienced downward mobility in their life. Therefore, he has suggested various ecology friendly mechanisms for their sustainable development which are quite useful for change agents and development practitioners.

Baiga is one of the primitive tribes of Madhya Pradesh. They are found in districts like *Anuppur*, *Shahdol*, *Sidhi*, *Singrouli*, *Umaria*, *Mandla*, *Dindori* and *Balaghat*. On the basis of both primary and secondary source data Y.G. Joshi observed that status of forest have deteriorated in these districts which have raised serious livelihood crisis for *Baiga*. The development initiatives by the state have increased over the time, but *Baiga* is far away from these projects. Also, in terms of literacy and education, health and nutrition, cleanliness, better quality of life, etc. *Baigas* are underdeveloped although over the time state initiatives have increased. The chapter concludes that there is gap between promises and performance at the village level.

In Madhya Pradesh, numerically *Saharia* is the largest PVTG, the *Saharias* constitute 4.01 per cent of the tribal population of Madhya Pradesh according to 2011 Census. This PVTG is concentrated in remote areas of Shivpuri, Sheopur, Ashok Nagar, Guna, Gwalior and Vidisha districts. Though, the PVTG is demographically preponderant, the irony is that only 28.7 per cent of them and 15.9 *Saharia* women are literate according to 2001 Census. The data on the education levels attained by *Saharia* show that the drop-out rate is high after primary level. It declines sharply from the middle level onwards. The chapter is an attempt to examine impact of four schemes under conservation-*cum*-development programme to ensure educational development of Saharia tribe. It is an outcome of a major study conducted by Y.S. Sisodia and T.K. Dalpati.

Chapter of Abhik Ghosh examines status of vulnerable tribes of Jharkhand state. To him these tribes are still engaged in hunting and gathering for their survival. The chapter is based on secondary source information, the chapter underlines that these tribes are the victim of alien development process. It has eroded their bases of livelihood by damaging biodiversity. Their indigenous knowledge have been ignored while formulating and implementing development projects for them. The chapter pleads for an effective use of their resources, in a holistic manner, for their sustainable development.

Diyadi is one of the vulnerable tribal groups of Odisha state. They are mainly concentrated in Kudumuluguma and Khairiput Block of

Malkangiri district. According to S.N. Tripathy even today this tribe holds all the traits of primitive tribe. He has made this observation on the basis of information obtained from both primary and secondary sources. And accordingly he has raised doubt on the relevance and functioning of development projects especially meant for them.

Is witchcraft superstitious or a reality? What is the content of current public discourse on witchcraft and related witch hunting? Is witch hunting a gender based violence/systematic killing of women or are men also the victims? Is it an imaginary crime with lawless armies settling scores and unleashing rough justice? Is it community, culture or region specific? How can such vulnerabilities of the victims be explained? Witch-hunting today poses a complex threat requiring not only the actionable solution, but also meaningful explanation. These are some of the specific issues which have been covered by R.K. Mohanty. The study is based on secondary source information with particular reference to Odisha state.

The chapter of V.K. Srivastava deals with the stages of declaring several tribes as primitive tribes with particular reference to Madhya Pradesh and Chhattisgarh from development perspective. The chapter denotes that in spite of several innovative steps, the condition of primitive tribes is not up to the mark, primarily because of apathy and reluctance on the part of local level bureaucracy and other change agents. He warned that under the given scenario it is difficult to think that status status of PVTGs of Madhya Pradesh and Chhattisgarh will improve in near future.

The chapter of D. Debnath focuses on all the three PVTGs of Madhya Pradesh namely *Bharia*, *Baiga* and *Saharia*. They have historically developed and retained symbiotic relationship with forests and the mechanism through which community consumed, sustained and conserved the environmental resources and maintained equilibrium with ecological system in the past. The chapter is an attempt to document their indigenous techniques which helped them to sustain and retain symbiotic relationship between them and the local environment since long.

The chapter of S.P. Sinha deals with *Asuras* and *Birjias* primitive tribes of Jharkhand state from vulneration and development perspective. It examines role and importance of their traditional economic life, role of forest in their life, their engagement in new occupation like bauxite mining, etc. The author concludes that today status of their traditional sources of livelihood is at pitiable stage. They have been forced to move towards insecurity and marginalization zone. And the new initiatives, both by the state and private players, are either indifferent or dysfunctional to their needs and concerns.

The chapter of S.K. Kolay, Mahant and Bhattacharya deals with socio-economic condition of Saharia Primitive tribe of Sheopur district of Madhya Pradesh. The chapter is purely empirical in nature. Conventional techniques of data collection were used. Attempts have been made to examine impact of schemes implemented to improve forest management in a pro-active and positive manner particularly from livelihood and food security point of view of Saharia tribe.

The chapter of Sajal Sammadar is on Toto tribe of West Bengal. It is based on both primary and secondary data. He has minutely documented traditional features of the tribe. Also, state of affair from developments; perspectives have been examined and it has been concluded that inspite of the presence of the state their socio-economic condition is not upto the mark.

The chapter of Manish Mishra and D. Debnath examines role of traditional healers in health and disease management among *Baiga* tribe of Dindori district of Madhya Pradesh. It covers role of tradition and local culture in the collection, process and use of traditional herbs and medicinal plants in disease management among *Baiga* tribe. They have documented various medicinal plants and herbs and described each of them in terms of its use and importance in curing various diseases.

Neelu Rawat argues that historically Baiga women played crucial role in economic life. But over the time, as interaction of *Baiga* in general and areas inhabited by them in particular with outside forces increased, status of sources of livelihood decreased. And with this status of Baiga women also decreased. The chapter also directs some ways and means to improve socio-economic condition of Baiga women under the given economic ad political context. Her study is based on primary and secondary source information, relating to *Baiga* tribe of Baiga Chak of Mandala district of Madhya Pradesh.

Sunil Kumar Yadav examines social and economic condition of *Bharia* primitive tribe of Chhindwara district of Madhya Pradesh from development perspective. The chapter is based on both primary and secondary source data. It examines status and roots of the presence of all the three indices of backwardness, on the basis of which *Bharia* was declared as primitive tribe, especially in relation to various steps taken by the state and civil society organizations in the contemporary context. To him if welfare schemes directed to their concerns are not formulated and implemented, keeping in view their concerns, these projects are likely to suffer and they are likely to stay at the receiving end.

On the basis of analysis of all chapters included in this volume it appears that PVTGs have still to move miles and miles to improve their quality of life. They are still underdeveloped and marginalized inspite of the presence of various innovative development projects. Their traditional support base is decreasing day-by-day. And modern sources of livelihood and dignity is at a distant place. This calls for serious debate on relevance development model and schemes being implemented among them. It also calls for serious debate on the methods followed in the implementation of welfare projects.

REFERENCES

Dhebar, U.N. (1961): *Report of the Scheduled Areas and Scheduled Tribes Commission*, Vol. 1, New Delhi: Government of India.

Government of India (1980): *Report of the Working Group on Tribal Development During Sixth Plan-1980-85*, New Delhi: Ministry of Home Affairs.

Government of India (1984): *Report of the Working Group on Development of Scheduled Tribes During Seventh Five Year Plan-1985-90*, New Delhi: Ministry of Home Affairs.

Government of India (2007-08): *Annual Report*, New Delhi: Ministry of Tribal Affairs.

Shilu Ao, P. (1969): *Shilu Ao Commission Report*, New Delhi: Government of India.

2

Problems of Classification and Enumeration Among the Primitive Tribes of Central India

Jagannath Dash

Development of a social groups always needs the proper or scientific understanding of its society and culture. They may tribe, primitive tribe or a non-tribe. The proper understanding of a tribe cannot be possible without its scientific classification and enumeration, in the context of several other tribes and non-tribes. Therefore, it is strongly asserted that development of a so called Primitive tribe cannot be possible without its scientific classification. As in the worlds of plants, animals and even non-living materials, where scientific classification has provided the basic identity and scope for further research and development, in the world of human beings also, there is a similar need for classification and identification. It is worth-mentioning that where as almost all modern men have been duly classified and enumerated, in case of tribals a systematic classification has not yet been possible completely. Though majority of them have found appropriate place in the table of classification and enumeration, few of them especially the PVTGS are found to be misplaced and neglected. This has been emerged as a great problem in the field of their right identification which, undoubtedly, influences their development now and in future.

It is needless to mention that since the colonial time onwards, continuous efforts have been made to use different nomenclatures for the tribal communities and their identity. It is also marked that from time to time they have been rectified for getting a better term and identity. Every term has been devised for a better and greater identity of the community failing which a community can never be understood in toto. Even though such efforts are continuing, somewhere some mistakes have been committed knowingly or unknowingly. Mistakes are always mistakes which may create hindrances and obstructions in several ways in the path of identity and development. In our country, for the classification as well as enumeration of tribal communities, the approval of Government authorities is badly necessary and unless the officers-in-charge are convinced, it becomes impossible for the acceptance of a right category and its approval. Therefore, it is quite natural to say that Government plays the most vital role in the fields of classification and enumeration. Of course, the role of researchers and academicians is sought by the Government in such processes. But it is never mandatory. Thus, for all research and official purposes, the scholars are bound to quote the classification and enumeration made by the Government authorities whether they are right or wrong. Under such circumstances, therefore, attempts have been made in the chapter to identify the mistakes committed in the classification and enumeration of the tribal communities especially the PVTGs. As already highlighted, this is the basic requirement for the tribal development anywhere and everywhere.

Soon after Independence, Government of India gave priority to economic development of the country for which various national policies emerged in the fields of industry, forest, mining, etc., but human factors were neglected. As in the fields of classification and enumeration of PVTGs, in the field of "National Policy for the Tribal's" also we had to wait for a long gap of time from 1947 up to 2006, about 59 years. At the outset, it is to be mentioned that Government of India had enlisted 75 tribal groups as Primitive Tribal Groups (PTGs) which is retermed as Particularly Vulnerable Tribal Groups (PVTGs) since 2006. It is quite stunning to mark that there are few tribes which are found distributed in more than one states. They come in the list of PVTGs for individual states. If we make an addition of PVTGs in all individual states, they are found to be 75 officially. The way they have been classified in this list, after the division/separation of three states if we follow the same method or way, perhaps it would be 86 (if counted separately for Jharkhand, Chhattisgarh and Uttarakhand as new states). However, as such a method has not been continued for these new states so far, with only 75 PVTGs the discussions have been maintained here.

From Table 2.1, it is observed that tribe *Birhor* has been found distributed in five states namely Odisha, Chhattisgarh, Madhya Pradesh, Bihar and West Bengal and in the total list for India it has been added not as a single tribe, but as four tribes, therefore, from total list of PVTGs there is a need to subtract three here. Similarly in case of the tribe *Savara*, it is found to be distributed in three states namely Odisha,

Table 2.1: PVTGs in Different States and their Population (2001 census)

Sl.No.	*Name of the States*	*Number of PVTGs*	*Population*
1.	Andhra Pradesh	12	1,34,402
2.	Bihar and Jharkhand	9	9,372 + 2,23,327
3.	Gujarat	5	36,903
4.	Karnataka	2	45,899
5.	Kerala	5	20,186
6.	Madhya Pradesh and Chhattisgarh	7	9,38,190 +1,21,392
7.	Maharashtra	3	4,08,668
8.	Manipur	1	1,225
9.	Odisha	13	7,30,3309
10.	Rajasthan	1	76,237
11.	Tamilnadu	6	2,12,429
12.	Tripura	1	1,65,103
13.	Uttar Pradesh and Uttarakhand	2	5,365 + 4,72,883
14.	West Bengal	3	85,983
15.	Andaman & Nicobar Islands	5	672
	Total	**75**	

Source: The figures have been drawn out from *Census of India Report 2001*, Office of the Registrar General & Census Commissioner, Government of India, New Delhi.

Bihar, and Jharkhand and Andhra Pradesh (as *Kondh Savara*). Here also, there is a need to subtract two from the total list of PVTGs. The tribe Lodha is found to be distributed in two States — Odisha and West Bengal and here there is a need to substract one from the total number of PVTGs. The tribe *Paraja*, in a similar manner is found concentrated in Andhra Pradesh and Odisha, and here also number one is to be subtracted from the total number of PVTGs. The *Gadaba* tribe also inhabits in Andhra Pradesh and Odisha. Here there is no need to substract the number from the total number as *Gadaba* is not a PVTG in Odisha. The tribes like *Dongria Kondh* and *Kutia Kondh* are found distributed in both the States as mentioned below and here there is a need to subtract two from the total number of PVTGS. Lastly, the tribe *Hill Kharia* is found to inhabit in Odisha, Bihar (with Jharkhand) and West Bengal and here also there is a need to subtract two from the total number of PVTGs. Such statistical information may be presented in Table 2.2 for reference.

In the above mentioned table a tribe-wise list has been prepared which signifies its state of inhabitation. But in the state-wise list as mentioned Table 2.3, everything in detail has been given where population as per the 2001 Census can provide us certain clues for further analysis. From this table the detailed accounts of all the tribes (PVTGs) may also add certain new observations with regard to classification and enumeration.

Table 2.2: Distributions of Some Tribes in Multiple States

Sl.No.	*Name of the Tribe*	*States where Inhabiting*	*Number for Deduction*
1.	*Birhor*	Odisha Bihar (Jharkhand) Madhya Pradesh (Chhattisgarh) West Bengal	–3
2.	*Lodha*	Odisha West Bengal	–1
3.	*Gadaba*	Andhra Pradesh Odisha	—
4.	*Dongria Kondh*	Andhra Pradesh Odisha	–1
5.	*Hill Kharia*	Bihar Odisha West Bengal	–3
6.	*Kutia Kondh*	Andhra Pradesh Odisha	–1
7.	*Savara (Kondh Savara)*	Andhra Pradesh Bihar/Jharkhand	–2
8.	*Korumba,* *Koraga* *Kolam*	Tamilnadu, Kerala Karnataka, Kerala Andhra Pradesh, Chhattisgarh, Maharashtra	–4

Source: The figures have been drawn out of *Tribal Annual Report 2012-13*, Ministry of Tribal Affairs, Government of India, New Delhi.

Table 2.3: Primitive Tribal Groups and their Population in India as per 2001 Census

Name of the States/UT	*Sl.No.*	*Name of Primitive Tribal Group*	*Population as per 2001 Census*
(1)	(2)	(3)	(4)
Andhra Pradesh	1.	*Chenchu*	49,232
	2.	*Bodo Gadaba*	NA
	3.	*Gutob Gadaba*	NA
	4.	*Dongria Khond*	NA
	5.	*Kutia Khond*	NA
	6.	*Kolam*	NA
	7.	*Konda Reddi*	83,096
	8.	*Kondasavra*	NA
	9.	*Bondo Porja*	NA
	10.	*Khond Porja*	NA
	11.	*Parengi Porja*	NA
	12.	*Thoti*	2,074
		Total	**1,34,402**

(*Contd.*)

Table 2.3 (*Contd.*)

(1)	(2)	(3)	(4)	
Bihar and Jharkhand			*Bihar*	*Jharkhand*
	13.	*Asur*	181	10,347
	14.	*Birhor*	406	7,514
	15.	*Birjia*	17	5,356
	16.	*Hill Kharia*	NA	
	17.	*Korwa*	703	27,177
	18.	*Mal Paharia*	4,631	1,15,093
	19.	*Pahariya*	2,429	20,786
	20.	*Sauria Paharia*	585	31,050
	21.	*Savara*	420	6,004
		Total	**9,372**	**2,23,327**
Gujarat	22.	*Kolgha*		NA
	23.	*Kathodi*		5,820
	24.	*Kotwalia*		—
	25.	*Padhar*		22,421
	26.	*Siddi*		8,662
		Total		**36,903**
Karnataka	27.	*Jenu Kurub*		29,828
	28.	*Koraga*		16,071
		Total		**45,899**
Kerala	29.	*Cholanaikayan*		NA
	30.	*Kadar*		2,145
	31.	*Kattunayakan*		14,715
	32.	*Koraga*		1,152
	33.	*Kurumba*		2,174
		Total		**20,186**
Madhya Pradesh and Chhattisgarh			*Madhya Pradesh*	*Chhattisgarh*
	34.	*Abujh Maria*	NA	
	35.	*Baiga*	33,2936	6,993
	36.	*Bharia*	15,2470	88,981
	37.	*Birhor*	143	1,744
	38.	*Hill Korwa*	NA	
	39.	*Kamar*	2,424	23,113
	40.	*Sahariya*	4,50,217	561
		Total	**9,38,190**	**1.21,392**
Maharashtra	41.	*Kathodi*		235022
	42.	*Kolam*		173646
	43.	*Maria Gond*		NA
		Total		**4,08,668**

(*Contd.*)

Table 2.3 (*Contd.*)

(1)	(2)	(3)		(4)
Manipur	44.	*Maram Naga*		1,225
		Total		**1,225**
Odisha	45.	*Birhor*		702
	46.	*Bondo*		9,378
	47.	*Chuktia Bhunjia*		NA
	48.	*Didayi*		7,371
	49.	*Dongria Kondh*		NA
	50.	*Juang*		41,339
	51.	*Kharia*		1,88,331
	52.	*Kutia Kondh*		NA
	53.	*Lanjia Saora*		NA
	54.	*Lodha*		8,905
	55.	*Mankiridia*		1,050
	56.	*Paudi Bhuiyan*		NA
	57.	*Saura*		4,73,233
		Total		**7,30,309**
Rajasthan	58.	*Saharia*		76,237
		Total		**76,237**
Tamil Nadu	59.	*Irular*		1,55,606
	60.	*Kattunayakan*		45,227
	61.	*Kota*		925
	62.	*Korumba*		NA
	63.	*Paniyan*		9,121
	64.	*Toda*		1,560
		Total		**2,12,439**
Tripura	65.	*Riang*		1,65,103
		Total		**1,65,103**
Uttar Pradesh and Uttarakhand			*Uttar Pradesh*	*Uttarakhand*
	66.	*Buska*	4,367	46,771
	67.	*Raji*	998	517
		Total	**5,365**	**47,288**
West Bengal	68.	*Birhor*		1,017
	69.	*Lodha*		84,966
	70.	*Toto*		
		Total		**85,983**
Andaman & Nicobar Islands	71.	*Great Andamanese*		43
	72.	*Jarawa*		240
	73.	*Onge*		96
	74.	*Sentinelese*		39
	75.	*Shompen*		254
		Total		**672**
All India		**Grand Total**		**3,26,2960**

Source: The figures have been tabulated out of Registrar General of India data.

In Central and Central-Eastern India, majority of the PVTGs inhabit mostly in the inaccessible forest pockets. In Bihar and Jharkhand, Madhya Pradesh and Chhattisgarh 9 and 7 numbers of PVTGs are found distributed respectively. So far as the numbers of PVTGs are concerned, Odisha is said to possess the largest number of PVTGs in the country. Such facts may be observed from the Table 2.4.

Table 2.4: Distribution of PVTGs in Central and Central-Eastern India as per 2001 Census

Sl.No.	*Name of the States*	*Name of the PVTGs*	*Population*
1.	Bihar and Jharkhand	1. *Asura*	181 + 10,347
		2. *Birhor*	406 + 7,514
		3. *Birjia*	17 + 5,356
		4. *Hill Kharia*	—
		5. *Korwa*	703 + 27,177
		6. *Mal Paharia*	4,631 + 1,15,093
		7. *Parhaiya*	2,429 + 20,786
		8. *Sauria Paharia*	585 + 31,050
		9. *Savara*	420 + 6,004
2.	Madhya Pradesh and Chhattisgarh	1. *Abujh Maria*	—
		2. *Baiga*	3,32,936 + 8,993
		3. *Bharia*	1,52,470 + 88,981
		4. *Birhor*	143 + 1,744
		5. *Hill Kharia*	—
		6. *Kamar*	2,424 + 23,113
		7. *Sahariya*	4,50,217 + 561
3.	Odisha	1. *Birhor*	702
		2. *Bondo*	9,378
		3. *Chukutia Bhunjia*	—
		4. *Didayi*	7,371
		5. *Dongria Kondh*	—
		6. *Juang*	41,339
		7. *Hill Kharia*	1,88,331
		8. *Kutia Kondh*	—
		9. *Lanjia Saora*	—
		10. *Lodha*	8,905
		11. *Mankirdia*	1,050
		12. *Paudi Bhuinya*	2,46,573
		13. *Saora*	4,73,233
4.	West Bengal	1. *Birhor*	1,017
		2. *Lodha*	84,966
		3. *Toto*	—

Source: The figures have been drawn out of *Census of India Report 2001*, Office of the Registrar General & Census Commissioner, Government of India, New Delhi.

Apart from the above mentioned tribal problems as regards the classification and enumeration of PVTGs which reveal the repetition of one tribe in several states and enumerated as more than one. In this way, the total number of PVTGs in India will be much less than 75. If we consider Madhya Pradesh and Chhattisgarh, Bihar and Jharkhand separately like other States, the total number PVTGs will be coming to 86. However, the nature of mistakes both in the counting of 75 and 86 are same. Therefore, if we count each tribe only once in the total national list, then the total number of PVTGs will be exactly 65 only. This is a great problem at the national level. But coming to the state level problems of classification and enumeration, the nature of the problems are found to be more interesting and complicated. While mentioning about the specific problems at the State level, one has to go first of all, by the criteria of selecting a PTG or PVTG. So far Government of India has depended on a threefold criteria which is as follows:

1. Pre-agricultural technology of the tribe.
2. Below 5 per cent literacy in the tribe.
3. Low growth rate revealed by the tribe (a stagnant population).

In addition to the above mentioned criteria of PVTG selection, there also few more characteristics considered in the selection procedure, they are:

1. Tribes living in inaccessible and difficult terrain.
2. Material belongings being few and very simple.
3. Prevalence of communal ownership of land.
4. Authority vested on village headman and all ritual functions performed by a religious head man.
5. No written law present except tradition bound customary laws.
6. Slow in adoption, change and development.
7. Very little economic diversification.
8. Strong belief in supernaturalism, sorcery, black magic and witchcraft.

Though the criteria and characteristics of selection are definite and need to be strictly followed at the State or micro-level, in some way, mistakes have been committed both by the researchers and census authorities. Coming specifically to the case studies from Odisha, one may find several examples a mentioned below for reference.

1. Birhor

Birhor is a Mundari speaking tribe and the term *Birhor* is derived from the Mundari terms *Bir* (forest) + *Hol* (man). Thus, it refers to "man of the forest". However, the tribe is specifically dependent on the rope-making and monkey hunting. Because of their monkey hunting which is a very peculiar practice in comparison to the neighbouring tribes and castes, local people use to address them as 'Monkey hunters' which in local Odia is '*Mankidia*'. This term has two derivations — '*Mankidi*' in Keonjher and '*Mankirdia*' in Sundergarh or Western Odisha. Thus very interestingly the same tribe *Birhor* is known by three terms and in the Census of India classification and enumeration they have been designated as two tribes — *Birhor, Mankidia* in different regions of the State as already mentioned. Scientifically speaking, if we use the tribe '*Birhor*' correctly it would come as one instead of two. Therefore, here a correction of (–1) is required from the correct list of PVTGs enumerated as 65.

2. Ujia

The case study of *Ujia* in Odisha unfolds another interesting situation here. Up to 1931 census the community was enumerated as a tribe and soon after it was found to be deleted from the list of the tribes of Mayurbhanj state. On empirical enquiry, it was revealed that another community with a similar name '*Ujia*' was noticed by the census people in North Balasore, a neighbouring district of Mayurbhanj. The '*Ujias*' in North Balasore usually depend upon fishing and belong to Scheduled Caste status. On the other hand The *Ujias* of Mayurbhanj who are primarily hunter-gatherers mainly live on the forest resources of Similipal Hills. Because of their scanty population (below 300) around Similipal Hills, perhaps Census authorities must have considered them to be the migrants from the neighbouring Balasore district. Even though the '*Ujias*' identify themselves as a fraternal community of the Hill Kharias, a well known PVTG in Similipal Hills, and maintain livelihood as a hunter-gatherer. Their identity has been ignored by the Census authority since long. In their socio-cultural practices too, they have been maintaining marital relation with the neighbouring '*Saaras*', an acculturated section of the traditional '*Savara*', an ancient tribe of Odisha. However, under the term '*Ujia*' they have been still designated as a Scheduled Caste community. Their request for rectification of their SC status to a ST one especially a PVTG one has been severely ignored and the *Ujias* around Similipal Hills are now undone and helpless.

3. Kamar/Paharia

The example of *Kamar/Paharia* is another interesting case study in Odisha in this order. This community is identified as '*Paharia*' in

Odisha mostly confined to the Sunabeda valley of Nawapara District (border line between Odisha and Chhattisgarh) belonging to Western Odisha, where as in the neighbouring Chhattisgarh they are known as '*Kamar*'. It is very interesting to note that both the groups belong to the same tribal community living on the border line of Odisha and Chhattisgarh. For generations, they have been maintaining marital relation among themselves as belonging to one endogamous group. It is quite shocking that where as the '*Kamars*' enjoy a PTG/PVTG status a few kilometers away from the Chhattisgarh boundary line, only because of a different local name, the same tribe within Odisha border is identified as a Scheduled Caste.

This discriminatory incidence has been due to the lack of empirical research on the community within Odisha. They are called '*Paharia*' after the name of a particular section of the community which is forest depended and named as '*Pahar*' (hills and forests) or *Paharia* group. As most of the forest resources have been depleted on the Odishan side of forest, they usually depend on basketry or bamboo-craft out of the bamboos collected from the surrounding forests in the Sunabeda valley. In Odisha, usually, the basket-makers belong to Scheduled Caste Status and perhaps the Census data-collectors might have been influenced by the occupation to finalize their caste status. In this context, one more tribe may be added to the total number of PVTGs for Odisha.

4. Hill Kharia

The case of *Hill Kharia* has nothing to add or substract. They have already been designated as a PTG/PVTG long back and included under the micro-project for availing special assistance. But the historical background may be very much eye-opening in justifying the primitive status of a community. Centuries back in the history, *Hill Kharias* are upland cultivators outside the Similipal hill range. Due to the historical defeat by the *Bathudis*, a settled agriculturalist in the neighbourhood, *Hill Kharias* are to take refuge in the dense forest of Similipal Hill range. Ultimately the language and religion of *Bathudis* are imposed on the *Hill Kharias*. On one hand, being away from the cultivation and compelled to live amidst natural resource, the *Hill Kharias* gradually became dependent on the hunting and gathering economy. The process has rightly been designated as the secondary process of primitivization. In a similar process of transformation also *Birhors* shifted from '*Jaghi*' (settled) status to '*Uthlu*' (nomadic) type and remain as forest dependent primary hunter-gatherers. Such a process of transformation is called an

'Oscillation' process of change. However, such transformations are nothing to do with the problems of the classification and enumeration of the PTG/PVTGs.

5. Saora and Lanjia Saora

Both the communities belong to the generic *Saora* tribe, which has several sub-groups or categories with the suffix '*Saora*'. However, *Lanjia Saora* mostly inhabiting the hill tracts of Seranga, Puttasing and Chandragiri in Odisha are identified as the primitive section of the generic group '*Saora*'. Therefore, the inclusion of *Lanjia Saora* under primitive category has been rightly justified. But the inclusion of '*Saora*' under the PTG/PVTG category does not seem to be a right decision.

6. Malhar

The case of '*Malhar*' is a very peculiar one. This tribe has not been included as a PTG/PVTG in Odisha so far. It has been associated with another tribe '*Koli*'. Very interestingly *Koli* and *Malhars* are also found in Maharashtra as tribes. There they are having a large population where as in Odisha they are significantly few and lead an economically backward life. Like *Hill Kharia* they collect honey and other plant resources from the forest and earn cash by selling them in the market. Like the *Birhor* they are landless and even do not possesses even the homestead land. They mostly inhabit the forest clad regions of Dhenkanal district. They usually speak a corrupt Odia language under the influence of the local Odia people. But in their word formation, non-Odia compositions are very much observed which might have been continuing from the original stock in Maharashtra. Therefore, they are presumed to be migrated from Maharashtra through the hill terrains and river courses of Madhya Pradesh to reach the river courses of Central Odisha in search of natural resources as food and other requirements. Such a backward, landless, and homeless forest dependent community is very few in number and has not been able to draw attention of the Government to get a primitive status as a PTG/PVTG. It is also extremely shocking that so far as no substantial research has been made on the tribe. The State Government is still continuing with a brief account of few paragraphs prepared on the tribe during the British rule. In this way, though the tribe is qualifying in every possible way to conform the criteria of a primitive tribe, it has not been possible yet. Definitely this is a serious draw back in our development approach for the primitive tribes. Our classification and enumeration of the so called primitive tribes have seriously failed in certain cases like that of the *Malhar* and *Paharia* (*Kamar*) who are severely neglected despite their required qualifications as per the criteria. This is really most undesirable and should be rectified with immediate effect.

7. Jhara

The case of *Jhara* is a bit different from rest others as mentioned above. At present, they belong to Scheduled Caste category with a traditional occupation of fishing. But looking at their inhabitation near the hill streams mostly in the forest clad regions, the status is assumed to be different in the past. Unlike other fishing communities of the State of Odisha, they mostly go for gold collection from the beds of hill streams and rivers. Anthropological research confirms that the *Binjhals* of Western Odisha were divided into three divisions, namely — (a) *Binjhwars*, (b) *Son Jharas*, and (c) *The Binjhia*.

The *Son-Jharas* are believed to be separated from the main tribal stock in search of gold in the hill streams. Therefore, it is believed that because of their movement away from the original stock has gradually identified them with fishing occupation and gradually the status might be changed from the Scheduled Tribe to a Scheduled Caste. Though the case of *Jhara* is not related to the problems of classification and enumeration of the PTG/PVTG, it may be a classic case of detribalization which no Census or Government record has noticed so far.

8. Korumba, Koraga and Kolam

Beyond of the State of Odisha, three more PVTGs, namely *Korumba*, *Koraga* and *Kolam* in South India also reveal similar problems of classification and enumeration. *Korumaba* is a primitive tribe found in two States Tamilnadu and Kerala. But in the list of PVTGs, they have been counted twice. Similarly, the PVTG *Koraga* is found inhabiting in Karnataka and Kerala; the PVTG *Kolam* is also found in Andhra Pradesh and Maharashtra both the States. There is no problem to classify and enumerate them in two or more States. They should be included in the respective lists of the States where they inhabit. But to count them as two tribes in two States is perhaps not right. Under such circumstances from the total number of PVTG list –3 more to be deducted. Therefore, the total number of PVTGs in our countries would be 60 only if we do not repeat them in two or more states simultaneously. If special enquiries will be made in other states, similar problems may be found more in number.

9. Koya, Gadaba and Paraja

Besides the above stated issues regarding the problems in Census classification and enumeration where the tribe like *Paharia* (*Kamar*) who in spite of belonging to a PVTG, was excluded because of misunderstanding created by their occupation. The *Birhor* also faced a peculiar situation. Because of certain local nomenclature instead of one tribe, they are classified as three tribes. The case of '*Malhar*' is the worst of all the problems. They are the most eligible tribe for inclusion in the list of PVTGs for Odisha. But due to severe negligence, they are not yet enumerated as a PVTG.

However, there are several other tribal groups in Odisha who need to be excluded from the list of tribes and others who also need to be included for their tribal features. Specifically, there are also few other tribes like *Koya, Gadaba* and *Paraja* who fulfill all the criteria for their inclusion in the list of PVTGs. The *Koyas* once upon a time were maintaining a pastoral way of life and now an agricultural way of life. They still maintain their cultural tradition and are least influenced by modernization. They definitely need to be included under PTG/PVTG category. The case of *Gadaba* is also equally strong. They have primarily two sections namely *Bada Gadaba* and *Ollar Gadaba*. Where as the *Bada Gadabas* are acculturated and maintain plains land agriculture, the *Ollarrs* maintain shifting cultivation and a backward as well as traditional life. At least the *Ollar Gadabas* are found to fulfill all the criteria and conditions for their inclusion under PVTG category. The case of *Paraja* also bears eligibility to be included as a PTG/PVTG. Besides their traditional culture and backward category, they also have several traditional subgroups like *Bondo-Paraja, Kondh-Paraja* who need the attention of the authorities for their inclusion in the list of PTG/PVTG. It is needless to mention here that some sections of *Gadaba* and *Paraja* tribes are also enumerated as PVTGS in the neighbouring state Andhra Pradesh.

So far as the present list of PTG/PVTGs are concerned, the *Hill Kharias, Mankidia, Birhor* belong to hunting and gathering economy where as tribes like the *Bondo, Didayi, Dongria Kondh, Kutia Kondh, Lanjia Saora, Saora, Juang* and *Paudi Bhuinya* maintain shifting cultivation as their primary occupation. On the other hand only two tribes namely *Chukutia Bhunjia* and *Lodha* depend on agriculture as their primary occupation. It shows finally that majority of the primitive tribes in Odisha are shifting cultivators.

Thus, in the list of the PTG/PVTGs for Odisha whereas *Saora* and *Birhor* have been twice mentioned, a few other tribes like *Paharia* (*Kamar*), *Malhar*, and *Chenchu* have not been included at all. It is also quite surprising that *Paraja* (*Bondo-Paraja, Kondh-Paraja, Parengi-Paraja*) and *Gadaba* (*Bada Gadaba, Gutob Gadaba*) have been denominated as PTG/PVTG in the neighbouring State Andhra Pradesh where as they are considered general tribes just on the other side of the boundary in Odisha State. In between Odisha and Chhattisgarh, as well as Odisha and Andhra Pradesh such discrepancies are intolerable. This is definitely more than a simple mistake. For the sake of the so called primitive tribes especially their development, classification and enumeration need to be done very systematically or correctly. The above mentioned mistakes, therefore, have misled the scholars and policy-makers on one hand, and on the other hand deprived the tribes, who have not yet been included under PTG/PVTG list of their development.

Besides the PTG/PVTGs, such problems of classification and enumeration especially in case of other tribes in Odisha are also equally prominent. In Odisha the total number of tribes is 62. But on the basis of correct classification and accurate enumeration, it may be less than that. For example, the tribe like *Banjara* in Odisha does not conform to a tribal status. In all possible manners they are acculturated, modernized and comparatively developed than even the local caste people. However, they maintain traditional culture and backward economy in few other neighbouring States where they have been recognized as a Scheduled Tribe. Similarly as already mentioned, Birhors have been enumerated twice in the list of 62 where as the *Saora/Lanjia Saora* are PVTGs in Odisha, but they are a general tribe in the neighbouring Andhra Pradesh. Similarly, *Chukutia Bhuinjia* in Odisha are a PVTG whereas in the neighbouring Chhattisgarh they are not. The tribe *Savar* is included as a separate tribe in the list of tribes of Bihar/Jharkhand but in Odisha they are lumped together with *Saora/Sabara*, though in Odisha they reveal completely a different socio-cultural tradition and language. Few more tribes in the list may put forth similar problems in other states too.

Conclusion

The problem of the PVTG classification and enumeration is a very serious one. Unless we classify or enumerate them correctly, how can we include them for development planning at this age of modernity and post modernity where accuracy either in number or character is badly required for each and every form of planning and policy-making. Unless we develop the information and knowledge system on any matter so accurately how can the required achievement would be possible. Therefore, the above discussed problems of the classification and enumeration can directly reflect the reliability of our information and knowledge systems regarding the PTG/PVTG, and in a similar manner it can speak of their development on the other hand. However, the cited information and facts in the chapter are primarily based in the tribal situation of Central and Central-Eastern India with specific reference to Odisha. It goes without further confirmation that in other states too, similar problems of classification and enumeration must be existing more or less. If attempts can be extended to other States with a similar purpose and approach, perhaps the problems of all kinds can be sorted out which undoubtedly help the planners, policy makers and above all, the Government authorities for the prosperity of the PTG/PVTG in future.

REFERENCE

Government of India (2004-05): *Annual Report*, New Delhi: Ministry of Tribal Affairs.

3

PTVGs in Central India: Status and Challenges

K. Gopal Iyer

Introduction

The Pre-agricultural economic groups generally have been included in the Primitive Communities. The highest form of technology in the case of these groups can be said to be practiced by shifting cultivators. Shifting cultivation is a stage of graduation from food gathering and hunting to settled agriculture. The following are the most important criteria:

(a) Pre-agricultural level of technology;
(b) Extremely low level of literacy, i.e. below 2 per cent; and
(c) Near stagnant or diminishing population.

With this end in view, 75 communities have been identified so far in 18 States and UTs. The tribal communities are placed in the list of Primitive Tribal Groups on the basis of certain criteria, e.g. Tribals' practicing shifting cultivation and collection of minor forest produce. The Government of India had requested the State Government on 16.07.1993 and 20.08.1994 to prepare comprehensive project report and action plan for each identified Primitive Tribal Group. The Primitive Tribal Groups were facing several areas of concern like poverty, economic deprivation and erosion in their subsistence based economy. Their subsistence, sustenance and survival is essentially based upon water and forest, which form their life-line as they provide source for agriculture, shifting cultivation and other natural resources for their day-to-day living.

The PTGs have been enumerated in various census reports from 1961 to 1991 which include 12 in Andhra Pradesh, 9 in Bihar, 5 in

Gujarat, 2 in Karnataka, 5 in Kerala, 7 in Madhya Pradesh, 3 in Maharashtra, 1 in Manipur, 13 in Odisha, 1 in Rajasthan, 6 in Tamil Nadu, 1 in Tripura, 2 in Uttar Pradesh, 3 in West Bengal and 5 in Andaman & Nicobar Islands. As per 1961 census, their total population at All India Level was 7,73,704, which increased to 24,12,664 by 1991. The census data reveals that in 1961, their population was 7.74 lakh which increased to 24.13 lakh, i.e. an increase of 84.67 per cent as compared to 1961 figures. This goes to show that there has been gradual increase in the population of PTGs as against the apprehensions expressed in several studies earlier of the gradual decline and extinction in their population. Such apprehensions were due to the adverse land and forest policies both during the colonial and post-colonial period. The survival and sustenance intricately linked to conservation and utilization of these resources. Corporate protectionism in terms of patents and Intellectual Property Rights (IPR) arising out of various international treaties/ instruments on trade and common property resources such as TRIPS under WTO represents a real threat to economic livelihood of these communities as well as a source of potential exploitation of their resource base as bio-diversity expressed in life forms and knowledge is sought to be converted into private property and is treated as an open access system for free exploitation. It has been argued that there is an urgent need to provide appropriate legal and institutional arrangement for recognizing the rights of Tribal Communities to such resources and knowledge.

PVTGs in India

The Government of India recognizes that these are the most vulnerable sections among Tribals and inhabit isolated, remote and difficult and scattered hamlets and habitats. Recognizing the urgency and importance, the Government of India in the Ministry of Tribal Affairs formulated a scheme of development of PVTGs w.e.f. 01.04.2015. These PVTGs have been acknowledged by Government of India to be declining or having stagnant population with low level of literacy, pre-agricultural level of technology and economically backward. This has led to the recognition of Seventy-five groups of PVTGs in 18 States and 01 Union Territory as PVTGs (Government of India, MoTA Letter F.No. 22040/ 37/2012-NGO effective from 01.04.2015). The MoTA recognizes that most of these groups have not attained significant level of education, economic progress and are having low health indices. Hence, priority has been accorded for their protection and improvement in terms of the social indicators like livelihood, health, nutrition and education so as to decrease their vulnerability. The scheme covers areas relevant to the PVTGs and their socio-cultural environment. MoTA has requested the State Government to prepare "Conservation-*cum*-Development Plan (CCD) for each PVTG of their State through Baseline and other specific survey to make an impact on the improvement in human development indices and infrastructure.

In this connection attention needs to be drawn to the characterization of PVTGs in their perceived 'primitivism' and 'backwardness' as evident in official discourse. The report of the High Level Committee (Virginus Xaxa, 2014, p. 41) notes that the highly derogatory term 'primitive' continues to be used by the Government, media and NGOs. The present author opines that the PVTGs could be designated under the broad rubric of '*Adivasis*'. However, the term PVTGs could be continued to be used in the official communications to stress the fact that in various indices of development like Health, Literacy, Poverty, Socio-economic status, they are highly vulnerable. It is a prerequisite that special efforts should be undertaken both by the respective State Government and Government of India to tackle the problem of their vulnerability in various dimensions so as to reduce the critical gap not only between the PVTGs and advanced Tribal groups, but also with the developed non-tribals. The PVTGs are gradually getting integrated into the mainstream culture due to the prevailing development path and Globalization and hence, the emphasis by MOTA to State Governments to formulate specific development plan for each PVTGs needs special consideration. It needs to be pointed out that the PVTGs are also placed as subalterns within the broader tribal framework.

Demography of PVTGs in India

The Ministry of Tribal Affairs, (Government of India) has identified 75 Number of PVTGs in different States as per figures given in Table 3.1.

The number of PVTGs are the largest in Odisha (13) followed by Andhra Pradesh (12), Bihar and Jharkhand (9 each), Madhya Pradesh (7), Tamil Nadu (6), Kerala and Andaman & Nicobar (5 each) and other states have less than 3 PVTGs. However, with respect to the Population of the PVTGs, the highest is in Madhya Pradesh (28.38%), followed by Maharashtra (14.76%), Jharkhand (13.99%), Tamil Nadu (7.87%), Tripura (5.96%) and other States have much less population of PVTGs in the Country, as per 2001 census (Table 3.2). The States with the lowest percentage of PVTGs are Manipur (0.04%), Andaman & Nicobar (0.03%), Uttar Pradesh (0.19%) and Kerala (0.73%).

Table 3.1: State-wise Number of PVTGs in India

Sl.No.	*State*	*No. of PVTGs*	*Sl.No.*	*State*	*No. of PVTGs*
1.	Andhra Pradesh	12	9.	Odisha	13
2.	Bihar*	9	10.	Rajasthan	1
3.	Gujarat	5	11.	Tamil Nadu	6
4.	Karnataka	2	12.	Tripura	1
5.	Kerala	5	13.	Uttar Pradesh*	2
6.	Madhya Pradesh	7	14.	West Bengal	3
7.	Maharashtra	3	15.	Andaman & Nicobar	5
8.	Manipur	1			
				All India Total	**75**

* The number of PVTGs in Jharkhand are the same as in Bihar, i.e. 9; similarly, in Uttarakhand the number of PVTGs is 2 which is the same as that in Uttar Pradesh. If we include these two states namely Jharkhand and Uttarakhand, then the number of PVTGs would be 86 at All India level.

Source: Ministry of Tribal Affairs, Government of India, (F.No. 22040/37/2012-NGO) Scheme of Development of Particularly Vulnerable Tribal Groups (PVTGs) (Effective from 01.04.2015).

There is consistence debate about the extreme vulnerability of some PVTGs facing extinction. This has to be seen in the context of the inter-censal figures of 1961 and 2001. This is depicted in Table 3.2.

Table 3.2: Intercensal Growth of PVTGs State-wise between 1961 and 2001

Sl.No.	*State*	*No. of PVTGs*	*Population as per 1961 Census*	*Population as per 2001 Census*	*Remarks (% at All India level as per 2001 Census)*
1.	Andhra Pradesh	12	1,23,269	3,34,144	12.02
2.	Bihar	9	2,57,288	10,873	0.39
3.	Gujarat	5	N.A.	1,06,775	3.86
4.	Jharkhand	9	N.A.	3,87,358	13.99
5.	Karnataka	2	10,005	45,899	1.66
6.	Madhya Pradesh	7	2,09,553	7,85,720	28.38
7.	Maharashtra	3	N.A.	4,08,668	14.76
8.	Manipur	1	N.A.	1,225	0.04
9.	Odisha	13	N.A	68,745	2.48
10.	Rajasthan	1	23,125	76,237	2.75
11.	Tamil Nadu	6	93,794	2,17,937	7.87
12.	Tripura	1	56,579	1,65,103	5.96
13.	Uttar Pradesh	2	N.A.	5,365	0.19
14.	Uttarakhand	2	N.A.	47,288	1.71
15.	West Bengal	3	45,906	85,983	3.11
16.	Andaman & Nicobar	5	N.A.	816	0.03
	All India	**86**	**7,73,684**	**27,68,322**	**Increase of 35.78%**

Source: *Statistical Profile of Scheduled Tribes in India*, 2013, Ministry of Tribal Affairs, Satistics Division, Government of India, pp. 159-62.

The figure of Table 3.2 shows that the over all population of PVTGs in 1961 was 7,73,684 which increased to 27,68,322, i.e. an increase of 35.78 per cent in the total population during the inter censal period of 1961-2001. However, there has been decline of some PVTGs population in Bihar which is mainly due to the bifurcation of the State into Bihar and Jharkhand. The State-wise/Population also shows gradual increase in the PVTGs population during the intercensal period. There has however been some decline in the population of *Birhor* in Madhya Pradesh, Kota in Tamil Nadu and among the 5 PVTGs population in Andaman & Nicobar Island. The relative increase of PVTGs population at State level and All India Level is a *silver lining* inspite of the severe malnutrition and infant mortality among them (*cf.* Appendix I).

The demographic vulnerability of some of PVTGS in India is still matter of concern. This will be revealed from the data in Appendix II which shows that the number of Vulnerable PVTGs with less than 1000 population are six in Bihar (*Asur*, *Birhor*, *Brija*, *Hill Kharia*, *Khurba*, *Sauria Pahria*, and *Savar*), Kerala (*Cholanaikan*), Madhya Pradesh (*Birhor*), Odisha (*Birhor*), Tamil Nadu (*Kora* and *Toda*), Uttar Pradesh (*Raji*) and Uttarakhand, Andaman & Nicobar (Great Andamanese, *Jarawa*, *Onge*, *Sentinelest*, *Shom Pen*). Special efforts are needed to tackle the acute vulnerability of such demographically endangered tribes.

Advasis in Jharkhand

It is obvious that Scheduled Tribe is not a monolithic group. Everywhere in the country the tribes show a great variation in economic, social, political, educational and health spheres even within the tribal group. The thirty tribes of Jharkhand were categorized by Vidyarthi (1958) in the following manner:

1. Hunter-gatherers — *Birhor*, *Korwa*, *Parhaiya*, etc.
2. Shifting Cultivators — *Sauria Paharia*, *Mal Pharia*, *Birjia*, *Asur*, etc.
3. Simple Artisans — *Mahli*, *Chik Baraik*, *Lohra*, *Karmali*, etc.
4. Settled Agriculturists — *Santhal*, *Munda*, *Oraon*, *Ho*, *Kharia*, *Kharwar*, etc.

The Tribals in Jharkhand can be classified into four-fold taking into account the changing social, economic and political perspective.

1. Settled Agriculturists
2. Simple Artisans

3. Neglected Tribes
4. Primitive Tribal Group

The settled agriculturists are the most populous and constitute nearly 87 per cent of the total tribal population. The "simple Artisans" Tribes are scattered throughout Jharkhand and they are the "Service Tribes". They provide the basic material needs to the Agriculturists like Utensils, Implements, Clothes, Tools and Weapons. In a single village only few families of these Artisan Tribes reside. They constitute 5.81 per cent of the total tribal population. *The Neglected Tribes* of Jharkhand are *Baiga, Banjara, Bathudi, Bedia, Chero, Gorait, Khond, Kisan*, and *Kora*. They are numerically insignificant, economically weak, politically ineffective and educationally scrawny. They have neither sufficient land nor assured means of livelihood. These tribes depend upon their more affluent brethren in the settled tribal groups for jobs in the fields as agriculture labourers and wage earners. They supplement their meagre income by collecting the Minor Forest Produce and working as contract labourers, rickshaw pullers, coolies, etc. They constitute 3.45 per cent of total tribal population, slightly less than the PVTGs. Their share of literates is only 2.39 per cent of total tribal literates in the State, marginally higher than the PVTGs. Though not pursuing hunting and shifting cultivation, their method of farming is quite primitive and their economic security is equally precarious.

The total population of the nine PVTGs according to 2001 census in the State Jharkhand is around 2.73 lakh. There are 32 tribes (2011) in Jharkhand of which Santhals are most numerous accounting for one third of the total tribal population followed by *Oraon, Munda* and *Ho* contributing more than 10 per cent to the total tribal population. Other tribes such as *Kharwar, Lohra, Bhumij* and *Kharia* have a share of less than 3 per cent each while *Mahli, Mal Pahariya, Bedia* and *Chero* have share of 1-2 per cent each. The tribes with less than 1 per cent contribution to the States tribal population include *Karmali, Gond, Chick Baraik, Generic* tribes, *Kisan, Sauria Paharia, Korwa, Kora, Paharia, Binjhia, Asur* and *Birhor*. The most marginalized tribes with less than 0.01 per cent are *Savar, Birjia, Gorait, Baiga, Bathudi, Banjara* and *Khond*. The *Birjias, Birhors, Korwa, Paryhaiyas* and *Asures* have been declared as the world's most endangered tribes in the country by UNESCO.

The PVTGs in Jharkhand are *Asur, Binjhia, Birhor, Birjia, Korwa, Mal Paharia, Parhaiya, Sauria Paharia* and *Savar* and they comprise of the hunter-gatherer and shifting cultivator groups. Their total population as per 1990-91 census was 2.30 lakh constituting 3.42 per cent of the total tribal population. The most numerous among them are *Mal Paharia* (86790), *Sauria Paharia* (48761), *Parhaiya* (30421), *Korwa* (23748), *Binjhia* (13090) and other PTGs namely *Asur*, *Birhor*, *Birjia* and *Savar* have less than 10,000 populations each. Their literacy percentage ranges from 5.74 per cent to 15.30 per cent as per 1990-91census. They depend for the livelihood on hunting, food gathering, fishing, shifting cultivation and collection of minor forest produce. Dwindling forest have made their traditional occupation totally unproductive. On the other hand, they are unable to adjust to the newer occupation because of their culture and tradition.

Pahariyas are one of the earliest inhabitant and PVTGs of the Santhal Pargana region. The PTVGs has now been pushed to the edge and is an ecologically and biologically endangered tribe. They go on hunting-expeditions, practice share-cropping as well as shifting cultivation. Most of the families live in mud houses, collect firewood from forest and practice herbal medicine. (Sanjay Ojha, "Jharkhand fails to Protect its Primitive tribes", *TNN*, July 17, 2013). The other PTVGs of Jharkhand, who are also living in the same deprived condition are *Asur*, *Birhor*, *Birajia*, *Korwa*, *Savar*, *Paharia* (*Baiga*), *Mal Pahariya* and *Souriya Pahariya*. The population of PVTGs in Jharkhand during 1991 was 2.30 lakh, constituting 3.42 per cent of the total tribal population in the State of Jharkhand. As per details given in Table 3.3.

Table 3.3: Population of PVTGs in Jharkhand as per 1991 Census

Sl.No.	*Name of Tribe*	*Total Population*	*Per cent to Total Tribal Population in the State*	*Literacy per cent as per 1991 Census*
1.	*Asur*	9,623	0.14	10.37
2.	*Binjhia*	13,090	0.19	14.52
3.	*Birhor*	8,159	0.12	5.74
4.	*Birjia*	5,191	0.07	10.50
5.	*Korwa*	23,748	0.35	6.14
6.	*Mal Paharia*	86,790	1.31	7.38
7.	*Parhaiya*	30,421	0.45	15.30
8.	*Sauria Paharia*	48,761	0.73	6.87
9.	*Savar*	4,264	0.06	9.55
	Total	**2,30,047**	**3.42**	**86.37**
	Average per tribe	**25,561**	**0.38**	

Source: Census of India 1991.

The PVTGs in Jharkhand have been characterized as economically backward and some on the verge of extinctions. The Birhors living in Tandas have very low literacy rate and they have very small plot of cultivable land among them per family 0.82 hectares. Their average monthly income is just between ₹ 500 to ₹ 1,000. They are severely dependent on natural resources for their livelihood. For ages they have been living in, and on, the forests. With the introduction of various forest protection laws their existence has become very precarious as these laws have hit them hard. Various studies show that, especially in the Reserved Forest areas and sanctuaries such as Betala in Palamau, and National Park in Hazaribagh, their life is cheaper than that of the animals. Dwindling forests have made their traditional occupation totally unproductive. They are unable to adjust to the newer occupations because their culture still is a product of the other traditions; and to the various development and welfare programmes instituted by the Government, because their ethos cannot accept these. They are suffering from an alarming malnutrition and high illiteracy. The Jharkhand administration has introduced certain developmental measures like housing scheme, public distribution system and other welfare schemes to protect them economically.

In October 2008, at least 20 people belonging to PVTG died in different districts of Jharkhand. While social workers and advisor to the Commissioner of Supreme Court (to monitor food for security programme) cite hunger as the cause of these deaths, the committee of secretaries appointed by the State Government *give food poisoning as the reason*. Of the 20 reported deaths of PTG, 17 belonging to *Birhor* and *Paharia* (*Baiga*) died along in Chatra districts two villages, in Hindiakala village of Chatra district, around 210 km. from capital Ranchi, nine members of *Birhor* tribe died in the first week of October 2008. The Hindiakala village death was followed by death of eight *Baiga* tribe members in Bhitaha village of the same district. Two members of *Birhor* tribe died in Koderma district and one death has been reported in Dumka district. The State Government had constituted a three-member Committee of Secretaries (CoS) to find out the facts and submit a report on the condition of primitive tribes and circumstances of death. Ruling out hunger as the cause of deaths the CoS indicated failure of Administrative system in implementing the Government schemes. "There was no post-mortem of the deceased and therefore the exact reason of death can only be a matter of conjecture". The *Birhors* took rice and *saag* (leafy vegetable) on the night they died. The suspected poisonous *saag* could be *bathua*. The report further says, Starvation death cannot happen in this pattern as the age of deceased varies from one-and-a-half-year to 60 years. The CoS also expressed unhappiness for not providing foodgrains to *Birhors* under *Antodaya/Annapurna* Rice Schemes under which Government supplies it to PTG at the rate of ₹ 3 per kg. It is unfortunate that *Antodaya/Annapurna* rice was not made available to the *Birhors* of Hindiakala for previous six months. The *Angnawadi Kendra* is non-functional for two years, while the nearest health centre is 12 km. from the village. After deaths of 20 primitive tribes Jharkhand Ex-Chief Minister Shibu Soren has announced to supply foodgrains to PTG free of cost. Keeping in view the extremely low life standards of these communities the State of Jharkhand has started Chief Minister's Special Food Security Scheme for Paharia Primitive Tribal Group. The State Government has started a scheme under which food grains (rice and wheat) are being made available free of cost to all families of Primitive Tribes. Under this scheme each family of Primitive Tribe will get 35 kg. of food grains rice per month.

Ranjana Agarwal (2013), Assistant Professor of Economics at IMT, Ghaziabad had undertaken a Research Study along with some Research Scholars on the initiative taken by Tata Steel under CSR initiatives of welfare activities for PVTGs in Jharkhand, (*AIMA Journal of Management and Research*, February 2013, Volume 7, issue 1/4 ISSN 0974-497 Copy right © 2013). According to their study, the Tata Steel Company is promoting the cause of 2 PVTGs, namely *Birhor* and *Savar*, residing in Patamda and Jamshedpur Blocks of Jharkhand. The sample size consisted of five villages each having a population ranging from 100-150. The data was collected during second week of June 2012. Tata Steel adopted these villages as part of CSR activities since 2008. Their houses are erected with bamboo, wood and mud walls. Their families are nuclear in structure. The usual way of acquiring bride is through bride-price. The main economic activities of *Savars* are basketry, collection of Minor Forest Produce, Lac cultivation and agriculture. Their village head is called *Manjhi*, who holds rent free land for his service. *Savars* occupy 0.05 per cent of the total tribal population in Jharkhand. *Birhors* constitute 0.6 per cent of tribal population in Jharkhand. Their population in 2001 was 4057. They are traditionally nomadic. *Birhor* is made up of two words, viz. *Bir* (Jungle) and *Hor* (Man), which means 'man of the jungle'; they are people belonging to forests. They consider themselves as descendents of the Sun. They live in groups known as '*Tandas*'. They are occupationally divided into two groups namely, *Uthlu Birhor*, who are *Nomads*, Hunters and Rope Makers; the other group is known as *Janghi Birhor*, who are settled as agriculturists. They are mostly landless and earn their living by rope making, hunting, food gathering and fishing. The Tata Cultural Society arranges bead and jute handicraft making, paper making, candle making, stone carving, etc. and promote Self-Help-Group (SHG) to make them economically self-dependent. The Tata Cultural Society also promotes education among the Tribal children and it also promotes tribal's scholarship. Women Self-Help-Groups have been trained in income earning activities like production of Bamboo, Cultivating Kitchen Garden and they are also providing medical facilities to them (*AIMA Journal of Management and Research*, February, 2013). They provide financial support worth ₹ 25 lakh to more than 493 meritorious tribal students each year since 2004. Fifty matriculate students are identified every year for coaching that prepares them for higher studies in accordance with the Affirmative Action Policy. In 2009-10, a total of 646 students were supported. To help underprivileged girl children enter the mainstream of learning, a camp school programme was initiated with the help of the Jharkhand Education project. The nine-month intensive learning course offered to students aged 9-14 makes up for education lost till the Vth standard and qualifies them for admission to class VI. In 2009-10, 200 girl children enrolled in the two camp schools. In the Villages under Tata Steel, TSRDC is providing health facilities. All villages have access to clean drinking water. All villages have at least one well and one hand pump. Post Offices are available in all villages while banks are available in seven villages. People have accounts in Banks to access NREGA funds. Many families have a mobile. Most of the selected villages have primary and upper primary schools, with Sarva Shiksha Abhiyan. The *Sabar* and *Birhor* families started kitchen gardens with support from TCS.

Study on Primitive Tribes in Odisha

The Tribes of Odisha are grouped on the basis of traditional economy as — (a) hunters and food-gatherers, (b) cattle herders, (c) simple artisans, (d) shifting cultivators, (e) settled agriculturists, and (f) industrial workers. The SCSTRTI, (Bhubaneswar, 2010), has included various tribal groups under different categories based on their traditional economy:

(i) The Tribes to be included in the *first group* are the *Mankidia*, *Mankirdia*, *Hill Kharia*, *Birhor*, *Malhar* and the *Korwa*; they exclusively depend on forests for their livelihood. They are semi-nomadic and mainly inhabit the forest areas of Sundargarh and Mayurbhanj districts.

(ii) Most of the tribes rearing domestic animals of different varieties, (namely, bullock and cow, goat, sheep, pig and fowl) are included in the second group. The only pastoral and cattle breeder in Odisha are the *Koya*, who are found in Malkangiri district. They also carry on slash and burn type cultivation in forests to supplement their income.

(iii) In Odisha, many of the tribal communities are proficient in several household crafts, like carpentry, leaf plate making, spinning and weaving broom stick and mat making. Mankidi in Mayurbhanj district and Juans in Angul district are making bamboo basketry and the Kol-Lohara in Sundargarh District are efficient as blacksmith.

The skills, techniques and material culture of PVTGs of Odisha are depicted in Table 3.4.

Table 3.4: Skills, Techniques and Material Culture of PVTGs of Odisha

STs/PTGs	*Manufacturing of Crafts and Art Objects*
Birhor/Mankirdia	Basket, rope making out of *siali* fiber, *sabai* grass and jute fiber, *khali* stitching and pressing
Bondo	Weaving of handloom cloth, carpet weaving, bead necklaces making and broomstick making
Didayi	Bamboo basketry and broomstick making, weaving of handloom cloths
Dungaria Kandha	Embroidery, wood carving and decorating, Comb making, wall painting
Hill Kharia	Collection and processing of honey resin, arrowroot, broom stick making, mat making and *khali* stitching and pressing
Juang	Wood carving, com making
Kutia Kandha	Wood carving and brook stick making
Paudi Bhuyan	Broom stick making, mat making and basketry
Lanjia Saora	Icon (wall painting) and wood carving.
Saora	Icon (wall painting), Wood carving and carpet weaving.
Lodha	*Sabai* rope making and herbal medicine.

Source: SCSTTRI, 2010, p. 48.

(iv) *Shifting cultivation* has been in vogue among several tribes, like *Bonda*, *Koya*, *Paroja*, *Diday*, *Gadaba*, *Koya*, *Dongana Kandha*, *Kutia*, *Kandha* and *Saora*, *Juang* and *Pauri Bhuiyan* of the State. They are either individually owned by family or lineage groups, or it is held under communal ownership at the village level.

(v) The major tribal people in Odisha are *settled agriculturists*, who also supplement their economy with collection of minor forest produce and wage earning. They are also numerically sizable tribes; the *Santhal*, *Oraon*, Plain *Bhuyan*, Plain *Kandha*, *Munda*, *Ho* and *Gond* carry on settled cultivation.

The PVTGs are mainly dependent on food gathering, hunting, shifting cultivation and procurement of NTFP. The Socio-Economic Status of some of the PVTGs like the *Bonda*, *Paudi Bhuiyans* are quite depressing. Infant mortality rate (IMR) among the PVTGs has been dreadful: at times, higher than 150 per thousand. Village sanitation practices have great deficiencies. Malaria menace in the hills keeps away the development agencies and functionaries indicating negligence of the area.

The *Bonda* tribe has a significant homicide rate accounting for nearly fifty murders a year. Many of the killings arise from clan rivalries which date back to several generations. Government interventions have created awareness among the *Bondos* who are victims of both backwardness and popular prejudice (bonded labour, hostile nature of homicide, drunkenness, etc.). 'Bondage of Bondos as intra-community practices of exploitation of the poor and vulnerable do exist, leading to indebtedness and bonded labour. The BDA officials and the Collector, Malkangiri are trying to fight that, but it has not been easy to check it completely.

Among the *Paudi Bhuiyans* one in every three households is landless. The land hungry *Paudi Bhuiyans* own undeveloped agricultural land and inadequate land for cultivation. Most of the landholders are marginal farmers. Some families have migrated from one village to another and settled there. Landlessness and migratory nature of people are limiting the implementation and execution of schemes.

"*Bondo* are now willing and eager to adopt improved practices in natural resources management as well as non-farm skills development for improving their lot" (Nayak, 2003-05). Educational development programmes have facilitated the *Bondos* for their socio-economic development. *Bondo* youth who have received some education and exposure have become powerful change agents within their community. Unrestrited tourism has led to unhealthy effects on the *Bondo* psyche. The young *Bondo* women are being bribed by the tourists and leading to corrupting their cultural practice.

During last one decade, the Government has distributed land to landless *Paudi Bhuiyans*, undertaken construction of land based irrigation projects, supply of pump sets for irrigation and horticulture development which have helped them to increase the yield of crops and income from agriculture. The *Paudi Bhuiyan* women participate more in activities like, wage earning and collection of MFP than their male counterparts. Level of participation, particularly among women and youths is gradually increasing and encouraging in various development activities including works/construction programmes. A sense of "we-feeling" is also growing up among the *Paudi Bhuiyan* people. Generally, the teachers posted in the schools in the PTG areas reported not interested to serve there. It is hard for some of the elder children to go to school as they are forced to look after the little ones. A significant number of children in the age group of 5-14 years are out of schools. Among School going children, the girls show the lowest profile of going to schools. As per the socio-economic conditions of the PVTG community, the girls are given household chores and not allowed to go to school by parents.

In this context, it would be worthwhile to highlight the positive achievement of *Odisha Tribal Empowerment and Livelihood Programme* (OTELP) which is implemented in most backward Tribal dominated District of Odisha having substantial Population of PVTGs in 7 most backward Tribal District of Odisha. The Tribals largely depend on shifting cultivation, procurement and marketing of NTFPs as the major livelihoods support; they exchange the NTFP with the local traders for important consumer items like Salt, Keroene, etc. They sell their horticulture produce like pumpkin, Jackfruit, tamarinds to traders for cash. Barter system is still one of the important medium of selling the NTFPs to local traders. They are thus exploited by traders which also results in their food insecurity, and starvation deaths.

In order to promote Collective Marketing on pilot basis, Marketing and Research Team (MART), Bhubaneswar has engaged a resource NGO since 15th April, 2006 in 56 Villages spread over to the District of Koraput, Kandhmal, Kalahandi and Gajapati. The main objective of this was to extend support to the SHGs in Collective Marketing for selected produces available in the villages. The Tribals were taken to the near by Market places and were facilitated to interact with the traders. The SHGs purchase the collection of produce from each household, so that, they can take it in a bulk to get adequate price directly from the traders. This resulted in reducing the exploitation of the tribals by the middle man and has also led to sufficient increase in their income and simultaneously contributing to establishing community waste growth centres.

Table 3.5 shows that more than 60 SHGs have gained substantial experience on storage, value addition negotiating with the Traders on rate fixation, etc. Four PTGs, i.e. *Bonda*, *Didayi*, *Lanjia Saora* and *Dongaria Kandha* reside in these villages. Their literacy rate of 36.58 per cent is very low 63.61 per cent and their Female literacy is only 24.72 per cent. In the PVTGs hills wet cultivation has come up alongside shifting cultivation.

The study was commenced during November 2007 and completed in 2008. The Research work was basically accomplished with the administration, academic and Research support of SCSTRTS. The TSP as an approach extends to the whole tribal areas of Odisha and it covers the entire tribal population in Odisha for development purpose. The universe of the study consisted of 21 ITDAs, 17 Micro-project, 46 MADA pockets and 14 CAPs in Odisha. It included many PVTGs area. The finding of the study observed that the tribals in the State cope with their natural and social environment by generating cultural richness combined with their local indigenous knowledge. Ganjam and Rayagada district are continuing with their expertise in the art of terracing hillsides and water management. *Dongaria Konds* girls are excellent in the art of cotton scarf embroidery work. The *Bonda* try to cultivate ascented rice in the small pockets of terraced land. The traditional tribal artifacts are still preserved like making combs, umbrellas, costums, ornaments, ropes, basket, musical instrument, hunting instruments. They are still practising traditional skills, Ethno medicines, and show their traditional skills, expertise, craftsmanship and artistery. The study also observed that the different development projects have acquired land which has displaced many tribal including PVTGs. The R&R policy has not been effective in the proper rehabilitation of the displaced tribals in Rayagada, Koraput, Jharsuguda and Jajpur. They have lost access to common property resources and faced marginalization. The study also mentions that the extremist activities in Odisha have spread to hilly and dense forest area which is inhabited by PVTGs it has spread to 12 of the 30 districts of the State. The extremist use the tribals as couriers and food soldiers, but they have not been able to make any positive contribution to the livelihood of the tribals. There is scarcity of drinking water in the studied villages though efforts have been made to provide drinking water through tube wells, sanitary wells, etc. Old age and widowed people are getting pension. There are 61 SHGs in the studied villages formed by both men and women which provide employment opportunity to the enrolled members. The main source of livelihood of the tribal people is agriculture

Table 3.5: Major Products Covered under Collective Marketing in Villages, OTELP

Sl.No.	*Product*	*Villages Covered*	*District Covered*	*Procurement Price*	*Sale Price*	*Total Quantity (qtls)*	*Total Turnover*	*Increment on Procurement Price (%)*
1.	Siali Leaf	9	Kalahandi/ Kandhamal	500	550	110	6,05,000	10
2.	Mustard	15	-do-	1,700	1,960	120	2,36,200	15
3.	Niger	33	Kalahandi/ Kandhamal	1,700	2,000	284	5,82,200	20
4.	Caster	6	Kandhamal	1,750	1,910	10	19,100	10
5.	Nahula	—	Kandhamal/ Koraput	1,000	1,250	220	2,75,000	25
6.	Nano Jelly	6	Koraput	3,000	4,200	21.22	89,124	40
7.	Oil Cake	3	Koraput	—	150	13.62	2043	100
8.	Kandul	4	Koraput	1,600	1,700	60	10,02,000	6.25
9.	Cow peas	3	Kalahandi	1,900	2,750	50	1,38,600	45
10.	Cashew	3	Gajapati	31.50	34.50	123.5	4,26,075	9.5
11.	Pumpkin	5	Gajapati	80	250	85.6	21,400	212
12.	Jackfruit	3	Gajapati	250	500	40	20,000	100
13.	Tamarind	—	Gajapati	—	600	556	4,72,600	41
				Total		**1,693.94**	**24,44,842**	**41**

Source: Annual Activities Report, 2006-07, OTELP, Bhubaneswar.

Table 3.6: Location of Micro-Projects for PVTGs with Population

Sl.No.	*District*	*Sl.No.*	*Name of the Micro-Project*	*Primitive Tribal Group (PTG) RTG Population Covered (as per 1991 Census*	*PTG Population*		
					1991	*2001*	*2007*
1.	Anugul	1.	PBDA, Jamadhi Pallahara	*Paudi-Bhuiyan*	5,433	5,022	5,633
2.	Deogarh	2.	PBDA, Rugurakudar	*Paudi-Bhuiyan*	2,467	3,108	3,655
3.	Ganjam	3.	Thumba Development Agency, Ganjam	*Soura*	3,057	3,362	4,040
4.	Nuapara	4.	CBDA, Sunabeda	*Chuktia-Bhunjia*	1,579	2,790	2,269
5.	Sundargarh	5.	PBDA, Khunagaon	*Paudi-Bhuiyan*	3,026	3,630	3,914
6.	Malkangiri	6.	BDA, Mudulipada	*Bonda*	5,050	5,565	6,008
		7.	DDA, Bayapada, Kudumulugma	*Didayi*	4,480	5,772	6,545
7.	Rayagada	8.	DKDA, Kurli Chatikona	*Dongaria Kondh*	5,181	5,680	6,036
		9.	DKDA, Parsali	*Dongaria Kondh*	2,485	2,319	2,567
		10.	LSDA, Putasinghi	*Lanjia-Soura*	3,544	4,534	5,774
8.	Gajapati	11.	LSDA, Seranga	*Lanjia-Soura*	4,043	4,822	5,441
		12.	SDA, Chandragiri	*Soura*	3,420	4,217	5,361
9.	Kandhamal	13.	KKDA, Belghar	*Kutia Kandha*	4,578	5,318	5,524
10.	Kalahandi	14.	KKDA, Lanjigarh	*Kutia Kandha*	1,901	2,385	2,549
11.	Keonjhar	15.	JDA, Gonasika	*Juang*	5,774	7,248	8,281
12.	Mayurbhanj	16.	LDA, Muruda	*Lodha*	2,052	2,265	2,840
		17.	HKMDA, Jashipur	*Khadia-Mankadia*	1,660	1,826	2,082
			All Total		**59,710**	**69,863**	**78,519**

Sources: 1. 1991 Census.
2. *Base Line Survey*, 2001 (SCSTRTI).
3. *Review of Tribal Sub-Plan Approach in Odisha* (SCSTRTI), Bhubaneswar, 2010, p. 366.

and horticulture plantation alongwith collection of minor forest produce and rearing of domestic birds. Over 90 per cent of the Tribal houses carrv on collection of minor forest produce. Still nearly 48 per cent of the PVTGs are depending on shifting cultivation. Agriculture and Agriculture labour continue to be important occupation of tribals. Most of the villages have no medical facility. Only one third of the cultivable area is irrigated. Some of the successful activities of the OTELP are Solar Lighting System by Tribal Women in a hill village namely Tingnaput of Narayhanpatna block in Koraput district promotion of collective marketing on pilot basis in 56 Villages spread over all the programme districts namely Koraput, Kandhmal, Kalahandi and Gajapati of OTELP.

The Status of PVTGs in Madhya Pradesh

Among all the States of India, Madhya Pradesh has the largest population of tribals, about one-fourth of India's total tribal population. The total number of PVTGs in the State during 1971 was 3,09,295 which constituted 22 per cent of the total PVTGs in India which is the highest amongst all the States. The Population of PVTGs in 2001 in the State increased to 7,85,720 constituting 28.38 per cent of their total population at All India level.

Rajesh K. Gautam and R. Jyoti (2003) in their study have discussed the status of *Baigas* in Madhya Pradesh. *Baigas* are widely distributed in the districts of Mandla, Dindori, Shahdol and Balaghat in Madhya Pradesh. They reside in deep unapproachable remote hilly tract of Satpura valley. Previously, they were undertaking shifting cultivation, but now they are on the process of settled cultivation. About 43 per cent of *Baigas* live in Shahdol district, 18.5 per cent in Mandla district, 17.5 per cent in Sidhi and the rest are in Bilaspur, Balaghat, Rajnandgaon and Surguja district. *Mahua* was an important source of food for *Baigas*. Nationalization of Forest, Forest Protection Act, Wild Life Protection Act and various other enactment of environment and biosphere conservation imposed the ban on shifting cultivation. Subsequently, they started settled agricultural practices. Their women work both as cultivator and agricultural labour. They also collect forest produce such as *harra, bahera, Chirota (Chakoda), resin, Tendu and mohlain* leave, and honey.

Table 3.7: Socio-economic Characteristics of the Primitive Tribes of Madhya Pradesh

Characteristics	*Bharias*	*Birhors*	*Hill-korwas*	*Kamars*
Type of household (%)				
Nuclear	64.1	88.5	62.4	79.6
Joint	35.9	11.5	37.6	20.4
Main occupation (%)				
Agriculture	39.6	19.2	12.4	5.1
Collection of forest produce	37.4	5.8	20.1	40.9
Labour	23.0	19.2	67.1	53.9
Rope making	—	55.8	0.4	0.1
Land holding (%)				
No land	12.8	42.3	13.5	8.2
< 5 acres	48.7	48.1	79.5	90.8
6-10 acres	12.8	9.6	7.1	1.0
10+ acres	25.7	0.0	0.0	0.0

Source: Pandey, G.D., and Tiwary R.S. "Some Aspects of Population Growth of the Primitive Tribes of Madhya Pradesh", *The Journal of Family Welfare*, Vol. 46, No. 2, October 2000.

The *Bharias* are found in Chhindwara, Seoni, Mandla and Sarguja Districts. The data for this study are were collected from 12 villages of Patalkot valley in Tamia Block of Chindwara district. In Madhya Pradesh, the population of *Birhors* was only 935 in 1992. They are mainly found in Raigarh district of Chhattisgarh. The *Korwa* tribe is mainly concentrated in Raigarh, Sarguja and Bilaspur Districts. The ecological setting of the villages inhabited by the *Hill Korwas* bears a definite nomadic character. Studies have reported a lower fertility of the tribe. The Kamars are a circumscribed tribe living in the hills and forest of the south-eastern part of Raipur district. The entire tribe seems to be struggling for survival under the changed circumstances and has been virtually reduced to drudgery. They have lost the freedom with which they used to work in the forest with unequalled vigour and zeal. Previously, when the *Kamars* had the free use of the forest, they earned their livelihood partly by utilizing indigenous methods of agriculture and partly from hunting, fishing and food collection from the forest. Now, under the changed situation, they are forced to seek new outlets for earning their livelihood.

The data in Table 3.7 clearly show the occupational features of the PVTGs in Madhya Pradesh. The *Bharias* depend on Agriculture and collection of forest produce, but the *Hill Korwas*, *Kamars* principal source of livelihood is labour while *Birhors* mainly depend on rope making. The study of Pandey and Tiwary (2000) points out that the *Birhors* 42 per cent are landless, but it was 12.8 per cent among the

Bharias and 8.2 per cent among *Kamars*. They mostly belong to the marginal and small family category. Their literacy rate range from 5 per cent to 22 per cent. Generally, the percentage of old people among the PVTGs is very low. Their death rates are higher. The major cause of their slow growth rate is not low fertility, but higher mortality. The State Government of Madhya Pradesh has banned sterilization among these tribes in 1978 through a Government Order. The infant mortality rate among the *Kamars* was 155 and among *Birhors* it was 154 which was the route cause of the lower growth rate among them.

Table 3.8: Population Characteristics of Primitive Tribes of Madhya Pradesh/Chhattisgarh

Characteristics	*Bharias*	*Birhors*	*Hill Korwas*	*Kamars*	*M.P. (Rural)*
Literacy rate (%)					
Total	21.5	14.3	3.5	9.6	42.1
Male	34.1	19.4	5.4	14.3	57.5
Female	8.9	8.7	1.8	5.3	25.1
Age (%)					
0-14	40.0	39.1	33.4	40.6	38.4
15-59	53.8	54.4	61.8	55.6	55.5
60+	6.2	6.5	4.8	3.7	6.1
YDR (%)	75.5	71.9	54.0	73.0	73.0
ODR (%)	11.5	11.9	7.8	6.8	10.8
TDR (%)	86.0	82.8	61.8	79.8	83.9
IA (%)	15.5	16.6	14.4	9.3	15.9
Sex Ratio	1,068	904	946	1,038	931

Note: YDR — Young age Dependency Ratio, ODR — Old age Dependency Ratio, TDR — Total Dependency Ratio, IA — Index of Ageing.
Source: National Family Health Survey, Madhya Pradesh, *IIPS*, Mumbai, 1995.

Arvind Solanki and Kailash Choubey (2014) have examined the prevalence of malaria among the *Bharia* tribe of Tamia, Chhindwara district of Madhya Pradesh. Tamia is surrounded by Hills and Forest and provide favourable environmental condition for occurrence of Malaria. The tribal community contributed 30 per cent of total malaria cases, 60 per cent of total falciparum cases and 50 per cent of total malaria deaths in the country.

Mithashri Mishra *et al.* (2006) undertook an empirical study to understand the nutritional status of Kamar Tribal Children in Chhattisgarh. They took a sample of 309 children (161 boys and 148 girls). Their major finding was that undernutrition in the form of underweight, stunting and wasting and low consumption of dietary intake (energy and protein) was found to be widely prevalent among *Kamar* tribal children. Therefore, an urgent dietary intervention programme is necessary.

In central India a great majority of tribal community show high prevalence of Child under nutrition. The *Kamars* are one of the five identified PVTGS of Chhattisgarh who live in district of Raipur and Damtari. About 80 per cent of the *Kamars* families are landless and still practice shifting cultivation. They have the skills of preparing Basket. Their population growth is very static. The study by Mithashri Mishra highlights that both boys and Girls of *Kamar* tribe suffer from under nutrition in the form of under weight, stunting and wasting.

Satwanti Kapoor *et. al.* (2010) conducted a study among *Saharias* of Madhya Pradesh. They took a sample of 168 males and 196 females to examine their health status. The *Saharia* tribe is socially and economically deprived tribal group in Madhya Pradesh. They have low level of literacy, primitive farm of agriculture and stagnant population. They had practiced shifting cultivation, hunting gathering, etc. Due to lack of cultivated land most of the *Saharias* have become labourers. The changing social-economic status have resulted in occurrence of high blood sugar level, high blood pressure and high fat percentage which is very recent phenomena among *Saharia* PVTGS. The Authors observe that on the one hand the *Saharias* are fighting with hunger and infectious disease and on the other they are burdened with costly treatment of diabetes and hyper tension.

PVTGs in Chhattisgarh

Sandeep Sharma *et. al.* (2007) have conducted a study to know the Socio-Demographic Profile of *Hill Korwas* a PVTGs in Chhattisgarh. They took a sample of 200 families from the districts of Jashpur and Surguja. Their female literacy was as low as 2.64 per cent and education did not make any impact among them. The occupation profile of *Hill Korwas* indicates that 34 per cent among them were dependent on agriculture and 20.50 per cent on labour, another 33.50 per cent on forest labour and rest on livestock labour, etc. Their major source of income was derived from agriculture, Forest and labour. Most of them are marginal and small farmers. The infant mortality rate among them is very high. They are very poor and located in isolation and remoteness.

T.K. Vaishnav (2004), undertook a study of *Kamar* tribe of Chhattisgarh. He studied the village of Garia bandh in Amjhar area; around 137 males and 142 females were studied. They constituted 50 households. Among them 24 per cent were landless, 56 per cent were marginal farmers, 8 per cent were small farmers and remaining 12 per cent were medium farmers. The principal crops were paddy and *Urud* gram. They eat rice, pulses, roots, herbs and wild animals. They also consume Mahuva liquor.

Their calorie consumption is 2600 during winter and comes down to 1547 calories during rainy season. It is even lower for their females.

PVTGs in Bihar

After the bifurcation of Jharkhand from Bihar, the conditions of PVTGs in Bihar are pathetic. Ganga Nath Shah (2014) has examined the Education and Health problems among the PVTGs in Bihar. He has focused his study on the *Sauria Paharia* and *Mal Paharia* of Bhagalpur and Banka district respectively. According to 2001 census only 9026 PVTGs remain in Bihar. The 8 vulnerable tribal groups of Bihar are *Asur*, *Birhor*, *Korwa*, *Birjia*, *Sauria Paharia*, *Mal Paharia*, *Parahariya* and *Sabar*. Earlier they were dependent for their food and fire wood on the forest but now they have lost their traditional ecological dependence. The PVTGs in Bihar are mainly inhabited in Bhagalpur, Banka, Madhepura, Supoul, Katihar, Kishanganj, Araria, Purnia, Nawada, Gaya and Bhabua district of Bihar. The *Mal paharia* have the largest population among all Vulnerable tribes. Subsistence of *Mal Paharia* and *Sauria Paharia* is based on laboring, animal husbandry and liquor selling, *Sauria Paharia* lives in very critical situation in respect of *Mal Paharia*. *Korwa* and *Birhor* still collect plants, roots, tuber, etc. of medicinal values which they sell in the market and earn money by which they survive. The *Parahaiya* of Gaya collects honey from the jungle and sell it in the market for their survival. The *Sauria Paharias* literacy rate is only 18.38 per cent, Male literacy rate is 20.04 per cent, while female literacy rate is 16.66 per cent. Mostly *Sauria Paharias* of Kahalgaon block including women also are seriously involved in liquor drinking. They are suffering from various diseases. Tuberculosis, Asthma, Pox, Skin disease, Itching, Diarhoea, Anaemia, Malnutrition, Jaundice, Gland T.B., Malaria, *kala-azar*, Cough, Liver problem and Leprosy are found in them.

The Health Status of PVTGs

UNESCO has already put *Asur*, *Birhor* and *Korwa* in the list of World's Endangered Languages. The area of concentration is around 150 km. of the Capital Town of Ranchi and is much closer to Bishunpur town. They are more numerously found in the Districts of Gumla and Latehar. These tribes were initially nomadic forest based hunting community, but were later forced by the Government to settle down in remote pockets and squeezed between the freedom of hunter gatherer and the skills of an Industrial Labour Force. Their lands and forests have been snatched away from them and they are forced to work as Agricultural Labourers, Marginal Farmers are getting exploited by outsiders. According to 2011 Census Figures, there are only 6000 *Birjias* left in the Jharkhand State while the number of *Savars* as 9000. The population of other PVTGs range between 10,000 to 1.35 lakh. The non-implementation of the Forests Right Act 2006 has added to the age-hold woes of the forest based rights. The Forest Regulations enforced during colonial time infringed upon the PVTGs rights over forest products. The issue of vulnerable tribes facing extinction can be addressed considerably with the implementation of Forest Rights Acts because it basically returns to them the rights of Forest Products, which they have lost over time. The experts have questioned the very rational behind forcing Nomadic forest dwellers into settled community and argue that the PVTGs should have the freedom to decide how and where they want to live and what kind of life they want to pursue.

The studies of Anthropologists and other experts have established that Tuberculosis, Malaria, Dengue, Chikungunya, Lymphatic Filariasis and Diarrhea and non-communicable diseases as Hypertension, Fluorosis, Cancer, Nutritional deficiency disorders and genetic disorders, etc. are major health problems in these tribes. Presence of these diseases coupled with illiteracy, poverty and malnutrition makes the situation more complex and tedious to the tribal group as well to the health functionaries to bring them to main stream so as to reach the targets of Millennium Development Goals (MDG).

Ramesh Sahani and Shyamal K. Nandy (2013) in their chapter have examined the major problem and the factors responsible for the present condition of PVTGs. They have found that the hepatitis infection was very much prevalent among the Andamenese tribes along with other diseases like Malaria, Tuberculosis, respiratory infection, diarrheal disorder, skin infection including leprosy and iron deficiency anemia among mostly in women and children. Similarly, they observed that the general health status of PVTGs have been found unsatisfactory in the ICMR Report. The ICMR study of 2003 have found that the infant mortality rate is as high as 84.2 in Odisha, mortality rate under 5 is 126.6, underweight among the children is 55.9 per cent, children with acute respiratory tract infection is 22.4 per cent, children with dysentery and diarrhea is 21.1 per cent and women with anemia is 54.9 for 1000.

The situations of *Baigas* are also very bad with one of the highest infant mortality rate, high level of infectious diseases and mal-nutrition (Sahani, 2009). The study of Ramesh Sahani shows that the incidence of sickle haemoglobin is found to be more than 30 per cent among the Irular and Paniyan and more than 22 per cent among the *Biagas*. He has also observed that the PVTGs like *Bondo*, *Didayi*, *Juang* and *Kutia Khonds* of Odisha are in critical situation relating to malnutrition (Chhotray, 2003-04). The adults among the PVTGs in Odisha like *Khond*, *Gadaba*, *Porja*, *Bondo*, *Kamar*, *Kolam* are also showing very serious and critical under nourishment situation. The study of Chhotray also reveals that 85 per cent of the *Paudi Bhuyan*, 40 per cent of the *Abhuj Maria*, 29 per cent of the *Birhor* and 42.2 per cent of the *Baigas* have severe anemia. The immunization assessment shows that in Tamil Nadu, DPT and Polio Vaccine coverage is around 99 per cent against its coverage of 59.7 per cent in the States of Madhya Pradesh and Chhattisgarh.

Ramesh Sahani observes that the high infant mortality rate, less life expectancy, high prevalence of anemia due to worm infestation are showing that the health status are not so good among the PVTGs. The study also observes that the height and weight are deficit among the *Kutia Khonds* in Odisha and Andhra Pradesh (Kupputhai and Mallika, 1993). Similarly, the nutritional status of the *Kamars* of Madhya Pradesh (Gangopadhyay, 2006) reveals that the consumption of all the nutrients is lower than the ICMR recommendation. It also quotes the study of Chetlalli *et. al.* (1991), which estimated that the average life expectancy of *Kutias* of Odisha was 46-49 years and for females it was 41-49 years. The main cause of sex-wise differential rate of mortality is ascribed to physiological stress and biological factors.

The study of Ramesh Sahani *et. al.* also comes to certain broad inference. One of the important observations is that the emotional attachment of PVTGs with their habitat acts against rehabilitation site in the new area. Most of the PVTGs feel isolated in the new rehabilitated area. The other is that the PVTGs settled across the State boundary should be brought under a common development agency. There should be bottom up approaches in terms of the specific PVTGs rather than top down approaches for their development. The existing studies bring out the extremely declining health status and socio-economic condition of various PVTGs of India, where the overall development is still needed in accordance with their existing biological and cultural scenario in general, but specific problems should be taken up for specific strategies of the development programmes.

G.D. Pandey and R.S. Tiwary (2001) provide the highlight of the health practices of Primitive Tribes of Madhya Pradesh particularly of *Abujhmarias*, *Baigas*, *Hill Korwas*, *Bharias*, *Kamars*, *Saharias* and *Birhors* (Tiwary, 1984). The authors consider some of their practices are good and can be utilized for strengthening reproductive health. The healthy practices are outlined below:

- They consider pregnancy a natural phenomenon and do their normal chores till the onset of labour pains.
- Avoidance of cohabitation during pregnancy.
- Pregnant women do not consume alcohol.
- Delivery is conducted in squatting position, which according to doctors, is less painful and more scientific if carried out carefully.
- Colostrum is given to the child, which prevents the child from various infectious diseases.
- Prolonged breast-feeding is beneficial to both mother and child in several ways, including birth spacing.

The authors also consider a number of their practices as not conducive to their reproductive health which are as follows:

- Preference for consanguineous marriages, which carry the risk of transmission of hereditary diseases in the progeny.
- No antenatal/postnatal care, which increases the health risk to mother and child. High infant mortality prevailing among these tribes could be attributed to this.
- The naval cord is cut and the stump is treated un-hygienically. This carries the risk of developing tetanus in the new born.
- Forbidding foods such as vegetables, wheat and grain for the mother for two months after delivery is an irrational belief that delays her recovery after delivery.
- Administering a few drops of alcohol to cure child diseases is an irrational and harmful practice.

The birth rate did not vary considerably (except among the *Hill Korwas*) and the death rate was generally higher. It was also observed that the higher death rates observed in the primitive tribes were mainly due to their higher infant mortality rates. In order to improve the situation, the level of accessibility and acceptability of maternal and child health care services have to be enhanced.

Arvind Solanki and Kailash Choubey (2014) in their paper entitled "Spatial Patterns of Malaria among *Bharia* Tribe of Tamia, Chhindwara

(M.P.), India" have explored the factors determining the special malaria pattern of *Bharia* Tribe, which lives in the tribal block of Chhindwara District in Madhya Pradesh. This tribe has been suffering with malaria for a very long time due to the environmental factors of Tamia block which is surrounded by hills and forests and provides favourable environmental conditions for malaria occurrence. The *Bharia* Tribe is mainly concentrated in the Patalkot valley of Tamia Block and its adjoining regions. The name *Bhumia* means "Lord of Soil" which is another name of this tribal group. They have adopted to the profession of shifting cultivation and also collect various forest products like tubers, roots and fruits. Their occupational characteristic show that 38.7 per cent among them are farmers, 37 per cent agricultural labourers and rest 24.3 per cent work as forest labourers. Only 11.6 per cent among them have acquired primary education and the rest are illiterate. The study shows the distribution of malaria patterns among *Bharia* tribe from 2006-2010. The total malaria cases suddenly rise during 2010 and almost five times of 2006 malaria cases due to development of resistance in mosquitoes and plasmodium parasite against anti-malarial chemicals and drugs.

Meena Radhakrishna (2009), who was Director (Research), National Commission for Denotified, Nomadic and Semi-Nomadic Tribes in 2007-08 has discussed how nutritional resources of people *on the move* might be gravely endangered through institution of new laws and policies by Government of India. They practice shifting cultivation, but this land has been declared as Reserve Forest in many parts of the country and the practice assiduously discouraged as it is considered an eco-unfriendly activity. *Curbing of the practice of shifting cultivation, almost entirely devoted to subsistence food crop farming, has led to large scale starvation or severe malnourishment.* Shifting cultivators used to and still grow maize, vegetables, potatoes, ginger, chillies, rice, millets, pulses, beans, sweet potatoes, oil seeds, yams, millets, mustard, sugarcane, sesame, pineapples, citrus fruits, bananas, jackfruit and so on. Restrictions under forest laws on shifting cultivation, hunting, gathering and fishing in the forests meant that the nutrition levels of these nomadic communities drastically fell. The incidence of "unnatural deaths among the PTGs" has become sufficiently grave. New forest laws have led to a large number of such communities being subjected to intense hunger for the following reasons:

(a) Lack of access to small game like fowl, rabbits, deer, monkeys which used to be staple diet for a large number of hunting communities.

(b) Lack of access to bark, roots, tubers, corns, leaves, flowers, seeds, fruits, sap, honey, toddy and other forest produce which was a regular source of nutrition for gathering communities.
(c) Lack of access to fish in ponds and streams in the forest which used to be a traditional source of food for forest dwelling nomadic communities.

All the forest dependent communities — shifting cultivators, hunter gatherers and pastoralists are also engaged in trade in the forest produce with outlying villages, and earn the cash income which has been cut off, resulting in shortage of food buying capacity. The establishment of wild life sanctuaries and parks has meant that a large number of communities who used to use the resources of the forest are no longer able to do so. Communities which were/are dependent on wild animals for livelihood are those which used to train bears, monkeys, owls and other birds, snakes and so on for street entertainment. The wild life conservation laws have destroyed their livelihood entirely and many members are not just constantly hungry but starving.

The general issues affecting the access to nutrition among nomadic people are the following:

(i) Lack of access to firewood for cooking becomes a regular reason for going hungry.
(ii) Constant pressure from the police and middle class neighbourhoods in the urban areas create inhibitions for the family to light *Chullah*.
(iii) The Public Distribution System does not effectively function for the Nomadic Communities because they do not possess BPL Card.
(iv) Government policy towards the Nomadic Communities has led to the family going hungry and is pushing them dangerously close to starvation.

The author recommends that the nutritional needs of all Nomadic Communities are required to be addressed through fresh policy initiative.

P.K. Sharma and P.K. Tiwari (2007) have studied "*Health Status of Sahariya Tribe of Central India*". The pilot study was conducted during the year 2005-2006 as an initial screening for TB prevalence in the three most populated tribal villages. The study reveals that 46 per cent of the samples reported positive for acid fast bacilli. The study concludes that none of the other Tribal Group in Madhya Pradesh has reported such a high prevalence of Tuberculosis.

Another rapid survey was conducted on Diet and Nutritional Status of *Saharia* Tribe in Rajasthan, which is also designated as a Primitive Tribe in the State. There were reports in the media regarding starvation deaths among *Saharia* Tribal Community in Kishanganj Block of Baran District. Consequent to this, a rapid survey was conducted among the *Saharia* Tribe during October-November 2004 to assess their nutritional status and to investigate the starvation deaths. The study covers a total of 200 children for the nutritional assessment among children of less than 05 years. The study covers a total of 08 villages from the 02 blocks of Shahbad and Kishanganj of Baran District covering 25 children from each tribal village. The majority of them was of nuclear families and 42 per cent among them were possessing land. The major occupation of the household was agriculture labourer. The study found that about 4 per cent of infants were emaciated, while an equal proportion had conjunctival xerosis. About 1 per cent of 1-5 year children had oedema (suggesting Kwashiorkor) and 5.7 per cent were emaciated. The prevalence of Vitamin D deficiency signs such as conjunctival xerosis (17.6%) and Bitot spots (8.3%) was much higher in these children than that reported earlier for the State of Rajasthan (0.3%). The prevalence of nutritional deficiency signs was observed to be negligible among adults. The study came to the conclusion that *Saharia* PTGs has a poor Socio-Economic Status and low literacy level. Their intake of various foods barring cereals and millets was very poor compared to the balanced diets. The intake of protective food such as green leafy vegetables and milk was very low, which was reflected in higher prevalence of micro-nutrient deficiency such as conjunctival xerosis and Bitot spots. They were availing the benefits of the Special Component Programmes also participating in supplementary feeding programme under ICDS and MDM. Premature delivery and infectious diseases contributed to a majority of the deaths among young children. Higher rate of illiteracy, ignorance, inappropriate infant and child feeding practices and lack of early treatment in case of morbidities seemed to have aggravated the situation.

Satwanti Kapoor *et al.* conducted a cross-sectional study among adult *Sahariya*, a PTG of Madhya Pradesh. The paper is entitled, "*Emerging Health Threats among a Primitive Tribal Group of Central India*". A sample of 364 persons (168 males and 196 females) ranging in the age group of 18 to 60 years were studied. The study observes that there is a drastic socio-cultural and economic shift among *Sahariya* from agriculture to daily wage labourer in urban sector adopting unhealthy diet which could have resulted in early appearance of obesity related health problem among the Primitive Tribal Group. This section of the population depends on nature based economy and consistent rainfall shortage leading to wage earning and migration and this phenomenon is quite alarming. The occurrence of pre-diabetic conditions in adult male and female *Sahariyas* led to poor dietary pattern with negligible intake of vegetables and fruits. Adult diabetic is a health problem which requires constant monitoring and regular medication.

Ganga Nath Jha and Bhaskar Kumar (2014) have examined the health status of PTGs in Bihar particularly of the *Sauria Paharia* and *Mal Paharia* of Bhagalpur and Banka district. According to 2001 census, a very scanty population of Primitive Tribal Groups remain in Bihar and they are the *Asur*, *Birhor*, *Korwa*, *Birjia*, *Sauria Paharia*, *Mal Paharia*, *Parahaiya* and *Sabar*. These PTGs still collect plants, roots, tuber, etc. of medicinal values which they sell in the market and earn money. The *Parahaiya* of Gaya collects honey from the jungle and sells it in the market for their survival. Lack of employment and resources, lack of awareness in relation to health and rampant drinking habit in addition to superstitious beliefs have made the life complex of these vulnerable group. Their literacy rate is very low. In Kahalgoan block of Bhagalpur District, *Sauria Paharia* Tribe were facing acute drinking water problem. Generally, they use self made wine (*Hadia*) prepared from *Mahua* and drink heavily. Due to water problem, liquor addiction, lack of cleanness, lack of awareness and lack of taking nutritional diet; they are suffering from various diseases, Tuberculosis, Asthma, Pox, Skin disease, Itching, Diarrhoea, Anemia, Malnutrition, Jaundice, Gland T.B., Malaria, *Kala-azar,* Clough, Liver Problem and Leprosy are found in them.

The SCSTRTI study is among the few studies of PVTGs inclusion in Tribal Sub-Plan Approach with systematic effort of implementing the Welfare and Developmental Programmes. The above table also provides the PVTGs population, a perusal of which points out that total population in Odisha during 1990-91 was 59,710 which increased to 69,863 in 2001 and further increased to 78,519 by 2007. This is consistent with the increase in the figures of PVTGs in other States as well.

Forms of Resistance of Adivasis and PTGs in Colonial India

The Felix Padel (1995), Archana Prashad (1910) and Felix Padel (2011) provide us an insight in to the forms of resistance by *Adivasis* and PTGs in Colonial and Post-Colonial India.

Felix Padel (1995) has made an incisive observation "... *advasi* struggles to protect their land, forest and mountains are the cutting edge of a grassroots movement to protect India's environment from a catastrophic *tipping point* of no return" (p. 316). This process commenced during British Rule and escalated since then. The author also calls the process of subjugation of the *adivasis* as "A Conquest over their Minds".

According to Felix Padel, the *Paharia*s, were among the first *adivasis*, who were raiding the Grand Trunk Road and resisted conquering their territory by the British. August Cleveland, the man who imposed colonial rule over them has stated that without bloodshed or terrors of authority, and only through the means of conciliation, confidence and benevolence, the lawless and savage inhabitants of the jungle territory of Rajmahal were subjected to conquest over their minds. As a matter of fact, Cleveland used military force to subdue the *Paharia* and publicly executed their chiefs during 1780-82. Felix Padel also compares it to the emergence of *Salwa Judum* in Chhattisgarh, which is a civil war in the south of Bastar (Dantewara and Bijapur districts) characterized by atrocities of Para-military forces and the Naxalites. The para-military organization is named as *Salwa Judum*. The civil war started in June 2005 and it was claimed as "spontaneous uprising against the Naxalites". Even a 'Gandhian People's Movement' which was non-violent in character was reckoned as a pro-naxal outfit. *Salwa Judum* forces had burnt several adivasis villages, forcing people to leave their villages and compelled them to stay in refugee camps, it was a big concentration camp of over 40,000 *adivasis*. It was alleged that the Bailadila mines had a terrible impact on the *Maria Gond* and other *adivasis*, and seriously polluted the Shankhini river. *Adivasis* in Bastar have a strong history of resisting plans for steel plants. In October 2001, police opened fire on tribal protestors against a NMDC steel plant which was to displace four villages at Nagarnar near Jagdalpur. Bastar has a long history of resisting the colonial rule and also in the era of globalization they are resisting the opening of steel plant. In the *Salwa Judum* encounters large number of tribals were seriously injured and hundreds of them were jailed including women. Similarly, the induction of Tata Steel Plant at Lohandiguda involved police intimidation, violence and arresting large number of them between July 2006 and February 2007. It has been acknowledged that the mining companies have been the main supporters of *Salwa Judum* operation. The involvement of the Naxalites has been against the system of endemic exploitation of timber *mafia* and corruption of senior officials. The tribal leaders found the Naxalites as a force to combat the corruption and exploitation. The author opines that Naxalite violence has undermined Tribal Society just as displacement has caused distress to the *adivasis*. Even in *Salwa Judum* encounters large number of PVTGs have been seriously affected as much as the other Tribals.

Felix Pedal remarks that during the years of East India Company, many tribal areas including the areas inhabitated by PVTGs were victims of burning of villages by Colonial rulers and use of force against those who resisted. The first senior administrator involved in the conquest of the *Konds* in Odisha favoured the promotion of market to wean away and subdue the *Konds*. This is the methodology of a '*conquest over their minds*' which draw *adivasis* into the market economy and addicted them to new tastes. The policy of exploitation of the tribals including the Primitive Tribals continues even today, which is amplified by providing license to corporate sectors in large areas including a magnificent forested mountain called Kandadhara, which is the Odisha's tallest waterfall and is considered sacred among the *Bhuiya* Tribe. Kalinganagar and Anti-POSCO Movement are a signal to foreign investors in India and instruments of displacement of the farmers and labourers. The system of '*endemic exploitation*' in India's tribal areas, have increased hugely during British rule and has escalated even more with industrial development. The process of extermination of the tribals during the colonial and during the post-colonial period through displacement mechanism is termed by the author as '*Cultural Genocide*'. During the colonial period, the case of 'Gold disturbances' was an attempt to establish a more centralized State Police Force which was even resisted by the tribals exemplified in *Bonai Gond Struggle*.

Archana Prasad (1910) highlighted '*Traditional Maria Protest and Forest Laws*' in Baster during 1910. The Marias of Bastar were among the initial *adivasi* groups to protest against the enforcement of Forest Laws in the feudal *zamindari* area. It was particularly marked by intensive protest by Marias between 1886 to 1892. The customary relationship between the *adivasis* and the Raja received a set back with the intervention of the British rule. Certain measures taken up by the British Residents and Diwan which was taken in the name of Raja were responsible for the Marias organizing collective protest against the State. In Bastar, the first Forest Rule was introduced in 1892, when large areas of forests were reserved and a Bewar type of cultivation was prohibited in forest areas. There were also restrictions on the access to fuel wood and other forest produce. The discontent got further escalated due to the exploitation by the forest officials. The Raja's administration had failed to protect the customary rights of the Marias in the forests. The British were also expecting '*bhet begar*' involving the carrying of luggage and building of houses without payment of any kind. The Marias also resented forms of exploitation by the lessees of the forests, the Hindu *thikadars* and the police. They were all considered '*foreigners*' in the region. The main slogan of the Maria protest was '*Bastar for Bastaris*'. Their anger was also directed on the police and forest officials. The Rajas misuse of customary power was very much resented. The Maria mutiny was targeted against the outsiders and exploitative elements and Maria identity was articulated as a traditional communitarian identity. All Marias were brought together through a system of communication, which was made the use of symbolic traditional form. The arrow was a sign of war, the red pepper implied urgency and the mango leaves mean meetings. Their assertion of identity took an aggressive form which involved the cutting of the supply of water, electricity and communication to the outsiders. The British recognized the Maria protest as a rebellion against the British Regime. In order to teach the Marias a lesson for their aggressive behavior Maria leaders were awarded stringent punishment like flogging and troops were called into repress them. The Maria protest postponed the inevitable application of the Zamindari Laws till the 1920s. The main impact of the protest was that it made the Raja of Bastar more dependent on the British for his survival. This was mainly because the Maria protest, despite its tacit anti-colonial content, was targeted more at the Raja and less at the British.

It would be appropriate to discuss here about the displacement scenario which had been thrust upon *Dongria Khond* pertaining to Niyamgiri hills. One sub-group of *Kondhas* is the *Dongria Kondhas*. They inhabit in Rayagada, Koraput and Kalahandi districts. Their major concentration is found in the blocks of Kalyansinghpur, Bissam Cuttack and Muniguda. They are called *Dongria* or dweller of *donger* ("hill" in Oriya) and settled in higher altitudes due to their economic demands. The *Dongria Kondh* call themselves *Jharnia* meaning those who live by the *Jharana* (streams). Hundreds of perennial streams flow from Niyamgiri Hill and there are hundreds of *Dongria* villages by the streams. The *Dongria* are considered the protectors of these streams, hills and jungles by the people of the nearby plain. Some *Kondha* tribes live in Gajapati District. *They now primarily depend on a subsistence agriculture, i.e. shifting, cultivation of slash and burn cultivation or Podu.* The *Dongria Kondhas* are excellent fruit farmers. The most striking feature of the *Dongria Kondhas* is that they have adapted to horticulture and grow pineapple, oranges, turmeric, ginger and papaya in plenty. Forest fruit trees like mango and jackfruit are also found in huge numbers, which fulfill the major dietary chunk of the *Dongrias*. Vedanta Resources, a UK based mining company, is threatening the future of this tribe *as their home the Niyamgiri Hill* is rich in bauxite. The bauxite is also the reason that there are so many perennial streams. In 2010 India's environment ministry ordered Vedanta Resources to halt a sixfold expansion of an aluminum refinery in Odisha.

Felix Padel (2011) — describes the ordeals faced by the *Dongria* Tribals on the displacement issue relating to the Niyamgiri Hills which is 5,000 feet high bauxite deposit. The Vedanta/Sterlite was trying to build a road up the mountains for mining the bauxite deposit on the top of Niyamgiri mountain and the local *Dongria* confronted the genocidal impact of mining the ore. The children in the Vedanta Nagar School had performed a show in front of Commissioners visiting the area on behalf of the Supreme Court in mid-2005, "*This country, this earth, is our mother. We will sacrifice ourselves in service of it, and make our nation proud of us*". *Adivasis*, who refused to be displaced, see the situation very differently. The company has showed no respect for their customs and deities, especially *Dharni Penu and Sora Penu*, their Earth and Mountain deities, and is '*flooding them out with money*'. The base rock of these mountains was named Khondalite by geologist T.L. Walker in 1900 — in honor of those fine hill men the *Khonds* in whose mountain jungles Khondalite is better developed than in any region hitherto described (1902:11). Felix Padel recalls a conversation a Census official had with *Konds* in 1941 and asked them "What is your religion?" and the answer was "Mountains". *Kond* religion is based on a performed understanding of the web of life. Their mountains are sacred entities of prime importance because they store monsoon water and release it in perennial streams, full of minerals, ensuring the land's fertility. Mine the mountain, and the constant supply of water ends forever. Mining a mountain's minerals sacrifices its ecosystem and the tribal culture that has utilized and channeled this for hundreds of years, to create short term profits through the metals trade.

The Supreme Court told Vedanta in 2013 that the *Dongria* must decide whether to allow mining on the Mountain. The *Dongria* answered with an unequivocal 'No'. In this context, it would be useful to quote from the Report of High Level Committee (Virginius Xaxa), "The Niyamgiri experience is ironic, demonstrating a clear break from before the time that the FRA was enacted. The *Dongria Khonds* opposed the mining, After two rounds of consideration by the Supreme Court, a hearing before the National Environment Appellate Authority, and two reports on the effect the project may have on the *Dongria Khonds*, the Supreme Court directed, on 18th April, 2013, that the *Gram Sabha* needed to consider the rights that were being affected by the proposed mining", (p. 324). The '*Palli Sabhas*' were held in Niyamgiri between 18th July and 19th August, 2013 in twelve hamlets in Rayagada in Kalahandi districts, which the State Government considered were likely to be affected by the mining. The proposed mining was unequivocally rejected by the twelve *Palli Sabhas* (Virginius Xaxa, p. 325). The Judge on hearing the case in 2013 remarked "You can't destroy the faith of those people. They believe their god is on the hilltop. Can you tell them, "take away your God to another place? Are you banishing the God?" — Judge on hearing the case, 2013. It would be apt to refer to the observations of Felix Pedal (2011) where he states that Killings of tribals such as at Maikanch and Kalinganagar and Symbolize a violent sacrifice and a psychic for *adivasis* that non-tribal peoples rarely understand. Underlying the cultural Genocide is the invaders' total lack of respect for tribal people's traditions and connection with the land (p. 334).

The struggle of *Dongria Kondh* could be successful because it received wide ranging support from the National and International Civil Society Organizations. This is a unique example to demonstrate that even PVTGs with their small numbers can resist giant Corporate Houses from grabbing the land which they considered as their cultural identity and heritage. This paper holds the view that land and forest are the issues of dignity and identity for the Tribals and they should combine their struggle alongwith the support of other tribal groups and Civil Societies.

The Niyamgiri hill range in Odisha state, eastern India, is home to the *Dongria Kondh* Tribe. Niyamgiri is an area of densely forested hills, deep gorges and cascading streams. To be a *Dongria Kondh* is to farm the hills' fertile slopes, harvest their produce, and worship the mountain god Niyam Raja and the hills he presides over, including the 4,000 metre Mountain of the Law, Niyam Dongar. Yet for a decade, the 8,000 plus *Dongria Kondh* lived under the threat of mining by Vedanta Resources, which hoped to extract the estimated $2 billion-worth of bauxite that lies under the surface of the hills. The company planned to create an open-cast mine that would have violated Niyam Dongar, disrupted its rivers and spelt the end of the *Dongria Kondh* as a distinct people.

The deep reverence that the *Dongria* have for their gods, hills and streams pervades every aspect of their lives. Even their art reflects the mountains, in the triangular designs found on village shrines to the many gods of the village, farm and forests and their leader, Niyam Raja. They derive their name from dongar, meaning 'hill' and the name for themselves is Jharnia: protector of streams. "*Niyam Raja is our god and we worship him*". The *Dongria* protested against Vedanta locally, nationally and internationally. They held roadblocks, formed a human chain around the Mountain of Law and even set a Vedanta jeep alight when it was driven onto the mountain's sacred plateau. But as long as the refinery sits at the foot of their hills, they do not feel their mountain is safe and will not give up their fight. Their determination, tenacity and success has won them international acclaim and inspired tribal peoples across the country and around the world.

High Rate of Rejections of Claims under FRA

The State of Jharkhand has 25 districts of which 18 are in Chotanagpur-*cum*-Ranchi region and 7 are in the Santhal Pargana region. As per the official figures submitted by Jharkhand Government, the number of PTG families in the 18 Chotanagpur District are 37,851 and their total number of Santhal Paragana region is 39,163 making a total of 77,014 families in the entire State of Jharkhand. The districts with the largest number of families are East Simbhum (13,797) and Pakur (11,897) followed by Garhwa (7,945), Sahibganj (9,806), Dumka (7,221) and Godda (7,889). In the entire state of Jharkhand, only 1,276 titles have been given to the PVTG families, which constitutes 1.66 per cent of the total families. This is in fact an absolutely low figure and ignoring the claims of the PVTG. The forests is one of the main sources of their livelihood and the Jharkhand Government should provide titles in the Forest Land in the areas of their habitation.

Major Issues Confronting the PVTGs in India

The Report of Prof. Virginius Xaxa (2014) has raised some basic issues relating to PVTGs in the country:

1. It provides a register of PVTGs with population of less than 1,000 persons and states that one of the criteria for their vulnerability is their small population. There are 19 such PVTGs spread to the different States of the country. Their lowest

number is 17 persons of the *Birjia* in the State of Bihar. These figures are based on the Census of India, 2001. The extremely low demography of the PVTGs is a matter of a grave concern which is also applicable to some of the Nomadic groups in India as has been indicated in the context of Jharkhand in this Paper.

2. It (High Level Committee Report of V. Xaxa) also identifies the following criteria for designating the PVTGs:

    (i) Forest Dependent Livelihood.
    (ii) Free Agricultural Level of existence.
    (iii) Stagnant or declining population.
    (iv) Low literacy rate and a subsistence based economy.

    As per the 2001 census, these 75 PVTGs have a total population of 27,68,322. The majority of the PVTGs live in 6 States of Maharashtra, Madhya Pradesh, Chhattisgarh, Jharkhand, Odisha, Andhra Pradesh and Tamil Nadu.

3. The vulnerability of PVTGs also stems from the loss of their traditional livelihood habitat and customary resource rights through the gradual exploitative inclusion of the market and the State in the form of Industrial Projects, conservation efforts, tourism and the forest bureaucracy. These have resulted in the loss of their land and resources resulting in chronic malnutrition, starvation and ill-health. The groups most affected are the *Jarawas* of the Andaman Islands, the *Bondos* of Odisha, *Cholanaickans* of Kerala, *Abujh Marias* of Chhattisgarh and *Birhors* of Jharkhand. Some PVTGs such as the *Paudi Bhuiyan* in Odisha are still not included within the list of Scheduled Tribes.

4. The issue of non-granting of ST status to some PVTGs is also a genuine discrimination against them. For example, the *Abujh Maria* has only recently been granted ST status in the State of Chhattisgarh. The rationale behind inclusion and exclusion must be made clear and all discrepancies must be immediately addressed. Further, of the States with PVTGs like Kerala, Karnataka, Tamil Nadu, Uttar Pradesh and West Bengal *do not have Scheduled Areas*, thereby accentuating their vulnerability as they lack the protections and rights offered by the Fifth Schedule and the Provisions of Panchayat (Extension to Scheduled Areas) Act 1996.

5. *Historical Injustices* — The High Committee Report (V Xaxa: 2014) observes that rather than granting them their autonomy and rights to address historical injustices, disastrous State Government Intervention in the name of their 'preservation' has contributed to immense harms to their social status. Among the historical injustices are the Forest Rights of the PVTGs and it needs to be mentioned in this context that the Forest Rights Act 2006 (pp. 288-96) has been very loosely implemented to correct the historical injustices faced by them. It also denies the members of PVTGs to make free reproductive choices. For example, *the Government of Jharkhand has provided titles of forest land under Forest Rights Act 2006 to only 1.66 per cent of the total PVTGs families in the State* (based on the data of Government of Jharkhand 2015). It sidesteps the real factors contributing to high mortality rate such as chronic malnutrition, starvation and lack of access to adequate health facility. Most of the PVTGs are Forest Dwellers and depends heavily on land and forest resources for their subsistence. Their habitat has been declared as reserve forest and protected forest making them vulnerable to displacement and eviction without compensation. For example, in 2009 nearly 245 *Biaga* families were moved out of the Achnakamar Tiger Reserve when it was notified under the project Tiger. The housing colonies built for rehabilitation began to collapse and they did not receive *pattas* for their new farm land. The *Biaga* families were re-located to an area where their traditional forest livelihood of collecting *Sal* and *Tendu* leaves as well as Bamboo was no longer available.

   Similarly in Tamil Nadu, the *Kattu Nayakans*, who lived on the fringes of the Mudumalai Wild-Life Sanctuary were prevented from collecting honey as well as produce from the forest area. The FRA Act 2006 recognizes the Forest Rights including community tenure of habitat and habitation for primitive tribal group. The report emphasis that the FRA provisions of habitat rights should be implemented for PVTGs. In Karnataka the 2,000 sq.km. of contiguous forest area spread across Tamil Nadu, Karnataka and Kerala is home to *Jenu Kuruba*, *Betta Khuruba*, *Soliga*, *Yerava* and *Paniyar* tribal groups. These tribals live scattered in the jungle and have an intimate knowledge of its flora and fauna. In the 1970's, that Karnataka Government acquired large area of forest land to construct dam over the rivers. It displaced the PVTGs from their traditional habitat but there were no rehabilitation measure for them. Further, the Karnataka Forest Act 1963 divided forest into Reserve Forest and Village Forest and besides this the Wild Life Protection Act (1972), and the declaration of National Park 1975 and 1986 were enacted *which declared the PVTGs as trespassers and evicted them out of the Forest.* They were even not allowed to collect forest produce like honey, fruits, medicinal roots, etc. The PVTGs resisted such attempts but were beaten, harass, their women were raped by forest officials and were also booked under the Law. As a result many of them moved outside the forest and were forced to reside in the proximity with non tribal resulting in the dilution of their cultural and religious practices. The .displacement from the forest deprived them of their traditional livelihood and they were forced to work as wage labour in coffee plantation, construction site and house building activities. They were also working as Bonded labourers and they were acutely indebted to the money lenders.

6. The FRA amendment Rules provides that "In view of the differential vulnerability of PVTGs, the District Level Committee shall ensure that all PVTGs are conferred habitat rights, in consultation with their concerned traditional institutions and that their claims for habitat rights are filed before the concerned *Gram Sabhas*". The report of the High Level Committee suggest that *the State Government should recognize habitat rights both over the Revenue land and Forest land.* Such habitat rights have been recognize for the *Madia* Community in Maharashtra, and the *Chuktia Bhunjia*, *Mankadia*, *Dongria-Khond*, *Juang* and *Khadias* in Odisha. Such efforts of providing habitat rights to PVTGs have also to be undertaken in other states which PVTGs habitation (pp. 281-99).
7. Literacy Rate among PVTGs are extremely low due to abysmal education infrastructure in Tribal areas, poorly trained teachers, lack of teaching in Tribal Languages. The Report observes that any educational policy or programme for PVTGs should take into account their distinct culture and pedagogic style suited to their traditional skills, cultural language.
8. Implementation of FRA has been weak particularly as the claims are being rejected without assigning reason. The High

Level Committee report observes that in 8 States the number of claims rejected under FRA was as much as 14.13 lakh. There is generally a big gap between the land claim and actual extent of titles issued to the claimants. In this connection it would be desirable to refer the Study of UNDP which conducted a study on High Rate of Rejections of Claims Under FRA, Especially in Jharkhand, Chhattisgarh and Odisha (2014). The Study observes that 38.2 per cent of the claims in Jharkhand and 26 per cent individual claims are rejected. Rejection is also high in Chhattisgarh. The average area per individual claims is as low as 0.57 acres in Jharkhand. The recording of claims at FRC level is almost non existent in the States of Jharkhand, Chhattisgarh and Odisha.

9. Poverty rate among Scheduled Tribes was quite high in 1993-94 at 65.9 per cent. However, there was overall decline in the poverty level between 1993-94 and 2004-05 but only the Scheduled Tribes lagged behind all social groups. Their poverty rate reduction during this period was only 3.7 per cent points, whereas for all groups it was around 8.5 per cent. By 2009-10, the reduction rates were substantial across all the groups between 2004-05 and 2009-10. It is heartening to note that the reduction rates were also significant for Scheduled Tribes, which was reduced by 16.9 per cent points. However, the poverty rates among the PVTGs is even lower to the general poverty rates of Scheduled Tribes in general.
10. The enactment of PESA of 1996 enjoins sufficient rights to *Gram Sabhas*, but it has hardly been extended to PVTGs.

Concluding Observation

The present chapter highlights some of the predicaments and dilemmas which the PVTGs are still facing. *It has been amply established that the major occupational dependence of PVTGs is on land, forest produce and forest resources.* The adverse impact of globalization and the so called developmental efforts have also contributed to the landlessness amongst the PVTGs. Their traditional dependence on shifting cultivation is also under stress. There are ample evidences to indicate that they are in the path of settled cultivation as also in the transition to proletarianization. There is necessity of providing land rights and homestead rights to PVTGs to facilitate them to the road to settled life. The isolationist policy is no more feasible and the path of globalization is also forcibly mainstreaming them to the path of cultural and social integration. There is *silver lining* of the PVTGs fighting for land rights. One such instance is the continuous protest by several Tribal Organizations under the leadership of C.K. Janu before the Kerala State Government for continuous 48 days protest leading to the State Government agreeing to distribute land to 252 landless families. This was followed by the exemplary Chengara Land Struggle in 2007, where the PVTGs were struggling for 120 days against Chengara Harison Malayalam State. This land struggle was jointly participated by landless *Dalits* and *Adivasis* as well as by OBCs from all parts of Kerala.

The recommendations made by Mota (2015) deserves attention:

1. Mota should facilitate especially designed status for the PVTGs which should also cover (in addition to enumeration) status of health, education and housing.
2. *Prepare vulnerability Indices* — PVTGs threatened with relocation from wild life areas and development projects should be identified and actionable strategies developed to prevent the same. Their Forest rights must be recognized. Wherever displacement and relocation becomes absolutely essential appropriate strategies be revolved for providing them appropriate rehabilitation. They should be made debt free.
3. There is need for recognition of the innate connection between PVTGs and their land and habitats is fundamental.
4. The status of implementation of Forest Rights Act (FRA) and PESA *vis-à-vis* PVTGs in various States should be monitored vigorously.
5. It is necessary to undertake an assessment of the statues of PVTGs who have been displaced with or without compensation/ rehabilitation and devise support mechanisms for ensuring their livelihoods.
6. Alienation of PVTG lands and habitats, even by other tribals, must be prevented and diversion/allocation of their lands for development projects must only be permitted with their prior informed consent as mandated by the Supreme Court Judgement of April 18, 2013 in the case of *Dongaria Kondhs* and as mandate by the FRA.
7. Allocation of land to displaced or relocated landless households among the PVTGs should be ensured, forest enclosures should be earmarked for the PVTGs.

8. Identification, release and rehabilitation of bounded labourers among the PVTGs be undertaken on priority.

REFERENCES

Foundation for Ecological Security (FES), (2014): *Study on High Rate of Rejections of Claims under FRA, Especially in Jharkhand, Chhattisgarh and Odisha*, Anand: FES.

M.V. Bijulal, Mishra K. Kamal (2012): *Chengara Land Struggle — Politics of Dalit Assertion in Kerala*, New Delhi: Indian Social Institute.

Meena Radhakrishna (2007): *Hunger among PTG and Non-PTG Nomadic Communities*, Delhi: MUKT-SAAD.

Ministry of Tribal Affairs (2015): *Scheme of Development of Particularly Vulnerable Tribal Groups (PVTGs)*, New Delhi: Government of India.

Ministry of Tribal Affairs (2013): *Statistical Profile of Scheduled Tribes in India*, New Delhi: Statistics Division, Government of India.

Mitra Mitashree, Kumar, P.V., Chakrabarty S. and Bharati P. (2006): *Nutritional Status of Kamar Tribal Children in Chhattisgarh*, Raipur: Pt. Ravishankar Shukla University.

Ota, A.B. *et. al.* (2010): *Review of Tribal Sub-Plan Approach in Odisha*, Bhubaneshwar: SCSTRTI.

Padel, Felix (1995): "In Lieu of an Afterword Mining Projects and Cultural Genocide: Colonial Roots of Present Conflicts", in Felix Padel (ed.), *The Sacrifice of Human Being: British Rule and the Konds of Orissa*, Delhi: Oxford University Press, pp. 23-24.

Padel, Felix (2011): *Sacrificing People*, Hyderabad: Orient Black Swan.

Pandey, G.D. and Tiwary, R.S. (2001): *Socio-Cultural Reproductive Health Practices of Primitive Tribes of Madhya Pradesh: Some Observations*, Jabalpur: Regional Medical Research Centre for Tribals.

Prasad, Archana (1997): "Unravelling the Forms of '*Adivasi*' Organization and Resistance in Colonial India", in Nandini Sunder (ed.), *Subalterns and Sovereigns*, Delhi: Oxford University Press.

Sahani, Ramesh *et. al.* (2013): "Particularly Vulnerable Tribal Groups in India: An Overview", *Journal of the Anthropological Survey of India*, 62(2): 851-865.

Sharma Sandeep, Makol Neelam, Manisha and Chakravarty Moyna (2007): "Socio-Demographic Profile of *Hill Korwas* of Chhattisgarh", *Indian Journal Prev. Soc. Med*, Vol. 38, Nos. 3 & 4.

Solanki, Arvind and Choubey Kailash (2014): "Spatial Patterns of Malaria among *Bharia* Tribe of *Tamia*, Chhindwara", *International Association of Scientific Innovation and Research (IASIR)*, USA, pp. 172-75.

Sunder Nandini (1997): *Subalterns and Sovereigns' — An Anthropological History of Bastar, 1854-1996*, New Delhi: Oxford University Press.

Xaxa, Virginius *et. al.* (2014): *Report of the High Level Committee on Socio-Economic, Health and Education Status of Tribal Communities of India*, New Delhi: Ministry of Tribal Affairs, Government of India.

APPENDIX I

State-wise Number of PVTGs and their Population between 1961 and 2001

Sl.No.	*States*	*Number of PVTG*	*1961*	*2001*	*Remarks (% of All India)*
1.	Andhra Pradesh	12	1,23,269	3,34,144	12.07
2.	Bihar	9	2,57,288	10,873	0.39
3.	Gujarat	5	—	1,06,775	3.86
4.	Jharkhand	9	—	3,87,358	13.99
5.	Karnataka	2	1,005	45,899	1.66
6.	Kerala	5	—	20,186	0.73
7.	Madhya Pradesh	7	2,09,553	7,85,720	28.38
8.	Maharashtra	3	—	4,08,668	14.76
9.	Manipur	1	—	1,225	0.04
10.	Odisha	13	—	68,745	2.48
11.	Rajasthan	1	23,125	76,237	2.75
12.	Tamil Nadu	6	93,794	2,17,937	7.87
13.	Tripura	1	56,579	1,65,103	5.96
14.	Uttar Pradesh	2	—	5,365	0.19
15.	Uttarakhand	2	—	47,288	1.71
16.	West Benal	3	45,906	85,983	3.11
17.	Andaman & Nicobar	5	71	816	0.03
	All India Total	**86**	**8,10,590**	**27,68,322**	Increase of 341.5 per cent, i.e. an increase by nearly 3 and half time between 1961 and 2001.

Note: The number of PVTGs in Bihar is 9 and in Jharkhand also the number of PVTGs is 9. The number of PVTGs in Uttar Pradesh is 2 and the same names of PVTGs is also included for Uttarakhand. This is the reason for the number of PVTGs increasing from 75 to 86.

Source: Census of India 2001.

APPENDIX II

Demographic Vulnerability of PVTGs in India

Sl.No.	*States*	*Name of PVTG*	*2001*
1.	Bihar	*Asur*	181
		Birhor	406
		Birja	17
		Hill Kharia	1,501
		Korwa	703
		Sauria Paharia	585
		Savar	420
		Total	**3,813**
2.	Kerala	*Cholamaikayhan*	—
3.	Madhya Pradesh	*Birhor*	143
4.	Odisha	*Birhor*	702
5.	Tamil Nadu	*Kora*	925
		Toda	1,560
6.	Uttar Pradesh	*Raji*	998
7.	Uttarakhand	*Raji*	517
8.	Andaman & Nicobar	Great Andamanese	43
		Jarawa	240
		Onge	96
		Sentinelest	39
		Shom pen	398
		Total	**816**
	All India	**Grand Total**	**9,474**

Source: Census of India 2001.

APPENDIX III

State-wise Particularly Vulnerable Tribal Groups (PVTGs) and their Population in India (1971 to 2001)

Sl.No.	States	Population			
		1971	1981	1991	2001
1.	Andhra Pradesh	1,95,264 (13.92)	1,89,968 (8.40)	2,86,078 (11.86)	3,34,144 (12.07)
2.	Bihar	2,85,716 (20.36)	5,23,545 (23.15)	3,70,638 (15.36)	10,873 (0.39)
3.	Gujarat	54,545 (3.89)	98,553 (4.35)	1,29,253 (5.35)	1,06,775 (3.86)
4.	Jharkhand	N.A.	N.A.	N.A.	3,87,358 (13.99)
5.	Karnataka	14,276 (1.01)	49,893 (2.20)	45,693 (1.90)	45,899 (1.66)
6.	Kerala	9,510 (0.67)	12,921 (0.57)	17,647 (0.60)	20,186 (0.72)
7.	Madhya Pradesh	3,09,295 (22.04)	5,84,998 (25.88)	6,73,068 (27.90)	7,85,720 (28.38)
8.	Maharashtra	2,56,246 (18.26)	3,59,425 (15.90)	3,50,046 (14.50)	4,08,668 (14.77)
9.	Manipur	5,123 (0.36)	6,544 (0.28)	9,592 (0.39)	1,225 (0.04)
10.	Odisha	30,538 (2.17)	77,267 (3.41)	58,225 (2.41)	68,745 (2.48)
11.	Rajasthan	26,796 (1.90)	40,945 (1.82)	59,810 (2.47)	76,237 (2.76)
12.	Tamil Nadu	1,05,032 (7.48)	1,44,366 (6.38)	1,95,332 (8.09)	2,17,937 (7.88)
13.	Tripura	64,722 (4.61)	84,004 (3.72)	1,11,606 (4.63)	1,65,103 (5.97)
14.	Uttar Pradesh	—	32,894 (1.45)	36,349 (1.50)	5,365 (0.19)
15.	Uttarakhand	—	—	—	47,288 (1.71)
16.	West Bengal	45,906 (3.27)	55,051 (2.43)	68,950 (2.86)	85,983 (3.10)
17.	Andaman & Nicobar	212 (0.01)	393 (0.01)	377 (0.01)	816 (0.02)
	Grand Total	**4,03,181**	**22,60,767**	**24,12,664**	**27,68,322**

Source: Statistical Profile of Scheduled Tribes in India 2013, Ministry of Tribal Affairs, Statistical Division, Government of India, New Delhi, pp. 160-61.

APPENDIX IV

Implementation of FRA 2006 in Jharkhand for PVTG

Sl.No.	*District*	*No. of PVTG Family*	*No. of Titles Given to PVTG*	*% of PVTG Family Given Titles*
1.	Bokaro	87	3	3.45
2.	Catra	1,375	—	—
3.	Garhwa	7,945	79	0.99
4.	Gumla	3,909	48	1.23
5.	Hazaribagh	672	60	8.93
6.	Latehar	4,025	73	1.81
7.	Lohardagga	526	7	1.33
8.	W. Singhbhu	200	0	1.00
9.	Palamau	2,982	134	4.49
10.	E. Singhbhu	13,797	26	0.19
11.	Ramgarh	145	36	24.83
12.	Simdega	225	0	0
13.	Saraikela	433	34	7.85
14.	Kodarma	347	109	31.41
15.	Ranchi	837	609	72.76
16.	Khuti	140	—	—
17.	Iridih	161	—	—
18.	Dhanbad	45	1	2.22
	Total	**37,851**	**1,219**	**3.22**
19.	Dumka	7,221	18	0.25
20.	Jamtara	816	188	23.04
21.	·Sahebaganj	9,800	72	0.73
22.	Pakur	11,877	78	0.66
23.	Godda	7,889	27	1.73
24.	Deohar	1,560	0	—
	Total	**39,163**	**57**	**0.15**
	G. Total	**77,014**	**1,276**	**1.66**

Source: Government of Jharkhand.

4

In Search of Sustainable Development: The Case of Lanjia Saora PVTG of Odisha

S.N. Ratha

I

The communities, officially known as Scheduled Tribes, constitute a little less than nine per cent of the country's population. For considerable part of history, most of them were left to themselves in their mountainous and forest habitats. They came under the serious administrative scan, when Acts, projecting the distinctness of their habitations and socio-cultural individuality, were passed in the closing decades of the British rule. However, with the country coming to be governed by its own Constitution, their multidimensional deprivation, such as, isolation, limited world view, scanty exposure to formal education, poor state of health, low life-expectancy, high rate of infant and maternal mortality, marginal farming, over-dependence on the forest — in short, low quality of their lives, compared to other communities around them, came to the focus; and administrative actions were initiated with the launching Five Year Plans and non-Plan Projects.

The initial actions, however, do not seem to be commensurate with the ground reality. In the First Five Year Plan (1951-56), Tribal Development input was through Community Development Projects. There were 56 such projects in the country. The Tribal development component constituted only 1 per cent of the Plan outlay. During the Second Five Year Plan (1956-61), 43 Special Multipurpose Tribal Development Blocks supplemented the Tribal Development Projects. Though it covered the entire country, the Tribal Development part was 0.9 per cent of the Plan outlay. During this plan period (May 1959), The Government of India Constituted a Committee to review the functioning of the Special Multipurpose Tribal Development Blocks. Verrier Elwin, an eminent Oxford trained anthropologist, headed it. The Report was submitted on 30 March, 1960. In the opinion of the Committee, the T.D. Block Programme did not have the desired effect. However, they were asked to continue for the Third Plan Period (1961-66) and extend it to cover more areas of tribal concentration. The projected expenditure for Tribal Development was 0.69 per cent of the outlay.

On the eve of launching the Third Plan, "The Scheduled Area and Scheduled Tribes Commission" (1960-61) was set up with U.N. Dhebar as Chairman. One of the major findings of this Commission was that "within Scheduled Tribes, there existed an inequality in the rate and level of development". The tribal situation was not uniform in the country. Therefore, uniformity in the approach to tribal development is not likely to hit the target.

The Fourth Plan did not take off in the usual sequence. Before it started (1969-74), there were three Annual Plans (1966-67, 67-68, 68-69). For this entire three year period, provision for tribal development was only 0.48 per cent of the budget.

With the launching of the Fourth Plan (1969-74), special programmes were launched for the tribal areas of Andhra Pradesh, Bihar, Madhya Pradesh and Odisha in the form of Integrated Tribal Development Agencies/Projects (ITDA/ITDP). It emphasized beneficiary oriented schemes. Funds allotted for tribal development was 0.5 per cent of the outlay (Rupees 7.5 million)

During the Fifth Plan (1974-78), a sub-plan strategy was initiated. Popularly known as Tribal Sub-Plan (TSP), it was a smaller plan contained in the State-Plan. This was a major paradigm shift in the strategy for Tribal development; and probably the beginning of a really serious attempt to hit the target. It sought to identify States with tribal majority Blocks to convert them into Integrated Tribal Development Projects (ITDP), to prepare individual project reports, keeping in view of the available resources, skills, needs, and the aptitude of the target population, to create an appropriate administrative structure for tribal areas and to adopt an appropriate administrative policy, and allot funds for tribal areas of the State, from general State Plan Sectors, on the basis of the ST population in an administrative unit. Thus, the most salient features of the TSP approach were: (1) the budget allocation for tribal development proportionate to the percentage of the Scheduled tribes, and that is not to be diverted for any other purpose; (2) quantification of funds from different sectors and fixation of targets in each sector, for speedy development; and (3) reflection of schemes and programmes relevant and beneficial to the tribes in the flow of funds.

The TSP strategy served to speed up the development of the Scheduled tribes; ensuring flow of funds to, and benefits from, programmes of each sector; and at the same time providing integrated delivery services to tribal areas. The strategy of the approach was the development of the area along with the tribal population living there in. It was designed to target individuals and families to benefit from income generating schemes in the spheres of agriculture, horticulture, and animal husbandry. Human resource development through education and building infrastructure had been a major component of the strategy. The approach envisaged an integrated development of the tribal area; and as such, all programmes, irrespective of their source of funding, functioned in unison to bring the area at par with the rest of the State. The various sources of funding were: (a) State Plan, (b) Special Central Assistance (SCA), and (c) Central and Centrally Sponsored Programmes (SCP).

II

The TSP approach necessitated a closer look at the quality of life of the tribal communities leading to a discovery of, what the Dhebar Commission had indicated that some tribes or sections of some tribes are in extreme difficult situations. The need to address to the special requirements was discussed in a "Workshop on Primitive Tribal Communities" in January 1975, organized by the Government of India, at New Delhi. The proceedings of the Workshop, put together in the form of a booklet entitled "Primitive Tribes — The First Step", was brought out. It provided guidelines to identify the problems and to concretize the approach to the Programmes of the Primitive Tribes. Subsequently, the Government of India "requested the State Governments to identify the groups and to have a quick survey to pin-point their habitations, their pressing problems, etc." (GoI, 1990a: 143). However, the State Governments did not seem to view the matter seriously. It is evident from a letter from the Joint Secretary, Ministry of Home affairs, GoI, addressed to the Commissioners/Secretaries of the States (Do. No. 29918/12/77; TD dated 4.6.1977). It was pointed out that the Government of India did not know "as yet the preparedness of the States in regard to the programme formulation and implementation for these groups", though the GoI had allotted some funds on *ad-hoc* basis in the year 1977-78 (GoI, *ibid.*: 143).

Almost two years later, the Joint Secretary, Ministry of Home Affairs, GoI, circulated "A Brief Note on the Primitive Tribes" to "help the State Governments in drawing up the Projects for Primitive Tribes". In the paragraph 2 of this note, criteria suggested to identify the Primitive Tribal Groups were:

1. Smallness in size, homogeneity, distinct cultural and ethnic identity, and diminishing number;
2. Backwardness and isolation;
3. Primitive technology in agriculture, pre-agriculture state of economy, small and marginal farming, forest collection; and
4. Very low literacy (Do. No. 20018/9/79-TD dated 26. 5. 1979, GoI, *ibid.*: 145).

A year after, the Joint Secretary (TD), Ministry of Home Affairs, GoI, had to shoot a reminder (Letter No. 20018/5/81-TD (A) dated 27.4.1980) inviting attention of the State Governments to the Ministry's earlier communications; and to a letter from the Planning Commission (No. PC/O 1/6ITSP/78 dated nil.6.78). The letter pointed out, that the basic approach to the problems of the Primitive Tribal Groups has three aspects. *Firstly*, identification of the primitive tribal groups to ensure that a genuine group does not get left out; and a group which does not qualify is not brought within the ambit of the programme; *secondly*, formulation of appropriate plan and strategy to enable a primitive tribal group overcome its peculiar problems; *thirdly*, effective implementation of the formulated plans through suitable administrative machinery (GoI, *ibid.*: 153). Repeating the criteria of identification, the letter noted that 52 communities were identified till the end of 1979-80. Further, the letter pointed out the necessity of studying each of them separately to formulate appropriate programmes. Guidelines were spelt out to prepare project reports avoiding stereotypes, so that, each is to be unique, related to the lifestyle, need and aspiration of the concerned group (GoI, *ibid.*: 153-54). This letter also indicated the need for competent, dedicated and sensitive personnel to man the projects. The Constitution of suitable administrative structures was left to the States. The GoI directed the States to take up the PTG programme as a priority item, complete the preparation of the project reports, establish the required administrative machinery and initiate programme before 30 September, 1981 (GoI, *ibid.*: 154).

More than five years after the issue of these directions, the Government of India noted (vide letter No. 20018/4/85-TD/R, Ministry of Home Affairs, dared 3.6.1985) "that comprehensive project reports on the identified primitive tribal groups . . . have not been formulated in many cases" and those which were formulated have not properly reflected "the perspective nature of development plan, touching upon resource endowment, skill and felt needs of the area" (GoI, *ibid.*: 155).

On the backdrop of this situation, the Government of India "decided that where the project report for a primitive tribal group has not been prepared or where the comments of the Ministry of Home Affairs have not been communicated or the report revised on the basis of such comments; core programmes relevant to the identified groups and the area, may be launched and implemented. . . . The core programmes to be undertaken for each group with the special Central assistance released by the Ministry from time to time should include family-oriented schemes designed to increase the income of the family by increased productivity in the field of agriculture, horticulture, cottage industries, etc. . . . besides all programmes relevant to the objectives, spelt out in the chapter on 'Objectives and Strategy' in the report of the Working Group in the chapter on 'Primitive Tribal Groups' should also be kept in view. It is suggested that the above programmes may be implemented in all cases without waiting for specific approval of the project report from the Ministry (where the project reports have been submitted). It is, however, reiterated that preparation and submission of comprehensive project reports for each group, as per the guidelines issued from time to time, should not be unduly delayed (GoI, *ibid.*: 155).

By the year 2005, 75 communities or sections there of had been identified as 'Primitive Tribal Groups' in different parts of the country (GoI, 2005: 174-76). Sometimes in 2006, they were redesignated as Particularly Vulnerable Tribal Groups (PVTGs). In the mean time, the Sixth Five Year (1980-85), the Seventh Five Year (1985-90), the Eighth Five Year (1992-97) and the Ninth Five Year (1997-2002) Plans were over and the Tenth Five Year (2002-07) Plan was in operation. Between the Seventh and the Eighth Plan, there was a Plan holiday stretching over two financial years (1990-91 and 1991-92).

The Tenth Five Year Plan document noted the "precarious conditions of the Primitive Tribal Groups" and set to prepare a National Plan of Action (NPA) for their survival, protection and development (pp. 462, 464, 466, 468).The projected expenditure for tribal development during this Plan was 0.09 per cent of the outlay. In the Eleventh Five Year Plan (2007-12) and the Twelveth Five Year Plan (2012-17), now in operation, the projected expenditure in the outlay remained at the same 0.09 per cent level.

III

From this account, it appears that the Government of India seriously began addressing itself to the plights of the tribes who were yet to cross the threshold of "primitiveness", prepared guidelines for their identification and "requested the State Governments to identify the groups, and have a quick survey to pinpoint their habitations, and pressing problems . . ." some times around 1975; and "expected that a clear picture will be available and it will be possible to launch a programme in 1976-77 itself". Some State Governments still dragging their feet and The Government of India in hot pursuit, had "allowed some money on *ad hoc* basis" in 1977-78; but soon decided not to continue with the programme on *ad hoc* arrangement, but address itself "to the specific problems of each of these groups as originally envisaged". It was 1979, "The programmes for the Primitive Tribes have not taken off yet, in spite of several discussions and correspondence in the past" wrote the Joint Secretary (TD), GoI, enclosing a comprehensive guideline for the State Governments to formulate, launch and administer projects (D.O. No. 20018/9/79-TD dated the 26 May, 1979, GoI, 1990: 145).

Odisha appears to have responded around 1984. By then 13 groups were identified. Among them, *eight* (*Chuktia Bhunjia*, *Birhor*, *Bondo*, *Didayi*, *Kharia*, *Juang*, *Lodha* and *Mankiridia*) are complete tribes. The *Kutia Khond* and the *Dongria Khond* belong to the *Khond* Group. The *Lanjia Saura* is the hill dwelling section of the *Saura* tribe. The *Saura*, a small part of the Plains section, inhabiting the Tumba area of Ganjam district. The *Paudi Bhuyan*, the hill dwelling section of the *Bhuyan* tribe.

The *Bondo* and the *Didayi* are in Malkangiri district. The *Lanjia Saura* are in Rayagada and Gajapati districts. The *Dongaria Khond* are in Rayagada district. The *Saura* are in Gajapati and Ganjam districts. The *Chuktia Bhunjia* are in Nuapada district. The *Kharia*, *Mankiridia*, the *Birhor* and the *Lodha* are in Mayurbhanj district. The Juang are in Keonjhar district (the *Dhenkanal Juangs* are not included). The Kutia Khond is in Phulbani district. The *Paudi Bhuyan* are in Sundargarh and Angul districts.

Altogether 17 Projects, 2 for *Dangria Khond*, 2 for *Paudi Bhuyan*, 2 for *Lanjia Saura*, 2 for *Saura*, 3 for *Paudi Bhuyan*, (ITDA/ITDP), one in which the *Kharia*, *Mankiridia* and *Birhor* clubbed, are in operation; and for the rest one each are in operation.

The TSP area of Odisha spreads over 118 Development Blocks in fourteen districts (Malkangiri, Koraput, Rayagada, Nabarangapur,

Gajapati, Phulabani, Kalahandi, Nuapada, Sambalpur, Deogarh, Sundagada, Keonjhar, Mayurbhanj and Baleswar) and is covered by 21 Integrated Tribal Development Agencies (ITDA) In an ITDA area, where the tribal population is 50 per cent or more, a tribal family is provided with a subsidy of 25-30 per cent for a family oriented development programme.

IV

The Ethnic group covered in this study is the *Lanjia Saora*, a section of the great *Saora* tribe. The *Saora* is a community of very long historical standing, mentioned as *Śabara* along with communities named as *Dasyu, Andhra, Pulinda*, and *Pundra* in *Aitarēya Brāhmana* (vii, 18:2) and *Śankhayana Srauta Sutra* (xv, 26:6), two Vedic Works related to the *Rig Veda* (Vedic Index, MacDonnel and Keith 1958: Volume I, p. 23; Volume II: p. 354). Their mention with the Andhra connotes that they have been in their present habitat since the Vedic times, if not earlier. They were noticed by Ptolemy and Pliny (Ramamurty, 1894:340); and "that at one time, they were distributed right across Middle and eastern India" and that they were the dominant people of the region "during the period 800 B.C., to A.D., 1200" (Elwin, 1958:33). Their present concentration, however, is in the districts of Rayagada, Gajapati, and Ganjam of Odisha; and the adjoining districts of Srikakulam and Vizianagaram in Andhra Pradesh.

The hill-dwelling section of the great *Saorā* tribe (GoI, 2005:105-06) is named as *Lānjiā Saorā* by the Odia speakers of the region. The name is derived from the loin cloth, their men used to wear, a loose end of which hung in front and the other on the back simulating a tail (*lānja* in Odia). In the Andhra Pradesh list of Scheduled tribes, the name appears as *Maliaya Savara* (GoI, 2000: 7). This name is said to have been derived from *māḷi*, meaning necklace of glass beads, profusely used to be worn by the women folk, covering their breasts. Presently, the dress and ornaments follow almost an all-India pattern.

More probably, the community is named after '*mālihā*', as their habitat on the Eastern Ghats is locally called. In official documents of Andhra Pradesh (2004:81), the name occurs as '*Koṇdā Sāvārā*. (In Telugu *Koṇdā* means hill). Elwin (1955) named them as '*Hill Saora*'. The people, however, call themselves as *Sorā*. Ramamurty (1931:vii), who studied their language, recommends the name *Sora* to be pronounced as *So:ra*; (using the symbols of the International Phonetic Association).

Saora, the spelling used here is from the 1931 Census (Volume XIV, Part 1, p. 286), which comes closer to the community's own pronunciation.

The habitat of the *Lanjia Saora*, spread over the north-east section of the Eastern ghats on the east of the Vansadhārā valley, "go by the local name *Māliha*" (Francis, 1909:146). Most villages are situated on hill-slopes/terraces overlooking the terraced farming area below. The forest behind, almost touches the village. Down below is a dale, not very wide, covered with paddy fields touching another hill, with or without another village and terraced fields. Villages on hill tops or at foot hills are rare. Invariably, a village is located close to a perennial water source. The settlements are fairly permanent and not easily abandoned. The hillocks vary in height from 700 to 1,500 meters from the sea level. Whenever a hii-rang takes a "v" or "^" turn throwing up a water parting line, there ensues a stream or rivulet. The entire area is full of such streams as it is with hillocks. Thus the geomorphology of the area is an intricate maze of hills and streams and magnificent terrace of paddy fields, forest and farming patches dotted with human habitations.

The climate is one of extreme type. The summer, spreading from March to June, is oppressive. May is the hottest month. The monsoon touches the area in middle of June and lasts, with intermittent rains, till the end of September. The mid-winter months, December and January, are very cold. The annual rainfall is around 1,400 mm. The temperature varies from around 12°C in mid-winter to 42-45°C in mid-summer. The soil in the higher contours is of lateritic origin. In the valley it is largely sandy and loamy, enriched from the forest droppings brought down by runnels and streams. Thus the valley, though narrow, is fairly fertile. A good amount surface water flowing through the streams help irrigation wherever land situation permits.

The villages vary in size from less than ten households to more than 60. From a distance a village looks like green patch. As one closes upon the spot, houses begin peeling from behind the trees. The houses may be independent of each other, each within its enclosure, securely fenced with their homestead land, or they may be side by side, such that a row faces another across the street like two blocks facing each other. Thus, a village may be agglutinated or a neighbourhood. In official records a habitat may figure as village or hamlet. For the inmates, however, it is a village.

Most villages are agglutinated, with one or two streets. When homesteads are scattered, their enclosures have space for kitchen gardening some fruit-bearing trees, like mango, jack, tamarind, *mohua* and sago-palm. Some agglutinate villages may also have one or more homesteads of this type, a little away from the main village Their "well kept fields" with numerous *mohua* (*Basia latifora*) trees scattered about them "have been likened to Italian homesteads surrounded with their dark olives" (Francis, 1909:157).

The villages, by and large, are permanent settlements. The boundary between two villages is marked by a sacred groove, normally on its southern fringe. It is known as *sandhi*. The presiding deity of the *sandhi* is worshipped once a year. A pig ling is sacrificed by piercing it through its chest over a fixed pointed stump. The sacrificial creature is left at the spot. The entire village participates. Women from every house dump their used earthen cooking pots at the sacrificial spot. Thus, the *sandhi* is a conspicuous spot with old trees, bushes and a heap of earthen pots and pot-shreds.

An eye catching landmark of a Saora village is its *guar*, the place of the secondary mortuary rites. It is cluster of stone slabs fixed erect on the ground, each representing a departed soul of the village. The Saora method of disposal of the dead is by cremation. *Guar* is an annual function when in a ritual, officiated by the community priest, the next of kin of a person, a year or more of age, dead during the preceding 12 months, erect a stone slab in his or her honour. This place has also the status of a sacred groove.

A wooden pole installed under an umbrella shaped thatched structure, at the entrance of the village, represents a deity named *jenaglaw*, regarded as the protector of the village from epidemics and evil spirits. A small cottage in middle of the village is devoted to the twin deity, *Gusadusung* and His consort *Kittisung*.

With the spread of Christianity, these land marks are giving way to churches grave yards.

The secular head of the village is designated as *Gamāng*. The decision making body of the village is the council of household heads under his leadership. Other functionaries attached to him are *Dalabehera, Mandal, Badarait* and *Barika*. The religious head is *Buiya*. All these, including the *Gamang* are hereditary positions, following the principle of male primogeniture. The *Gamang* and the *Buiya* enjoy considerable status in the society, live in large and better houses, own more land and wealth; and often have more than one wife.

A typical house is built upon a plinth of about 2-5 feet in height from the ground. Most houses are strongly built. The walls are made of stone slabs held together with specially processed mud plaster. The ceiling is made of wood and mud. The roof is of thatch. Bricks, cement and corrugated iron sheets have already made their way into the villages as building material. Well to do houses are stone and brick walled, cement plastered, concrete or corrugated iron sheet roofed. A humble house may have wooed stakes fixed to ground and plastered with mud for walls with thatched roofs without ceiling.

The houses are open to the street. Some have also back openings line with the front. There are no windows. Specific places for all relevant activities of the inmates are built into it. The cattle shed stands separated from the dwelling quarters by a solid wall. Poultry birds and pigs are safely lodged in cubicles specially made for the purpose under the front verandah.

Wall painting is an integral part of a *Saora* dwelling. In the language of the community it is called *idital* (*idi* = picture or painting, *tal* = wall).The inner surface of a side wall is painted with pictures, symbolizing plants, animals, human beings, Sun, Moon, and stars as well as some geometrical designs. A picture is drawn arranging straight lines, circles, triangles, etc. in specific orders to produce the desired result. Some anthropomorphic figures are supposed to represent the ancestors in one set. An *Idital* specialist is called *Kudang*. The painting is to be executed by the *Kudang* and consecrated through an installation ritual *before* occupying a new house.

The painting is a graphic presentation of the Saora's known universe; and is supposed to represent the family deity. All edibles to be eaten for the first time in the season are first offered to the *Idital*. It is taken care of with reverence due to a deity as long as the house remains inhabited.

V

The livelihood pursuit of the *Lanjia Saora* is based upon land and forest. Their careful method of cultivation was noticed by the author of the *Vizagapatam District Gazetteer* who wrote, "They are known for their industry with which they cultivate. They terrace the steep hill-sides with great revetments of stone, often fifteen feet deep. . . . preserve every pound of fodder by cutting the crops close to the ground . . ., and utilize for irrigation every rill . . ." (Francis, *ibid.*). A substantial part of land on hill slopes is terraced. The terraces are built with great ingenuity with inputs of substantial input of manual labour, the most important asset of the *Lanjia Saora*. The magnificence of the terraces bears ample testimony to the meticulous, skillful and optimum use of this asset. The terraces come under the best quality of land. The lower terraces gradually merge with the land in the valley down below. They are better and more productive than those on the upper contours. The terraced plots are smaller in size than those in the valley. Small plots, at different heights are used for crops suited to their location. The upper terraces are rain fed. The lower terraces having the benefit of irrigation from the perennial streams yield two to three crops annually.

Rainfed crops are different types of millets (finger millet, fox-tail millet, pearl millet, barnyard millet, *kodo* millet, little millet, etc.), *sorghum*, pulses (red, black, green and horse grams) and oil seeds (gingli, sesame) in addition to *kharif* paddy.

Each household owns a sizable plot of land around or close to it. The plots are securely fenced. They are some thing like kitchen gardens. They normally contain some fruit bearing trees and the space between trees is used to cultivate seasonal vegetables.

The terraces and homestead land are privately owned. The unterraced hill slopes, flat-topped hills constitute a part of the common property resources controlled by the patrilineal extended kin groups called *birinda* or the village as a whole. Though such land is actually State property, the users have been enjoying usufructuary rights for generations where they practice shifting cultivation (*podu*). The upper contours are used for the cultivation of minor millets. The lower contours are used for raising maize, *sorghum*, finger millet, pulses and oilseeds. A good quantity of turmeric and ginger is also cultivated for external market.

In addition to these seasonal crops, long-term plantation of tree crops is also practiced. These include mango, tamarind, jack, *mohua* (*Basia latifora*) and *sago* palm. These are planted singly or in clusters planted on *podu* land, homestead land or any suitably available land. These bring in reasonable cash income and provide a safety cover against food scarcity. Stray *mohua*, and mango plants in the forest, on the public land or on the road-side are treated as common property; whereas tamarind, *karanja* (*Pongomia glabra*), *kusum* (saffron flower or *Carthamus tinctonus*), date palm, and sago palm have their individual owners, wherever they stand and such are scrupulously respected by the community.

A substantial quantity of tamarind, *mohua* seeds and flowers makes its way to the external market. Mango kernel and tamarind seeds are processed to make them edible in times of scarcity. Sap tapered from the sago and the date-palm is a soft drink for all occasions, social, religious or casual. A hard drink is distilled from *mohua* flowers. Oil is extracted from *karanj, kusum* and *mohua* seeds. *Kusum* wood is used exclusively to make agricultural implements, especially the plough. Felling any edible fruit bearing or otherwise useful tree is a taboo, the violation of which brings in divine wrath in the form of famine, drought and epidemic, etc.

The forest constitutes a complementary as well as a supplementary source of livelihood. It also enriches the food basket. A number of items, such as *mohua* flowers and seeds, a number of edible leaves and tubers, mushrooms, berries, and wild mangoes are collected in different seasons. Hunting is an annual ritual. Fishing is a leisure time activity to add to dietary delicacy. A lot of fish is collected from the paddy field when, just before harvest, the water from the field is let out to render the field dry to facilitate reaping.

There are a few artisan groups among the *Saora*. The weavers are called *Arsi/Arisi*. The basket makers are *Kindal/Kundal*. The *Muli/ Luara/Lohara* are iron-smiths. There are good carpenters and masons among them.

VI

The nuclear family, consisting of a man, his wife and child/children, is the basic unit of *Saora* social structure. This is normal rule, if not compounded by polygyny. A polygynous household consists of more than one hut, each men for a wife and her children. It is patrilineal in descent, patrilocal in residence, and patriarchal in decision-making. After marriage, a daughter leaves her parental family to live with her husband; whereas a son breaks from the parental family his own nearby. Thus, a cluster of *Saora* households, be it a hamlet or a village, is a patrilineal and patrilocal residence group named as *birinda*. It is a very well-knit kin-group. The member families help each other in land preparation for cultivation, transplantation, weeding, harvesting, house building, etc. The social life centers a round the family and the *birinda*.

In spite of its patriarchal nature, women enjoy considerable freedom. They work side by side with men in cultivation sites, performing such jobs as, clearing the site, sowing, weeding, harvesting, etc. suited to their physical ability. There is no discernible gender based division of labour, except that women do not plough. Forest collection is largely a feminine activity.

Children are treated with great deal of indulgence and are never physically punished. They enjoy a carefree childhood. Filial affection is exemplary. From a very early age, the *Saora* is oriented to the values of truth, honesty, hard work, fellow feeling, hospitality, respect to elders and fear of God. From the age of six years children accompany parents to the work sites and the forest to learn associated skills. They join the work force around the age of 11 years.

Boys get married around the age of 18 years and girls around 15. The *birinda*, often coterminous with a village or hamlet, is exogamous. Marriage with a matrilateral cross cousin is preferred. Giving due consideration to the preference of the boy and the girl, initiating a matrimonial negotiation is the responsibility of the boy's parents. The negotiation is concluded with the payment of a bride price. On an auspicious day, fixed by the priest, the prospective groom goes to the bride's house. A small group of relatives, carrying a reasonable amount of home made liquor, accompany him. The girl's parents treat the party to a feast, and then hand over the bride to the groom. When the party returns, the boy's parents treat the village to a feast. The marriage is complete. No ritual is associated with it. A girl, even after marriage, continues to be a member of her parental *birinda*.

Plygynous marriages are not rare. In secondary marriages, levirate and sororate, wherever possible, is preferred. An exceptional form of secondary marriage, where a young widow is married to her step-son, is found in this community. It is termed as *yoyāngkoi*.

Divorce is a simple affair. A martially dissatisfied woman can simply return to her parents, or to another man of her preference. In the latter case, the new husband is expected to compensate the deserted husband, normally amounting to the bride price paid earlier if the man initiates the divorce, he does not get back the bride price that he might have paid. If there are children, the infants go with the mother, and grown-up s stay with the father.

VII

Death is regarded as a supernatural punishment. The *Saora* do not associate death with any disease. The normal disposal of the dead is by cremation. In case small pox or cholera is the immediate cause, the disposal is by burial.

The body bathed, groomed and dressed with a piece of new cloth, before carrying it to the cremation yard. The pal bearers are women, while men carry out other associated functions. Before the body is consigned to flames, a cock is offered in sacrifice, the meat is cooked with rice; and the preparation is offered to the spirit of the dead. The victual then is partaken by the mourners, a part of which is carried home for others to share. The following day, selected family members accompanied by the community priest (*jāni* or *Kurānmārāng*) and his female counterpart (*Kurānboi*) go the cremation spot to decipher the immediate cause of death from the marks appearing on the spread out ash. The ashes are then gathered into conical heap. The party then retuns home after taking a purificatory bath on the way. At home a grown-up spinster of the village is chosen to assist the family in the performance of the death related rituals. In this capacity she is called *idoiboi*.

After a few days or weeks or months or even years, the ceremony called *Guār*, is performed, singly or with several other families which are also perform the ceremony. It is an expensive affair, as it is mandatory to offer goats and buffalos in sacrifice. The ceremony enables the dead to join their deified ancestors as equals.

VIII

The *Saora* visualize their existential position between what they see and feel around and the Powers that made their seen world possible. They constantly feel the presence of a number of divinities and deified ancestors, who, provided they are treated with humility and reverence, make them breath, keep them and their domestic animals healthy, provide them with food, maintain the fertility of their fields, equip them with strength, ensure a good harvest, ward off droughts and epidemics, pour sufficient rain, bestow conjugal bliss, bless them with good, strong, obedient, skillful and hardworking children, provide a safety cover against malevolent spirits; and finally conduct them to the abode of their ancestors.

The abode of these divinities is spread over human habitations, homes, farming sites, hills and forest and the under world. They are in constant move to observe human behaviour and are watchful of all human activities. Therefore, the *Saora* are careful enough not to annoy them by any untoward conduct and behavior. An annoying behaviour or conduct is *erāsi* (*Saora* equivalent of sin). Infuriated Super naturals are likely to play *havoc* with human life and environment. The *Saora* constantly endeavour to keep all divinities in good humour through sacrificial offerings in every undertaking, such as, house building, land preparation, sowing, transplanting, harvesting, eating first a season's fruits or produce. This symbiotic or complementary relationship between the human and the divine constitute the essence of *Saora* religious and moral life.

The Supreme God of the *Saora* is *Kitung* (the *Saora* equivalent of Creator), is regarded as the principal creator of the earth and every thing it contains. *Jenanglaw*, installed at the entrance of a village, protects it from epidemics and evil spirits. *Gusadusung* and his consort *Kitisung*, believed to be the defied progenitors of the community, installed in a hut inside the village, guide the inhabitants in their day-to-day activities and protect children when the parents are out on work. *Idital*, literally wall painting, ritually done on the inner surface of a side wall of the house, represents the presiding deity of the household.

The principal ritual specialist of the village is *Buyāng*. He prescribes the day for all religious and secular undertakings. *Kudāng* is the ritual healer. He is also the specialist painter of the *idital*. He divines for the causes of illness and other difficulties. If it is found to be the consequence of committing an *erāsi* (sin), he prescribes remedies and performs curative *rituals on behalf of his clients*. The *Jani*, a lesser diviner (*Kurangmarang and his female counterpart Kuranboi*, both are called by a generic term *Jāni*), often does the preliminary job of identifying the spirit responsible for the affliction, before the *Kudang* takes over.

IX

The great *Saora* community is in the process of polarization into two distinct religious groups. The hill dwellers have been exposed to Christianity for more than a century. The plains section, popularly known as *Suddha* (pure) *Saora*, has successfully insulated itself against Christianity. In the early decades of the twentieth century, under the leadership of Mangai Gamang of Marichiguda village, in Gunapur subdivision of Rayagada district, the *Suddha Saora* projected the individuality of their culture and language. It is said that Mangai meditated for 21 days on a small hillock near his village. When on deep meditation, he claimed to have "seen" 24 letters, set in four groups in digital order, and 42 digital numbers, inside a figure resembling the letter "*Om*" in Sanskrit, on the flat top of a boulder.

Mangai adapted the letters as basic alphabets and created a script for the *Saora* language. He established a printing press and produced some religious literature linking *Saora* religion with Lord Jagannath based upon popular legend where, Viswabasu, a *Saora* king appears as the original worshipper of the Lord. He interpreted that the figure symbolized a dictum, "ever alert", "vigilant" and "move forward". In *Saora*, the terms are *mat, tar, bnam*. The Sun is supposed to symbolize ever alertness, the Light stands for vigilance and the Earth for moving forward. Thus, the '*Om*' like figure has come to represent the Sun, Light and Earth in a composite symbol, carrying the message, *Mat tar bnam*. Each letter contained in the figure is believed to represent a deity of the *Saora* pantheon. Thus *Māt-tār-bnam*, named as *Dagri*, has become the guardian deity and center of the *Saora* neo religious movement. He has been receiving a wider approval, following His installation in a separate shrine in the precincts of Sri Jagannath Temple (Śabara Śri Kṣetra), Koraput. The boulder, on which Mangai had "seen" the symbol of *Māt-tār-bnam* in his meditation, is now a center of pilgrimage, not only of the *Saora*, but also of the other communities of the region.

In the mean time, the non-Christian *Saora* of the plains and hills of the South Odisha districts, have, together, set up an organization called The "Śabara Samāj". A village is a unit called *Maṇḍaḷi*. More than one hundred *mandlis* have already been set up. New temples of God and Goddesses of the Hindu pantheon have already come up in many villages. The *Samāj* organizes it annual conference in one of the constituent villages in rotation.

The substratum of the *Saora* belief system is that every thing Kiting (God) has created is for human benefit; and that he dwells in every unit of His creation. Thus, the *Saora* visualizes God in water, air, fire, cultivated and cultivable land, hills, forests, in trees, and what not. This belief prevents the *Saora* from purposeless cutting of any tree; and cutting a fruit bearing tree a sin (*erāsi*).Thus, one comes across centuries old edible fruit bearing trees, such as Mango, Tamirand, Jack, etc. in human habitations.

X

The Principal focus area of our study is the Lanjia Saura Development Agency, under the ITDA, Gunupur in Rayagada district. The other projects covering the *Saora* are the Lanjia Saura Development Agency, *Seranga*, the Saora Development Agency Chanragiri, both under the ITDA, Paralakhemundi in Gajapati district, and Tumba Development agency, Tumba under Patrapur Block (non-TSP area) in Ganjam district.

Registered under the Societies Registration Act No. XXI of 1860 (No. 152-13/1984-85 dated July 10, 1984), the project started functioning from April 1, 1984. It is spread over an area of 39 square Kilometers coterminous with Sagada Gram Panchayat containing 8 revenue villages with their 11 hamlets. The population covered was 3080 persons drawn from 534 households (from the project records). It is a part of the

1200 ft. plateau to the north-east of the ITDP headquarters, Gunupur in the Vansadhara valley (300 ft. above the mean sea level).

Resource Base

Land

The project area is hilly and interspersed with narrow valleys. Land under cultivation, on the eve of launching the project, was 870 acres, of which 250 acres were in the valley and the rest was on hill slopes. 132 acres had the benefit of irrigation from hill streams. There were 704 acres of cultivable waste land and 1,174 acres of uncultivable waste. About 6,350 acres of forest land was under shifting cultivation. Average land holding per household was around 1.60 acres. Land available to each household for shifting cultivation was about 10 acres.

Education

A study conducted by the NCERT in late sixties found education of the *Saora* in a "deplorable condition" and the School functioning in this area for more than 40 years "has not been able to produce even literates" (Srivatava, 1971:43). On the eve of launching the Project in 1984 the literacy was 2 per cent. There was an Upper Primary School at Sagada, the G.P. Headquarter since 1963.

Livelihood and Associated Skills

The livelihood of the people in the project area revolves around farm and the forest as is the case with the rest of the tribe. The people have successfully responded to the stimulus of their immediate geomorphologic environment. Since land available for cultivation is not of one type, they resorted to a kind of agro-diversity and multiple dietary habits. They have been able to render a substantial part of the available land suitable for cultivation by terracing the hill slopes, check soil erosion and manage water from the hill streams for irrigation. Even their practice of shifting cultivation is a sort of stimulus-response syndrome of environmental determinism. Consequently, the skills developed are such that they provide optimum support and sustainability to the livelihood.

The worker constituent in the population of 3,080, at the time of launching the project, was 1,830 (900 male and 930 female), excluding children below 10 years and adults above 60 years of age.

There is hardly any gender based division of labour, except that women do not plough. Children learn life-skills from the parents at the work place.

House Structure

Traditionally, the houses are built with stones, mud and thatch. A man is his own architect. The working unit is husband-wife combine, the man performing the role of a mason and the woman as mate. The cultural rule of residence after marriage expects a man to establish his own household soon after he gets his wife to live with him. Therefore, house-building is the first major post-marriage activity. The man gets help from his younger siblings and *birinda* members who make use of the exposure as augmentation of their capacity building training.

A householder makes the wooden accessories for his agricultural implements, doors and door frames of his house. The sons or the younger brothers work with him as mates and learn the trade. Thus, almost every adult male has expertise in masonry and carpentry, sufficient to build and maintain his house and agricultural implements.

Foraging

The *Lanjia Saora* habitats, so to say, are forest villages. The normal tenure of life of a person is almost equally divided among three sectors of activity — the household, the farm land and the forest. The people of the project area regard the forest as a supplementary and some times as a complementary food basket. Edible items collected from the forest consist of five to six kinds of tubers, ten to twelve kinds of berries, four to five kinds of mushrooms, and several kinds of green leaves; apart from wild mango, tamarind, wild jack, *mohua* flowers and oilseeds (*Mohua*, *Karanja*, *Kusuma*, *Bahada*) seeds.

Foraging is a round the rear activity. Different items are collected in different seasons. Mushrooms and green leaves are collected during the rains. The mushrooms are capricious elements. Some are deadly poisonous. One has to learn to distinguish the edible from the poisonous.

Similarly, edible leaves are to be recognized, particularly when the structure of the leaves of more than one plant is alike, when only one of them is edible.

The knowledge of what to collect, how, when and from which part of the forest, is to be acquired by the novice from their parents and elders. One should know where to look for what and the spots to avoid.

The forest is not merely a conglomeration of trees, herbs and shrubs and wild animals, it is also a sanctorum of many divinities, some among whom are evil. One is supposed to be familiar with spots supposed to be sacred and indulge in sucu activities there to attract supernatural displeasure and wrath. One is also supposed to pay obeisance to the presiding deity of the place while passing by. These deities are believed to provide the necessary safety cover in the forest and lead the collector in the right direction.

Food Preservation and Processing

Pre-consumption processing and preservation of certain kinds of wild tubers, mango kernel, tamarind seeds are skills, largely developed by women and passed on to daughters. Such skills enables a household to tide over scarcity of normal food items, to contain physical hunger, and ensures a reasonable food security.

The people of the project area thus acquire life-skills and build their capacity step by step, as they grow up and step into adulthood. The boys are found married around the age of 20 and girls around 16. By that time they are supposed to have gained sufficient confidence and capacity to lead the remaining part of life.

Development Inputs

Officially, the Project began functioning from April 1, 1984, based upon an annual presentation of an action plan by asking for fund allotment for projected expenditure under various heads, such as income generation, education, health, etc. Our study of the project is confined to its activities from 1984-85 to 1998-99. Consolidated expenditure statements for various development activities in three phases are available. The first phase was from 1984-85 to 1989-90 (six years), the second phase was from 1990-91 to 1991-94 (four years), and the third phase was from 1994-95 to 1998-99 (five years). Our data base is limited to these fifteen years of development input.

An amount of rupees 2,23,85,600 was spent during these fifteen years. 45.68 per cent of the expenditure went to income generation schemes (Agriculture, horticulture, soil conservation, irrigation, ploughs and bullocks). 34.54 per cent was spent on development schemes other than income generation (surface communication, education, health and drinking water, awareness building, electrification, etc.).

The principal area development input was for income generation. It is one of the three factors used by the United Nation Development Programme (UNDP) to measure human development, the other two being education and longevity. The Project sought income generation to be grounded in the form of horticulture by planting various kinds of fruit bearing trees. The project authorities targeted forest land under shifting cultivation. They sought to wean the people away from shifting cultivation and at the same time to prevent soil erosion, while keeping able bodied men and women engaged in plantation activity. Cashew, a plant new to the area was selected for the shifting fields; and the grafted varieties of some traditional species, such as mango, lemon, orange, coconut, pineapple, banana, etc. were chosen for the private and homestead plots.

Apparently, it was thought to be a soft strategy to gain entry into the community to enlist its participation. It was not be so. We have noted that the legal ownership of the forest land under shifting cultivation is vested in the Government. The users have been simply enjoying usufructuary rights, so far overlooked by the Government. So, the initiative to cover such land by plantation was suspected to be an administrative trickery to establish/reinforce control and deprive people their rights. However, people were found cooperative with the horticultural intervention through the traditional species, precisely because the *Saora* believe that all edible fruit bearing trees are the abodes of their ancestors and by their grace and for the benefit of the descendents the trees are enabled to bear fruits. Consequently, a taboo is built to protect such tree and never to fell them. The Cashew being unknown to them, they played truancy with cashew plantation. Participating in planting the cashew saplings, they would stealthily uproot and threw away the plants. They never knew that cashew as a fruit bearing plant.

An imaginative Project officer temporarily halted targeting the shifting cultivation land for plantation and added cashew saplings to the traditional ones for plantation on the private holdings. He then befriended some community leaders, took them, now and then, on pleasure trips to the near by town, showed them cashew plants bearing beautiful, fleshy fruits. When they tasted the fruits and nuts, id dawned upon them that cashew, like any other fruit bearing tree, should be covered under the taboo for the prevention of felling or harming edible fruit bearing trees. In the meantime, the Project staff had been convincing people that the intention of the Government was not to interfere with their traditional rights. On the contrary, the ownership of the trees planted would be formally vested on the people with special Record of Rights. Ultimately the traditional village councils began cooperating with the Project programmes and income generation through horticulture registered signs of success from 1996-97.

In education and health were included in the group of programmes other than income generation. The money spent here was to the tune of 34.54 per cent of the total expenditure, in which education received 25.42 per cent and health 0.8 per cent. However, of the total expenditure incurred, education received only 0.8 per cent and health 0.003 per cent. The drinking water programme, an integral part of the health programme, received 1.31 per cent.

Of the projected expenditure on educational development, 7 per cent remained unspent. On health the unspent amount 77.93 per cent. The records show that the programme was touched during the years from 95-96 to 97-98. Thus, education and health emerge as weak spots of the Project. 69.37 per cent of the projected expenditure remained unspent under the awareness building programme.

Surprisingly, under the undefined 'Development Programme' the amount spent was five times more than the allotment.

When the target group has a limited exposure to the world at large, it is imperative that the people are adequately made aware of the development process; so that, it becomes participatory. Only 0.53 per cent of the input goes to awareness building programme.

Development Output (From the Project Records)

The major preoccupation of the Project had been with income generation to be achieved through horticulture utilizing forest land under shifting cultivation and cultivable waste land, owned by people notionally or actually. An area of 5,548.20 acres (rounded to 5,550) was brought under plantation coverage. Of this 4,270 acres (about 77 per cent) were used for cashew. The benefits covered 2163 persons/households (54.35 per cent). The other trees, in descending order are coverage in acres, 109 acres are orange (495), lemon (335), mango (106), pineapple (88), coconut (70), jujube (67), banana (8), and cinnamon (2). There were also mixed plantations covering.

Individual/household oriented large scale plantations were largely confined to cashew, orange, lemon, pineapple, jack, to some extent grafted mango. Saplings were freely distributed among beneficiaries for backyard and sporadic plantations. Raising such other trees as guava, jackfruit, papaya, pomegranate, custard apple, drumstick, sapeta was also encouraged through the distribution of seedlings. Fruit bearing and traditionally grown useful trees like tamarind, pongomia, *mohua* were also covered by the plantation scheme to augment cash income.

Next to plantation, agriculture received some attention in terms of improved method irrigation, soil conservations of cultivation, introduction of high yielding crops, land development, soil conservation, helping four households with ploughs and drought animals, 2,544 have availed the befit of supply of fertilizer, pesticide, and improved seeds.

The Project authorities claim that they are able to check shifting cultivation (*podu*) to the extent of "90 per cent" and "covered almost all hill-slopes" with plantation of various fruit bearing trees. Consequent upon these inputs, it is claimed that 350 households (48.21%) were able to cross the poverty line.

In the area covered by the project, there were seven Government primary schools when the project started. Subsequently four schools were established under the DPEP scheme. The Project upgraded the GP Headquarters School, adding class IV, V, VI and made provision for six teachers in place earlier two and attached to it a 40 bedded hostel. Further, 17 *chatsali* schools and 17 adult literacy centers were established. Three hamlets still lacked in-village school facility. All students were provided with text books and other learning material, school uniform, mid-day meal to the day scholars and free boarding and lodging to hostellers.

In 1998-99, fifteen years after, a survey by the Project authorities, found that there were 1,750 literates (39.09%) in a population of 4,375.

When the project started, there was a Government hospital at Puttasingi, the Project Headquarters. The Project added a Primary Health Centre, sometimes around 1988 with 2 Multipurpose Health Workers (one male and one female). It was located at the GP Headquarters. Periodic health camps were organized in collaboration with the Zilla Swasthya Samiti. It is claimed that all babies below the age of five, were immunized against measles, diphtheria, tetanus, and polio.

19 out of 21 habitations avail the benefit of potable water supply. 16 are tube wells. 3 are ring wells.

XI

Observations, Suggestions and Conclusions

The major problems, sought to be addressed for development of the target group, are, diminishing number, backwardness, isolation, small and marginal farming, forest collection and very low literacy.

Among these backwardness and isolation are qualitative indicators, which cannot be meaningfully dealt with small time quantitative inputs. It requires a long-term psychological participatory input. Therefore, we propose to examine here the sate of population (diminishing, static or increasing), outcome of income generating efforts, educational, health and health related inputs.

The Project area population, around the time of launching the Project, was 2,644 (1,295 male and 1,349 female) drawn from 533 households. Around 1998-99, it increased to 4,372 (2,104 male and 2,232 female) drawn from 726 households. Around 2000-2001, it went up to 4,534 (2,257 male and 2,277 female) drawn from 756 households. A SCSTRTI study (2002a:42) found the population 4,547 (2,221 male and 2326 female). Thus, there is steady increase of population from 2,664 to 4,547, an increase of about 71 per cent in 25 years. The male-female ratio also remained steady, from 1,042 females for 1,000 male to 1,047 female to 1,000 male, between 1981 and 2001. The population dynamics in the Project area seems to be satisfactory.

If the initial figures are correct, the beneficiaries strode from a household income of 1360 in 78-79 to 12,660 around 1998-99; and then to 15,843 by 2001-02. The annual average per capita in the project area had moved up from ₹ 274 to ₹ 2,672. 34.16 per cent of the population could cross the poverty line.

Giving due allowance to the rate of inflation during this period, it is a perceptible achievement. What is more important is that income generation had been possible with a little more than marginal tilt towards horticulture with the newly introduced cashew plantation within the parameters of the traditional land based livelihoods only.

XII

Population Size

- Too much emphasis need not be laid on population growth. However, efforts to ensure child and maternal health need to be increased.

Income Generation

- Availability of cultivable land being limited, land based income generation should not be stretched too far. In stead, appropriate vocations are to be encouraged. In case of the *Lanjia Saora*, Masonry and carpentry can be picked up for skill-up gradation through workshops and short-term training programmes to enable the beneficiaries better employment opportunities away from the village.

- Cashew plantation should be limited to land under shifting cultivation or any other degraded land.
- Eco-diversity of the area needs to be maintained. It should include protection, efficient management and optimum use of the existing forests, and if possible, reasonably expand it in conformity with the National forest policy.
- Existing agro-diversity, born out of the people's response to the stimulus of the local geomorphology, need not be interfered with.

Education

- The objective of education built into the development process should depart from its obsessive attachment to simple literacy.
- Applying an appropriate method of social marketing, people are to be made to realize the importance of education. Demand for quality education should become a people's movement.
- The level and content of education should be such that it should be able to act as a pull factor and extricate a section of the population from land based and other traditional occupations; so that, per capita land holding and produce there from sustains those dependent on land.
- A properly managed Primary school within a reasonable distance from the village with resident teachers should be the essential step in building up the educational infrastructure. A strong foundation at the primary level may motivate the learners to go for higher education at their own cost, at least from APL households.
- The medium of primary education should be in the language of the learner. The pedagogy is to be learner friendly.
- Course content, school timing, and holiday schedules should also be learner friendly as well as culture friendly.
- Appropriate life skills should form additional but integral part of school curriculum.
- The Village Education Committee (VEC) should have full control over the functioning of the school and its teachers.
- The truant teachers should be summarily dealt with.

- Girls' education should receive optimum priority. A reasonably educated mother never lets her children remain uneducated.

Health

- The health delivery institutions and personnel should be user friendly and be available within an approachable distance.
- The traditional community health providers can be suitably motivated, trained and co-opted in their localities.
- People should be made aware of the causal connection between polluted water and water-borne diseases.

Conclusions

Data from the *Lanjia Saora* case enable us to identify the premises within which the development paradigm can be set; and to build strategies to motivate people to participate in their own development.

We have noticed the difficulties faced by the development implementers in enlisting the participation of the beneficiaries till they stumbled upon a taboo in their belief system that edible fruit bearing plants are the abodes of their ancestors. On the back drop of this cultural value, targeting fields subjected to shifting cultivation through cashew, an edible fruit bearing species, became easy to ensure participation of the people. Secondly, shifting cultivation is a joint venture of men and women. In fact the latter's' contribution is more. Therefore, targeting shifting fields automatically involved women whose participation is complementary in any participatory development programme. Thirdly, cashew, though new to the area proved to be an eco friendly and local resource friendly (soil and land type) species for the area.

Thus an eco-friendly intervention through the frontiers of a culture friendly, local resource and human resource friendly soft ware enlisted people's participation and yielded reasonable amount of success in the priority area of intervention, namely income generation; and achieved some amount sustainability. It follows that development intervention to become people participatory, should be

- Culture friendly,
- Eco-friendly,
- Local resource friendly, and
- Should make optimum use of the local human resource, including women power.

Limited physical resources in the primary land based sector, however, may, in course of time, render the human resource surplus, an inevitable outcome of population growth. Therefore, for sustainability to become a long term reality, material resources generated in the primary sector are to be judicially and optimally utilized in developing the surplus human resource through capacity building for employment sectors, not based upon land. This can possibly be achieved through employment-market oriented educational planning and implementation on one hand, and social marketing of the relevance of education on the other. In this process, the primary resource utilizing sector shall be able to maintain its sustainability while providing the necessary support base for its increasing human resource to spread out to various other employment sectors. Thus sustainability to become long lasting, prospective human resource planning emerges as another parameter of sustainable development.

Intra human relations, human-nature/environment relations, and human-divine relations are all conditioned and regulated by norms and values formulated through the accumulated experience of several generations in all culturally homogeneous and autonomous human societies, such as the tribal communities. Such norms and values consolidated as beliefs guide and fix the premises of most human activities. For the believer, the beliefs are unarguable absolutes beyond the normal comprehension of any other person, other than their adherents. In this scenario, a non-participant observer, however keen one may be, cannot comprehend the logic behind all activities of the observed. Thus in any culture, there are two broad areas — the seen or the tangible part, which any one can see and understand and an unseen part which only the insider can "see" and take the guidance from. To locate a culture friendly area for entry, the development interventionist should either be an insider, or a sensitive participant interventionist, or should take guidance from the latter.

Participant intervention is an action oriented technique developed by Cultural Anthropologists. It is not very difficult to learn. The learning inputs are:

- Wisdom to observe human situations with an open mind, for every human situation is unique and in the process develop a genuine love for watching and talking to people.
- Ability to "see" what has always been there, but has gone unnoticed (what other have failed to or comprehend because they stopped looking too soon).

- Ability to listen to ones own intuition.
- Sharpen the power of deductive reasoning in developing hypotheses about the emotional underpinning of observed human behaviour.
- Restraints to "judge" human conduct.
- Insight to focus on the left brain analytical skills in drawing inferences.

On the basis of this case, we feel confident enough to conclude that a field model to ensure peoples' participation for sustainable development can be built, provided that the pre-intervention exercise emphasizes upon:

- Identification of the right community.
- An ethnographic depth study of the identified community, carefully documenting its felt needs, soft areas of culture for smooth intervention, resistant areas of culture to avoid possibilities of clash, map local material resources in use as well those utilizable, but yet unused, human resources that would include local knowledge and skills.
- Identification of the development sectors and inputs, strictly in accordance with the findings of the study.
- Orienting the development agency and personnel to respect and accommodate the views of the people, make use of their knowledge, and skills, treat them as partners, not simple beneficiaries.

Satisfaction of the people in the changed situations of their lives, consequent upon the development inputs; and the bureaucratic satisfaction in the success of their administrative acumen, must be looked upon as co variables in any situation of State induced development intended to be sustainable. There does not seem to be any difficulty to conflate peoples' interest with those of the development administrator, provided the people are willing to rise above their beneficiary status to that of partnership; and the administrator is prepared to step out of the bureaucratic frame with a sense of involvement, for involvement is said to be the hall mark of efficiency.

The present case has demonstrated this possibility to a considerable extent. The experience can be replicated, and can be made use of, to design a methodological module to be employed to micro level development interventions.

Finally

The technique of reaching the message of development to the beneficiary be so designed in language and content that every targeted beneficiary can understand and internalize it to participate in the process.

REFERENCES

Dhebar, U.N. (1960-61): *Report of the Scheduled Areas and Scheduled Tribes Commission*, Vol. 1, New Delhi: Government of India.

Elwin, V. (1955): *The Religion of an Indian Tribe*, London and Mumbai: Oxford University Press.

Elwin, V. (1958): *Myths of the North-East Frontier of India*, Vol. 1, Arunachal Pradesh: North-East Frontier Agency.

Francis, 1908:146.

Francis, W. (1909): *Vizagapatam District Gazetteer*, New Delhi and Chennai: Asian Educational Services (reprint: 1992).

Government of India (1966-67): Annual Plan, New Delhi.

Government of India (1967-68): Annual Plan, New Delhi.

Government of India (1968-69): Annual Plan, New Delhi.

Government of India (1975): "Primitive Tribes — The First Step", proceedings of workshop on *Primitive Tribal Communities* organized by Government of India.

GoI, 2005: 174-76.

GoI, 1990.

GoI, 1990a: 143.

GoI, 2000:7.

McDonnel, A.A. and A.B. Keith (2007): *Vedic Index and Names and Subjects*, Vol. I and II, London: Matilal Banarsidas.

Ota, A.B. and S.C. Mohanty (2007): *Lanjia Saora*, Bhubaneswar: Scheduled Castes and Scheduled Tribes Research and Training Institute (SCSTRTI).

Ramamurty (1894:340).

Ramamurti, G.V. (1931): *A Manual of the So:ra (or Savara) Language*, Chennai: Government Press.

Srivastava, L.R.N. (1971): *Identification of Educational Problems of the Saora of Orissa*, New Delhi: NCERT.

SCSTRTI Study (2002a:42)

5

Status and Social Change Among the Baigas of Madhya Pradesh

Y.G. Joshi

Background

Baiga is one of three tribal communities that have been identified under the category of 'particularly vulnerable groups' in Madhya Pradesh. It is a smaller group as compared to the major tribes of the State, constituting only 2.7 per cent of the entire tribal population of the State, as per the Census data of 2011. The *Maikal* Range of the *Satpura* hills is their abode. However, the entire *Baiga* population is scattered in 1143 villages of 22 development blocks. Though the largest numbers of *Baigas* dwell in Shahdol district, the typical *Baiga* culture is observable in the *Baiga Chak* patch. It is a 1,649 sq.km. path located on the thickly forested Maikal plateau in Dindori district.

The objective of the present chapter is to outline the existing ethno-demographic and economic status of the *Baigas* on the one hand, and to trace the social change which has taken place over time, on the other. The chapter is based on field level studies conducted during two time periods. The first one was conducted in the year 2002 with D.K. Verma at Dr. Babasaheb Ambedkar Institute of Social Science, Mhow in which 40 *Baiga* villages from the undivided Madhya Pradesh were surveyed. The project was sponsored by the Ministry of Home Affairs, Government of India. The second study was conducted in 2013 under the Senior Fellowship Programme of ICSSR, New Delhi at M.P. Institute of Social Science Research, Ujjain. This study was conducted in 9 tribal villages of Eastern Tribal Belt of Madhya Pradesh, assisted by a Ph.D. scholar. In the above referred studies three types of schedules were canvassed to collect the primary data, namely, Village Observation and Group

Discussion Format, Household Schedules and Ethnographic Schedules. The information for village schedule was filled up by recording observations and conducting group discussion with village elite and other knowledgeable persons. The household schedules were filled-up by holding discussion with the selected household in person. The ethnographic schedules were filled up in 5 selected villages by a separate team of students having a sound background of anthropology.

As per the above stated objectives the subject matter has been divided into following two sections:

I. Ethno-demographic and socio-economic status.
II. Social Change.

I
ETHNO-DEMOGRAPHIC AND SOCIO-ECONOMIC STATUS

Identity, Origin and History

The name *Baiga* commonly applies to anyone who serves as a village priest and is locally known as '*Panda*' (a Priest). *Baigas* claim themselves '*Bhumiaraja*' or '*Bhumijan*' ('Lord of Earth'/'Soil') and are recognized with that title. They are also known as sorcerers or medicine-men and consider themselves masters of 'wild life' and 'magic'; inventors of 'love charms'; controllers of 'natural calamities' and 'health'; and observers of 'purity of kinship'. Their practice of '*Baigari*' (slash and burn cultivation) is also considered, particularly by *Gonds* and other inhabitants of the region, for their nomenclature. They are also known as '*Dewar*' meaning knower of Gods.

The *Baiga* tribe inhabiting the *Maikal* Range of *Satpura* hills represents the hill culture of ancient times. *Baigas* can be easily identified by their scanty dress and tangled hair (*girda*) on their head. Their long hair is the typical identity. They are light brown complexioned, below medium to short stature with a long and narrow head, thick lips and a flat nose. Hair dressing is a typical identity of *Baigas*. They usually wear their hair long or shave the front part of the crown, cutting it back into a perfectly straight line. In both the cases, the hair at the back are allowed to grow very long and are tied into a *jura* (a bun) which hangs down on the left side of the head.

Baigas are considered to be a branch of primitive *Bhuiya* Tribe of Chhotta Nagpur (Elvin, 1939). It is also opined that *Baigas* were a tribe of Chhattisgarh region and were dominant in the Chhattisgarh plains and hills surrounding it with adjoining Chhotta Nagpur, the home of the

Bhumiyas. Later on they were expelled by Rajputs to hill areas. According to Russel and Hiralal (1916) the earliest settlement of *Baigas* is marked in Chhattisgarh region from where they migrated to Chhotta Nagpur and entered into Satpura Hills. Their mother tongue is '*Baigani*, but it is seldom known outside *Baiga chak*.

The origin of *Baigas* cannot be ascertained on the basis of historical facts. Many stories and folk-tales are prevalent with regard to their origin. Most of them hold "*Nanga Baiga*" as their ancestor. Russel and Hiralal have quoted a story that God first created '*Nanga Baiga*' and '*Nanga Baigin*' who lived in deep forest. After some time they got two children. The elder son was a *Baiga* and the younger son was a *Gond*. The progeny of these two were respectively the *Baigas* and the *Gonds*. *Baiga* trace the mythological strength to support *Bevar* and hold that God instructed their ancestors to cut trees, clear bushes fire them and grow food grains (Shifting Cultivation). *Baigas* were allowed by the British to lead their traditional life in forest villages which were important areas for resource exploitation by the latter. *Baigas* enjoyed their right to '*Bevar*' up to 1935 after which the practice of shifting cultivation was restricted.

Population and Socio-demographic Characteristics

Baiga is a smaller tribal group and represents only 2.7 per cent of the tribal population of Madhya Pradesh. Their concentration is in *Maikal* hill ranges and plateau. Nearly 52 per cent of *Baiga* population was concentrated in the previous undivided Shahdol district which is now represented by Shahdol, Anuppur and Umaria. As per the Census Report of 2011 nearly 96 per cent of *Baiga* population is concentrated in 8 districts of the Eastern Tribal Belt of the State (Table 5.1).

Table 5.1: Major Districts of Madhya Pradesh with Baiga Concentration — 2011

Sl.No.	*Districts*	*Population*	*Percentage of Total Baiga Population*
1.	Anuppur	30,211	7.29
2.	Sidhi	26,392	6.37
3.	Shahdol	99,299	23.95
4.	Singroli	45,142	10.89
5.	Umaria	87,177	21.03
6.	Mandla	43,331	10.45
7.	Dindori	42,109	10.16
8.	Balaghat	25,226	6.09
	Total	**3,98,887**	**96.23**

Source: State Primary Census Abstract for Individual Scheduled Tribes, 2011.

In spite of the fact that Shahdol has the highest *Baiga* population, 38 per cent of the *Baiga* villages of the *Baiga* Development Authority are located in the Dindori district. Some of the available demographic indicators for *Baigas* available in latest Census data, as compared tc scheduled population of the State as a whole, are depicted in Table 5.2.

Table 5.2: Comparative Picture of Available Demographic Indicators of *Baigas* with Total ST Population of Madhya Pradesh — 2011

Sl.No.	*Attribute*	*Baigas*	*Total ST Population*
1.	Total population	4, 14,526 (2.7%)	1,53,16,784
2.	Sex ratio	996	984
3.	Growth of population 1991to 2011 (%)	56.3	50.3
4.	Per cent urban population	4.9	6.8
5.	0-6 age group (%)	18.8	18.4
6.	Per cent literate among 6 year and above	47.17	50.55
7.	Female literacy among 6 year and above (%)	37.90	47.47
8.	Total workers (%)	51.4	49.9
9.	Main workers (%)	49.7	63.7
10.	Marginal workers (%)	51.3	36.3
11.	Cultivators (% of main workers)	28.2	41.5
12.	Agricultural labourers	52.4	45.4
13.	Household industry	1.5	0.7
14.	Other workers	17.9	12.4

Source: State Primary Census Abstract for Individual Scheduled Tribes, 2011.

Table 5.2 depicts that though the *Baigas* represent only a tiny section of States tribal population, their growth rate in between 1991 to 2011 has been slightly higher than the tribal population in general. The tribal population in general represents a higher sex ratio being 984, as compared to State average of 931. The baigas represent even higher sex ratio of 996. Against the State average of 27.6 per cent of urban component this percentage in the tribal population is merely 6.8 and it is even lower at 4.9 among the *Baigas*. The population of 0 to 6 years among *Baigas* is the same as in tribal population in general. The per cent literates is slightly lower than the tribal population, however, it is perceptibly lower at 37.9 per cent as compared to 47.47 per cent, as far as the female tribal literacy is concerned. Work participation among *Baigas* shows some interesting trends, in that, though the percentage of work force is 51.4 per cent, being marginally higher than the tribal population (49.9%), the percentage of marginal workers (51.3) is significantly higher than the tribal population of the State which is 36.3 per cent and the State of 28.1 per cent. This clearly depicts a sorry state of affair with respect to the condition of average working population among *Baigas* who are out of work for quite a long duration every year. The data also shows high incidence of landlessness among *Baigas* where only 28.2 per cent of the main workers are cultivators, as compared to 41.4 per cent for the tribal as a whole.

Material Culture

Settlement and Neighbourhood Pattern: *Maikal* plateau, where *Baigas* are mostly found, is a region of multi-ethnic groups. It represents a collective culture and identity which has crystallized over a long period. The *Maikal* plateau, girdle of *Maikal* ranges and the upper Narmada basin had been an abode of pre-historic man. In the ancient times, the *Pulind, Shabir, Kapali, Druhya, Aamir, Kirat, Malechchha* tribes, etc. had been the aborigines of the region. These people had been the ancestors of the present day aborigines like *Gond, Baiga, Kol, Pradhan,* etc. Traditionally, *Baigas* are dense forest dwellers. The particular geography of difficult hill terrain and practice of shifting cultivation have resulted in a typical type of physical culture among *Baigas*. Though *Baigas* are commonly found in eight districts of the State, the '*Baigachak*' is their typical abode where villages are small and are mostly located at Hill Slopes in difficult terrain. *Baiga* settlements are separate and their houses are usually constructed in rows called '*Tolas*' (colony). There can be more than one '*Baiga tola*' in a village. Earlier *Baigas* used to live in spherical *Tolas* surrounding a plain ground. All dwelling units used to face the ground and there was only one entrance into the *tola*. At the backside of each dwelling unit there used to be a *Bari* (courtyard). But now such settlements are not seen.

Dwelling: *Baigas* construct their dwelling units with wood, bamboo, grasses and plaster made of mud and cow-dung. They themselves construct their houses. All members of the *tola* help in house construction. *Baiga* houses are rectangular in shape and are usually 8 to 14 feet in breadth and 20 to 30 feet in length. Earlier there used to be a uniform pattern of *Baiga* houses, having a small *katchha* (temporary) construction with a narrow entrance with no panels in doors and without any provision for windows. Now, there exists much variation in house construction.

Most of the houses are semi-*katchha* in construction with a medium-height entrance provided with doors. Windows have also become a regular feature in houses. Roof is thatched. Walls are made up of wood and plastered with mud. Every house has a *varandah* (courtyard). Earlier there used to be only one entrance in the house, but now two entrances, one in the front and another in the backyard, have become common. In each house there is a long *Kotha* (room) and a *Randha Kotha* (corner kitchen). On one side of the house there is *Darba/Suar* (pig/hen house). In front of the house is *Sar* (cattle shed)) for keeping cows. In that place Baigas do not feed their cows and it is kept clean.

Dress and Ornaments: *Baiga* wear minimum clothes. They prefer unbleached hand-woven cloth. Earlier neither men nor women used to wear shoes. But now men particularly young men wear plastic slippers or shoes. Men usually wear '*Partani*' (also called '*Patka*' or '*Lungi*'). It is worn between the legs and tucked in front and at the back under a waist-string. Male usually wear a shirt. Often a sheet called '*Pichauni*' is wrapped up around the waist while chest and shoulders are left bare. It is taken off while working in the field. Young children do not wear much clothing. They tie a small piece of rag over their private parts.

The main garment of *Baiga* women is called '*Lugra*' (also called '*Dhoti*' or '*Kapchi*', '*Kakshi*'. It covers the body from the waist to the knees. The *Lugra* is a long strip of cloth about three to four feet wide which for dressing is folded into two unequal portions. The fashion of covering the body, beginning with the doubled end at the back, is peculiar to *Baiga* women, who could be easily identified as *Baiga* by the triangular flap of their *Lugra* hanging down over their buttocks. Half of the *Lugra* is also made use of as a bag, called '*Bagapana*' to carry child. The women folk keep their children in *Bagapana* while working. The *Lugra* of *Baiga* women is always of unbleached cloth. *Baiga* women seem to be conservative in the fashion of arranging their *Lugra*. There is a tradition that the ancestors had decreed that *Baiga* women should wear only unbleached cloth to distinguish them from the women of other communities.

On special occasions male wear '*Dhoti*', Shirt, Jacket and '*Phatka*' (turban) and women wear '*Mungi*' (cloth woven with alternately white and red yarn), '*Bigara*', and '*Chagdaria*'. These sarees are woven by a particular sub-tribe '*Panka*' whose traditional occupation is weaving. Young boys and girls have started wearing under garments also. *Baigas* who have settled in villages near townships have started wearing normal garments as worn by other villagers.

Baigas particularly women are very fond of ornaments. Because of their low economic status they make and decorate their bodies with locally available materials. *Baiga* women wear '*Guriya*', a necklace of red and black glass beads. Other types of necklaces are '*Hawal*' (made of gold or silver coins), and '*Sutia*' (silver made). They also wear

'*Tarkul*' made of wood which is considered a symbol of marriage. Women usually do not wear any nose ornament. Young women wear tops of various designs in their ears. Modern ornaments like ring, bangles, Payal, tops, etc. have also become common among *Baigas*.

Male usually wear German metal Bangles (*Chudha*). On arms they wear *Nagmuri*, and *Banwatha. Mundri* (Ring) is worn in fingers. *Chutki* (a kind of ring) is most liked by *Baigas*. Earlier *Baigas* used to make ornaments on their own from the locally available materials, but now ready-made ornaments usually made of Gillet and available in weekly markets are in common use.

Food and Drink

Baiga diet consists of wild edible roots, fruits and tubers, rice and coarse grains. They are non-vegetarians and eat chicken, crab, mouse, ducks, pigs, fish, goat and flesh of nearly all kinds of animal except beef. In particular places *Baiga* eat red ant (in Bilaspur district) and if available monkey and beef also. They are very fond of eating rats. A *Baiga* may devote his whole day for searching rat in agricultural fields. They rarely consume milk, but are fond of drinking *mahua* liquor.

They eat three times a day. *Kodo* (a kind of millet) and *Kutki* (a kind of grain) is their main stay. First, in the early morning about eight, at the meal called '*Juara*', they usually drink *Pej* of *Kodon, Kutki*, siker or rice. *Kodo* is small millet (*Paspalum scribulatum*) and *Kutki* is a small grain (*Panicum miliaceum*). *Kodo* or *Kutki* is prepared in two ways. It is husked and then boiled to a broth called *pej*. If the grain is boiled till the water has evaporated, it is called *Bhat* (boiled rice). Husked *Kodo* is called *Kodai*.

The second meal, which also consists of *Pej*, is taken at about four in the afternoon, and is called '*Marriaiya*'. The third meal is called '*Biyari*' (*Biyaru*) is rather taken in the evening and consists of *Kodon* and *dal* with vegetables and sometimes bread of wheat or *Marria. Pej* is the foundation for other food. Among fruits most popular is mango. Other fruits eaten by them are *Jamun* (*Eugenia jambolana*), *Bel* (*Aegle marmelos*), *Ber* (*Ficus bengalensis*), *Bohar* (*Cordya myxa*), *Tendu* (*Diospyros tomentosa*), and *Aomla* (*Emblica officianalis*).

Mahua (*Bassia latifolia*) is the most valuable fruit tree because its flowers, fruits and seeds are used by them for food and preparing liquor. It flowers in the month of May. Early in the morning they go to the forests to collect the sweetly smelling blossoms and gather them in baskets. At home they dry them up in the sun, and then store them in bins for use as food or to distil them into liquor. The *Baigas* have always been rather strict in matters of food and drink. They consider it safer to avoid social intercourse with people who eat beef. A *Baiga* may take certain kind of nourishment from anyone, even from a Muslim like boiled milk, cooked sweetmeats, fresh fruits, *mahua* liquor, tobacco and cigarettes, and all kinds of dry and uncooked food. Children can eat with anyone and anywhere until they are married. Women do not eat with anyone outside the tribe. They also avoid eating with anyone outside their own sub-tribe.

Utensils

Baigas possess very few utensils. These are usually made of Brass; German silver; or Mud. Plates and bowls are made from leaves of Mahlon tree. These days stainless steel utensils have also come in use. Women collect Mahlon leaves from the forest areas. Food is served in the plates made from the leaves and *Pej* and other drinks are also taken in bowls made from the leaves. Other kitchen items include grinders made of stone for grinding grains.

Family, Clan and Other Analogous Divisions

Baigas are patriarchial, patrilineal and patrilocal. Monogamy is a rule, but polygyne is observed. Earlier polygyne was very common among *Baigas*. Nuclear family pattern is common. However due to shortage of space and resources sharing of the same dwelling area with additional rooms for married couples is becoming popular. They call their family name or linearity as '*Jat*' (Caste). Every '*Jat*' has a '*Garh*'. It is a saying that '*Jatka Jat Hai Tat ka Garh*' (The one who has a caste has an ancestral place).

Baigas are endogamous and the endogamous tribal division called *Biladeri* (Brotherhood) or *Jat* (Breed) is sub-divided into exogamous family groups which are organized in a twofold manner. The social system which Baigas call *Kher* (site of an ancient village) is understood by them as a relationship of persons who once inhabited the same village. They are in some way conscious that they belong to one big family. Thus *Kher* forms one regional unit and represents a territorial division. The other system of relationship is *Gotra* or *kur*. It is the relationship of persons descending from a common ancestor in the male line.

At present these two systems exist in such a manner that a certain *Gotra* includes a limited number of *Kher*. Among them the objection to marriage within the same *Kher* is more pronounced than to marriage within the same *Gotra*. However, the marriage within the same *Kher* can be legalized by the mere payment of fine. Earlier the *Baiga* tribe was sub-divided into following sections: the *Bhumia, Bharotia, Binjwar, Narotia* or *Nahar, Bharia, Kurka, Bhaina Rai* and *Kath* (*Bhaina*), *Kondwan* or *Kundi* and *Gondwania* (Russell and Hiralal, 1916, Vol. II, p. 80). In the current Scheduled Tribes list *Bhumia, Binhwar, Bhaina* and *Bharia* are identified as separate tribal groups.

There are more than 100 *Goti* or *Gotra* among *Baigas*. Most commonly known among them are '*Marwani*'; '*Dhurva*'; '*Makran*'; '*Parteti*'; and '*Tekan*'. *Baiga* trace their *Gotra* mostly with the places/ regions associated with their ancestors. Earlier they used to suffix clan names to their names but now they have started using surnames like Ram, Lal or Panda. In school almost all *Baiga* children were found using suffix *Baiga* to their name.

The kinship system of the *Baiga* is of the usual classificatory type although this is not immediately apparent owing to the fact that they speak a broken dialect of Hindi and in consequence use some of the customary Hindi words for their relations. A *Baiga* husband calls his wife *Bai* or *Dauki* (woman) while the wife calls her husband *Dau* or *Dauka* (Child's father). Other terms in the language of *Baiga* are Father: *Bap, Baba, Dada*; Father's Father: *Budha, Daji, Dada*; Father's Mother: *Aji*; Mother: *Dai*; Elder brother: *Dau*; Daughter: *Noni*; and Daughter's daughter: *Noni Bai*. The kinship term *Mama* (Maternal/Paternal Uncle) is used both for the father's sister's husband and mother's brother. The father's sister and mother's brother's wife are described by the same term, *Mamee* (Maternal/Paternal Aunt).

Most men of the same generation, a man's own brothers, his mother's brother's sons his mother's sister's sons, his father's brother's sons, his father's sister's sons, are classed together as brothers. The term *Bhai* is used if they are younger than the speaker, *Dada* if they are older. A woman calls her husband's elder sister's husband *Soudhua*, and his younger sister's husband *Bhai*.

Baigas speak '*Baigani*' language which is a synonym form of Chhattisgarhi dialect with a number of words and expressions from '*Gondi*' dialect. In Bilaspur and along Maikal hills they speak ordinary Chhattisgarhi. In Mandla and Jabalpur it is *Awadhi* mixed. In Balaghat it is a mixture of *Baigani*, *Marathi* and *Gondi*.

Resources and Economy

The general terrain in the *Baiga* belt is hilly and the agricultural land is undulating with patchy fields. Land resources with *Baigas* are even poorer as compared to other tribes and non-tribal residing in the area. Most of the fields cultivated by them are small in size are situated on slopes with less retentive *Bharra* soils. In terms of water resource, due to higher rainfall of 150 to 170 cm., the availability of both the surface and ground water is better. However, due to sloppy terrain water holding capacity is lower resulting in quick run-off and resultant soil erosion. Compared to western tribal belt the area has rich forest resource that provides some subsistence to them. The area is rich in mineral resources, but their contribution in the tribal economy is nil, on the contrary it has negative fallout in terms of environmental degradation and displacement.

Baigas who once upon a time lived in deep forests, quite isolated and unconcerned with the people of the plain areas, had their abode on hill tops. Traditionally, *Baigas* practiced slash and burn cultivation, known as "*bewar*", on hill slopes and patch cultivation on level lands. The economy was subsistence and need based. They produced coarse varieties of paddy, "*Kodon*", "*Kutki*", "*Rai*" and "*Ramtil*". They collected flowers, leaves, shoots, fruits, roots and tubers from forest to supplement their food. Occasional hunting was a source of food and recreation. Domesticated livestock like pigs, cows, goats and poultry birds augmented their means of livelihood.

With the advent of new forest laws during the eighties based on rigorous forest policy, a number of restrictions were imposed on the use of forests and forest produce. This changed the entire situation of food gathering, hunting and primitive farming prevailing in *Baiga* economy. The total economic set-up which was tuned with the forest economy has therefore undergone a drastic change. Large-scale exploitation of coal and other minerals has also adversely affected both the ecology and economy of *Baiga* homeland of Madhya Pradesh.

The level of economic development in the eastern tribal belt of Madhya Pradesh is relatively lower than the western and central belt, and despite cent-per-cent assistance provided by the Central Government for the economic development of *Baiga* community, they lie on the lowest ladder, as compared to land owning *Gond* and *Kawar* tribes within the *Baiga* territory. *Baigas* once upon a time lived in deep forests on hill tops, quite isolated and unconnected with the people of the plane areas. They had a subsistence economy based on shifting cultivation. The *Gonds* who were settled in the Baiga region to acquaint them with settled agriculture cornered all the good quality land of the area. Today due to stoppage of shifting cultivation and dwindling access to the forest resources, the economic base of *Baigas* has shrunk. Nearly 40 per cent among them are landless and those who possess some land, the size are small, the quality of soil is poor and access to irrigation and farm inputs is meager, resulting in low agricultural productivity. Besides paddy, maize, wheat, gram and rapeseed, a sizable land is devoted to minor millets like, *kodo* and *kutki*. Among the work force, skill component is nearly missing. A large percentage of work force is engaged as manual workers in forest department, in MGNREGA and in the fields of other farmers. The incidence of poverty among them is very high and nearly 75 per cent may be put below poverty line. The quantum of seasonal migration is relatively lower among them. The percentage of marginal workers is comparatively high and unfortunately a sizable percentage of workers among them are of school-going age of 10 to 19 years. The inter-generational occupational mobility shows a negative trend, in that; more and more farmers are joining the workforce of unskilled labourers. Besides agriculture and manual labour selling of firewood and forest produce in nearby towns and distillation and selling of country liquor provide some sustenance to them. Though nearly all of them rear animals, rearing milch cattle for dairying is not popular among them.

For their economic development *Baigas* are covered under centrally sponsored 'Baiga Development Agency' with its headquarter at each district place that are linked with the adjoining Integrated Tribal Development Projects (ITDP). Each agency has a governing body headed by a Chairman which has to be a *Baiga*.

II
SOCIAL CHANGE AMONG BAIGAS

Theoretical Perspective

Social change is an ongoing process. No society can remain static, though the rate and magnitude of change may vary from time to time, from place to place and within different segments. Social change in itself is a complex process which has been analyzed by hundreds of authors with anthropological, economic, political, geographical, historical and behavioural perspectives. The views expressed in the classical theories of social change may broadly be divided into three categories: (a) linear, (b) cyclical, and (c) dialectic (Hynson, 1974:100-101). In the first category falls the theories put forward by Comte, Spenser, Durkheim and Tonnies. Comte's theory explains social change as the outcome of man's intellectual development in a progressive sequence from theological, metaphysical to positivism, and believed that eventually man would be able to measure empirically and explain conclusively all forms of social behaviour in the latter stage. Spencer borrowed the biological evolution formulations from Darwin and applied it to society. He also emphasized the necessity of studying the interrelationship between different elements of society with a view to examine how the parts influence the whole and *vice-versa*.

Two other models are of Durkheim and Tonnies. Durkheim spoke of a division of labour in the modern society which has become more specialized, resulting into a shift from a 'mechanical solidarity' where there was homogeneity of individuals based on kinship norms in the traditional society, into 'organic solidarity' of the modern complex society where the differentiated units are highly interdependent on other components due to division of labour and specialization. Similarly, Tonnies also talked about the transformation from a predominate community life of the past, to the business life of the present society.

The second category of classical views of change is 'cyclical' in which the dynamics of social change has been viewed as cyclical in nature, though the notions of 'change', 'evolution', 'development' and 'progress' are sometimes confused, or are combined in a single concept (Sharma, 2000:42). Greeks were the first to utilize the cyclical model and a similar view was expressed by Spengler, though his model was biological, rather than astrological. Culture, according to him arises, develops, ripens, and falls, never to return back. Toynbee, who also predicted a similar model, introduced an element of hope into it, in that, according to him the cyclic change may be interrupted by the creative minority. More recently Sorokin considered that the society follows a trendless cyclic pattern, that is, like a pendulum and culture has three distinct systems of truth, viz. ideational (coming from God), idealistic (coming both from God and senses), and sensate where only sensate truth is valid. The combination of cyclical and linear approach is reflected in Max Weber who says that social development follows a cyclical course while cultural development takes a linear path (Dube, 1992:54).

The third category of the classical theories of social change, referred to as 'dialectic', is represented by Hegel and Marx. As per Hegel every idea and all the history goes through the dialectic process, where by a 'thesis' is challenged by 'antithesis' and merges into 'synthesis'. This synthesis then becomes the thesis and the process begins all over again.

Marx also viewed history as moving in a dialectic pattern from slavery to feudalism, from feudalism to capitalism, and from capitalism to socialism. However, here the prime mover is economy and class conflict. It has been asserted here that all changes in the society arise from development of its inner contradictions. In Marx's theory of social change two element of social life have a pre-eminent place; the development of technology (Productive forces) and relationship between social classes. As per him, the continuing development of productive forces change the relationship between classes and the conditions of their conflict, and in due course the hitherto dominated class is able to overthrow the existing mode of production and the system of social relationship to establish a new social order (Sharma, 2000:41).

Most of the above classical theories of social change are speculative and somewhat subjective, when compared with contemporary analysis. Furthermore, the theories fail to account for extraneous or intervening variables (Hynson, 1974:100). In the modern period dominant conceptions of change itself have changed. In the contemporary situation due to globalization, urbanization, rapid population growth, information technology and penetration of market forces, the process of social change has become more complex, and thus, a condition applicable to one situation may not be applicable to the other. As such, generalizations made on the basis of overall factors become meaningless. Today the theories of social change have been expressed with different perspectives, such as, 'Critical Theory', 'Functionalism', 'Conflict Theory', 'Gender' and the like. The pattern of analysis being followed is also different; some are isolated studies dealing with attitude change, local social dynamics, policy intervention, etc. while other try to relate social change with factors, like, population change, urbanization, and globalization. Under such condition the notion of one grand cause of social change is a myth. The postmodernists treat different theories, merely as conflicting narratives or incommensurable perspectives, rather than as portrayals of factual realities that can be judged in accordance with inter subjective standards and procedures for determining valid knowledge. They also reject the very concept of a coherent social order (Antonio, 1994). After review of various theories of social change Dube also questions whether our quest for a single theory of social change is valid and meaningful in view of human cultural variability and complexity of social life? He advocates that the acceptance of multi-causality of change will yield more satisfactory answers and it will be more valid to ask what kind of factor-mix in specified situation, results in a particular type of change

(Dube, 1992:62). Yogendra Singh also does not agree with the generalized conceptual view of social transformation and change in the Indian context and argues that the generalized models and their operationalization cannot be transplanted from one culture to the other, without distortion (Singh, 1993). In the present chapter also the dynamics of social change has been viewed in a framework of multi-causality with chain reaction.

Social change among the tribes of India is to be viewed with somewhat different perspective. Firstly, the scheduled tribes are not a sociological category, but are represented by a variety of ethnic and cultural groups. Even within Madhya Pradesh there are 43 designated tribal groups which are at different levels of socio-economic development, from primitive to those who have integrated (assimilated) with the main stream societies. Secondly, the ecological conditions, the level of connectivity and contact with other population are also different. It is further to be recognized that though the tribals in India are not different people, due to centuries of isolation and limited contact, their way of life has evolved differently. Therefore, the debate on the integration of tribals revolves around the breaking of this isolation. The general view held by anthropologists about the Indian society is that two societies dwell in India (a) caste society and (b) tribal society. Caste society is hierarchical and segmented, based on the notion of purity and pollution, while the tribal society is essentially a kin society and is divided between blood kin and marital kin (Sharma, 2008:14). In general the process of social change among the tribal society is viewed by the anthropologists as a process of integration due to loss of isolation and through a closer interaction with the mainstream societies. During post-independence period the policy intervention of the State which is aimed at ensuring and increasing their access to mainstream education, health care and income generation to improve their quality of life (Government of India, 1996:1) also assumes greater significance as an agent of change. The political participation in the democratic process has also paved the way towards faster pace of integration. Sociologists have used terms like '*sanskritization*', '*hinduvization*' and '*kshetrialization*' for this transformation, though there is difference of opinion among them with respect to their use. More generic terms like 'acculturation', 'assimilation' and 'absorption', have also been used for this process. One of the dominant modes in which the transformation of this society has been conceived is in terms of tribals getting absorbed into larger Hindu society which represents civilization. Ghurye has termed them as 'backward Hindus' (Ghurye, 1963). Both the historians and the anthropologists have made similar observations in the past; Kosambi has referred to tribal elements being fused into general society (Kosambi, 1975) and Bose has also made a reference of their fusion into Hindu outfit (Bose, 1941). Xaxa has argued against this general anthropological view that when the tribe looses isolation and through close integration with the wider society, sooner or later, transforms into a caste. He advocates that this may have happened prior to independence in the historical past, but not now. As per him, the change in occupation and lifestyle or formation of classes among them, based on occupation or income level does not mean that they have come in the caste fold and have lost tribal identity (Xaxa, 2008). Sharma has also contended that the contemporary situation of tribals in India is that, on the one hand they are ready to take the benefits of the new forces of transformation, manifest in globalization and new capitalist agriculture, but at the same time they are obliged to maintain their cultural and tribal identity (Sharma, 2008:171). Besides Hinduism, conversion to Christianity has also played a role in the transformation process, especially in the North-East. However, this also did not alter the distinguishing feature of tribalism and tribal ethos (Hasnain, 2008: 284).

Long back Wirth had conceptualized the transformation of minority communities into four types, namely, 'pluralistic' in which a minority desires existence side by side with the majority and other minorities, secondly, 'assimilationist' in which minority desires absorption in the dominant group and the majority accepts the idea, thirdly, 'secessionist' wherein a minority seeks both cultural and political independence, and finally, 'militant' in which the minority goes beyond the desire for equality and seeks domination (Wirth, 1945). Doshi while analyzing these four types, places the transformation process of the Central Indian tribes into assimilationist mode because they have largely shown their acceptance to the broader economic policies of the Nation (Doshi, 2005:63).

Observed Ecological and Socio-economic Changes

Though *Baiga* was referred to as Primitive Tribal Group during Fifth Five Year Plan and was considered to be on the bottom of the development process with pre-agricultural level of technology, during post-Independent period the society did not remain static, but on the contrary due to opening up of the area, integration of the economic process and large scale policy interventions of the state, it has undergone various transformations which are clearly observable at the ground level. However, there are various micro level variations. The process of change has been slowest in the *Baiga Chak* and faster out of Mandla-Dindori districts, especially at locations closer to urban centres. Noticeable changes which were observed during field work and came to light during detailed group discussions in the sample villages may be summarized as follows:

- There has been a perceptible decline in the forest cover. Against the Land Records data of 72 per cent area under forest for Mandla, satellite data records only 49 per cent of forest cover. In nearly all of the visited villages people state that at present they have to travel larger distance to collect forest produce for their livelihood. The forest which once bordered the village site has now receded and the border area is converted to barren plateau.
- Though forests still provide some livelihood to people, their proportion in the household income has declined. Hunting has been banned and fishing is also restricted to few locations. The relative earning from selling of firewood and the collection of *tendu* leaves and other minor forest produce has declined due to both the increased pressure on available forest resources and various restrictions imposed on them by the forest functionaries.
- Due to decrease in forest cover, higher pressure on agricultural land and enhanced mining activity, land degradation has increased. Due to mining activity silting of river beds has been reported at many sites.
- Eastern tribal belt receives relatively higher rainfall of 150 to 170 cm, and therefore the availability of both the surface and ground water is better, despite higher runoff on sloppy terrain. Previously drinking water had to be fetched from longer distances from streams and springs but now a day hand pumps have been provided to all the village sites. Due to the construction of a number of check dams and ponds and the provision of loan and subsidy for digging wells, the availability of water for irrigation has perceptibly increased in the area, though other land-owning communities of the area have been benefitted more than the baigas, who are either landless or possess land on sloppy terrain. Due to lager extraction of ground water the ground water level has receded, resulting in water scarcity during summers in the villages situated on the plateau. A new problem of increased fluoride content in the hand

pumps has also crept in making the water from a large number of hand pumps unfit for human consumption. The use of water from these hand pumps, despite warning, is causing fluoride related disorders in the area.

- Earlier *Baigas* used to live in spherical *tolas* surrounding a plain ground but now a day such *tolas* are no more planned in a circular manner, but look like any other rural colony, particularly in those villages which are situated on main roads or near to towns. In the past there used to be only one entry in the house, but now there is provision of two doors and more windows. Outside Mandla-Dindori districts *pucca* houses are also coming up, especially under Indira Awas Yojana.
- Especially during last two decades there has been a significant improvement in the village infrastructure and connectivity due to construction of roads, increased number of private vehicles and increased mobile connectivity. Due to the availability of funds to the village *panchayats*, a number of villages have constructed *kharanja* or cement roads within their villages. There is also a visible improvement in the drainage of the villages. The *Pradhan Mantri Sadak Yojana* has contributed significantly towards the connectivity of villages with the towns. Mobile connectivity has improved significantly, resulting into replacement of once popular transistor radio with mobile. There has also occurred general improvement in the infrastructure related to public utilities like, schools, *anganwari*, ration shop, post office, *panchayat*, PHC, etc.
- Nearly all of the villages are now electrified, and despite poor support system a majority of *Baiga* households could acquire one point domestic power connection under the Government scheme meant for BPL families. Those who have irrigation facility could acquire power connection in their fields under the loan and subsidy schemes of the Government.
- The overall reach to village and town markets has increased. Previously in the *Baiga* belt of Mandla there was no provision of village *Hat Bazar*. Alternatively, within two or three villages *Madhahi Melas* were organized where the villagers participated with festivity. In the *Melas* villagers also purchased necessary items. Now, with increased access people prefer to go to nearby bigger villages and towns to purchase necessary household items. Some weekly markets are also being organized in some areas. As

the surplus generated by an average *Baiga* is meager as compared to other farmers of the region, their participation in the marketing system is also quite restricted. Some *Baigas*, besides selling fire wood, also sell medicinal herbs collected from forests in nearby towns.

- Noticeable changes in land use, cropping pattern and agricultural technology have occurred in the eastern tribal belt after 1991, of which *Baiga* is a part. Irrigated area increased by 87 per cent with consequent increase in the double cropped area, that is, area under wheat and gram in the *rabi* season. The area under course millets has decreased by 35 per cent, while the area under rice increased by 28 per cent. There has been a significant increase in the use of chemical fertilizers, pesticides and the use of modern farming technology in the region, resulting in increased per hectare productivity. Though it may not be said that these changes of the eastern tribal belt have not affected the *Baigas*, however, as compared to other farming communities of the region, including the *Gonds*, the transformation had been slowest among them, in spite of financial and technical support provided by the Government. This is due to three reasons, firstly 40 per cent of the *Baiga* household are landless, secondly those who possess some land, its size is small and the quality of soils is poor and thirdly the capacity to absorb innovation in farming is comparatively very low among them.
- With increasing population, slow growth in agricultural productivity and decreasing access to forest resources, the onetime livestock, land and forest based self-sufficient economy of the *Baigas* has undergone a change. Though in the *Baiga Chak* area livestock, forests and agriculture still dominates the livelihood scenario, outside this tract the self-sufficient economy has largely shifted to wage paid employment. Wages earned from unskilled work with farmers and contractors and under different Government run programmes now forms a major component in the household income of an average *Baiga*, especially among 40 per cent of those who are landless or are small and marginal farmers. In spite of high participation rate the labour productivity is very low due to absence of skill component and non-availability of work throughout the year; unfortunately more than half of the workers are marginal workers. A negative trend in the three-generation occupational mobility has been observed, in that, more and more

of onetime *Baiga* farmers are converting to unskilled labourers. Though seasonal labour migration among *Baigas* is much lower as compared to scheduled castes of the area, its rate has significantly increased in last two decades, though the distance travelled is relatively shorter. Besides the traditional sources of livelihood, during field work it was revealed that brewing and selling of country liquor has also cropped up as a new livelihood source and in a number of surveyed villages its contribution in the household earning was found to be nearly ten per cent. Though at present some *Baiga* boys could acquire Government jobs as school teachers and *patwaries*, compared to total population, this proportion is quite meagre.

- Besides changes in the income sources, a change has also been noted in the expenditure pattern. As compared to the past, the proportionate expenditure on marriages and social functions has increased. More and more among them are spending money for purchasing motorcycles, mobiles, televisions and other fashion goods, especially among the younger generation. An increase in the level of indebtedness has also been reported. The expenditure incurred on illness of some family member constitutes a significant component of the amount of loan taken.
- There has been a marked improvement, both in the availability and access to school-level education in the area, though the quality is poor. This has resulted in a perceptible increase in the general literacy level of the *Baiga* population. The general literacy among the *Baigas*, as per Census data of 2011 is 47.1 per cent (Table 5.2) and the gap between them and the tribal population of Madhya Pradesh has narrowed down to mere 3.38 per cent. However, this gap is nearly 10 per cent, as far as female literacy is concerned. There has been a marked change in the attitude of the parents towards sending their wards to schools, including the girl child. Mid-day meal programme and the financial support provided by the Government has also contributed significantly towards increase in the general literacy level. However, drop out level after class tenth is high, especially among girls. The rise of literacy level, however, could not make any contribution to skill development. Unfortunately a sizable number of boys of the school-going age were found to work as labourers. Of course some educated *Baiga* boys could acquire Government jobs in nearby towns.
- Due to establishment of Primary Health Centres (PHCs) in the area *Baigas* have started approaching available health facilities.

Still nearly 45 per cent were found to go to their traditional healer *Gunia* in normal ailments, but for serious ailments patients are taken to nearby PHC or to the nearest town. Due to poor quality of service and indifference at PHCs a sizable number take the services of unqualified *Jhola Chhap* doctors, illegally operating in the region. Despite Government effort under *Janani Suraksha Yojana*, nearly half of the deliveries are still taking place at home, even without the help of midwife. A significant number of deaths have been reported in the *Baiga* belt to have been caused due to preventable diseases like malaria and diarrhea. The vaccination programme has been totally successful in the area, however construction of toilets in the house could not be popularized and a majority defecates in the open fields.

- Though lower than relatively advanced tribes, like *Bhil* and *Gond*, life style changes are clearly observable in *Bagas*, especially among younger generation. The dress of younger generation is no more like typical *Baiga*, but they have started wearing pants, bush shirts and under garments like other rural inhabitants. Women are fond of jewellery available in the *hatbazars*. Young women appear in common sarees. Shoes and slippers have become a common feature. The traditional popularity of *gudna* is receding. There has been change in the traditional food preference and the marriage functions are increasingly been organized like others in the village. Motor cycle and mobile is the latest craze among the youngsters.
- The political consciousness among the *Baigas* has significantly increased during past decades and their participation in polling during last Assembly election was found to be no less than other population. Due to provision of reservation to scheduled tribes and women, quite a significant number among them could acquire position of *panch* or *sarpanch*. Their representation in the Baiga Development Council has also been assured. Thus with regard to political participation the difference among them and the other population is fast disappearing.
- Under the influence of Hindu culture they have started worshiping Hindu Gods and Goddesses like *Bajarangbali, Durga mata, Hardev Lala, Narayan Dev*, etc. The Hindu festivals of *Dashahra, Diwali,Holi* are also celebrated with great zeal and fun-fare with other communities of the village. This does not mean that the importance of their traditional gods and festivals has receded; though the system of animal sacrifice is slowly loosing popularity.

Larger adoption of Hindu way of life in no way means that they are diluting their identity or the tribe is transforming into caste.

REFERENCES

Antonnio, R.J. and Kellner, Douglas (1994): "Postmodern Social Theory: Contributions and Limitations", in Dickens, D. and Fontana, A. (ed.), *Postmodernism and Social Enquiry*, New York: Guilford Press, pp. 127-52.

Bose, N.K. (1941): "The Hindu Method of Tribal Absorption", *Science and Culture*, (7), pp. 188-94.

Doshi, S.L. (2005): "A Sociological Analysis of Political Unification Among the Scheduled Tribes of Rajasthan", in Chacko and Priyaram, M. (ed.), *Tribal Communities and Social Change*, New Delhi: Sage Publication, pp. 134-47.

Dube, S.C. (1992): *Understanding Change: Anthropological and Sociological Perspectives*, New Delhi: Vikas Publishing House.

Elvin, Varier (1939): *The Baigas*, London: John Murray.

Ghurye, G.S. (1963): *The Scheduled Tribe*, Mumbai: Popular Prakashan.

Government of India (1996): *National Tribal Policy (Draft)*, New Delhi: Ministry of Tribal Affairs, Government of India.

Hasnain, Nadeem (2008): *Tribal India*, Lucknow: New Royal Book Company.

Hynson, Lawrence McKee (1974): "Classical Theories of Social Change", *Proceedings of Oklahoma Academy of Sciences*, Vol. 54, pp. 100-101 (https://Climateandsecurity.files.wordpress.com/2012/04/femia-stemberg-werell-seton-hall-journal-of-diplomacy.pdf).

Kosambi, D.D. (1975): *The Culture and Civilization of Ancient India in Historical Outline*, Delhi: Vikas Publishing House.

Russel, R.V. and Hiralal (1916): *The Tribes and Castes of the Central Provinces of India*, London: MacMillan Co., Reprint (1975) by Delhi: Cosmos Publications, Vol. II, pp.77-92.

Sharma, S.L. (2008): *Emerging Tribal Identity*, New Delhi: Rawat Publications.

Sharma, S.R. (2000): *Process of Social Change Among Tribals*, New Delhi: Manak Publications.

Singh, Yogendra (1993): *Social Change in India: Crisis and Resilience*, New Delhi: Har Anand Publications.

Wirth, Louis (1945): "The Problem of Minority Groups", in Relph, Linton (ed.), *The Science of Man in the World Crisis*, Columbia: Columbia University Press, pp. 347-72.

Xaxa, Virginius (2008): "Transformation of Tribes in India: Terms of Discourse", in Choudhari, S.K. and Patnaik, S.M. (eds.), *Indian Tribes and the Mainstream*, New Delhi: Rawat Publications.

6

Implementation of Welfare Schemes for Development of Education Among Saharia in Madhya Pradesh

Yatindra Singh Sisodia and *Tapas Kumar Dalapati*

Introduction

Tribal communities in India are characterized by primitive lifestyle, geographically isolated habitation and shyness in social interaction with the mainstream society. After six decades of planned development, still they remain educationally and economically marginalized. Tribal communities live in about 15 per cent of the country's areas in various ecological and geo-climatic conditions ranging from plains to forests, hills and inaccessible areas. Tribal communities are at different stages of social, economic and educational development. While some tribal communities have adopted a mainstream way of life at one end of the spectrum, there are 75 Particularly Vulnerable Tribal Groups (PVTGs), who are the most vulnerable communities with respect to all parameters of human development.

After Independence welfare paradigm of National Government introduced several measures to facilitate the reduction and removal of the gap in the Human Development Indices of the Scheduled Tribe population *vis-à-vis* the general population and help empower socially and economically the Scheduled Tribes to enable them to exercise effective control over their life style, their natural resource base and their human development. The Indian tribal development approach attempted to remove disparities between tribal and other developed areas and also to improve the quality of their life. These twin approach aims at forcing area development with problem solving with greater emphasis on (i) increase in productivity and income, (ii) development of human resources, (iii) elimination of exploitation, and (iv) infrastructure development in the tribal areas.

After six decades of planned development in tribal areas, it is observed that development initiatives are not percolated down to all tribal communities in an equitable manner. In fact, there are certain communities, which are at a much lower level of development even as compared to the other Scheduled Tribe communities. It is also observed that in the matter of devolution of funds for the development of STs, the major share is taken by those communities that are more assertive and in a better position in demanding such benefits. As a consequence, the marginalized STs are left out in the process of development. In order to ensure development of these marginalised communities, certain groups were identified for the first time in 1975-76 and thereafter in 1993, which are regarded as the poorest of poor amongst the STs and are called Primitive Tribal Groups (PTGs). The criteria fixed for identification of such PTGs are: (i) pre-agricultural level of technology; (ii) very low level of literacy; and (iii) declining or stagnant population.

With the advent of the Fifth Five Year Plan, a fresh diagnosis was made and it was decided to adopt a new strategy for the development of the tribal communities living totally a secluded life. These communities faced different type of problem due to their ecological settings, and were at a different level of agricultural development. Efforts were made to identify such primitive tribal communities on the basis of recommendations of the working group on Tribal Development, Planning Commission, GoI (1984) deciding three criteria to identify primitive tribal community, viz. (i) stagnant or diminishing population; (ii) pre-agricultural level of technology; and (iii) extremely low level of literacy. In this context, having small size of the community, pre-agricultural stage of economy, high extent of isolation, low level of literacy, etc. 75 tribal communities among all tribal groups of India have been scheduled as primitive tribes. In 2006 the Government of India proposed to rename 'Primitive Tribal Group' as 'Particularly Vulnerable Tribal Group'. PTGs have since been renamed particularly vulnerable tribal group by the Government of India. In Madhya Pradesh, three tribal groups have been declared as PVTG on the basis of these criteria during the Fifth Five Year Plan: (a) Baigas of Mandla, Dindori, Shahdol, Umariya and Balaghat districts of Madhya Pradesh. (b) Saharia of Gwalior and Chambal Division of Madhya Pradesh and (c) Bharias (of Patalkot) of Chhindwara district of Madhya Pradesh.

Table 6.1: Literacy Among Saharia (%)

Literacy Rate	*All ST (MP) 2001 Census*	*All ST (MP) 2011 Census*	*Saharia (2001)*
Persons	41.2	50.6	28.7
Females	28.4	41.5	15.9

Source: Census of India, 2001 and 2011.

In Madhya Pradesh, Saharia is the largest PVTG demographically; the Saharias constitute 4.01 per cent of the tribal population of Madhya Pradesh according to 2011 Census. This PVTG is concentrated in remote areas Shivpuri, Sheopur, Ashok Nagar, Guna, Gwalior and Vidisha districts. Though, the PVTG is demographically preponderant, the irony is that only 28.7 per cent of the Saharia and 15.9 Saharia women are literate according to 2001 Census. The data on the education levels attained by Saharia show that the drop-out rate is high after primary level. It declines sharply from the middle level onwards.

Table 6.2: Educational Status of Saharia (%)

	Literate without Education	*Below Primary*	*Primary*	*Middle*	*10th/Higher Secondary/ Intermediate*	*Tech. and Non-Tech. Diploma*	*Graduate and Above*
All ST MP	10.8	46.5	24.8	9.7	6.6	0.1	1.4
Saharia	15.4	62.2	16.1	4.0	1.8	0.1	0.5

Source: Census of India, 2001.

Etymological origin of Saharia expresses that the word '*Saharia*' is the combination of two independent words like '*Sa*' (companion) and '*Haria*' (tiger) which means companion of tiger. In every dispersed Saharia village, hamlet or '*falia*' is regarded as the first ecological unit. Most of the Saharia tribals depend on local natural resources, which play an important role in forming their economic structure. The past-economic history implies that they traditionally practised shifting cultivation, hunting, gathering, pastoralism, etc. and sometimes adopted nomadic life also. Nevertheless, in the present time, most of the Saharias have become daily wage earners instead of their traditional way of occupation. Most of them are landless and poverty-stricken. Bread is considered their staple food. Nevertheless, sometimes, due to unavailability of wheat, they consume roots, tubers, leaves, etc. which are collected from the nearby forest. They are very much addicted to drinking local wine. They usually face shortage of water. Even their useable water from well and sometimes from tube-well is neither clean nor purified. Most of the Saharia are dominated by nuclear families. Saharia are strictly clan exogamous and tribal endogamous. They generally practice negotiation and monogamy form of marriage at very early age. Influencing with their low socio-cultural pattern, most of the Saharia prefer to have a male child. Modern family planning contraceptive methods are rarely adopted among them. Literacy rate of Saharia is 23.2 per cent, it accounts for 28.2 per cent and 17.7 per cent for male and female Saharia respectively. Low level of literacy and lack of adequate skill to adapt with the degrading traditional livelihood resources is the biggest challenge for this community.

Although there was progress as per Human Development Indices in the conditions of the STs, yet the benefits were not percolating to the Particularly Vulnerable Tribal Group (PVTGs), that lived in not only far flung regions, but in remote and inaccessible areas and in small numbers. Therefore, in 1998-99, a Special Central Sector Scheme was introduced with the objective to cover those items/activities which, though very crucial for the survival, protection and development of PVTGs (at that time named as PTGs), are not specifically catered to by any existing schemes, State or Central or by guidelines governing the utilization of funds under Special Central Assistance to Tribal Sub-Plan and Article 275(1) of the Constitution. Such items/activities cannot be exhaustively identified at the Central level as they may differ from State to State and even within a state, and from project to project. However, funds under the scheme could be used for helping the beneficiaries of the project to cope with extremely adverse pressures, which threaten their survival and protect them from various forms of exploitation thereby bringing them to a stage when they can demand and receive specific assets and services.

Education is a pre-requisite for human development and is essentially concerned with the well being of mankind. The UNDP Human Development Index (HDI) comprises three components, i.e. education, health and income generating capacity. As Saharia's livelihood is mostly dependent on primary activities and forest based resources, depletion of the forest based resources is the biggest challenge to sustainability of their livelihood. Vulnerability of majority of Saharia's have been further aggravating as they are illiterate and not skilled enough to take up non-farm skilled jobs to enhance their livelihood opportunity. Education is a vital aspect for any kind of society. It involves acquisition of knowledge and learning skill and also helps to shape moral values of the society. Explaining function of education in society Durkheim says education a social phenomena and relative to needs and structures of particular societies, it is the means by which the society perpetually recreates the conditions of its very existence (Durkheim, 1961). Talcott Parsons on the other hand defined education system as an important mechanism for selection of individuals for their future role in society. He stated that education functions to allocate the human resources within the role structure of the adult society (Parsons, 1961). In the same perspective Kingsley Davis and Moore stated that education system is a proving ground for ability and hence selective agency for placing people in different statuses according to their capabilities (Davis and Moore, 1967). In the pre-literate society, family and communities are the agents of education and that type of education is sufficient to sustain the community. In present situation modern education system is developed and implemented in tribal areas and planners believe that tribal has to accommodate with it in order to integrate with mainstream society. The changing ecological as well as socio-economic changes around the tribal communities also require penetration of modern education in tribal areas. However, an important question very often arises that is the mainstream educational process is relevant enough and proper yardstick to measure modern education indicators and status of education in the tribal area. The answer is certainly negative, because forceful thrust of any alien element can be threat for cultural traits and identity of a tribal community. Therefore, modern educational policies should only become useful to tribal communities, if the pedagogy is tribal friendly and truly devised to enhance their capabilities according to their socio-cultural worldview.

There are several studies about just implementation of educational schemes in tribal areas. In this context Rudolf C. Heredia firmly reiterated that, if the developmental dilemma that confronts our tribal is to be successfully addressed, tribal integration will require their mobilization not just to preserve their cultural autonomy, but also to redress their minority status. In this context tribal education will have to play necessary and crucial role to solve the problem. He advocated for a liberal pedagogy for social transformation among tribal to empower themselves. He also reiterated that it is also necessary to make the tribal able to participate in their own transformation through innovative educational policies (Heredia, 1995). To stream line tribal educational policies K. Sujatha emphasized that educational backwardness of tribal cannot be solved with half hearted short term strategies, it should be planned according to the culture and local environment in totality. It is important that planners take a long-term view which is embedded in a meaningful policy framework. The prime focus should be on provision of quality education that makes tribal communities economically effective and independent. In the tribal context, it is essential that the school schedule be prepared as per local requirement rather than following a directive from the State. It has been found that vacations and holidays are planned without taking into consideration local contexts, and thereby, unnecessarily antagonize tribal communities and keep them out of school. Though it has been highlighted by scholars, no concrete step has been taken to provide locally relevant material to tribal students. Availability of locally relevant materials will not only facilitate faster learning, but also help children develop a sense of affiliation to school. In order to make education effective and sustainable, building partnership between the community and the Government is important. Environment building is of immense importance in the context of educational development among tribal communities. Community awareness and community mobilization, which are its core elements, should receive adequate importance and attention (Sujatha, 2000).

Keeping in view the educational backwardness and upcoming livelihood crisis among Saharias under the conservation-*cum*-development programme for Saharia PVTG, Government of Madhya Pradesh initiated four educational schemes to ameliorate educational backwardness and illiteracy among the Saharia community. The initiated schemes are coaching in tribal hostels; Saharia teacher; Saharia nursery teacher; compensation for sending girl child to school.

(i) *Coaching in Tribal Hostels*

In the Saharia dominated areas, the Tribal Development Department has established hostels to ensure all-round educational development of Saharia. In these hostels there are provisions for coaching, for the subjects, in which Saharia students are not performing well.

(ii) *Saharia Teacher*

Education is a very subjective matter, to ensure interest among the Saharia students. For this purpose appointment of a Saharia teacher is introduced to impart a subjective understanding of education in consonance with Saharia culture (Saharia dialect).

(iii) *Saharia Anganwadi Teachers*

Education of tribal children and their health and hygiene are ensured through *Anganwadi* centres through ICDS Department. To ensure Saharia children education and nutritional diet, there is a provision for the appointment of Saharia Anganwadi Teacher in the Saharia concentrated villages. In the Saharia dominated areas *Saharia Anganwadi* teachers are recruited by the Women and Child Development Department to ensure community participation and involvement of the Saharia women in the nutrition enhancement project.

(iv) *Compensation to Parents for Sending their Girl Child to School*

Majority of Saharia live amidst economic penury and engage their girl children in home chores and taking care of their siblings. Compensation for sending girl children to school meant for encouraging the parents of Saharia girls who do not stay in Ashram School/Hostel and is regular day scholar student in a school. In this schemes the parents are compensated ₹ 100 and ₹ 200 monthly respectively for sending their girl child to class 5th and 8th respectively.

The chapter is based on the evaluation of the performance of above mentioned welfare schemes related to education for the conservation-*cum*-development of Saharia PVTG of Madhya Pradesh. The salient objectives of the paper is to analyze the operationalization of the education schemes; assessment of the impact and effectiveness of the services; level of participation of Saharia people in the education schemes; and the practical problems of implementation of the schemes for the enhancement of educational status of the *Saharia* tribe in Madhya Pradesh.

Background of Field and Methodology

The major concern of the study is to comprehend the implementation of educational schemes for Saharia PVTG in Madhya Pradesh. The locale of the study is Gwalior region of Madhya Pradesh. Three districts of the region are selected for the micro-level study on the basis of Saharia PVTG concentration. Sheopur, Shivpuri and Guna districts were identified for this study. The Saharia population of identified three districts are Sheopur (1,44,600), Shivpuri (1,91,243) and Guna (65,352) according to 2011 census.

In order to evaluate efficacy of education schemes among Saharia, the selection of villages has been done based on operationalization of various education schemes operational in the villages specifically meant for the Saharia PVTG. Beneficiaries of the schemes are the unit of observation for this evaluation study. There are four schemes related to promotion of education, viz. compensation to parents for girl child, coaching in hostel and Saharia teacher and Saharia Nursery/Aanganwadi teacher. Out of these four schemes in operation, 50 Saharia parents, 25 Saharia teachers interviewed for evaluating the Saharia Teachers Schemes, 25 hostel students were interviewed for hostel and coaching schemes and 25 Saharia parents were interviewed for evaluating the compensation to parent's scheme. In order to supplement the quantitative data and understand the community participation separate focus group discussions sessions were also organized with the beneficiaries of the educational schemes.

Implementation of Education Related Schemes for Saharia PVTG

Saharia Teacher

Education is a very subjective phenomenon, it is not only meant for achieving higher qualification for awareness generation and maintaining a livelihood, but also it is meant for perpetuation of cultural values which are functional for survival of a community. The basic problem of Indian education system is that it has not incorporated in its pedagogy a culture specific orientation and that is responsible for large-scale drop out from tribal communities. Saharia is a primitive community and these tribals are shy in nature and their culture is rooted in a forest and agriculture based livelihood structure. Due to this reason Saharia children find themselves helpless when they are unable to cope up with the alien jargons of mainstream language. In this situation an interpretation of the text in Saharia dialect is necessary to visualize the content and meaning of the text in the psyche of Saharia students. In this background appointment of Saharia teacher is a unique initiative to help Saharia children to come out from the cultural shock they usually confront in the schools.

In the Saharia dominated Gwalior region of Madhya Pradesh, appointment of Saharia teachers is not made simultaneously in the entire targeted districts. In all the districts, the targets were not fulfilled due to non-availability of 10th pass Saharia applicants. Some of the Saharias are educated up to high school level, but they do not belong to the local area. For this reason they are not given any chance to teach the Saharias. Those who are working as Saharia teachers are not getting their remuneration regularly. However, the impact of the scheme is significantly encouraging. It is found that the Saharia teachers are regular and attract students from Saharia communities. A Saharia teacher teaches his/her students in Saharia dialect with the result that student drop out has decreased after Saharia teachers started teaching in Saharia villages.

It is stressed by the Saharia teachers and parents that Saharia teacher should be appointed for a period of three years instead of one year contract. There should be no delay in appointment and the teachers should be appointed with the beginning of the academic sessions. Where locally educated Saharia are not available, Saharias from other blocks should be appointed and their remuneration should be enhanced and regularly paid. Such a step would be open doors for the betterment of Saharia students.

In Madhya Pradesh *Eklavya* society is developing new models of pedagogy in local dialects for different subjects. Instead of directly recruiting Saharia teachers search for educated Saharia should be made who can effectively teach Saharia in local dialect. They should be regularly posted through Education Department after adequately trained from organization like *Eklavya*. In this regard, new coordination and understanding between Tribal Development Department and Education Department is need of the hour.

Saharia Anganwadi/Nursery Teachers

To ensure community participation and effective implementation of various nutrition and health related programmes, appointment of Saharia Anganwadi/Nursery teacher are provisioned under the conservation-*cum*-development plan for the Saharia primitive tribal group.

The main problem in the implementation of the scheme is the unavailability of 10th class pass Saharia women for the post of teacher. In Karahal block, it targeted to appoint 248 Saharia Anganwadi Teachers, but due to lack of qualified women only 43 nursery teachers were appointed during the year 2008. It is mandatory to impart training to work as Anganwadi teachers after appointment, but because of not arranging timely training even Anganwadi teachers could not join their duties.

In the case of appointment of Saharia nursery teachers, there is lack of necessary instructions from the higher authorities. Therefore, despite the financial allocations, the scheme is not implemented adequately. It is advised that keeping in view the level of literacy among Saharia women, the qualification for the Anganwadi teachers should be kept as Class 5th pass instead of high school. It is also advised that the programme should be extended to other Saharia dominated district of Gwalior region of Madhya Pradesh.

Coaching Facility in Hostel

The Saharia students usually can not perform at par with the general students in the school. Therefore, under the conservation-*cum*-development plan special coaching facilities are provided in some subjects, wherein tribal students are unable to perform well. It is found that in most of the tribal hostels coaching is being imparted in English, Mathematics and Science subjects. The Saharia students are also unable to understand social science and Sanskrit language in the school. Therefore, coaching should be imparted in all subjects.

In the hostels teachers come there for coaching at the same time and teach one class in one day. This makes it difficult for the Saharia students to maintain continuity in the subjects. Further, due to different methods of teaching of teachers Saharia students very often get confused. It is advised that if possible the teachers of the same school should be given extra incentives to teach Saharia students after the school. This will also provide them monitoring and extra time to track the performance of the weak students.

Compensation for Girl Child Education

Under the conservation-*cum*-development plan for the Saharia primitive tribal group, it is envisaged that girl literacy should be advocated seriously to enhance the all round socio-economic development of the Saharia tribals. In Saharia community girl's hands manage several household chores and due to their involvement in these household activities they are very often not able to attend school. To ensure Saharia girls attendance in the school, it is planned that each parent/mother of Saharia girls who are not residing in any tribal hostel would be given ₹ 100 and ₹ 200 whose girls are studying at class 5th and class 8th respectively. To implement the scheme ₹ 170 lakh has been sanctioned in Gwalior region, but not a single parent has given money for the same as yet.

The main bottlenecks in successful implementation of the scheme are lack of awareness among the Saharia parents about the scheme and apathy of local administration. The other problem in the implementation of this scheme is lack of bank account in the name of Saharia families whose girls are studying in the schools. It is therefore recommended that the Saharia parents should be distributed the money along with the fellowship of the girl child and awareness campaign should be encouraged to check and retention of girl attendance at school.

Along with this scheme special incentives should be given to Saharia girl child along with her educational attainment at class 8th and class 10th.

Constraints in Implementation of Programmes

The bottlenecks in smooth and effective implementation of programme under the scheme are lack of staff at block headquarters and lack of monitoring and evaluation by the schemes by functionaries. Allocated money remained unutilized because all the schemes related to the Saharia are attached to different departments like ICDS, education and health. All these, Department are also facing problems like lack of staff and one functionary holding responsibilities of many Departments. Under this inadequate man power structure, a sensitive programme of conservation-*cum*-development of PVTG like Saharia cannot be achieved smoothly. Therefore, Tribal Welfare Department should strengthen its man power base to coordinate and monitor the implementation of the scheme at the community level.

Conclusion

Saharia is a PVTG that has its own cultural norms. Their integration with mainstream society and their development in education totally depends upon how they visualize importance of education in their world-view. Widespread illiteracy among Saharia is a result of cultural alienation from the mainstream society and its education system. Their dependence on primary activities like hunting and gathering, and their socialization process with forest based livelihood give them disenchantment from an alien education system that we are thrusting upon them. Though, their cultural way of life is different, it is the task of Central Government to understand their culture and initiate development programmes to bring them at par with the mainstream society. In this context, introduction of Saharia teacher is a unique step towards attracting Saharia students towards education. In this study, it is found that appointment of Saharia teacher is not taken seriously by the local administration and teachers are being appointed in a very haphazard manner. The Saharia teachers should be appointed regularly for a three year term instead of one year and they should be given training as how to teach a subject from specialist organization like *Eklavya* society for capacity building of the Saharia teachers. Their emoluments should be regular and at par with the regular teachers of the Education Department because it is found that Saharia teachers are more regular than other teachers in Saharia dominated areas.

Saharia students are found generally weak in grasping the subjects taught in the school. Therefore, for educational development of Saharia students, coaching and hostel facilities are very much necessary. It is found that there is lack of educated Saharia to act as Saharia teachers in the Saharia dominated areas. In fact, Government should identify meritorious Saharia students from class 5th onwards and undertake special support programmes to impart higher education for the sake of producing able teachers. In Marki Mau village a class 10th pass Saharia is imparting private tuition to Saharia students. As the education facility in the village is not functioning properly at all due to indifferent attitude of the teacher posted there, it is therefore the task of the Government to encourage Saharia teacher to educate the Saharia in the Saharia dominated areas.

In the Saharia Society role of a girl in household chores is very important. In fact women are equally responsible for managing livelihood in a forest based economy. In the case of Saharia, they do not visualize the need for girl literary. The scheme introduced for compensation to the mothers of the school going girl child is not properly functional in the study areas and technical problems like non-availability of bank accounts of Saharia parents is the major setback according to the functionaries working there. The scheme of compensation is implemented half heartedly and there is no campaign to popularize girl child education in the study areas in spite of giving compensation in terms of money only to school going girl child. A long term incentive programme in consonance with education (like *Ladli Laxmi Yojana*) should be introduced to attract more girl children towards education.

Despite all such efforts, it is very clear from the study that there is an urgent need to create awareness, sensitization and capacity among the Saharia PVTG for understanding the requirements of development and Governmental efforts put in place. The education related schemes need to be reformulated on the basis of local needs of the Saharias. There is a culture of silence among the Saharia PVTG society and therefore, the need of the hour is to make the society aware and responsive, so that, they can become active participators in the educational development process.

REFERENCES

Davis, K. and Moore, W.E. (1967): "Some Principles of Stratification" in Bendix and Lipset (eds.), *Class, Status and Power*, London: Routledge and Kegan Paul.

Durkheim, Emile (1961): *Moral Education*, New York: Free Press, 1961 (First French Edition, 1925).

Government of India (1984): *Report on Working Group on Tribal Development during the Seventh Plan*, New Delhi: Planning Commission.

Heredia Rudolf, C. (1995): "Tribal Education for Development: Need for a Liberative Pedagogy for Social Transformation", *Economic and Political Weekly*, Vol. 30, No. 16.

Parsons, Talcott (1959): "The School Class as a Social System: Some of Its Functions in American Society", in A.H. Halsey *et al.* (eds.) (1961): *Education, Economy, and Society: A Reader in the Sociology of Education*, New York: The Free Press of Glencoe.

Sisodia, Y.S., Ashish Bhatt and Tapas Dalapati (2010): *Evaluation of Scheme related to Education and Health for the Conservation-cum-Development of Saharia Primitive Tribal Group: A Study in Gwalior Region of Madhya Pradesh* (Mimeo), Bhopal: Commissioner, Tribal Development, GoMP, and Ujjain: Madhya Pradesh Institute of Social Science Research.

Sujatha, K. (2000): *Education Among Scheduled Tribes*, New Delhi: CED.

7

Hunter Gatherers as Vulnerable Tribal Groups: Some Current Issues from Jharkhand

Abhik Ghosh

Introduction

Particularly Vulnerable Tribal Groups (PVTGs) have had a checkered history in India. In inception, they began by being tribes, Hinduised tribes, criminal tribes, ex-criminal tribes, denotified tribes, among other things before being pejoratively labeled as primitive tribal groups before donning this latest label. In criminology, such 'titled' groups are often called 'labelling', after some Chicago School theorists. Anthropologists found it very difficult to get past this label because they considered the term 'primitive' to be pejorative and thus politically incorrect. Today, the Indian Government has found 75 communities to be worthy of being labelled in this manner. This label has then become a matter for targeted intervention programmes to improve their health, education, and other matters relating to sustainable livelihoods and development.

The Background to the Problem

It would be beyond the scope of this chapter to go into all the details of the issue, but it has been a running battle of concepts between the Government, experts and the tribals of India. In September 2004, a national assembly of indigenous peoples in New Delhi rejected the draft National Policy on Tribals that had been framed. They claimed that the document violated their rights and showed a lack of respect for their unique culture. The tribals also claimed that 'mainstreaming and assimilating' them was a violation of their rights. The document also referred to tribals as being 'primitive'. The tribals reiterated that this word was not synonymous with 'backwardness'. Finally, they claimed that tribal knowledge systems need not conform to ideas of 'mainstream' development notions. The tribals felt a need for some statement on the adverse impact of the policy of liberalization, privatization, globalization and structural adjustments on them. This document also did not recognize or promote tribal, indigenous and Adivasi customary laws, practices and governance systems, using definitions and descriptions that were derogatory and offensive (Krishnakumar, 2004).

Some of things that this statement complained about were taken care of in part by the Forest Rights Act later. This included a clear recognition of rights to ancestral lands, territories and natural resources. Some authors believe that it is the Government's fault that the term 'tribe' is ill-defined. Actually, Anthropologists all over the world have yet to find a very sharply defined definition of the term. In such a situation, working definitions abound. Anthropologists use some that have been found to be very useful. The Government of India uses another set to define Scheduled Tribes (STs). Some of these latter ones claim 'primitive' traits, distinctive culture, shyness with the public at large, geographical isolation, low literacy rates, pre-agricultural economy, stagnant or declining populations, as well as social and economic 'backwardness'. They were all seen as 'primitive races' in the draft policy.

A 1950 notification of STs had also referred to tribes in India as being 'primitive'. In 1961, the Scheduled Areas and Scheduled Tribes Commission report termed all STs as indigenous peoples under International law. It was pointed out by the Asian Centre for Human Rights in New Delhi in 2004, that the use of terms like 'Primitive Tribal Groups' in the draft policy was 'insensitive' and 'derogatory'. It did not see them as being dignified and equal to other human beings by referring to them in this manner. The term 'indigenous and tribal peoples' and the definitions should be used since India was a signatory to the International Labour Organization (ILO) Convention Numbers 107 and 169. In fact, the ILO Convention Number 169 on Indigenous and Tribal Peoples as well as International law since 1957 emphasize the need to move away from the idea of assimilation of these communities since this violates the cultural and social rights of the groups.

The point was that, according to the Declaration of 2004, tribal lifestyles were seen to be 'primitive'. This meant that the tribals were amenable to change their way of life. This was simply not true. The Declaration gave the example of the Jarawas of the south and middle

Andamans who (among six tribes of the region) shunned modern lifestyles and lived as hunter-gatherers. This was the case with 75 tribes classed as Primitive Tribal Groups who are now re-classed as Particularly Vulnerable Tribal Groups who are now more than 2.5 million people and represent 0.3 per cent of the country.

Not understanding the tribes as they are not helped in their development. In spite of several Government programmes to develop them over the last 65 years, has often led to failure, often creating 'a second-rate copy of ourselves' as Nehru had said. Many of these communities still live on the margins. Sometimes, development schemes have left them environmentally, socially and economically worse off. These issues rarely come to the fore. There is an emphasis on giving inputs from outside when many have their own systems in operation, as with much of their medical systems. Profit-sharing of products derived from their knowledge has been patchy and rare in implementation. Unlike the original idea of *panchsheel*, framed by Jawaharlal Nehru, the tribes are developed in a way that often does not suit their own 'genius and tradition'.

The Tenth Plan document describes the PVTGs in this manner:

> "A decline in their sustenance base and the resultant food insecurity, malnutrition and ill-health force them to live in the most fragile living conditions and some of them are even under the threat of getting extinct. Prominent examples in this context are the Bay-Islanders such as the Great Andamanese, Shompens, Jarawas and Sentinelese of the Andaman & Nicobar Islands. Even some of the mainland groups, such as the *Bondos* of Odisha, *Cholanaickans* of Kerala, the *Abujhmarias* of Chhattisgarh and the *Birhors* of Jharkhand are dwindling".

A similar situation has also happened with the classed set of communities called 'Denotified Tribes'. They were classified as 'Criminal Tribes' due to their 'criminal tendencies' by the British through the Criminal Tribes Act in 1871. In 1952, this Act was denotified, but a similar Habitual Offenders Act was enacted. In fact, for a time they were called Ex-Criminal Tribes. They both go against the idea that 'human beings are born free and equal'. Several tribes are booked for crimes they have committed under this Act. Unfortunately, their lifeways have been destroyed by successive forays by different states as a result of which they seem to have picked this mode of life. The First Five Year Plan allocated ₹ 3.5 crore, the Second Five Year Plan allocated ₹ 2.94

crore, the Third Five Year Plan allocated ₹ 4 crore, and the Fourth Five Year Plan ₹ 4.5 crore for the resettlement of these communities and the consequent retraining. Needless to say these have not succeeded, least of all because clarity was not present. By the Third plan period, the Planning Commission commented that:

> "In view of the small results achieved thus far in rehabilitating denotified tribes, it is considered that their needs should be studied in each area at close range and suitable programmes should be formulated, keeping in view the long-term and complex nature of the problems".

In 2002, the National Human Rights Commission and the National Commission on the Review of the Working of the Constitution had some specific ideas on the Denotified Communities and the Nomadic and Semi-Nomadic Tribes. By 2011, the Census operations enumerated the Nomadic and Semi-Nomadic Communities separately for the first time.

Many of these tribes have been facing adverse conditions due to their shrinking economic arena today. The British had created isolationist policies with respect to the tribals to increase revenue. Today, the post-Independent Governments have increased the battle for the lands belonging to the tribals, expropriating them under various guises. Even with the Forest Rights Act in being, tribal rights in forest are being decimated in the name of overall development and industrialization. This has resulted in tribals being 55 per cent of those displaced by development projects even though they constitute only over 8 per cent of the total population. Tribals who protest such forms of development are alleged by the Government as being trouble-makers, opposition political party supporters, supporters of Maoist groups or just a hindrance to general development. Though the Fifth Schedule sees tribal displacement from land as a violation of the Constitution, it was seen to be an inevitable consequence of development today.

Thus in many ways, the tribes are being forced away from their own cultural roots — by displacements, by educating them in a different way, by extending other kinds of healthcare, by giving them jobs far away from their homes, and so on. Alternative methods are rare and rarely used.

The PVTGS of Jharkhand: An Outline of the Issues

On 3rd March in New Delhi, the National Commission for Scheduled Tribes asked Jharkhand Government to submit a status report on the living conditions of PVT communities. A head-count, literacy rate and socio-economic status are among the information to be collected for this purpose, according to the commission chairman Rameshwar Oraon. It was also a move to find out whether Government development programmes were reaching these groups. At present the State Government is implementing ten development schemes for tribal communities in health, education, social and economic development, and so on. Some of these are funded by the centre. However, it has been claimed that only 20 per cent of this money reached the target groups. These funds either remained unutilized or were diverted to other purposes. Queries by different agencies often receive no replies. One researcher has also commented that classifying the tribes as being cultivators or agricultural labour hid the actual occupations followed by the tribes (Sukanya, 2015). A look at some of the cases given here would outline some of the major problems faced by these communities today.

One of the biggest problems of these communities is access to potable water. Without any other resources, these communities depend on streams. The implementation of the Forest Rights Act 2006 may have solutions but sometimes it has increased these problems. Sometimes healthcare issues are not dealt with adequately due to lack of staff at health-care centres. If the State is developing them by changing their lifestyle, then water, food and health-care should be delivered to them feel many NGOs working in this arena. Activists have also questioned the logic of settling nomadic communities in specific areas without giving the community a choice (Our Correspondent, 2014).

Biodiversity and Risk in Jharkhand

Jharkhand has been known from a long time ago as being bio-diversity rich due to its variety of physiographic and climatic conditions. Located between 21°58'10" to 25°18' N Latitude and 83°22' to 87°57' E Longitude, Jharkhand includes part of the Chhotanagpur plateau. This is part of the Deccan Peninsula Biogeographic Zone. Reserved forest in the state amount to 4,387.20 sq.km., protected forest to 19,184.78 sq.km. and unclassified forest to 33.49 sq.km. The forest covering is 23,605.47 sq.km. which is about 29.6 per cent of the total geographical area of the State. The forest consists of tropical dry deciduous, moist deciduous, dry peninsular and dry mixed deciduous forests. It has wild, semi-wild and cultivated regions. They also involve the catchment areas of the three main rivers, namely, Koel, Damodar and Subarnarekha.

As seen from some of the comments given above, Jharkhand is rich in natural resources with nearly 50 per cent of the minerals of the country being located in this zone. Many of the minerals are in this forested zone. The State has 97 varieties of trees, 46 varieties of shrubs and herbs, 25 varieties of climbers, parasites and orchids and 17 kinds of grasses. Some of the trees include *Shorearobusta* (*Sal*), *Dalbergiasissoo* (*Shisham*), *Madhuca indica* (*Mahua*), *Acacia nilotica* (*babool*), *Azadirachta indica* (*Neem*), *Terminalia arjuna* (*Arjun*), *Bombax ceiba* (*Semul*) and *Butea monosperma* (*Palash*). There are also 39 species of mammals, 170 avian species, 12 reptilian species with 8 snake species and 4 lizard species as well as 21 insect species from these forests. Some of the mammalian fauna include tigers, leopards, sloth bears, elephants, wild boars, Indian bisons, hyenas, wild monkeys, langurs, wolves, deer and antelopes.

Recent data was collected in the Jamshedpur region in May-June 2010 with the help of the Department of Forests in seven wildlife zones (Udhuwa lake wildlife sanctuary, Topchanchi wildlife sanctuary, Koderma wildlife sanctuary, Hazaribagh wildlife sanctuary, Lawalong wildlife sanctuary, Simdega forest and Dalma wildlife sanctuary). The study showed the following trends:

Table 7.1: Forest Fauna in Jharkhand over the Years

	Mammalian Species	*Avian Species*	*Reptilian Species*	*Invertebrate Species*
2000	45	205	15	45
2005	41	201	14	43
2010	35	168	11	48

Source: Ministry of Forests and Environment, Government of Jharkhand: May-June 2010.

The causes for this decline has been attributed to constant pressure of unsustainable harvesting of these species, habitat destruction and fragmentation, impact of pollutants, as well as competition with colonizing, invasive, exotic species. Anthropogenic activities like agricultural activities, stone quarrying, industrialization, urbanization, grazing, mining, railway track laying, road building, dam construction, development activities as well as some of the ethnic activities of tribes. Threatened wildlife of Jharkhand are the endangered *Elephas maximus* (elephant), the vulnerable *Melursus ursinus* (sloth bear) and those that cause the least concern *Ratufa indica* (Indian giant squirrel). Isolated populations of birds like *Phaenicophaeustrististristis* (green-billed *malkoha*) and *Macronousgularisrubicapilla* (pin-striped tit babbler) are recorded here as the southern-most edge of their distribution range. Among the reptiles, *Chamaeleozeylanicus* (Indian chameleon) is listed in Schedule II of the Indian Wildlife (Protection) Act of 1972.

Understanding this variety and the risk of loss of species can help in mitigation and reduction of the loss of these species due to anthropogenic activities. Habitat loss itself presents a loss of biodiversity. Losing species as well as the ecosystem leads to losses in genetic diversity. This could lead to changes in agricultural practices. New, species introduced like rice, wheat and corn have already pushed out many local and indigenous varieties from the 1950s onwards at a very quick rate. In my fieldwork conducted in 1991, many indigenous species seen and used by the tribals of Jharkhand at the time were no longer seen to be used by the same communities by 2011. Eventually, then, the 39 mammals, 12 reptiles and 15 insect species need urgent protection by the State.

The Government was still failing to implement the Scheduled Tribes and Other Traditional Forest Dwellers (Recognition of Forest Rights) Act. The N.C. Saxena Committee constituted by the Ministry of Environment and Forests found that only 7,207 forest dwellers had been granted land rights under the Act while 11,054 claims had been rejected by August 2010.

Biological and Cultural Diversity: The Human Component

In the same way that flora and fauna need to be conserved in order that we may survive in the future, it is even more important that biological and cultural diversity is maintained for the same reasons. It is in this context that the PVTGs need to be looked at in Jharkhand, if not for the rest of India. The PVTGs found in Jharkhand are mentioned in Table 7.2.

Table 7.2: Particularly Vulnerable Groups of Jharkhand

Sl.No.	*Name of Tribes*	*Population*	
		2001	*2011*
1.	*Asur*	10,347	22,459
2.	*Birhor*	7,514	10,726
3.	*Birjia*	5,365	6,276
4.	*Hill Kharia*	1,64,022	1,96,135
5.	*Korwa*	27,177	35,606
6.	*Mal Pahariya*	1,15,093	1,35,797
7.	*Pahariya*	20,786	25,585
8.	*Sauria*	31,050	46,222
9.	*Savar*	6,004	9,688
	Total	**3,87,358**	**4,88,494**

Source: Census 2001 and 2011, Government of India, New Delhi.

The total tribal population in 2001 was 27 per cent of the total population of 2.70 crore. The PVTG population at the time was 2.23 lakh. Four of the tribes — *Birhor*, *Birjiya*, *Baiga* and *Sauriya*, *Pahariya* — were declining.

By 2011, Birjiya and Sabar communities were declining, each being less than 10,000 members. The total population of the others was about 4 lakh. The literacy rate was about a little over 20 per cent with a State average of 66 per cent. The average monthly income of the household was between ₹ 1,000 and ₹ 1,500.

PVTGS and Maternal Health in Jharkhand

One of the most crucial aspects of PVTGs are their health issues. Among these issues include the reproductive, maternal and child health, since increase in their absolute numbers is a crucial issue.

Since 2005, the Government of India began a series of programmes to improve health issues of women. These include the Janani Suraksha Yojana (JSY) and the JSSK. Country-wide SRS surveys show that maternal mortality was coming down in all the States in the last decade. This included Jharkhand. By August 2013, there were descriptions of 23 maternal deaths in one year among poor tribal women (especially PVTGs) in two blocks of Godda district, Santhal Parganas division in Jharkhand in EPW. An NGO called National Alliance for Maternal health and Human Rights conducted a fact finding mission in the area. Three villages were selected. They found home deliveries were the norm and even when deaths occurred, women preferred to deliver at home. Literacy rates were very low. There was no knowledge of health schemes and a lack of outreach programmes. The land is hilly and much of the area is not connected to the roads. People usually thus connected better with the Dom, Ojha or the RMP.

Basic services like ANC, immunization services for children was unavailable, especially for the PVTG. ANMs often did not visit homes for child-births or for ante-natal care. The health-sub-centre was not easily accessible. VHND was not taking place in many areas due to shortage of human staff and transportation. There was no functioning of blood storage and transfusion facility in the entire district. Tribal women had high degree of anaemia and those who needed service had to go to Bhagalpur in Bihar. There was a lack of Anganwadi centres and Supplementary Nutrition did not reach lactating or pregnant women. Among the *Sauria Pahariya*, health problems were still not being taken care of adequately till recently (Jha and Kumar, 2014).

The PDS was being used by the community even though the concerned distribution centre was far. The scheme refused to acknowledge the local grains which were having better nutrients. Traditional foods included forest foraging and the practice of mixed organic farming in the forest has been ruined by the PDS. Iron tablets are preferred to be given to the women while the local iron-rich foods are ignored. Health services often cannot reach deep in the forest. An earlier tribal health system based on local herbs is ignored. This creates barriers between the two health systems and tribals of the area mistrust the system which is being promoted. Such tribal practices, seen as ignorant and uneducated, are often looked down upon in the region.

In this connection our own study in Palamau and Latehar areas shows a different trajectory. We had gone to study the health and nutrition of the Cheros. We ended up peripherally noting issues relating to the adjacent Parhaiyas. In both cases we found hidden malnutrition. We are calling it hidden because traditional medical services could not diagnose it easily. The local health system was working very well. The medical officer was very well acquainted with each village in the region. He knew the names of the workers there as well as other senior villagers. He knew the precise number of households of each tribal community in each household. The health centre was neat, clean and better than many hospitals. A cold chain was maintained with UPS, batteries and back-up. The waiting area had fans, AC and a TV for patients. The free ambulance service was working very well. Malnutrition was being checked. Where it was found, the mother and child were shifted to a special area, where they were treated, fed and observed on a full time basis until they were well enough to be sent home. Check-ups at villages were routine and weighing machines were mandatory.

We found that *Parhaiyas* often lived deeper in the forest than the Cheros in the Betla and other forest areas. The *Parhaiyas* were then in the link with the Maoists. They were also linked to the Cheros, since they gave foods from the forest to them, including medicinal plants, herbs, small animals, and the knowledge of other foods and medicines. This is what will be lost as the *Parhaiyas* get geared to a different economy.

Demography and PVTGs

As shall be described here, the demography of the PVTGs shows a steady rise. The Onge (Andaman & Nicobar Islands), *Birhor/Mankirdia* (Odisha), and other PVTGs from Jharkhand, Manipur and Uttarakhand showed an increase. The *Thoti* of Andhra Pradesh had decreased in number. State Governments have been asked to form a Conservation-*cum*-Development (CCD) plan between 2012 and 2017, suiting the requirements of the PVTGs. Such CCDs were to focus on welfare and economic development.

In Jharkhand one group called the *Kumarbhag Pahariya* disappeared from the Rajmahal Hills of Santhal Pargana region due to official apathy. In the 1971 census they numbered 7,568. In the 1981 census they were no longer mentioned.

In October 2008, 20 people of PVTG communities died. Social workers and advisor to the Commissioner of Supreme Court (to monitor food for security programme) claim this was caused due to hunger, the Committee of Secretaries appointed by the State Government claim it was caused by food poisoning. Initially, nine *Birhors* had died in the first week of October. Then 8 *Baiga* members of Bhitaha village had died. Two *Birhors* then died from Koderma district followed by one from Dumka district.

Between 24 August and 30 August 2010, 10 members of the *Pahariya* tribe, including four children, at Duggu Karma Tola village in Barhet Block of Sahebganj district died due to a lack of basic medical facilities. The first case came to light on 24 August when Dharma Pahariya, aged 45 years, the Gram Pradhan, died of some ailments. The next day the BDO had written orders to inspect the village and set up a health camp, which was not done till the 28th August. Stringent action was recommended against the doctors for the delay but no action was taken. Apparently the *Birhors* eat rice and *saag* or leafy vegetable of *bathua, gandhari* and *kantela*. Such a diet should not have caused starvation from an age of one-and-a-half year to 60 years. The *Antyodaya* scheme of providing grains to the *Birhors* for ₹ 3/kg was not available to them for six months. The *Anganwadi Kendra* was not running for two years and the health centre was 12 km. from the village. According to the Jharkhand Advisor to the commissioner of SC, Balram, the *Birhors* had not eaten rice since April and out of hunger ate *gaithi* which was a poisonous root. With its inaccessibility and lack of roads, the area is well-known for its population of Maoist rebels.

Males among the *Paharias* do not adopt sterilization. One family, after six of their children survived the initial five years went to the State's health department where their case was refused since, they were *Paharias*. The *Paharias* are thought to be dwindling and thus, the Government had decided to stop sterilization to increase their numbers.

In other words, for many people, this right to reproductive choice was removed from the whole community. Rational thought in this regard was not a matter of choice but of decree. Male sterilization has been decreasing but female sterilization in the area has steadily increased. NFHS data from 2005-06 shows that female sterilization was 66 per cent of the total in Jharkhand. NFHS 2 and NFHS 3 show a reduction in male sterilization from 0.8 per cent in 1998-99 to 0.4 per cent in 2005-06. In 2011-12, the targets set by the Government of Jharkhand were 30,000 for male sterilization, 175,000 for female sterilization, and 300,000 for Intrauterine Device Insertions. Thus, targets are also higher for female sterilizations and IUD insertions. Yet, male sterilization is simpler, less time consuming, requiring almost no surgical interventions. For *Paharias*, among others, large families lead to a larger stock of human resources that can work for the family. This puts greater pressure on women to reproduce. As a result, their health suffers. The fact has also been pointed out that the *Paharias*, instead of becoming extinct, have increased from 8,800 in 1991 to 13,500 in 2001 to 16,000 in 2011 approximately. Therefore, instead of using a method best suited to flora and fauna, it would perhaps be useful to look at the historical marginalization and structural deprivation in these communities. The entire programme thus re-entrenches patriarchal structures since such programmes preferentially use women's bodies as sites for deprivation and action rather than male bodies. The Planning Commission asked the Chhattisgarh Government in 2012 to revoke this order which had been passed in 1979. They claimed that the order was misconstrued and those from the PTG community who wish to be enrolled for sterilization cannot be denied (John, 2013).

A study of 5 Birhortandas in Giridih showed a literacy rate of just 16.87 per cent against the state average of 54 per cent. The average cultivable land is 0.21 hectare/family as opposed to a State average of 0.82 hectare/family. The average family monthly income was between ₹ 500 and ₹ 1,000.

In fact, many researchers were initially of the opinion that the tribes of Jharkhand were showing a decline due to large losses in younger ages or other health issues during their lifetime. Demographic data shows otherwise. Their fertility rates are not much different from other communities and their mortality figures are often better. So, it seems that perhaps long-term migration for work from the region may account for a slow rate of growth till the last decade (Maharatna and Chikte, 2004).

Problems of Resettlement

80 *Birhor* residents had been resettled by the Government in Buki Balara hamlet in 2007 in 17 two-roomed huts under the Birsa Awas Yojana, about 35 km. from Ranchi, a few metres from the Getelsud dam catchment, Angara block, Ranchi district. Today, this group defecates in the open since the huts neither had a toilet nor did they have a common toilet. In fact, this has been a hallmark of *Birhor* resettlement in the region. They were often chased with sticks from doing so in the neighbouring fields by the owners of these areas. They were abused, threatened and forced to clean up. The men could move around more and were luckier while the women who were often tied to their households and children suffered more. There is also only one hand pump for water which is in front of the hamlet near the road. It has no electricity. Many still sell forest herbs.

For many, the hunting-gathering economic life has been seen to be something from a past time, a throwback to the past that need not be continued. For many anthropologists, this is not true. For them, a hunting-gathering economy is a very advanced mode of economy that is as advanced as a modern day economic system that we see around us today. For one thing, it occupies the community fewer number of work hours per day to make a living than an office-goer. Hence, this situation shows the truth of the statement that they were the 'original affluent society', after Marshall Sahlins. The *Birhors* of Jharkhand have also advanced and changed over the years. They use the produce of the forest to exchange it with other communities around them for things that they need like rice and other tools. In fact rice was a very important part of the *Birhor* diet and is seen in their cosmology. The *Birhors* seem to have interacted with other communities regularly, yet avoided the attentions of the State over the centuries. For them, perhaps, all it meant was going deeper into the jungles they knew so well about. All anthropologists know of their leaf-huts or *kumbhas* they have still continued to build. They use leaves and jungle creepers to also fashion ropes, mats and nets for sale. Today, they also use jute or even plastic fibres to create the same products. The creepers or bark fibres (*chope*) used are from *Bauhinia scandens*. *Birhors* were first discussed by Edward Tuite Dalton. Hunting now involves longer time of travel into and out of the forest, sometimes also increased by rehabilitation and resettlement. Their favourite tool is the axe. Larger animals are caught and dispatched in the forest to save space in transporting them to the market averting the eyes of the forest guards. Clearings at the edges of forest areas make for the best hunting areas. After finding such a spot a large number of nets are used to cover large areas between trees. Loose nets were then tightened by hooking them to sticks or poles. The animals in a particular area of the forest are then beaten and scared out into these nets. Catching hares, collecting bundles of firewood, wild greens, mushrooms, tubers, fruits, quails, honey and lac are some of the collectibles from the forest. After Alpa Shah, one may even call them 'eco savages'. *Birhor* resettlement structures are made of concrete, roughly built, poor quarters for living in, closed, airless and already crumbling. Since they sell the meat, their diet has become extremely vegetarian. They also sell medicinal plants and animals to other communities (Moon-Little, 2014).

It may also be seen by looking at the data on the *Birhors* from the census that they have been seeking different kinds of work. From hunting and gathering there was a shift towards rope-making and now towards different kinds of labour. This is more pronounced in districts where the forest cover is being stripped away (Firdos, 2005).

This data may be seen to be supported by detailed fieldwork conducted on the *Birhor* by a number of researchers. In fact, there has been a major shift from being *uthlu* (nomadic) to being *jaghis* (settled) among the *Birhor* (Pankaj, 2008).

Hunger and Starvation Deaths: Twists in the Tale

Since October 2008, till January 2009, there were 35 deaths of *Birhors* in Hindiyakalan, panchayat Narayanpur, block Pratapur, district Chatra. There were massive irregularities and fraud related to the *Antyodaya* scheme cards which ensured basic minimum of food to each of these families. Further officials were frequently transferred at random. Such starvation death reports from Jharkhand have been coming in since 2002 (Khera, 2009).

These issues have become even more highlighted due to the increase in laws and their strictness in demarcating and keeping forest and Protected Areas clearly outlined and safe by the government. Many of the PVTGs still hunted even when it was banned, often to stave off hunger, or to sell for money to buy food. This seems to be an on-going process that has been years in the making. For some, protecting wildlife has taken a bigger importance than protecting human beings (Radhakrishna, 2009).

Tilra village on the Ranchi-Patna highway houses the *Birhors* who had been resettled from a hunter-gatherer lifestyle. In September 2011,

Ratni Birhor had died at the age of 55 years of starvation. This had triggered outrage and hence some Government intervention. Gopi Nath Ghosh, a Ranchi-based human rights activist, had led a fact-finding team to Tilra, had filed a complaint with the Jharkhand Lokayukta. Ratni's husband Bhola was 60 years old and he was partially paralyzed after a recent illness. The nomadic *Birhors* were attempted by the Government to be settled and created brick houses for them. Now about 50 huts have been built alongside these. After this, the Government forgot about them. Ratni's MGNREGA job card was empty — she had not received a single day of work. PDS grains were also not supplied. The villagers were also not getting pension or health benefits. The Lokayukta agreed and proposed the setting up of a committee to monitor them. Food grain supply and health care services improved after the death of Ratni. Most of the Government houses did not have doors. Further no new schemes have come up. As the next generation came up, the older people moved into worse dwellings to give way to their children. The Government provided quilts in winter but a family of ten found it difficult to make do with one quilt. Many *Birhors* settled near Bokaro, but there was a lack of employment opportunities for them. Thus, the youth were migrating to other states, even though they were getting new skills from the Industrial Training Institute (ITI).

In July-September 2010, ACHR documented deaths of many due to starvation. In April 2010 poor parents put red-hot iron rods into malnourished and hungry children's bodies to stave off hunger and disease in Mirgitand village of East Singhbhum, thus killing and infecting many of them.

On 25 September, 2010, Yugeshwar Bhuiya, 45 years old, died of starvation at Semarhat Tola of Dokra village under Chainpur Block of Palamau district. Apparently, there was no food in the house for several weeks and they were surviving on some herbs. The BDO S.N. Upadhyay refused to accept this and claimed that the death was caused due to illness.

On 16 August, 2010, Laxmi Devi, 32 years old, with her three children jumped into a well to escape from hunger at Harlagora village in Bokaro district. Laxmi Devi was rescued by villagers but her three children died. She claimed that she attempted suicide when she had nothing to eat in her house for a week and could not bear it when her children asked for food.

It is surprising to see that the same tribe which helps other neighbouring tribes to survive in times of drought and hunger, are those that have now been forced to starvation themselves since, they cannot access their own traditional means of survival or even the knowledge that makes it all possible.

Losses and Gains in Traditional Lifestyles

The Asurs of Jharkhand are now slowly losing their traditional occupation. Laldeo Asur is now 70 years old of Polpol Path village and he practices iron-smelting, something which their tribal community is well-known for. This has now become economically unviable and obsolete today. At one time, it is these communities which provided iron ingots and raw pig iron to the developing civilizations in the region, including the Indus Valley Civilization, who had shifted to an iron age on the backs of such suppliers. The Asurs today number about 22,000 members and the UNESCO has classed the Asur language as being definitely endangered with only 7,000 speakers left. The community was basically a hunting-gathering one with an added element of iron-smelting. A little more than half are settled in the pat area near Netarhat. From the British Forest Acts of 1865 onwards the Asurs have traversed a history of being alienated from the forests they had once hunted in. Today, the Government of India forced them to settle down to an agrarian life. Smelting also requires wood from the forest for charcoal. When this became unavailable, they started shifting to agriculture.

The smelting method uses crushed stones rich in iron ore and charcoal in a cylindrical furnace fanned by deer-skin bellows. They made farming implements and household tools for sale in the market. The younger Asurs now work in the bauxite mines of the region. Some have become cultivators or agricultural labour. Power supply is low, mobiles are non-functional and they live in old still mud houses with mud tiles. The health centre is 50 km. away and drinking water is obtained by walking up a steep and narrow path. For the Asurs the big companies who have taken over their forests have never given anything back. They would have preferred small-scale industries that use their skills.

The Asurs seem to be able to recognize three different kinds of iron ore. *Pola* is magnetite, *Bichi* is haematite while the haematite found from the laterite is called *Gota*. Experience and observation tells them where to find these different kinds of iron ore (Kumar, 2010). The NGO Vikas Bharti at Bishunpur attempted to revive the tradition and so did the IGRMS at Bhopal. Today, very few Asurs are actively doing this kind of traditional smelting. There are very few takers for this product. Cheaper, better machine-made tools are now available.

By March 2015 at the *Dol Jatra*, or festival that is conducted at the time of *Holi* or spring festival, the *Asura* tribe of Netarhat have taken up the job of smelting iron again in a joint meeting. They claim to have done this since no alternative job has been given to them by the Government. This meeting was held at Polpolpat in Bishunpur block of Gumla district. Other PVTGs like *Birjiya*, *Korwa* and *Birhor* also attended the meeting. It was presided over by Bimal Asura, of the *Adim Janjati Yuva Jagriti Sangh* — Polpolpat.

The *Sabar* are a PVTG from Saraikela district in Jharkhand. They are also found in Chhattisgarh and West Bengal. Initially, they were classified as a criminal tribe by the British in 1871 for their resistance against them which then became denotified. The Jharkhand Government has begun Project Palash to train them to weave eco-friendly, designer products out of bamboo, cane, *Kanshi* grass, etc. for their livelihood. A collaboration with NIFT for training these artisans led them to diversify their products. As a result, instead of earning ₹ 150 every month, they are now earning ₹ 4,000 every month. It is claimed that this Project has weaned away many from the Maoists and has also caused a decrease in deforestation since this way of life is sustainable. They may now participate in events like the prestigious IITF (India International Trade Fair). The Government hopes to adapt all this in tune with their own culture (Tiana, 2015).

The State Art and Culture Department of the Jharkhand Government is attempting to revive the livelihood skills, art forms and forgotten rituals of the PVTG of Jharkhand. To help in this regard, a five-day workshop-*cum*-festival would be organized soon. The nine PVTGs of Jharkhand amount to 4.8 lakh of the population. The Government planned to document the lives of these PVTGs to give a fresh impetus to their endangered customs and traditions. The festival is being co-hosted by the Department of Tribal Languages at Ranchi University. One of the examples stated of such knowledge is that of the *Asurs*, who had the knowledge of smelting and creating rust-free products, like the iron trident (*trishul*) at Tanginath in Gumla district. It was important that such knowledge was passed on to the next generation. Since, these technologies had a scientific basis, they could be the answer to the future problems of mankind. At present, only 6,276 *Birjias* were left while only 9,688 *Savars* were left in the state. Other tribes ranged from 10,000 in number to 1.35 lakh. The UNESCO had put the *Asur*, *Birhor* and *Korwa* languages in the list of the world's endangered languages. Even *Birhor* was seen as being 'critically endangered' with only 2,000 speakers left. It was also felt that colonial regulations on forests imposed restrictions on the way of life of these communities which has eroded their societies (Our Correspondent, 2014).

Some studies on the *Parhaiyas* show that some of their current problems have been due to incorrect implementation and lack of attention at local government development bodies as well local government bodies like the *panchayat* [Kumar and Kapoor, 2004, 2005(a), 2005(b), 2013].

Conclusions

It is a fact that many researchers as well as organizations have published works on so many of these communities in recent times. The Jharkhand Tribal Welfare, Training and Research Institute at Morhabadi (earlier called Bihar Tribal Welfare Research Institute) has been exceptional in creating booklets and monographs as well as research papers which have been published by them. This provides an on-going database for research into these communities in Jharkhand (Mahto, 1993; Mohan, 1993; Verma, 1993; Vikram, 1993; Oraon, (1994(a), 1994(b)). However, other organizations and publishers have also lent a hand in this enterprise (Halder and Roy, 1998; Doongdoong, 2007; Richard, 2008).

At the end I would like to summarize what we have learnt from this exercise and to give some recommendations:

1. The PVTGs have mostly been very flexible in the past with regard to their livelihood. This is part of the anthropological definition of tribes. This flexibility has made them good survivors. It is this survivability that is now being tinkered with due to anthropocentric changes in the social as well as the physical environments.
2. A majority of these PVTGs have been hunter-gatherers, having additional qualities, abilities or skills. These additional features have made them good neighbours with other communities. Anthropologists working in Jharkhand have called them 'service tribes'. It is in this context that the *Mahlis*, *Lohras* (Noamani, 1993), *Parhaiyas* (Das Sharma, 1996) and the *Kumarbhag Pahariyas* need to be included into the list of PVTGs of Jharkhand. Perhaps the *Banjaras* found camping in different parts of the state are also a broken remnants of one such group from the past. Other communities that have come into such an

ambit have been the *Bhuiyas* (Herbert, 2010), *Binjhias* (Kerketta, 1996) and the *Bedia* (Shukla, 1997). In January of last year, the centre accepted the state's plea to accept four more communities as tribes within the State — these being Gounjhu, Bhokta, Puran and Tamaria communities. All four of these communities practice agriculture (Sukanya, 2014).

3. The Government has not only taken away this basic survival from their own culture, life and traditional knowledge, they have made them even more vulnerable. Their resettlement programmes has made many rethink about going back to their own original lifestyle that they understand and feel better about. For instance, the *Birhors* have created leaf huts inside the bare concrete dwellings that they have been granted by the Government.
4. The bio-diversity and knowledge of these communities — perhaps key issues for our future survival — are being ignored and destroyed and needs urgent rescue. This includes the ideas that are already being used by many communities for their survival. For instance, *Birhors* are selling medicinal herbs and trading other items of use to neighbouring communities as are the *Parhaiyas*.
5. Destroying such community knowledge may not only lead to a flow of goods and knowledge across communities, but may also lead to vulnerability growing as a cascade among multiple communities. Thus, this kind of community knowledge must be seen as a set of issues that cannot be separated from the zone within which they are located. They are all linked into a web of transactions that benefited all.
6. Often, it is difficult to argue about hunting in this day and age. However, hunting-gathering communities hunt conservatively when they are doing it only for their own use. Also, as top carnivores disappear, lower mammals increase exponentially causing other kinds of harm. There is a necessity for their culling. USA, Canada, Australia, Germany and other countries have allowed for this kind of culling through either hunters or by giving permits to their tribal and indigenous peoples. Such a proposal already seems to be on the cards [Dhaliwal, 2015; PTI, 2015(a), 2015(b)]. We may think of this as an option.
7. Teaching of skills to those who wish to learn is not bad. Learning from those who know is also a necessary part of this

process. Those who wish to lead a way of life should be encouraged and facilitated, if only that we may know how to survive our terrifying, climate changed future. This knowledge may perhaps be the only edge required for our survival in the future!

8. Understanding and acknowledging our joint knowledge, trade and future would be the first stage in acknowledging the history of relationship of the hunter-gatherers with us and giving them back their dignity and self-worth.
9. Many may also become resource persons in helping us or others learn survival skills. Those who are knowledgeable may also be a part of disaster management teams. This kind of survival game activity has become predominantly at the level of corporate board elites in very well-off business organizations as a mode of team survival. It has also been showcased by the more affluent environment-related channels like Discovery and National Geographic. Perhaps now they can be made essential for others as part of pre-emptive disaster management.
10. It is time to sensitize the administrators, bureaucrats, forest officials and the general public that such people are not to be looked down upon. Rather, they are to be looked up to for a whole new range of skill sets that we need and a culture that has often been claimed as 'the original affluent society'. Funds and resources for the continuing study and recording of the knowledge of PVTGs should be a matter of Government policy rather than as something that needs to be argued out by researchers every time. A freely available database on researches on such communities should also be a matter of priority. That is what can become a baseline for planning, administration, action and research.

At the end, it would be important to stress that the issues covered in the sections above cannot be taken as being independent of each other. They are all linked and a holistic outlook needs to be the correct attitude for dealing with the issue of PVTGs as hunter-gatherers.

REFERENCES

Banerjee, Soumik, Priya John and Sanjeev Singh (2013): "Stairway to Death: Maternal Mortality Beyond Numbers", *Economic and Political Weekly*, Vol. 48, No. 31, 3 August.

Chhandosree (2015): "Hamlet Without a Toilet", *The Telegraph*, 13 January.

Das Sharma, A. (1996): *The Parhaiyas of Palamau: An Ethnographic Study*, Ranchi: Bihar Tribal Welfare Research Institute.

Dhaliwal, Sarbjit (2015): "Allow Hunting of Animals Ruining Crops, Wildlife Department Tells Government", *The Tribune*, 23 June, p. 2.

Doongdoong, Antony (2007): *The Kherias: Identity and Modernity*, Ranchi: Ranjit Pascal Toppo.

Firdos, Sohel (2005): "Forest Degradation, Changing Workforce Structure and Population Redistribution: The Case of Birhors in Jharkhand", *Economic and Political Weekly*, Vol. 40, No. 8, 19-25 February, pp. 773-78.

Haldar, Asesh Kumar and Kanchan Roy (1998): *The Sauria Paharia: A Study of Ethno-Medical System*, Bidisa: Rarh Samskriti Sangrahalaya.

Herbert, Tony (2010): *A Cultural Journey: With the Bhuiyas of Central East India*, New Delhi: Indian Social Institute.

Jha, Ganga Nath and Bhaskar Kumar (2014): "Education and Health Problems Among the Primitive Tribal Groups of Bihar", *Asian Mirror — International Journal of Research*, Vol. 1, No. 1, February, pp. 1-6.

Jharenvis (2014): *Depletion of Biodiversity in Jharkhand*, Ranchi: Department of Forests and Environment, Government of Jharkhand.

John, Priya (2013): "The Irony of Targets: Sterilizations in Jharkhand", *Kracktivism*, 14 June.

Kerketta, Sushil (1996): *The Binjhias: A Little-Known Tribe of Chotanagpur*, Kolkata: Institute of Social Research and Applied Anthropology.

Khera, Reetika (2009): "Starvation Deaths and 'Primitive Tribal Groups'", *Economic and Political Weekly*, Vol. 43, No. 52, 27 December-2 January, pp. 11-14.

Krishnakumar, Asha (2004): "A 'Primitive' Perspective", *Frontline*, 23 October-5 November, Vol. 21, No. 22.

Kumar, Mrityunjay (2010): "Situating Asurs of Jharkhand in Socio-Economic Perspective" in M.C. Behera and Jumyir Basar (eds.), *Interventions and Tribal Development: Challenges before Tribes in India in the Era of Globalization*, Delhi: Serials Publications, pp. 550-66.

Kumar, Rajeev K. and A.K. Kapoor (2004): "Dimensions of Development Among Parhaiya: A Primitive Tribe of Jharkhand", *Man and Life*, Vol. 30, Nos. 1-2, pp. 11-22.

Kumar, Rajeev K. and A.K. Kapoor (2005a): "Social Organizations in Parhaiya: A Primitive Tribe of Jharkhand", *Man and Life*, Vol. 31, Nos. 1-2, pp. 53-60.

Kumar, Rajeev K. and A.K. Kapoor (2005b): "Some Aspects of Health and Role of Public Health Services in a Primitive Tribe of Jharkhand" K.K.N. Sharma (ed.), *Health Problems in Rural Areas of India*, Delhi: Academic Excellence, pp. 552-67.

Kumar, Rajeev K. and A.K. Kapoor (2013): "Role of Tribal Development Administration in Development of Parhaiya of Jharkhand" in *International Journal of Social Science and Interdisciplinary Research*, Vol. 2, No. 12, December.

Maharatna, Arup and Rasika Chikte (2004): "Demography of Tribal Population in Jharkhand 1951-1991", *Economic and Political Weekly*, 20 November, pp. 5053-62.

Mahto, Bijal (1993): *Birjiya* (in Hindi), Ranchi: Bihar Janajatiya Kalyan Evam Shodh Sansthan.

Mohan, Hari (1993): *Korwa* (in Hindi), Ranchi: Bihar Janajatiya Kalyan Evam Shodh Sansthan.

Moon-Little, Edward (2014): "The Life of Two Birhor Brothers: A Photo Essay", *The South Asianist*, Vol. 3, No. 1, pp. 5-17.

Noamani, H.R. (1993): *Lohra* (in Hindi), Ranchi: Bihar Janajatiya Kalyan Evam Shodh Sansthan.

Oraon, Prakash Chandra (1994a): *Bihar ke Birhor* (in Hindi), Ranchi: Bihar Janajatiya Kalyan Evam Shodh Sansthan.

Oraon, Prakash Chandra (1994b): *Bihar ke Asur* (in Hindi), Ranchi: Bihar Janajatiya Kalyan Evam Shodh Sansthan.

Our Correspondent (2014): "Revival Pill for Primitive Tribes", *The Telegraph*, 13 October.

Pankaj, Rajesh (2008): "The Changing Economy of the Birhor of Jharkhand", *Indian Anthropologist*, Vol. 38, No. 2, July-December, pp. 75-82.

PTI (2013): "India's Endangered Tribal Groups See Rise in Population" *The Economic Times*, 25 August.

PTI (2015a): "Hunting Neel Gai to be Legalized?", *The Times of India*, Tuesday 9 June, p. 9.

PTI (2015b): "Overpopulated Animals May be Marked 'Vermin'", *The Tribune*, Tuesday, 9 June, p. 18.

Radhakrishna, Meena (2009): "Starvation Among Primitive Tribal Groups", *Economic and Political Weekly*, Vol. 44, No. 18, pp. 13-16.

Richard, V. (2008): *Tribal Development Strategy: Mal Paharias of Dumka, Guhiajori, District Dumka*, Jharkhand: Shanti Nivas.

Saha, Abhishek (2015): "Jharkhand: Vulnerable Birhor Tribe Suffers as Government Schemes Fail", *The Hindustan Times*, 3 January.

Shukla, Chandrakant (1997): *Bihar ke Bedia* (in Hindi), Ranchi: Bihar Janajatiya Kalyan Evam Shodh Sansthan.

Shukla, Nityanand (2008): "Despite Schemes, Primitive Tribes Die Unnaturally in Jharkhand", *India Today*, 5 November.

Sukanya, Sumi (2014): "4 New Tribes Get Counted", *The Telegraph*, 31 January.

Sukanya, Sumi (2015): "National Panel Seeks Status Report of Tribes", *The Telegraph*, 4 March.

Tiana (2015): "Project Palash for Sabar Tribe of Jharkhand", *Forum IAS Home*, 2 January.

TNN (2015): "Jharkhand's Asur Tribe Losing Traditional Skills to Modern Times", *The Times of India*, 12 March.

Verma, Umesh Kumar (1993): *Sauriya Pahariya* (in Hindi), Ranchi: Bihar Janajatiya Kalyan Evam Shodh Sansthan.

Vikram, Kirti (1993): *Mal Pahariya* (in Hindi), Ranchi: Bihar Janajatiya Kalyan Evam Shodh Sansthan.

8

Social and Economic Life of Didayi Primitive Tribe of Odisha

S.N. Tripathy

Backdrop

The total Scheduled Tribes population in the country, according to the census 2011 was 8.8 per cent of the total population of the country. The States of Madhya Pradesh, Chhattisgarh, Maharashtra, Odisha, Jharkhand and Gujarat have more than half of the total tribal population of the country. One of the most and largest tribal concentrated states of Indian Union is Odisha. The primitive tribal groups usually live in secluded forest habitations where in the forest resources harmoniously contribute to their socio-economic and cultural lives.

Displacement and Deprivation of Tribes

The process of industrialization in India since the advent of twentieth century, the Tata Iron and Steel Company, Jamshedpur (Jharkhand), The Bokaro Steel Plant (Jharkhand), The Rourkella Steel Plant (Odisha), have detrimental impact on the tribes resulting in alienation of land, displacement and deprivation of this poverty-stricken community. Though the development activities in Odisha surged as early as 1950's, there were about 8,117 displaced families from 1,446 villages because of development projects during the period 1950 to 1993.The UNDP estimates that till date more than one lakh people in Odisha have been displaced while 20 lakh have been effected by development projects. Industrial projects like Rourkella Steel Plant (RSP), The Hindustan Aeronautics (HAL) and National Aluminum Company (NALCO) have displaced mainly the tribes (Fernades, 1994; Tripathy, 2003).

Displacement is a multidimensional phenomenon not confined to physical relocation; it reduces the "quality of life" of the communities into sub-human conditions. This understanding of displacement highlights: (i) the alienation of the individual and community legal and customary rights and dislocation of the social and economic organization; and (ii) the politics of legal and policy instruments that sanctions such disenfranchisement.

Cernea's impoverishment risk and reconstruction model proposes that "the onset of impoverishment can be represented through a model of eight interlinked potential risks intrinsic to displacement". These are: (i) Landlessness, (ii) Joblessness, (iii) Homelessness, (iv) Marginalization, (v) Food Insecurity, (vi) Increased Morbidity and Mortality, (vii) Loss of Access to Common Property, (viii) Social Disintegration, (ix) Loss of Access to Community and (x) Violation of Human Rights (Cernea, 1988).

Thus, if we trace the historical process of development intervention by the Government in the tribal areas; one can perceive a very illogical, insincere and shortsighted attempt at defining 'development' in the hill regions. Government policies have always been in contravention to the laws of the scheduled areas and never been implemented. Moreover, the abundant resources of land, water or forests have been utilized for the benefit of external societies and people, but never was there development of the local communities. Further, evidences are there which depicts that with regard to the establishment of development projects may be irrigation, drinking water, electricity or any other, the tribes have been displaced, and even experienced the plight of multiple displacement with meager or no compensation for their loss of resources or livelihoods. Vivid presentation on the plight of Didayi because of their displacement from their local habitat has been made in the subsequent paragraphs.

Socio-cultural Life of Didayi — The Vulnerable Tribal Group

Like *Saharias* of Madhya Pradesh and *Chenchus* of Andhra Pradesh, *Didayi* is one of the Vulnerable Tribal Groups found in the hilly terrains mainly concentrated in Kudumuluguma and Khairiput block of Malkangiri district of Odisha and nowhere in our sub-continent (see Table 8.1). *Didayee* as an ethno-cultural group settled in Malkangiri on the both sides of the river Machhakunda in the centre of Kandakamberu hills.

Didayi is one of the most deprived, economically backward and vulnerable tribes with low level of education, pre-agricultural technology and insecure/declining livelihood opportunity. The aggressive industrialization and mining activities in tribal dominated areas of Odisha have added to the deprivation of tribes by their forceful mass displacement, land alienation and related atrocities. In the context of the *Didayi*, who were settled in the valley, on construction of Balimela Hydro-electricity Project in 1962, to generate hydro-electricity power from the river Sileru, displaced as their land got submerged with the reservoir water. Most of them shifted to higher ridges (hill top) and some were rehabilitated in Odisha Government's rehabilitation colonies. Didayis protested against the construction of Balimela Hydro-electricity Project.

Ironically, these tribals first displaced by the 1st Hydro Power Project of Machhkunda inaugurated by the first President of India Dr. Rajendra Prasad way back 1948. After 11 years of Independence of India another Hydro Power Project was taken over at Balimela than these villages once being displaced by the Machhkunda Power Project cut-off from the mainstream by the Chitrakonda Reservoir (meant for generating power at Balimela). Since then the people of these villages don't have even the basic amenities like drinking water, health and education. The cut-off areas are essentially eight gram panchayats of Kudumulugumma Block separated from the mainland district by Balimela reservoir constructed in 1977. Due to the dam project, over 33,400 people in 151 villages were separated from the Odisha mainland though they were connected on the other side to Visakhapatnam district of Andhra Pradesh. Lack of a bridge has hindered any developmental work in the cut-off areas, helping the Maoists spread their base.

To recapitulate, *Didayi* or *Didayee*, a little known tribe, is an important tribal race with rich heritage. The term *Didayi* which means wild people has been given to them by their Oriya neighbours. They are trilingual; among themselves they use the Didayi language which belongs to the Austro-Asiatic family of languages, and with others they speak in Telugu and Oriya, though they use the Oriya script. In recent years some researchers (Mahapatra, 2011; Mohanti, 2009; Guha *et al.*, 1970) have attempted to focus on the socio-cultural life, and the plight and precarious conditions of *Didayi* tribe of Malkangiri. Based on an empirical study, K.K. Mohanti (2005) in his chapter, "The Didayi Development Perception", highlights socio-cultural, political and economic life of the community and focuses on development interventions carried out among them by the Micro Project *vis-à-vis* the development perception of the community on their own standard of thinking.

The relationship of the *Didayis* of the *Bonda*, *Paraja* and the *Gadava* is very intimate and matrimonial relationships between the *Didayi* and others, though clandestine in nature, are not found wanting. In spite of all these they maintain their distinctive identity and cannot be regarded as a part of any tribe. They have been enlisted as a scheduled tribe. *Didayees* live in five *panchayat* of Kudumulugumma Panchayat Samiti. *Didayees* have their own language. They live in houses made of wood and bamboo. They color the walls of the houses. Their houses are very neat and clean, hunting, fishing and cultivation are the main occupation of *Didayees*.

Didayis are very religious in faith. The cultural life, hospitality and method of treatment of diseases are most praiseworthy. Their costume consists of a loin cloth for men while the women wear *saris*. They are occasional non-vegetarian and *ragi* is their staple food. They eat pulses such as peas and beans, and niger seed and sunflower oil are their cooking media. The men regularly drink home-made alcohol while women do so only occasionally. There is an increase in the consumption of vegetarian food among them.

The *Didayi* women folk play a vital role both in household activities and supplementing income. They actively participate in the formation of self-help group and micro-finance activities. Comparatively the *Didayi* women in the cut-off and hill region are less advanced than the women living in the plain foot hill regions. A study conducted by a group of researchers of Anthropological Survey of India under the stewardship of Smt. Uma Guha classify the Didayi under three economic groups (Guha *et al.*, 1970, p. 26).

(i) Permanent agriculturists who own fertile lands and who have a surplus domestic economy;

(ii) Cultivators who have a hand to mouth existence either because of the land they possess is inadequate and inferior in quality; and

(iii) Landless labourers who work on the land of the other rich farmers mostly of their own group or engage themselves as wage earners in forests.

Developmental Intervention for Tribes

Efforts taken for the development of tribes are multifarious. The creation of separate tribal development blocks in the Second Five Year Plan (1956-61) and a Tribal Sub-Plan (TSP) within the state plan in the Fifth

Table 8.1: Name of the Particularly Vulnerable Tribal Groups (PVTGs) (Earlier called as Primitive Tribal Groups) in Andhra Pradesh, Madhya Pradesh and Odisha

	Name of the State		*Name of PVTGs*
1.	Andhra Pradesh	1.	*Bodo Gadaba*
		2.	*Bondo Poroja*
		3.	*Chenchu*
		4.	*Dongria Khond*
		5.	*Gutob Gadaba*
		6.	*Khond Poroja*
		7.	*Kolam*
		8.	*Kondareddis*
		9.	*Konda Savaras*
		10.	*Kutia Khond*
		11.	*Parengi Poroja*
		12.	*Thoti*
2.	Madhya Pradesh (including Chhattisgarh)	13.	*Abujh Marias*
		14.	*Baigas*
		15.	*Bharias*
		16.	*Hill Korbas*
		17.	*Kamars*
		18.	*Saharias*
		19.	*Birhor*
3.	Odisha	20.	*Birhor*
		21.	*Bonda*
		22.	*Didayi*
		23.	*Dongria-Khond*
		24.	*Juangs*
		25.	*Kharias*
		26.	*Kutia Kondh*
		27.	*Lanjia Sauras*
		28.	*Lodhas*
		29.	*Mankidias*
		30.	*Paudi Bhuyans*
		31.	*Soura*
		32.	*Chuktia Bhunjia*

Source: Compiled from the web-site of Ministry of Tribal Affairs, Government of India, New Delhi.

Five Year Plan (1974-79), and formation of a Large Scale Multi-purpose Cooperative Societies (LAMPS), tribal development agency, Integrated Tribal Development Area Project (ITDA), Modified Area Development Approach (MADA), micro-project for primitive tribal group (PTGS), are some of the measures undertaken during the course of tribal development administration in our country.

Approaches and strategies like top-down approach, regional planning, target group approach, integrated development, participatory development, joint forest management, watershed management, and poverty alleviation programmes, etc. have constituted the part of tribal development approach.

The concept of sustainable development propelled a paradigm shift in development discourse. Sustainable development as a concept was originated from the World Commission for Environment and Development (The Brunt land Commission) in its 1987 report, 'Our Common Future'; 'the ability to meet the needs of the present generation without compromising the ability of the future generation to meet their own needs'.

In the context of development of *Didayi* tribe, dwindling/depleted forest resources have put serious pressure on economic vulnerability among the *Didayee* tribal communities. Thus, onslaught of impact of river valley projects and other developmental activities, penetration of urban entrepreneurs particularly the multinationals companies with vested interests and impact of globalization coupled with trajectory of economic growth has led to the fierce controversies about the purpose of forestry and forest management. It has also polarized conflicting views between human right activists and conservation professionals in respect of livelihood issues of tribals and sustainable management of forest resources.

According to Amartya Sen, development means expansion of people's capabilities or psychological dimensions of development. He considers freedom as a vital element of the individual centric capability approach (CA) of development. "*The purpose of development is to enrich human lives, not richness of economy which is only a part of it*". Thus, Sen's capability theory of development revolves around the people — who are both the means and the end of development and their capabilities. As a serious alternative model of progress and development the CA accepts that people's abilities are influence by external factors — other people, social arrangements, access to infrastructure and public services, freedom to speak and participate, and so on. Being adequately nourished; having shelter; being literate; able to work, rest; enjoying good health, living long, being happy, having self-respect, and participating in social and political activities, etc. are closely related to capability. People's opportunity to have and use economic resources or entitlements, known as economic facilities, people's ability to access health and education services, opportunities to participate in social processes and activities referred to social opportunities and social protections of the vulnerable people so that they don't fall into abject deprivation.

Therefore, According to Sen, "*Poverty must be seen as the deprivation of basic capabilities rather than merely the lowness of incomes*". To Sen "capability deprivation" is a better measure of poverty than lowness of income. Sen asserts that poverty should be seen "as a deprivation of basic capabilities, rather than inadequate income" (Sen, Amartya, 2000).

This deprivation has taken place in the context of *Didayi* tribe. Because, in the matter of devolution of funds for the development of Scheduled Tribes, the major share was taken by those communities who are more assertive and in a better position to demand their rights. As a consequence, the marginalised Scheduled Tribes have been systematically left out of the process of development.

In order to ensure the development of tribal communities, certain groups were identified, for the first time in 1975-76 and thereafter in 1993, which are regarded as the poorest of poor amongst the STs and were called Primitive Tribal Groups (PTGs). The criteria fixed for their identification was the presence of pre-agricultural level of technology; very low level of literacy; and declining or stagnant population.

There are 75 tribal communities identified as PTGs spread over 17 States and one Union Territory. State Governments submit proposals for identification of PTGs in accordance with the prescribed criteria and their proposals are examined by the Ministry for Tribal Affairs in consultation with Planning Commission. The National Tribal Policy proposes to use the alternative term Particularly Vulnerable Tribal Groups (PVTGs) instead of 'Primitive' Tribal Groups. Upliftment in all aspects of Didayi people and providing basic in respect to livelihood under the Didayi Development Agency, Kudumuluguma has been the avowed objective of the Government of Odisha. Kudumuluguma and Govindapalli (presently known as Khairiput) blocks were converted as tribal development blocks during the third plan period. The main objective was to accelerate the process of development of tribes by supplementing funds for development.

Of late in the eve of the Fifth Five Year Plan, the Government of India realized that the most backward tribal groups living in the isolated and inaccessible areas have hardly benefited from the various economic development programmes undertaken earlier under different Five Year Plan programmes. The main objective was to accelerate the process of development of tribes by supplementing funds for development.

The various developmental programmes executed through different development agencies including Community Development Block and Tribal Development Blocks and Projects particularly the primitive tribal groups living in inaccessible and isolated hills and forest areas, cut off area had hardly derived any benefit worth the name. This was probably due to absence of necessary sociological bias and special approach to setting up the development programme which did not offer much to the primitive tribal groups to participate in their execution.

It was, therefore, resolved to start with afresh and to created special development agencies for the primitive tribal group for making special efforts to execute suitable programmes and the identified primitive tribal families in the light of their cultural compulsions, social taboos and social sanctions. These development agencies were called Micro Projects. On the basis of the guidelines issued by the Government of India, Ministry of Home Affairs (currently, Ministry of Tribal Affairs) during Fifth Five Year Plan, Didayi communities living very close to in Malkangiri District of Odisha were identified as primitive tribal communities for their age-old primitive method and pre-agricultural level of technology, small and almost near stagnant population with remarkable lower growth rate and low level of literacy for the purpose of special attention for their socio-economic development.

Besides these above mentioned criteria, certain other co-related characterization like language spoken by them and proficiency in regional language, self-sufficiency to the extent of satisfying their needs with the help of local resources and communal ownership of property to the extent that everything seems to belong to everybody were also taken into account while identifying these communities as primitive.

For intensification of the development programmes, among the Didayi community living on hills, a Micro-Project named as Didayi Development Agency (DDA) was launched during the year 1986-87. Didayi Development Agency is operating since 1986 in 37 villages under three G.Ps of Kudumuluguma block and one G.P. of Khairaput Block. Out of total 37 villages are in the cut off area, i.e. inside the Balimela reservoir 17 villages are in the Hilly area of Ghat area and 06 villages are in plain area or located in the foot-hills. The plain Didayi are comparatively better and advanced than the Didayi living in cut-off areas. Because the Didayi living in cut off areas are relatively isolated, inaccessible and less exposed to modernization. *Didayi* are considered to be the primitive tribe. But the Ghat is in 200-4,000 feet above the main sea level (MSL), all the villages of this area are very difficult, inaccessible without proper communication.

Profile of District and Block Under Study

A pre-requisite for the formulation of a development plan of an area is the analysis of the basic information pertaining to the area in respect of physiographic, demography, socio-economic features, etc. It gives the base to overview the broad changes that have occurred in some of these features in the recent past and to identify the factors which have influenced the socio-economic life of the people in general and the under-privileged class like tribes in particular. This serves as a backdrop in reviewing the existing development programmes and in either modifying, improving the existing programmes of in proposing new programmes for better results. With this objective, an analysis of the profile of district and block has been presented below.

Malkangiri District is located at the southernmost tip of Odisha. The states of Madhya Pradesh and Andhra Pradesh on two sides outline as its neighbouring borders. Malkangiri is considered to be the most backward district of Odisha. The district Malkangiri — carved out of undivided Koraput district in October 1992 with a population consisting mainly of *Bonda*, *Koya*, *Poraja* and *Didayi* tribes, apart from Bengali settlers — has long been a synonym for Government apathy and neglect. Locals blame coastal leaders for their woes, saying that coastal districts have traditionally dominated Odisha politics. Successive Governments, they hold, have largely ignored the underdeveloped regions of the State, a charge that the State Government denies. Some argue that Naxalites, who clamour for tribal development, have actually contributed to Malkangiri's underdevelopment. Roads may be the vehicle for development, but they also give access to security forces. So, the rebels allow very few roads to be built or repaired across the 1,045-village district. The Maoists come in the way of building culverts and bridges too. The 100 km. long Malkangiri-Jeypore road, the district's only link to the rest of the State, is a case in point. The road is a never-ending stretch of craters, some of them deep enough to swallow a small car. Officials also acknowledge that connectivity is the main problem plaguing the district, once part of the Dandakaranya project set-up in September 1958 to rehabilitate displaced Bengalis from what was then East Pakistan and is now Bangladesh (*The Telegraph*, 2011). There are a number of distinctive factors in the underdevelopment of Malkangiri. In 2011, Malkangiri had population of 6,13,192 of which male and female were 3,03,624 and 3,09,568 respectively. In 2001 census, Malkangiri had a population of 5,04,198 of which males were 2,52,507 and remaining 2,51,691 were females. Its small population gives it a much lower population density as per census 2011, of 106 people per sq.km. than any other district in the State. This low population density spread over difficult terrain severely limits the ability of any development interventions to reach a critical mass.

As has been pointed out earlier, the district has received a large influx of refugees since the 1960s, mainly Bengalis from East Pakistan, (Presently Bangladesh) but also some Tamils from Sri Lanka. This has dramatically changed the face of Malkangiri creating problems that exist nowhere else in Odisha, nor for that matter, in India. In the district of Malkangiri there are seven blocks which have broadly three district clusters, Kudmulugumma, Malkangiri and Korukonda regions forming one cluster, Maithili and Khairput region being the second and Podie and Kalimela being the third. The total geographical area of Malkangiri district is around 6,190 sq.kms. of which nearly one-third is under forest, most of which are deciduous. Blocks with more than one-third of their area under forests are Khairput, Kalimela and Kudumuluguma.

Due to undulating terrain, presence of hills and ghat ranges, rivers and streams, the net sown area is just around one-fourth of the total surface area. While in plains net sown area constitutes more than one-third of the total area, in ghats areas, it is even less than one-tenth (as in Kudumuluguma block). Since, the area is thinly populated, relatively a higher proportion of the area is under cultivable waste (15.3%). In the two blocks, i.e. Kudumuluguma and Podia, this component constitutes more than one-fourth of the total area. As the area has got good forest coverage, the extent of permanent pasture and grazing lands is relatively low.

Malkangiri has 13 tribal communities that constitute 58.36 per cent (2,46,214) of the total population. The total population also includes 84,208 Scheduled Caste (SC) (19.96%), a large chunk of which are refugees who have been resettled in the district under the Dandakaranya resettlement project initiated in the early 1960s.

Geographically, it is the most isolated district in the State. No railway exists (although the construction of a railway was part of the Dandakaranya Development Project). The extent of electrification is well below the other undivided Koraput-Bolangir-Kalahandi (KBK) districts with only 35.35 per cent of villages electrified.

Objectives and Methodology

The specific objectives of the present study is to understand the social identity of the *Didayi*, to evaluate the Government programmes on their socio-economic conditions and finally, to find out an alternative strategy for Didayi's development.

Methods adopted were both secondary and primary. While secondary sources of data were collected from various published sources, primary sources of data were mainly accumulated through brief interview and focus group discussion with the community in two plain villages Oringil and Purunagumma were selected purposively due to their accessibility. The study was made by the researcher during June 2013.

The *Didayi* tribe, inhabit in 37 villages located in three distinctly marked sub-areas of Malkangiri district. Its population numbered 3,055 in 1971 decreased to 1,978 in 1981 and again increased to 5,471 and to 5,471 in 1991, 7,371 in 2001 and 8,890 in 2011 (GoI, 2013, p. 206) Oringil and Purunagumma have 127 and 42 *Didayi* households respectively where as non-*Didayi* households are 10 and 31 respectively in the said selected villages. The members of SHGs, field functionaries of micro-projects, school teachers, NGO activist working in the area were the key informants who participated in the focus group discussion.

The Economy of Didayi

The *Didayi* have a subsistence economy, but some families are found below subsistence level. The number of households below poverty line is preponderant in hills area, followed by cut-off area and plains area. In brief, as high as 70 per cent of households in the entire *Didayi* inhabited area is below poverty line. There is absence of elaborate division of labour in their community and in other words, their simple division of labour is based on age and sex. The labour is inalienable and often organized through cooperation on kinship orientation. Their concept of capital (both in shape of cash or kind) is simple. All the economic pursuits are labour intensive and there is absence of entrepreneurship. They derive their subsistence mainly through the exploitation of natural resources. In the interior areas, goods as well as services are directly exchanged. Their technology is by and large indigenous and simple. The magnetization of economy has already made in-road in the *Didayi* area. Their market exchange is concentrated in nearby weekly markets (Mohanti, 2005). Besides economic exchange, there is popularity of extra-economic exchange in their community in the shape of gifts and presentations. The production decision is taken at the household level devoid of any motive for profit-making. Ragi is the principal food of the *Didayi* and rice, suan, edible roots and tubers; fruits, green leaves, vegetables, etc. supplement their diet. With regard to the custom of food taking it is manifested that the housewife generally eats her food after all members of household have eaten. In all economic pursuits, *Didayi* women's contributions to the household economic pool is significant, substantial and are found to be harder working, more responsible and more honest. Thus, the primary economy of the district is agriculture followed by forest produce. About 28 per cent of the total cropped area has protective irrigation. The net sown area in the district is 1,26,777 hectares. Crops such as rice, maize, wheat, a number of minor millets and oil seeds, varieties of pulses and vegetables are grown in the fields. Some aboriginal communities such as the Bondos, Didayis, Koyas, Gadabas, mostly *podu* cultivators inhabit in the district. It is interesting to note that notwithstanding functioning of the statutory *panchayats*, the traditional village Council leaders, such as the Nailk (the secular headman), the Pujari (the sacerdotal head or priest) and the Disari (the medicine man-*cum*-magician) are still enjoying confidence of common men in their community. The *Palli Sabha* opens opportunity for the participation of the traditional leaders. Therefore, it may be interpreted that among the *Didayi* the old and the new system are more complementary than conflicting. It reveals that the *Didayi* people have maintained the statutory system and simultaneously retained their love for the traditional socio-political organization (Mohanti, 2005).

Table 8.2: Nutritional Health Indicators of Tribes in Terms of Body Mass Index, Anemia and Child Malnutrition

	SC	*ST*	*OBC*
Stunted Children under 3 years (%)	44.1	44.3	39.2
Wasted children under 3 years (%)	20.5	25.7	18.9
Underweight children under 3 years (%)	52.2	56.7	46.4
Women whose Body Mass Index is below normal (%)	39.5	46.6	32.6
Men whose Body Mass Index is below normal (%)	33.7	38.0	27.7
Children age 6-35 months who are anaemic (%)	82.3	85.1	79.7
Ever-married women age 15-49 years who are anaemic (%)	58.8	69.2	55.2
Ever-married men age 15-49 years who are anemic (%)	26.5	39.7	22.0

Source: National Family Health Survey III.

Table 8.2 reveals that at the national level, nutritional indicators such as body mass index, anemia and child malnutrition of tribes are consistently worse off than dalits and caste Hindus. In the context of our micro-study in Malkangiri, the field study demonstrated that facilities for health are conspicuously absent in the study villages. The tribes are victimized by a series of diseases and for treatment they mostly depend on local medicine man known as '*Disari*'. The deaths with Malaria are quite common in the area.

Findings of the Study

(i) It is inferred from the study that when the basic needs of a population are denied, the state is expected to intervene with remedial measures, mostly in the mode of welfare schemes. But, there can be three ways which (mis) lead eligible beneficiaries out of the purview of their rights to food: (a) Lack of awareness about the schemes themselves; (b) an eligibility criteria with selection in the hands of local elites; (c) tardy programme implementation; and (d) corruption and pilferage of development funds; of course, invariably manifested in all tribal regions of the country with variation in degree — all exclude the needy and poor marginalized tribes.

(ii) As per census 2011, the literacy level of tribes in Odisha is 52.2 per cent out of which male literacy is 63.7 per cent and female literacy is 41.2 per cent. In case of *Didayi* tribe the corresponding figures are 34.6 per cent, 43.9 per cent and 26.6 per cent. However, it was found that the literacy rate of the study villages stood at 10 per cent for male where as it was 4 per cent among the females. Opportunities for education in the area are inadequate and mostly teachers remain absent resulting in large scale illiteracy, low level of awareness and exploitation by middlemen/business men in weekly markets while selling/exchanging their products. According to census 2011, the sex ratio of tribes as a whole in Odisha stood at 1,029, but in case *Didayi* it is 992.

(iii) Unbelievably, there are high percentages (about 70%) of Below Poverty Line (BPL) families. In fact, in blocks such as Korukonda, Kudumulugumma, the number of BPL families is above 80 per cent. Kondakamberu plateau and Machhakunda River, all of which are cut-off from the main land because of the reservoir of Balimela Hydro-Electricity Project and hence, one can only be able to access such villages with the help of motor launch or county boats.

(iv) There are 44,915 hectares of cultivable wasteland and 49,371 hectares of uncultivable wasteland. Besides, there are 19,774 hectares of grazing land. The average operational land holding in the district is 1.81 hectares in comparison to the State average of 1.34 hectares; third highest in the State.

(v) The per capita food grain availability in the district is 264 kg. which is the 8th highest average in the State and the State average of 203 kg. of per capita. Now about 34 per cent of the agricultural land comes under protected irrigation, which is high in comparison to the other KBK district, but almost exclusively accessed by the refugees.

(vi) The *Didayi* economy basically being a self-sufficient one at its subsistence level, the organization of economic activities revolves round the family — the basic unit of production and consumption. Economic performances with an intention to earn profit and engaging labour and capital in the enterprises to that end is not found among them. The family being the basic unit of production, production decision is taken by the family members mainly the head of the family.

(vii) The *Didayis* have a subsistence economy and their major activities centre round the quest for food. *Ragi* is the staple food supplemented by rice, edible roots and fruits. The whole family take their meals together and do not waste their food. Salap, the palm juice of caryta tree is used as their drink.

(viii) The non-timber forest produce (NTFP) collected by *Didayi* tribe are usually sold at a very lower price due to lack of cooperative or Governmental agency to procure them at a remunerative price. Supply of agricultural implements, introduction of high-yielding varieties of seeds, development of kitchen gardens, etc. were promoted by the DDA. But it was also reveled that a sizable amount of development fund is misappropriated/leakages of fund by Government officials and development functionaries.

(ix) The *Didayi* derive the maximum income out of agricultural practices which forms about 37 per cent of their total income followed by food gathering, 26 per cent and wage-earning 20 per cent and the lowest income derived from petty business (17%).

(x) The *Didayi* is a small community where each member is a valuable asset for the community. There exists mutual love and cooperation among them. They are honest, hospitable, tolerant, and more receptive and open-minded people. Non-payment of debts is not found among them.

(xi) The *Didayi* passionately love their children and land. They give prominence to their women counterparts. In the management of household affairs, women play the crucial role. Live and let live is the underlying philosophy of *Didayi* life.

Concluding Observations

The development paradigm pursued since Independence has aggravated the prevailing discontent among marginalized sections of society. This is because the development paradigm as conceived by the policy-makers has always been imposed on these communities, and therefore it has remained insensitive to their needs and concerns, causing irreparable damage to these sections.

The benefits of this paradigm of development have been disproportionately cornered by the dominant sections at the expense of the poor, who have borne most of the costs. Development which is insensitive to the needs of these communities has invariably caused displacement and reduced them to a sub-human existence. In the case of tribes in particular it has ended up in destroying their social organization, cultural identity, and resource base and generated multiple conflicts, undermining their communal solidarity, which cumulatively makes them increasingly vulnerable to exploitation.

Displacement deprives of the vital sustenance of the tribal people who are dependent on the land, forests, common property resources (CPR), for their livelihood and finally their long term sustainability is also endangered. Whereas the tribes constitute 8.08 per cent of country's population, they are 40 per cent of the total displaced/affected persons by the projects (GoI, 2008, p. 22).

The key factors explaining the highest incidence of poverty in tribal regions are: (1) tribal's' low bargaining capacity; (2) their low degree of political representation and poor quality of local governance; and (3) constrained access to forest, land, and water. The issue of control, power and access to natural resources is contentious both at economic and political level for tribal groups, apart from deep rooted corruption and massive pilferage of development funds by the Government officials (Tripathy, 2014).

In the case of *Didayi* tribe in particular, development project resulted in displacement and has ended up in destroying their social organization, cultural identity, and resource base and generated multiple conflicts, undermining their communal solidarity, which cumulatively makes them increasingly vulnerable to exploitation. The prevalence of high percentages of Below Poverty Line (BPL) families among the *Didayi* tribe (about 70%) and the percentage is as high as 80, in blocks such as Korukonda, Kudumulugumma, marks the testimony of their exploitation and plight.

From the above discussion it also transpires that despite development efforts the Didayi Development Agency (DDA) has not succeeded in bringing about perceptible socio-economic changes among the *Didayi*. Hence, the development schemes and programmes have to be people centred, eco-friendly, and hand in hand with their culture, to make a significant dent in the development process of the Didayis.

Thus, the benefits of development has not percolated to the local Didayi tribe, rather adversely affected their life style, leading to the violation of human rights, miserable living standard of tribes, restricted the community rights over natural resources, and their own forest resources, and finally, culminated to identity crisis of the tribes. The reckless and indiscriminate exploitation of natural resources by the non-tribes who dominate the Government machinery in the tribal area results in not only a threat to tribal survival, but is also leading to depletion of resources in the tribal regions.

Thus, it can be inferred that despite positive political, institutional and financial commitment to tribal development, there is presently a large scale displacement and biological decline of tribal communities, a growing loss of genetic and cultural diversity and destruction of a rich resource base leading to rising trends of dwindling forests, crumbling fisheries, increasing unemployment, hunger and conflicts.

It has been observed that non-recognition of tribes over resources and restrictions on their use, alienation tribes from the means of production, denial of due entitlement of labour, distressed payment of wages, and misappropriation of development funds, have kept the tribes in the web of misery and starvation. In tribal dominated States in India, the life support system of the local tribes has been snatched away by non-tribes and State institutions, through the imposition of restrictions on the use of forests. As a result, tribal movement originated in fierce struggle of their rights (Tripathy, 2000).

Suggestions

On the basis of the above study and observations made, we can forward some suggestions for ameliorating the socio-economic conditions of *Didayi* tribes.

1. There are provisions for positive discrimination in favour of tribal groups under many anti-poverty and livelihoods. It is important that *Didayi* tribe is identified on objective criteria, especially because of their enormous proneness to malnutrition,

hunger and starvation. Hence, to ensure food security, there is a need to introduce mobile ration shops in all the Particularly Vulnerable Tribal Groups (PVTGs) areas, where ration dealers are unable to establish their shops, and ensure their regular distribution of food grains on fixed days coinciding with the weekly *haat* or tribal market.

2. Cashew plantations in the hill slopes, grafted mango tree plantation, pine apples, banana, lemon and papaya, etc. are essential for as horticulture develcpment to generate additional sources of income of the *Didayi* tribes.
3. In Particularly Vulnerable Tribal Groups (PVTGs) areas it is essential to recruit local *anganwadi* workers and helpers from amongst the local PVTG itself. All PVTG households should be given job cards under priority, and 2 members of the family entitled to get employment under NREGA. To prevent further indebtedness, all released bonded workers should also be permitted to draw their full entitlement of grain on credit from PDS shops every month. This should be adjusted against one-third of their daily wages once NREGA works are commenced.
4. The *Didiyi* tribal youths need to be imparted training for upgradation of technical competence for their development, improve the quality of human resources essential for effective administration, to ensure free from exploitation and finally, enrich the quality of life. The training component should include leadership management, natural environmental protection, maintenance of health and hygiene, household management, child care, etc. for bettering their way of life. Tribes evolved local specific livelihood strategies based on their indigenous knowledge. Boosting animal husbandry practices in a scientific manner is required as the *Didayi* possess the indigenous skill in rearing of animals.
5. Joint forest protection committees should be constituted in all PVTG areas, giving full rights over NTFPs to these communities, and taking their active support to prevent timber *mafias*.
6. A special task force should be created in all tribal districts to ensure time bound implementation of laws to restore land illegally appropriated from PVTG members. There is need to change the school curriculum with reference to the richness of tribal culture to arrest the drop-out rate of PVTG children.
7. There is a need to ensure full implementation of the Panchayats (Extension to Tribal Areas) Act 1993 (PESA) in PVTG areas,

which give control over forests and other commons to tribal communities. A single-window approach to make all social security schemes to reach out PVTGs through the tribal *panchayats* need to be adopted.

REFERENCES

Behura, N.K. and K.K. Mohanti (1998): "Vulnerable Ethno-cultural Groups (VEGs)", *Adivasi*, Vol. XXXVIII, Nos. 1 and 2.

Cernea, Michael M. (1988): *Involuntary Resettlement in Development Projects: Policy Guidelines in World Bank Financed Projects*, World Bank Technical Paper No. 80, Washington, D.C.: World Bank.

Chowdhury, B. (1990): *'Didayi' in Tribes of Odisha*, Bhubaneswar: Scheduled Castes and Scheduled Tribes Research and Training Institute, pp. 98-102.

Fernades, W. (1994): *Development Induced Displacement in Tribal Areas of Eastern India*, (mimeo), New Delhi: Indian Social Institute.

Government of India (2008): *Development Challenges in Extremists Affected Areas : Report of an Expert Group to Planning Commission*, New Delhi: Planning Commission.

Government of India (2013): *Statistical Profile of STs 2013*, New Delhi: Ministry of Tribal Affairs.

Mahapatra, Bhagyalaxmi (2011): *Development of a Primitive Tribe: A Study of Didayis*, New Delhi: Concept Publishing Co. (P) Ltd.

Mohanti, K.K. (2005): "The Didayi Development Perception", *Adivasi*, Vol. 45, No. 1, June.

Mohanti, K.K. (2009): *On the Social Life and Customs of Didayi Tribe from Malkangiri District of Odisha*, Bhubaneswar: Scheduled Castes and Scheduled Tribes Research and Training Institute.

Sen, Amartya (2000): *Development as Freedom*, Anchor.

State of the Adivasis in Odisha 2014: *A Human Development Analysis*, (2014), Skill Share International India, Sage Publication.

The Telegraph, Kolkata, Sunday, February 27, 2011.

Tripathy, S.N. (2014): 'Naxalism and the Development of Tribal Youths', in *Tribal Studies: A Journal of COATS*, Vol. 2, Issue 2, December.

Tripathy, S.N. (2000): *Glimpses on Tribal Development*, New Delhi: Discovery Publishing House.

Tripathy, S.N. (2003): "Problems of Displacement and Development", (ed.) S.N. Tripathy, *Economic Development and Problem of Displacement*, New Delhi: Anmol Publishing.

Uma Guha, Muhammad Khalil Abbas Siddiqui, Palghat Ramaswamy Govindan Kutty Mathur, (1970): *The Didayi, a Forgotten Tribe of Orissa*, Kolkata: Anthropological Survey of India, Government of India.

9

Actualizing the Reality or Intellectualizing the Occurrence: Victimology of Witch Hunting Cases in Tribal Mayurbhanj of Odisha

R.K. Mohanty

Introduction

The influence of new technology, and advances in science and medicine appear to have made miniature impact on evil practices and superstitious beliefs leading to scapegoating, mass hysteria, lynching and gruesome homicide. This time-honored wisdom has often led to the academic dismissal of the continued relevance of the belief in witchcraft and magic, not only for the marginalized in society, but also for the people in mainstream. It is too crude and misleading to portray the scientific advancement as a period of intellectual and social leaps. It should rather be seen as a period of subtler renegotiation between cultures, and a period when the relationship between private and public beliefs became more problematic and discrete, and therefore more difficult for the social scientists to investigate (Davies and Blécourt, 2004:4). The study of witchcraft and magic provides us with an important means of exploring these broad trajectories of social relations and mentalities, just as it has done much to help our understanding of social relations in primitive and present society.

There are a couple of issues at stake. Is witchcraft superstitious or reality? What is the content of current public discourse on witchcraft and related witch hunting? Is witch hunting a gender based violence/ systematic killing of women or are men also the victims? Is it an imaginary crime with lawless armies settling scores and unleashing rough justice? Is it community, culture or region specific? How can such vulnerabilities of the victims be explained? Witch-hunting today poses a complex threat requiring not only the actionable solution, but also meaningful explanation. Hence, an analysis of Victimology of witch hunting seemed not just necessary but also an urgent starting point for understanding the dimensions of the problem and recommending intervention for addressing the problem, and for rescuing and rehabilitating those who are suffering from the impact of such targeting.

This study is an attempt to examine the literature in their theoretical methodological and substantive aspects along with the case data from the field on witchcraft and related witch hunting with the aim to demarcate the boundaries of witchcraft research into its current dimensions and dynamics. The emphasis is not so much on witchcraft beliefs as such, but on the aftermath of suspicion, not so much on the persecution of witches but on the prosecution of cunning-folk, not so much on supposed divining the relations with the devil, but on strategic pacts towards instigation, less on the declining belief in witchcraft and magic and more on the continuance of related killer aspects across the regions of their occurrence.

There are four sources of data that this study is based on — (a) case data (total 39 from 2010-2014) about the accused/victims, involved in witch hunting collected from District Police Office, Mayurbhanj in Odisha; (b) Newspaper and electronic media reports and the reported judgements of Courts in India on cases of witch hunting; (c) Key Informant Interview with police authorities and local influential; and (d) Scholarly articles, research reports and books published on the subject.

Against the above back drop, this chapter divides itself to nine parts: (i) The Witch Concept, (ii) Review of Theoretical Perspectives and Substantive Literature, (iii) Methodological Issues in Literature, (iv) Etiology of Witch Hunting, (v) Typology of Harms Caused by Witchcraft, (vi) Legal Prohibitions on Witch-Hunting in India, (vii) Witch-hunting in Mayurbhanj of Odisha, (viii) Overview of Findings and (ix) Suggestion of Remedial measures.

I

Defining the Witch Concept

The term "witch" has its origin in the ancient Anglo-Saxon word "wicca", which itself is derived from the word "*wicce*" meaning "wise", and ultimately from the Germanic root "*wic*" meaning to "bend" or to "turn". Ancient Roman and Greek authors applied it to 'uncivilized' people outside the Classical world (Wikipedia.com). The early Church used it in its campaign against the pagan religions which it ultimately outdone. In Reformation Europe the word became a confessional swear word used by Protestants to characterize Catholic devotional practices, meanwhile the Catholic Church also used it against its own laity who daıed assume clerical powers or who resorted to unsanctioned forms of piety. This confessional use of 'superstition' was still prevalent today, but as several researches tend to show and the term also underwent a process of secularization (Davies and Blécourt, 2004:4). Nandini Sundar calls it Divining Evil (2001:425). Sau (2003:5325) brands it 'swamps of superstitions' fuelled through 'politics of populism'.

Witchcraft is the supposed power of a person to harm the other by occult or supernatural means. A witch or a *Dayan* is a female supposed to be holding such powers. Witchcraft calls upon the powers of the devil much like a believer prays and believes in the power of God. Witchcraft power is used to influence the health (longevity, sickness, drowning, death), or behaviour of another person (the witchcraft victim) or to cause a physical action (e.g. drought, earthquake) or social event (unemployment, family discord, road accident) in the victim or the witch's society (Adinkrah and Adhikari, 2014:315). The physical characteristics of persons vulnerable to witchcraft accusation include emaciated bodies, wrinkled faces, stooping posture, toothless, gray hair, reddish and yellowish eyes and "ugly" appearance. Women who have little to no head hair or have facial hair are also susceptible to witchcraft accusation and subsequent physical torture and abuses (Adinkrah, 2004; Sah, 2007). Witches are typically seen as particularly active after dusk, when law-abiding mortals are asleep. The witches are believed to have had a secret identity. A sorcerer, magician, or "witch" attempts to influence the surrounding world through occult (i.e. hidden, as opposed to open and observable) means.

Witchcraft has been defined in many different terms such as: (a) the use of various types of magical or mystical or supernatural powers; (b) the practice of sorcery, enchantments and intercourse with spirits; (c) a cultural ideology which explains human misfortune by blaming it either on a supernatural entity or on a known person in the community; and (d) magical and shamanistic practices, generally dealing with spirits or deities, the afterlife, magic and ritual. For the purpose of The Odisha Prevention of Witch-hunting Act 2013: (a) "Witch" means a woman, locally known as "*Dahani*", "*Dayan*" or otherwise, who has been identified by any person or persons believing her to be in possession of, or is having, any evil power for causing any harm to any person or his property; (b) "Witchcraft" means use of supernatural or magical power with evil intention to call up spirit or cast spell or discover the whereabouts of stolen goods and includes such other similar practices which are locally known as '*Guni*', '*Jhada phunka*', '*Cot Bidya*', '*Bata Bidya*', '*Kula Bidya*', '*Nakha Darpana*' or by any other name; and (c) "Witch-doctor" means a person who claims to be a *Gunia, Tantrik, Kalisi* or by any other name called and claims or is believed to be having supernatural or magical power to control or to cure a witch or by performing rituals to free a woman from evil spirit or bless a woman with a child or performs any ritual on behalf of any person with an intention to harm a person.

Indeed, there were "witches" of all ages and sexes. Witches and sorcerers are usually feared as well as respected, and they used a variety of means to attempt to achieve their goals, including incantations (formulas or chants invoking evil spirits), divination and oracles (to predict the future), amulets and charms (to ward off hostile spirits and harmful events), potions or salves, and dolls or other figures (to represent their enemies). Witches seek to gain or preserve health, to acquire or retain property, to protect against natural disasters or evil spirits, to help friends, and to seek revenge. Sometimes this magic is believed to work through simple causation as a form of technology. For instance, it is believed that a field's fertility can be increased by ritually slaughtering an animal. Often the magic triggers an effort to construct symbolic reality. Sorcery is sometimes believed to rely on the power of gods or other spirits, leading to the belief that witches use demons in their work. Witch hunt is the process of prosecution/execution of a witch, often involving mass hysteria and lynching. Witch hunt is the process of identification, prosecution and systematic elimination of witches (largely women). The ferocity of witch-beliefs and consequent witch hunting, however, knows no frontiers. This may also seem a lot for an imaginary crime with lawless armies unleashing rough justice. In September 2009 the UN identified witch-hunting as "a form of persecution and violence that is spreading around the globe" (*News X*, 24 September, 2009).

II

Review of Theoretical Perspectives and Substantive Literature

To Soma Chaudhuri (2013) and Nandini Sundar (2001), the two authorities on witch hunting studies, sociological explanations of witch hunts have relied on pre-modern European and colonial American witch hunts to provide most of the explanations for why witch hunts occur in some societies. Major theoretical perspectives on witchcraft related witch hunting as found in the literature are: (a) Feminist and Gender Perspective, (b) Religious and Cultural Perspective, (c) Theory of Persecution, (d) Theory of Dual Deviance, (e) Scapegoating Theory, (f) Labelling Theory, and (g) Victim Precipitation Theory. A brief explanation of these perspectives is brought in order here below.

(a) ***Feminist and Gender Perspective:*** Feminist explanations of witch hunts depicting them as gendered violence, where men target women in power in economic wealth, spiritually, or through social positions, have become increasingly popular. Barstow (1995) writes that a typical witch in Europe was a woman who possessed the power of healing and the power to kill as well. Similarly, women healers, who helped during illnesses and childbirth procedures, were common targets during witch hunts. The witch craze in Europe helped in reinforcing the traditions of misogyny and patriarchal control and demonized the image of the woman (Barstow, 1995:13). Inheritance in colonial America was a major factor in targeting women as witches. Most accused women had no legitimate male heirs in their immediate families and therefore were in a position to inherit or did inherit the property left by their father or husband (Chaudhuri, 2013:319).

Nathan, Kelkar and Xiaogang (1998:1) quoting Archer (1974:292-93) analyze the gender nature of a Santhal tribal myth such as women as witches and men as witch finders as per the blessings received from *Maran Buru — Their God* "Grand-father". The Santhal myth of the origin of witchcraft ascribes it to the struggle between the genders, between men and women, in the family and in Santhal society as a whole. Once myths are mythologized, these notions continue to play a role in people's understanding of contemporary events. Looking at the Santhal myth of the origins of women as witches and men as witch-finders, one can tend to argue that the violence of witch-hunting and killing was instrumental in turning gender difference into gender hierarchy (*Ibid.*). Thus, this function of the violence of witch-hunting may be viewed as instrumental — that is, violence employed to establish a patriarchal gender-hierarchy and its belief system. The idea that women had some power which was subsequently stolen from them by men, and then guarded carefully by them, is quite frequently seen in the myths of different tribes. Nathan, Kelkar and Xiaogang (*Ibid.*) argue that witch hunting in Jharkhand has been both instrumental in changing gender relations, as well as constitutive of gender relations, initially instrumental and then constitutive. The contemporary condition of indigenous peoples is one of rapid change, a change from subsistence economies to one of accumulation. The former is characterized by relative stability and the latter by instability and growing inequality. Nathan, Kelkar and Satija (2013) also opine that there is some variation in this gendered picture among the major indigenous communities of Jharkhand, with an almost entirely female incidence among the Santhal, Ho and Munda, but less so among the Oraon people, concentrated in the tribal-dominated states of peninsular India. Similarly, Adinkrah and Adhikari (2014: 315) maintain that witchcraft-related violence against putative witches is a form of gendered injustice mounted against socially and economically marginalized groups of innocent victims, most of whom are women — elderly, extremely poor, widowed and unmarried — who are treated as scapegoats for myriad individual, familial and community misfortunes.

However, other literature on witchcraft accusations in India point to factors other than the gendered nature of conflict (Chaudhuri, 2013:323). Sundar (2001) argues that in Bastar the accused do not fit any pattern of gender, age, dependency, or kinship, and thus attempts to understand these witch hunts should be placed within the context of the contemporary changes that these communities are facing. F.G. Bailey (1992) depicts the interlocking relationships of kin, caste, politics, and religious beliefs which focus on the witch hunt incident in the village of Bisipara in Odisha. The villagers found Susila's death quickly after fever suspicious and feared being the result of a malevolent *devata*, or godlike spirit that can be kept for good luck. Holding an investigation to find someone to blame, the village council carried out a hurried inquiry. They eventually agree on the identity of a culprit and exact from him a large fine. The accused felt that he is falsely implicated and mustered courage to defy. That led to a tension between collective judgement and individual freedom. From one aspect the offender is seen as a heroic individual who has broken from the chains of the past, a dissenter standing up for his rights against an entrenched and conservative establishment. From the opposite point of view he is a troublemaker who rejects the moral order, on which society and the good life depend, a man who has trespassed outside his proper domain. From Bailey's perspective, the offender's conduct threatened those in power; their determined and successful effort to punish him was an attempt to protect their own privileged position. In doing so, of course, they could say they were defending the moral order of their community. Bailey had originally dismissed discrepancies between religious beliefs and behaviour as annoying hypocrisies only to realize later that it is precisely the tension between belief and action that forges the structures of cultural life.

(b) ***Religious and Cultural Perspective:*** Religious explanations of witch hunts were also popular in explaining the colonial American situation. Puritans viewed witches as doubly wicked: witches were not only threats to their neighbours' physical and economic well-being, but they were also heretics. Witchcraft was thus viewed as a rebellion against God. The constant fear in New England Society was the devil's success in recruiting people to help destroy Puritan churches. The witch in New England was a human with superhuman powers. Foremost among these was her ability to perform "maleficium", that is, to cause harm to others by supernatural means (Karlsen, 1998). The hunts were studied as an exotic ritual in alienation to the socio-political events. In the same vein, the entire purpose of Evans-Pritchard's (1976) work on witchcraft among the Azande was to demonstrate, through functionalist reasoning, how witchcraft beliefs led to a stabilizing influence on the moral and social system: a form of control system with a negative impact. By comparison, the postcolonial accounts of witchcraft are treated as a reaction of the traditional societies toward a changing moral, economic, and social order, where witchcraft beliefs do not disappear with the advent of modernization, but adapt, change, and reemerge in newer forms.

The Norwegian missionary, Bodding, who in the later eighteenth century recorded the myths of Santhal life, wrote, "I am inclined to think that the practice of witchcraft by Santhal women is, to a certain extent, really secret worship, resorted to by women because they are not permitted to take part with the men directly and personally in ordinary public worship", (1979: 224). Some scholars go on to argue (Nathan, Kelkar and Xiaogang, 1998; Bosu-Mullick, 2000; Mishra, 2003; Nathan, Kelkar and Satija, 2013) that there was a conflict between women-centred and men-centred religious practices among various indigenous people. As for example, The Santhal and Munda both have myths of the manner in which the women-centred religious practices were relegated to the margins or came to be denounced as negative.

Elwin's book (1977) 'Maria Murder and Suicide' is an examination of the cases which give the Bison-horn Maria their reputation for violence, and an attempt to work out motives in terms of the community's culture. The factors which usually led to women being branded as witches in medieval Europe still hold chillingly true for India. Undoubtedly, it is superstition which inspires people to see witches in women but this belief often has its roots in very practical issues, like those involving property disputes, political or caste affiliation and the denial of sexual favours. Witchcraft and magic, marital infidelity, the desire to eliminate (various inconvenient persons), disputes about property, crime in the relationships of family life, alcohol, fatigue, revenge, crimes of women, criminal lunacy are the major triggers behind tribal practice of witch hunting among Marias and Kotas of the Nilgiris. Elwin reports on the authority of various old Marias that formerly witches or men found practicing black magic had their teeth "knocked out" or "broken" and suffered other punishments of various sorts. The Kotas of the Nilgiris believe that Kurumba sorcerers who step out of line should have their front teeth knocked out. The reason given is that they are thereby prevented from saying spells correctly (Elwin, 1977:185).

Some scholars relate it to Indian discourses on the jungle and marginalized groups (Kakar, 1982; Bailey, 1997; Wardhaugh, 2005). The Indian fear of the jungle predates the British colonial period. The popular belief was that the jungle is a place where ghosts, spirits and witches have traditionally been thought to live; they reside in forests and "enchanted groves" (Kakar, 1982: 4-5). The jungle is also the place to which deviant and marginal groups traditionally have been banished. According to Bailey (1997: 126) in his anthropological study of Bisipara village in Odisha:

> *. . . forest and village stand at the two ends, representing the extremes. At one end is order and civilization, things under control, certainty: but the forest is the place of uncontrolled and uncontrollable forces, the negation of the idea of the ordered community. Consequently, what is a threat to the community is suitably expelled to the forest".*

Nandini Sunder (2001: 425) analyses an early work of Raghubeer Prasad, manager of the Bhopalpatnam zamindari (estate) entitled "The Aborigines of Bastar", who wrote in 1908, "tremblingly wander in a world of sorcery and witchcraft of which imitative magic forms a part. . . . Whenever a man or his child gets sick it is not ascribed to bad food or bad climate or some such cause, but it is often put down to sorcery and witchcraft". Commissioned by Rai Bahadur Hiralal — to write a monograph on magic among the Gonds of Bastar, Raghubeer Prasad came up with a detailed list of charms and spells to cause rain or to bewitch a newly married girl, several different cures for doing away with malignant glances, omens, and agricultural superstitions.

(c) ***Theory of Persecution:*** Other explanations found in literature relating to the strategic attempts to harass those who are the threats to the social order, include the theory of persecution and the theory of dual deviance (Chaudhuri, 2013; Barman 2002). The term 'persecution', is widely popular among feminist scholars and Western scholars on witch hunts. The term persecution is said to mean harassing to afflict or injure because of a group's beliefs or characteristics. Acts committed against a religious group's beliefs may be deemed persecution by observers or by believers, while people committing those acts may see them as necessary to preserve social order and safety. Thus, the concept of persecution refers to strategic attempts encouraged by the dominant powerful groups in a society, erected at groups that threaten them (Jensen, 2007). The targets of ritual violence in persecution are symbolic of real targets, that is, the targets are symbolic of a group or category that constitutes a real threat to the persecutors. In others words, where witch hunts are categorized under persecution, the accused witches are symbolic of the female threat to patriarchy (Jensen, 2007). The planned and calculated attack on the threat group is also another defining characteristic of persecution that does not end with a single attack. Rather, in persecution, the strategic attacks culminate in a mass wave of attacks toward the threat group. Prior Conflict and previous enmity are other triggers. The names of witches that people called out were all pre decided.

Barman (2002:1), one among the few anthropologists studying witch hunts in contemporary West Bengal, argues that witch hunts are a form of "persecution" toward widows, who face "a condition of marginality culminating in total exclusion from society". Her analysis, based on the case study of Malda district in West Bengal, India, confirms the findings of previous works on the subject: witch hunts in India are an outcome of property disputes involving widows and husbands' kin (A.B. Chaudhuri, 1981; Kelkar and Nathan, 1991; Kelkar and Warrier, 1997; Nathan *et al.*, 1998; Chaudhuri, 2013 and 2013a). The accused women are mostly childless widows, who have a life interest in lands (meaning the right to control the land and its production), which will pass on to their nearest male relative after their death. By accusing them of practicing witchcraft, these men inherit the land immediately. This persecution, according to Barman (2002), is part of a calculated assault on women's traditional rights, which results in the successful establishment of a patriarchal order that forces widows into a subordinate position to the men. The right of a widow to the property of her husband is denied, according to the tribal laws, if her husband's kin are able to prove that she is a witch.

(d) *Theory of Dual Deviance:* Dual deviance occurs when both the "accusers of witchcraft" and the individuals who are labeled as "witches" are categorized as deviants. The deviance is construed as the "normal" response to "abnormal" social conditions. The concept of dual deviance involves deviance at two levels. The dual construction of deviants: *dains* become deviants from the perspective of their fellow villagers and accusers, while the accusers themselves are viewed as deviants from the perspective of the police and legal codes. This consists of two groups: the deviant group and the moral entrepreneur group (the labelling group). The deviant group is the group whose actions (regardless if these actions are factual or assumed) are considered to be a threat to the moral order of the community that this deviant group and the moral entrepreneurs belong to. The moral entrepreneur group is the group that seeks to maintain the moral boundaries of the community, and is also assigned the task of labelling the deviant group as deviant. Becker coined the term moral entrepreneur in Outsiders (1963); it consists of rule creators and rule enforcers. Rule creators can be seen as moral crusaders, who are chiefly concerned with the successful persuasion of others based on what they think is moral (and therefore defining deviance), but are not concerned with the means by which this persuasion is achieved. Moral crusaders must have power and public support, generate public awareness of the issue, and be able to propose an acceptable solution to the problem that is enforced by rule enforcers (Becker, 1963).

Violence is often used as a means to disrupt order (riots, genocides), and it is often the beginning of anomie. However, in the context of witch hunts, the violence against the accused is symbolic: getting rid of the plague that is responsible for the misery. Violence can thus be both disruptive (from the point of the police, the State, and the so called moral entrepreneurs or accusers) and restitutive (justice for the wronged, in this case the tribal community). Thus, the tribal workers look toward the *dain* as the image of misery, an image that can be destroyed and shamed through the witch hunt, and the community can restore its honor.

(e) *Scapegoating Theory:* Scapegoating refers to the punitive or negative treatment of people or groups who are held accountable for crises or problems they did not cause. In scapegoating, the target takes the blame for the crisis that is threatening the group, either "as an intentional diversionary tactic or as a cathartic displacement of anger and frustration" (Jensen, 2007, p. 53). While the practice of witchcraft accusations and the witch hunts have continued throughout the years, the practice has changed in form.

(f) ***Labelling Theory:*** Every case of witch hunting presupposes labelling a person as witch rightly or otherwise. While society uses the stigmatic label to justify its condemnation of witch actions, the witches are branded, named or labelled accordingly real or purported. Labelling satisfies the society's need to control the behaviour that outrages the society. Howard Becker (1963) says "Social groups create deviance by creating the rules whose infraction constitutes deviance and by applying those rules to particular people and labelling them as perpetrators".

The labelling theory asks why some people committing some actions come to be defined as deviant, while others do not. Labelling theory is also interested in the effects of labelling on individuals. Once someone has been successfully labelled as criminal or deviant, the label attached may become the dominant label or 'master status' which is seen as more important than all the other aspects of the person. He or she becomes a 'hooligan' or 'thief' rather than a father, mother or friend. Each label carries with it prejudices and images and this may lead to others interpreting the behaviour of the labelled person in a particular way. The witch is labelled as bad and dangerous and is attempted to be excluded.

(g) ***Victim Precipitation Theory:*** Another line of thought in trying to understand victimization is the idea that victims may precipitate or provoke their own victimization consciously or unconsciously. The classic criminological statement on this perspective was provided by Marvin Wolfgang (1958). Wolfgang's analysis of homicide in Philadelphia found that a substantial percentage of murders resulted from a victim — offender interaction that actually began with aggressive actions on the part of the eventual homicide victim. Wolfgang implied, therefore, that the victim's actions are presumed to provide criminal motivation for the offender. As applied witch hunting is the post-effect of killer attempt made by the victims as witches.

Though criticized as a theory of victim blaming, there was and still remains substantial empirical evidence that victimization and offending behaviour are correlated and that many criminal events involve retaliatory violence. His idea was that violent victimization — in particular, homicides and physical assaults — emerged from a pattern of interaction (a transaction) between victim and offender that typically starts with an insult of some sort and eventually escalates to a violent outburst. However, the insult rarely immediately precipitates offender violence. Instead, a "back-and-forth" occurs between victim and offender whereby insults are followed by counter insults as efforts to "save face". Eventually, this dynamic, which revolves around the protection of honor, may lead to actual violent victimization.

III

Methodological Issues in Literature

The subject at hand has attracted some interest in the last few decades, and increasingly so in the last few years. At present, no single academic discipline dominates the study of witchcraft and magic. In reality pragmatic and mystical explanations of events usually exist in parallel or combination, but operate in different contexts and at different levels. Witchcraft explains the diseases whose causes are unknown, the mystery of death, and, more generally, strange and inexplicable misfortunes. There is thus no inconsistency in the actions of the sick persons in the area who consults both a medical doctor and a witch doctor. The first is believed to treat the external symptoms, while the second uncovers the hidden causes. Thus, the great interest now being displayed in the culture of continued persistence, including its occult aspects has rendered this theme of pressing concern. In the absence of a lack of interdisciplinary conversations on the topic, each way of looking at it becomes an important piece of the puzzle on why witch hunts occur (Chaudhuri, 2013:320). As a result, scholars and researchers of witch hunts are left with a one-sided view of the phenomena, a view that is blurred by the theoretical framework dominant in their disciplines. Despite the criticism, some scholars have been able to transcend disciplinary boundaries through historical perspectives (e.g. Comaroff and Comaroff, 1993; Geschiere, 1997; Skaria, 1999) toward an understanding of how witchcraft beliefs are explained. Frankfurter (2006) in his book, Evil Incarnate, traces the construction of evil throughout history, and in different contexts, up to the late twentieth century. He demonstrates that evil, moral panics, ranging from witch hunts to genocide, are a reaction to getting rid of malevolence and its cohorts.

Moreover, the difference between cultural genera and specifica is a major issue as well, which often blend other concepts such as magic, sorcery, religion, folklore, theology, technology, and diabolism together. Some societies regard a witch as a person with inherent supernatural powers, but in the West witchcraft has been more commonly believed to be an ordinary person's free choice to learn and practice magic with the help of the supernatural. The answer to the old question "Are there such things as witches?" therefore depends upon individual belief and upon definition, and no single definition exists. One thing is certain: the emphasis on the witch in art, literature, theatre, and film has little relation to external reality.

In contrast to the popularity of African and Western witchcraft, the study of witchcraft accusations in India is much neglected. In the last three decades of the twentieth century, most of the research on witch hunts was carried out in the African nations by white Western historians who were driven by a need to understand the newly Independent modern states (Hutton, 2002). There arose an abundance of scholarly work by historians on the European and colonial American witch hunts (Chaudhuri, 2013). Although much of this research on colonial and European hunts consists of a close study of a single case or community, Hutton criticizes this research as it rarely studies data outside the Western world. He considers the colonial witch persecutions as "trivial affairs", when the duration and the number of victims are considered, compared to the hunts in the non-Western world (Hutton, 2002, pp. 16-17). Of the few studies on contemporary witchcraft accusations in India, the bulk of the research is conducted primarily by social anthropologists (Bailey, 1992; Bosu, 2000; Carstairs, 1983; Desai, 2008; Kelkar and Nathan, 1991; Nathan *et al.*, 1998; Sundar, 2001), where the focus is on the tribal regions in central India, particularly Madhya Pradesh, Chhattisgarh, Jharkhand, Bastar, and Bihar if not Odisha and Andhra Pradesh. Soma Chaudhuri (2013:320) emphasized and worked extensively on the need for studies on the witch hunts among the tribal migrant communities of tea plantation workers in Jalpaiguri.

Further, historians and scholars of literature who have studied the theme have become particularly interested in narratives. This involves a concern to reconstruct the role played by conflicts over the use of contested terms (such as 'witch'), and the provision of alternative stories of what was happening in a specific case. But it also involves an interest in the inter textuality of witchcraft cases, that is their shaping by reference to previous stories, authorities or cultural models of how, for example, a possession might develop and be resolved. Most accounts are written in a detached mode, exhibiting little outrage over the horrific destiny that so many of the accused have met. Few scholars mostly from civil society through their research have words of sympathy for the women, men and children who have been murdered.

The major issue concerns the need for case studies and qualitative analysis. Available literature have a near consensus that witchcraft must be studied as a conjectural phenomenon, operating at a whole series of levels and affected by the interplay of a variety of institutions, interests, ideologies and languages. While these can all be analyzed separately, it is equally crucial to study their interrelationship and this, for the moment at least, is best done in specific settings where the evidence survives to allow a full reconstruction of the development and resolution of a witchcraft menace.

IV

Etiology of Witch Hunting

Analyzing the causes of witch hunting has not been as simple as it appears to be. For the sake of brevity, the causes of witch hunting can be examined under two major heads: (1) The reasons for naming people as witches; and (2) the causes of post-accusation witch hunting.

Several causes motivate accusations and labelling. Sometimes, the victim is thought to have caused illness, death, or a bad harvest (Saxena, 2009). Despite this diversity, modern observers have identified several common threads in harmful witch-hunting practices across India. The victims of witch-hunts are usually marginalized members of society and the women, and they are usually blamed for any ailment or misfortune that befalls the community or their members. The practice is most widespread in areas of lower socio-economic development. In other cases, she is being punished for refusing sexual advances or challenging the authority of the community elders, (Bhaumik, 2008). In many cases, a woman is accused of witchcraft in order to dispossess her of land she owns: once the woman has been killed or driven from her village, her attackers are free to confiscate her property. Since most of the fatalities of these witch-hunts are widows, this scenario seems especially likely. Mita Barman notes that because the incidence of witch hunting is rising in some communities, even those that had no history of witchcraft, witch hunting is likely used as an excuse for violence and dispossession of property (Barman, 2002).

Today, witch hunting takes place primarily among the indigenous tribal people, especially in Santhal, Oraon, and Munda, Ho, and Kharia communities (Saxena, 2009). Among these communities, women's property rights are either extremely limited or non-existent. Only the Santhal give women, even widows, property rights; the Munda and Kharia merely allow women to maintain property owned by a man. Further, witch-hunts take place for the most part in rural areas with little access to medical care, sanitation, and education, as it is in these areas that traditional tribal beliefs are most widespread and superstition gains a force of its own (Saxena, 2009). The *ojha/gunia*, a spirit healer or witch doctor, in a community may sometimes accept bribes to name a woman as a witch. The traditional healers or witch doctors have seen their social status boosted by the collapse of public health care and the rising number of related deaths. Their authority reconstituted, many have made it a lucrative business to posture as witch-finders.

In remote parts of India, illness, a poor harvest or just plain bad luck can sometimes mean only one thing: a curse in the family. Villagers will often consult an *ojha*, or witch doctor, who they believe has the power to undo evil spells and identify those who supposedly placed the curse. Accusations originate with the ill-will of the accuser, or, more often, the accuser's fear of someone having ill-will toward him. Land disputes and abuses of power are often other triggers of such accusations — with women and their families falling prey to false accusations and being driven off their land and house. "The trigger could be a death [or] a series of bad luck, but we have also seen that witch hunts are also triggered by motivated and vested interest. These are communities and areas [where] there is much impoverishment going on, so, there is a constant sort of stress. And it does not take long for the community to start gossiping and then also coming together and getting support against the 'witch'. And the witch hunt then becomes sort of a representation for stress relief. You go, you eradicate the woman or you beat her, or you make her confess — and the stress is relieved a little bit" (Chaudhuri, Soma 2013).

The tribal belts of India have some of the worst health facilities in the country and this concomitant with illiteracy, marginalization and Government corruption results in a reliance upon *ojhas* (traditional healers) when diseases such as malaria or cholera strike. The *ojhas* serve as both medicine man and mediator, dealing with the daily troubles of the people. What is more, they are viewed as religious leaders, whose closeness to God and special skills and knowledge allow them to play an active role in saving their communities from epidemics.

These important religious, political and social figures legitimize witch hunts by confirming the supposed involvement of witchcraft in any ill fortune, while village level politics serve to further support and encourage villagers in their hunt for witches. The accused women are subjected to extreme torture both physical and mental. In a majority of cases, the women have to suffer silently as most are unable to reach out for help, given the lack of education and poverty. The result is that they either have to flee the village leaving their house and land behind, or be subjected to humiliation, torture and death at the hands of the villagers. In these tribal communities, accusations of witchcraft are sometimes made by neighbours against neighbours against whom they bear a grudge or with whom they do not get along (Sah, 2007). Sometimes witchcraft accusations against neighbours stem from the envy or jealousy of accusers themselves. For instance, envy from a neighbour's economic success may spark an accusation against the more successful neighbour. Even rivalry among co-wives may cause one woman to accuse another wife of witchcraft.

The most common and simplest reason is that of ignorance and underdevelopment of scientific temper in these regions which easily fuel superstitions, wherein rural folk throw the burden of their miseries — be it bad crop, ill health, natural disasters, unnatural deaths and the like, upon the 'evil spirits'. Moreover, witch-hunting has become a customary practice, glorified by the upper class 'witch doctors'. Other reasons include backwardness and herd mentality. However, the root of this practice goes way deeper than this.

Local tribals believe that much more is at stake than 'tradition' and 'superstition'. At the same time, many accusations are evidently manufactured to rob people of their property and particularly of their land. Indeed, land plays such a key role in the present witch-hunts that it is tempting to hypothesize that they are primarily a means of land grabbing. Those most vulnerable to this sort of expropriation are single, and more specifically widowed or divorced women. Typically, women whose husbands have died and who insist on keeping the land the couple has acquired are accused of being witches by the relatives of the deceased. While multiple factors have combined to produce a climate in which the fear of witchcraft thrives, there is a consensus that at the root of the witch-hunts there lies a struggle for survival (Federici, 2010:23).

Witch hunting has spared neither men, nor women, nor children. Nevertheless, there is no doubt that those most frequently attacked have been women, and in particular disadvantaged and elderly women. It is also argued that the abuses (Federici, 2010:22) inflicted on 'witches' serve to discipline all women, thereby preventing them from asserting their rights. Sometimes, this practice is also adopted to show the woman her supposed 'place'. It could be any woman — the one who dares to speak against the patriarchy, or who is outdoing others in the community, or is self-sustaining, or someone who refuses to return sexual favours to the socially dominant.

V

Typology of Harms Caused by Witchcraft

Witch hunting as a blood-curdling violation of human rights is neither a dead nor a redundant practice of the past. Instead, it is very much persistent, accepted and tolerated in society and what is more of concern is that the number of instances of witch-hunting in India is on the rise. Typology of harms caused by witchcraft may fall into two categories: (a) The harm caused by the so-called witches; and (b) The harm caused to the witches who are accused of having caused harm to the perpetrators. Perceived losses suffered by witchcraft victims can again be grouped under the following three categories: (1) material damages, (2) personal damages, and (3) intangible damages.

1. Material damages may include harms such a bad crop harvest, sickness and death of farm animals (poultry, cattle, pigs), loss of personal property through theft and fire damage, loss of home and other material property through adverse climatic changes and natural disasters.
2. Personal damages may include pain and suffering caused by illnesses, injuries from accidents and premature death in the family.
3. Intangible damages may include mental illness, infertility, sexual impotence, alcoholism, divorce or marriage failure, failure to find spouses, imbecility and even failure in school examination.

The helpless 'witches' are hounded and punished by being stripped naked, paraded around the villages, their hair is burnt off or their heads tonsured, their faces blackened, their noses cut off, their teeth pulled out (they are supposedly defanged) so that, they can no longer curse, they are whipped, they are branded, sometimes, they are forced to eat human excreta and finally, they are put to death (the victim is hanged, impaled, hacked, lynched or buried alive). Surprisingly, such stomach-churning, toe-curling torture takes place not in dingy, shadowy places, but mostly in vast, open village lands where the cheering crowd can fill a modest stadium. Where these women are left to live, they are considered inauspicious and malevolent, socially ostracized and forced to forego their livelihood. Where they don't end up losing their life, they are made to lose their mental balance (Singh, 2011).

These hunting also aim to rob the woman of her property. Sometimes it is also directed as punishment for turning down sexual advances or even to settle any grouse that some person with say in village politics might nurse against that woman. Those who seek to rob the woman may be her own family. But in situations where the woman is unprotected, i.e. she is a widow or a single woman, there's no shortage of people eyeing her land. Witch-hunters (or property-hunters), irrespective of being family members or outsiders, often use the services of '*ojhas*' or 'witch-doctors' to further their cause. In many rural communities with limited or no access to health care, these *ojhas* become powerful figures. Police investigation has found, in many cases, that the local *ojha* has accepted a bribe to name a woman as a witch.

One easy way to break a strong woman is to call her a witch and punish her. Lata Sahu, a *Dalit* woman in Raipur, Madhya Pradesh, contested the polls against the wishes of landowning castes. She was condemned as a witch, stripped and beaten (*The Telegraph*, May 25, 2008). The perception of what constitutes a 'strong' female, or 'a female challenge' could be less obvious than in the case of Lata. Identifying *Dalit* and tribal women as witches helps preserve caste structures or maintain upper-caste hegemony. When they turn rebellious, they are silenced by this gender-based violence, indicating that 'women' must stay within their '*lakshman rekha*' (crossing limits). Witch-branding is also a useful tool for political lobbies that use the obscurantist *ojhas* to influence the community — since these lobbies have their own contemporary brand of obscurantism to push.

VI

Legal Prohibitions on Witch-Hunting in India

There is no national law or legislation against witch hunting in India except Indian Penal Code (IPC) and some state-level laws that cover the acts and behaviours of the perpetrators. Until 2012, the IPC was totally inadequate for addressing sexualized and gender based violence including witch hunting. Acts of forced disrobing, parading, stoning, tonsuring the hair, blackening face and so on were dealt with as simple hurt (Section 323 of IPC), outraging the modesty (Section 354 of IPC) and word or gesture to insult the modesty of woman (Section 509 of IPC), all trivial in comparison to the gravity of the violence, the humiliation inflicted and the resulting long term ostracism that follows. Some of these have changed with the recent changes brought about by the Criminal Law (Amendment) Act 2013 which gives due recognition to forced disrobing as a serious offence, strengthens the older provision on outraging the modesty (Section 354 of IPC). These amendments even introduce the right to compensation and medical treatment for victims. The compensation available should neither be linked to conviction of the accused, or his financial capacity to pay fine — but be disbursed immediately by the State to help the victim recover. The parading of women, tonsuring the hair, blackening face are forms of violation that involve more than physical injury, as they intend and result in humiliating the victim, destroying her social standing and dignity in her community. These can only be part of the penal code, not a special law, as they are particular, but not limited to witch hunting; indeed, such victimization is typical of community reprisal against social and sexual deviance by women. In the case of the perpetrator accusing a woman of witchcraft so that he may obtain her property, Section 382 of IPC provides a ten year prison sentence for "whoever commits theft, having made preparation for causing death, or hurt, or restrain . . . in order to the committing of theft . . . or in order to the retaining of property taken by such theft.

When the witch-hunts resulted in the death of the victim, the perpetrators were often charged under Section 302 of IPC pertaining to murder". It was also quite common to bring charges under Penal Code provisions on concealing or destroying evidence, kidnapping or abducting in order to murder, and acts done by several persons in furtherance of a common intention. Charges were also brought under Sections 324, 325, and 326 of the Penal Code, which relate to voluntarily causing hurt and grievous hurt, and under Section 448 on house-trespass".

The increasing graph of crimes against women under the pretext of them being witches has compelled some States in India to formulate necessary legislation against this appalling practice. Bihar, for all its backwardness, was the first state in India to pass a law against witch-hunting. The Bihar Government passed a law in 1999 called the Prevention of Witch (*Dayan*) Practices Act 1999. Jharkhand followed it with the Anti-Witchcraft Act in 2001. The Chhattisgarh *Tonhi Pratarna* Bill, 2005 (Chhattisgarh Prevention of Atrocities on Women in the name of *Tonhi*) was formulated in 2005. Rajasthan followed the suit in 2006 and Odisha Prevention of Witch-hunting Act came in 2013.

The Odisha Prevention of Witch-hunting Bill, 2013 was passed by the state Assembly in December 2013 before becoming an Act in February 2014. It describes witch-hunting as an act of omission, commission or conduct on the part of any person identifying, accusing or defaming a woman as a witch, or harassing, harming or injuring such a woman mentally or physically or by damaging her property. Every offence under the Act is cognizable and non-bailable. Under the law, anyone indulging in an act of witch-hunting, or abetting or provoking such an act could be punished with a prison term extending up to three years and a fine of no less than ₹ 1,000. Similarly, anyone who forces a woman, while branding her as witch, to drink or eat any inedible or parades her with her face or body painted, or commits acts derogatory to human dignity, or displaces her from her house, will be punished with a jail term of no less than one year, which may extend to five years along with a fine. The law also empowers the State Government to chalk out schemes to create awareness against blind beliefs and evil practices like witchcraft.

However, the effectiveness of laws has been blunted by poor enforcement, insufficient penalties, and peculiar court rulings. In many cases, FIRs reporting incidents of witch hunting are not getting lodged at all, due to the social taboos relating to the practice of witch hunting, community guarding against not to report to police as well as the unwillingness of the police to get involved in cases of witch hunting against community sentiment. The fact that no protections are given to witnesses of the crimes further acts as hindrances to the lodging of FIRs. The crimes that the perpetrators of witch hunters are booked under are often paltry offences when one observes the nature of the atrocities committed against women in these circumstances.

Exact figures are lacking, for many instances except murder are not reported. As mentioned, the authorities generally fail to punish or even pursue the witch-hunters, though these often act openly and in the presence of bystanders. In some cases, witch-finders have gone from village to village, invited by local chiefs, submitting everyone to frightening interrogations and punishments (Federici, 2010:23). What the law fails in doing is to take a proactive stance. One thing which is clear is that witch-hunting is an out and out violation of human rights enshrined in several international conventions and the Constitution of India, like Right to Equality, Right to Life, Right to Protection against All Forms of Gender Discrimination, Right to Security, Right to Subsistence, Right to Adequate Housing, Right to Access Law and National Tribunals and the like. Law has grossly failed in sensitizing people against this practice. Neither the mechanisms for adequate identification of the problem, nor for the rehabilitation of the victims is in place. To add to this, are the evidentiary and procedural glitches in the criminal justice system as well as lack of adequate legal awareness of one's rights in the areas where such practice has laid its clutches on.

The jurisprudence in Indian courts on witch hunting is relatively limited and has resulted in mixed outcomes. Several cases in Jharkhand and Bihar High Courts have indicated the courts' willingness to punish those who injure and kill suspected witches, but in others, courts have reduced or eliminated the punishment for those accused of causing harm through witch hunting.

In spite of laws being in place, the malady is deep-rooted and widespread. One is reminded here of an observation by D.D. Kosambi: "Ideas (including superstition) become a force, once they have gripped the masses" (Kosambi, 1975:10). Apparently, the spell of witchcraft had once swayed the masses, and it has continued ever since.

VII

Witch-hunting in Mayurbhanj of Odisha

The practice of witch hunting/killings is present in a number of states in the country, and these are generally the regions located in central and eastern India. In India, the incidence of witchcraft-related crimes is occurring regularly in Odisha, Andhra Pradesh, Bihar, Chhattisgarh, Jharkhand, Uttar Pradesh and Madhya Pradesh. Meanwhile, Government of India has decided to declare all forms of witchcraft illegal to stop the practice. For it generally happens in places where there is almost no economic development, with meager or no access to basic education and health care. In this kind of an atmosphere, people tend to develop very strong superstitious beliefs and anything bad that might befall these villagers like bad crop, diseases, sudden and unexplained death of someone in the family, or drying of well tend to be considered the work of some evil 'witch'. Thus, begins a witch hunt to locate the person responsible, real or purported.

Table 9.1 shows the number of cases of murder and causing death and attempting to cause death due to witchcraft from 2009 to 2013.

Table 9.1: No. of Cases of Murder and Causing and Attempting to Cause Death due to Witchcraft 2009-2013

States	*302/304/308 IPC*				
	2009	*2010*	*2011*	*2012*	*2013*
Andhra Pradesh	27/00	26/00	28/01	24/00	15/00
Jharkhand	37/00	15/00	36/00	26/00	54/01
MP	23/02	18/00	15/00	10/00	11/00
Odisha	28/08	31/03	39/02	32/00	24/00

Source: Compiled from NCRB (New Delhi) Data 2009 to 2013.

Table 9.1 reflects those states taken where number of cases has been $\geq$ 20 per year in 2009. Data for available last 5 years have been compiled from NCRB New Delhi Statistical Tables from 2009-2013. Data for 2014 is yet unavailable. All these states are the bordering states of Odisha and more over Jharkhand and Odisha, the two tribal dominated states, are the very ill famous in the matter relating to witch hunting as can be understood from the figures in the table presented. Such crime are recorded under three sections of Indian Penal code by NCRB: (a) 302 IPC: Cases of Murder/culpable homicide; (b) 304 IPC: Cases of causing death not amounting to culpable homicide; and (c) 308 IPC: Cases of attempting to commit culpable homicide. However, Karnataka State had the unusual highest number of 77 cases of such murder in 2011 as against near zero in other years (only 1 each in 2009 and 2010. Haryana had 32 cases in 2009, 58 cases in 2010, only 05 in 2011 and nil reports both in 2012 and 2013.

For the purpose of analysis it has been decided to include only one tribal district namely Mayurbhanj in North Odisha. The rationale behind choice of the district is the following: (1) This district bordering Jharkhand state is the worst witch hit and has the highest witch hunting occurrences in the state of Odisha. (2) The tribals of Odisha mostly inhabit this land locked district, mainly in close proximity to forests worst deprived in terms of accessibility to health care, education, road and transport and the allied basic service facilities. (3) This is the district in which 53 Tribal Groups out of total 62 types of tribals of Odisha live for centuries, being far away from the mainstream in their relatively isolated, inaccessible, less fertile and less agriculturally productive regions of forests, hills and mountains. For better appreciation, a brief profile of the district is given below.

Mayurbhanj is situated in the Northern boundary of the State with a total geographical area of 10,418 sq.km. and the district headquarters at Baripada. The district is bounded in the North-East by Midnapure district of West Bengal, Singhbhum district of Jharkhand in the North-West, Baleswar district in the South-East and by Kendujhar in the South-West. More than 39 per cent of total geographical area (4,049 sq.km.) is covered with forest and hills and the district is governed under 32 police stations. The population density of Mayurbhanj district for 2011 is 242 people per sq.km. as against 213 people per sq.km. in 2001.

Mayurbhanj is a tribal dominated district. Mayurbhanj district has the highest proportion of STs (58.72%) followed by Malkangiri (57.83%)

in the State of Odisha in 2011. The major tribes found in Mayurbhanj are: the *Santhals*, *Kolha*, *Bhuyan*, *Bathudi Bhuyan*, *Gond*, *Bhumija*, *Munda*, *Khadia*, *Mankadia* and *Lodha*. The tribes constitute 57.67 per cent of the total population of this district. Though the population of Mayurbhanj is only 6 per cent of the State's total population, the tribal population shares a 15.42 per cent of the state's total S.T. population. As per 2011 Census tribal population of Mayurbhanj District comprised of total 14,79,576 out of which 7,30,487 were male and 7,49,089 were female. Bhumija and Kolha live scattered throughout the district. Their concentration is more in Khunta, Bijatala, Jamda, Tiring and Thakurmunda blocks which varies from 70 per cent to 80 per cent of the total population of the respective blocks. The *Khadia*, *Mankadia* (nomadic food gatherers and hunters) and *Lodha* (a criminal tribe) are the Particularly Vulnerable Tribal Groups (PVTGs) and the erstwhile primitive tribals (PTGs) of the district. The *Santhals*, another tribe are mostly marginal farmers and agricultural labourers.

During the period from 2010 to 2014, a total number of 39 cases of murder and related abuse of victims were reported and cases registered. Detailed summary of the type of cases registered, profile of the victim and the accused, the sections of Law invoked are give appendix (Table 9.2). Following table gives a picture of PS-wise No. of Cases registered in Mayurbhanj district during last five years from 2010 to 2014.

Table 9.2: Police Station-Wise No. of Cases (2010-2014)

Sl.No.	*Police Station*	*No. of Cases Registered*
1.	Jashipur	5
2.	Tiring	5
3.	Rairangpur	4
4.	Bisoi	4
5.	Karanjia	3
6.	Others	18
	Total	**39**

Source: Field Survey Data.

Tiring, Jashipur, Rairangpur and Bisoi police stations which have more than 4 cases during the period of study are in the Jharkhand boarder. More than 80 per cent in these police station areas are inhabited by tribals. There is a Jharkhandi impact on the instances of witch hunting as believed by the people of the area. As and when the local *gunias* fail to cure the illness or heal the hazard, the local people tend to move to Jharkhand in search of a more effective healer or *Ojha* (witch doctor). In this table police station with more than 3 no of cases between

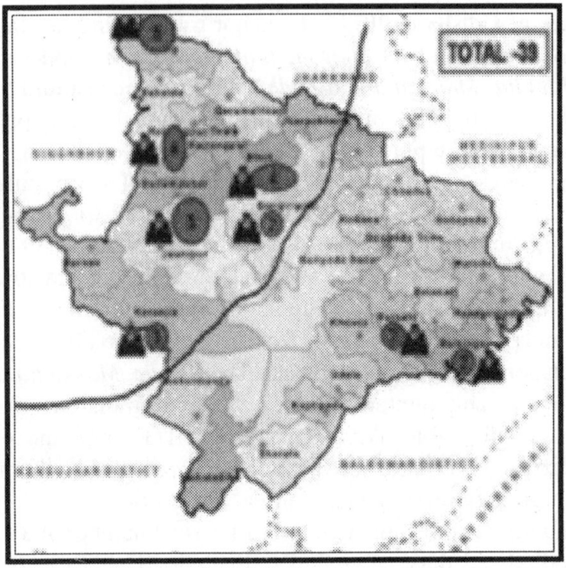

Figure 9.1: Police Station Wise Witch Hunting in Mayurbhanj, Odisha (2010-2014)

2010 to-2014 have been shown. Other police stations with less than 3 cases include Bangiriposi, Kaptipada, Badasahi with two each. In the same vein Jamda, Jharpokharia, Badampahar, Gorumahinsihani, Baisinga, Uddala, Baripada Sadar, Thakurmunda, Betanati, Raruan, Rasagobindapur and Sarat police stations have registered one case each. More number of cases is found in upper Mayurbhanj (Beyond *Baban Ghati*) numbering 21 out of total 39 cases. Out of total 39 police stations, 19 police stations have registered witch hunting cases terminating in murder.

All 39 cases are specially reported cases. Sensational cases like witch hunting and resultant murder are given a special status under the orders of Superintendent of police of the concerned district for the purpose of careful investigation by a senior officer under proper supervision. Reports available on record show that all cases except two related to Murder (302 IPC) or attempt to murder (307 IPC) turning to murder due to subsequent death. It was a matter of curiosity to know from the police authorities regarding the non-registration of public humiliation, attempted/physical violence and torture and property violence. It could be ascertained that such cases are not reported to police and are being sorted out at the village level amicably or through *gram sabha* (village level committee). A great number of cases are never taken to the police. Though Odisha Prevention of Witch-hunting Act, 2013 has come into force since February 2014, not a single case has been booked under the said Act in the District. Some of the police officers are yet unaware of the provisions and the background circumstances under which such Act was promulgated in the State of Odisha.

Efforts were made to locate and tabulate the distance of place of occurrence from police station as can be seen from Table 9.3.

Table 9.3: Distance of Place of Occurrence from Police Station

Sl.No.	*Distance*	*No. of Police Station*	*%*
1.	Upto 15 Kms	15	38.46
2.	15-25 Kms	11	28.21
3.	25-35 Kms	6	15.38
4.	35+ Kms	7	17.95
	Total	**39**	**100.00**

Source: Field Survey Data.

It can reasonably be established that none of the places of occurrence of cases of witch hunting appear to be nearer to the police station. Place of occurrence being at the least distance was 4 kms away from the police station and the highest being at a distance of 97 kms. Three police stations show to have a distance of more than 50 kms from the place of occurrence. More distant is the place from police station, greater is the occurrence of witch hunting resulting in homicide. Police also went on to say that some of the places of occurrence are so inaccessible that it becomes difficult to make a prompt rescue of the victim of torture. During the witch hunting, some of the locals guard and prevent others not to inform the police. The community warns the people not to inform the police. The community in a mob like situation also prevents the police from rescuing the victim.

This can be well appreciated from Jashipur PS Case No.1 dt.10.01.14 u/s 302/34 IPC, Specially Reported (SR) Case No 10/14) in which a 45-year-old widow was recently killed by two men who had been led to believe that she was a witch responsible for the death of their relatives. The places and the details of the crime differ but the victim targeted is a woman, usually from an impoverished background, whose fraught position in terms of gender, class and economy makes it easy for her community to eliminate her by giving her a convenient name whether of a person of loose morals or of a witch.

The incident took place in Kuaribil, which is among the most inaccessible regions within the Simlipal forest. The police could reach the village several hours after the murder took place because the reporting, done by the victim's 12-year-old daughter, who was an eye-witness, involved a number of detours before it reached the police outpost in Gudgudia *via* the professional messenger of the forest, the *dakua*.

From Kuaribil, the nearest public health centre is 35-40 kilometers away there is no public transport system connecting the village to the PHC. The local school has reportedly remained closed for six years because no teacher is willing to suffer the exile. Incidentally, Kuaribil is also known for the large number of infant deaths, which had attracted the attention of the human rights authorities in 2006-2007 (Mukherjee Anusua, 2014).

The prevalence of witches in Odisha is expectedly connected to this lack of health facilities, since a 'witch' is very likely to be a woman suffering from psychological ailments, which cause her to behave abnormally. While a young woman is likely to be labelled a witch if she is too smart, sassy or pretty, an elderly woman suffering from, say, epilepsy or dementia, is also an easy target. When families do not want to undertake the medical expenses of an aged, ailing relative, they throw her out. It becomes easier to drive her out of her home and property if the family members get social sanction for the act by branding her a witch.

The lacunae created by the insufficient State healthcare system are also the spaces where the witch-doctors, in their various avatars as *gunias, ojhas* or quacks, step in. In another case, encouraged in his belief by the local *gunia*, the husband, aided by his parents and sisters, stuffed turd in his wife's mouth, plucked out her teeth and drove her out. Malaria and diarrhea epidemics, two diseases and the resultant deaths are not uncommon in these areas. The rest of the villagers keep vigil over the family members of the accused. When some of the family members of the accused totally horrified try to escape from the village to inform the police, the rest of the villagers prevented them, using threats and physical assault.

The narratives of witch hunting reminds Hobbsian brutish barbarism, illiteracy, blind faith, particularly amongst tribals, when all these features are neither exclusive to a specific community, nor is there sufficient evidence to conclusively establish the existence of all these aspects in every case of witch hunting. Table 9.4 explains the community status of the victim and the accused.

Table 9.4: Community Status of Victim and Accused

Community	*Victim*	*%*	*Accused**	*%*
Non-tribal	5	12.82	4	10.26
Tribal	22	56.41	21	53.85
PVTG	12	30.77	14	35.90
Total	**39**	**100.00**	**39**	**100.00**

*Accused may be an individual or in groups.
Source: Field Survey Data.

It is found that 87 per cent of the total victims are tribals out of which 31 per cent of the victims belong to particularly vulnerable tribal groups and the most marginalized tribals. Out of total 5 non-tribal victims 1 each belonged to general and scheduled caste category respectively and the rest of three victims were held from socio-economically backward classes (SEBC). Allegations about use of 'supernatural' powers are invariably present in cases of witch-hunting. But marginalization, vulnerabilities and settling scores over previous enmity, tend to emerge as underlying factors in a significant number of cases. The high rates of lack of formal education among the victims and the perpetrators on the one hand and the large number of health issues which surfaced as pretexts for labeling men and largely women as witches indicate the links between witch hunting and the larger issue of governance and development.

There is a very broad spectrum of violence that a victim of witch hunting has to face: stigma, isolation and ostracism being the most prevalent and persistent forms. The victims and their families are also subject to serious social and economic deprivations as a consequence of the labelling and ensuing violence. In most cases, while the immediate family members both support the victim and suffer the consequences of the labelling, the neighbours and the larger community are complicity in the victimization process. The local governance bodies also do not seem to unequivocally stand by the victims, often aiding the perpetrators.

Similarly about the accused it is evident that 97 per cent of the total accused persons are tribals out of which 36 per cent of them belong to particularly vulnerable tribal groups and the most marginalized tribals. Out of total 4 non-tribal accused 1 each belonged to general and scheduled caste category respectively and the rest of two were held from SEBC category. Our study revealed the accused as a very nebulous category. The people of the region certainly have a strong belief in the existence of such men and largely women who practice a different form of worship labeled as witchcraft, and thus — as per popular belief to which they are completely and unquestionably committed — gain certain powers to cause harm. To them there are really such practices as gathering at night, in the sacred grove, where it is otherwise forbidden for women to enter, usually on the night of a new moon (*amavasya*), dancing, possibly naked and uttering unknown chants. These are the people who also narrate their experiences of the actions of and the harm caused by witch(s) and witch hunting so called is an attempt to execute and eliminate them. This conclusive aspect, if subscribed to, may run close to the victim precipitation theory. Even some of the police authorities and the local media persons at Baripada district headquarters vehmently establish the existence of witches and the harm caused by them to the public in the area. Again, there are also such people who take advantage of such belief within the community and settle their scores with their enemies. Witch-hunting as a form of violence also surfaces in contexts of family disputes and stresses. This idea goes on to support the labelling theory.

Rasgobindapur PS Case No. 83 dt.17.06.14 is one example which goes as follows. Mirza Baske's wife was selling 'handia' (country liquor) in the area and Mirza was of help in the sale process. All the three accused Hempa, Hemlal and Udhab used to drink handia from Mirza's shop. Once after drinking handia, Hempa suffered fever and stomachache. The type of local medicine Hempa was used to, did not work and he suspected some witch attempt by Mirza. Premlal Hembram happened from Jharkhand had settled in the village after being married to Udhab's sister. They had a daughter who suffered disease and later died. Premlal consulted local Gunia and villagers who made him to believe some witch attempt by Mirza. He also suspected Mirza Baske.

Udhab works in Chennai as labour and also takes handia from baskes wife during his visit to the village. Udhab once suffered similar problems like Hempa and also similarly suspected Mirza Baske. One day they decided to eliminate Mirza and the brutal murder took place. Hempa being local was nabbed by police. Udhab and Premlal appear to have been hiding at Chennai and Ranchi respectively.

An attribution of a person as a witch is nearly always negative, fearful and destructive. Although such attribution draws upon what may be treated as superstition, it does not necessarily arise from superstition. In many cases, interpersonal animosity, rivalry and conflict over various material sources may lie behind the labelling of a person as a witch. Once a person is labelled, whether or not such labelling is malicious in nature, a complex set of reactions and fear are invoked, making it very difficult for the women (sometimes men) targeted as witch to defend themselves. It is believed that diseases caused by witchcraft cannot be cured by conventional medicine. However for the purpose of brevity and precision it becomes difficult to draw a line between a witch real and one fictitiously labelled as a witch. But one thing is clear from the data as such that witchcraft and related witch hunting are predominately found in tribal areas mostly among the tribes. Overwhelming majority of victims and the accused are adult married/widowed tribal men and largely women.

Then, an attempt was made to disaggregate the intra- and inter-community status of both the accused and the victims in order to establish if there is any relationship between the community status and the gruesome practice of witch hunting. Data on nature of collective offense and group identity was none the less revealing as can be seen from Table 9.5.

Table 9.5: Nature of Collective Offense and Group Identity

Category	*Yes*	*No*	*Total*
Accused in Group	21	18	39
Accused and Victim from same clan	38	1	39
Women among Accused	3	36	39
Child Accused	1	38	39

Source: Field Survey Data.

With witch practice ruling the roost in the tribal hinterland of Odisha, villagers young and old continue to be tortured and killed on the suspicion of practising witchcraft. The cases involve more than one accused or individual accused under popular support, so that, this public nature of violence is executed by a group rather than an individual. Out of 39 cases total 21 committed murder collectively in a group and 18 were individual accused. There were three cases in which women formed part of the murder accused group. Soon after the suspicion spreads, a group of people organize to attack the witch and sometimes single individuals muster courage with necessary support from the community commit witch hunting. Individual witch hunters are sometimes instigated to commit as happened in case of Gourangi Murmu who was led to believe that her brother died of fever and later she plucked the high school examination (the only child accused of Bisoi PS Case No. 33 Dt. 10.05.11) due to witch action of Ratani Marandi. Nearly all of the accused and victims belonged to the same clan, community and the village. The distribution of victims and accused according to social groups do not present any varied or diverse picture. A significant intra-community if not inter-caste/inter-community dynamics can be discerned in this study of cases of witch-hunting as a whole. Our work nonetheless found that the accused is generally related to the victim through kinship, community or neighbourhood ties. Moreover, the accused and the victim seem to belong to comparable social and economic strata. In a very small number of cases, the members of women's natal families, their sons or their daughter's marital families were also involved in labelling and targeting women as witches. In the remaining cases the largest set of cases consist of perpetrators who are neighbours of the victims and the remaining few cases consist of perpetrators who are residents of the same village in which the victim resides.

The first step in a series of events which constitute the victim of witch-hunting is that of labelling someone as a witch. Although, often there are complex and long term issues which shape the process of labelling of a woman as a witch, there is usually some incident or allegation that provides the trigger for the process to take a tangible form. In the case studies collected by us, in an overwhelming number of cases, the immediate trigger for labelling someone as a witch arose from the illness or death of a human or an animal and the attribution of this to the victim with or without the intervention of a sorcerer (variously labelled as a *gunia* in Odisha and an *ojha* or *baiga* of Jharkhand). Except for three cases in which the immediate triggering event was bad crop, a snake drinking milk, and a missing object from a ritual site, in all the remaining cases, the victim was held responsible for an actual or alleged illness (ranging from stomach aches, fever, paralysis, mental problems including hysteria, skin eruptions, joint pains, etc.), inability to conceive a child, deaths due to illness or even murders (committed by someone else) and suicide.

Physical contact or verbal statements made by the victim as well as sheer evil intentions are often mustered up as evidence of the victim's responsibility for the undesirable incident. This process of labelling is also often aided by the intervention of the local sorcerers who are approached to ascertain the cause of various modes of suffering. In at least 19 out of the 39 cases available, a *gunia* was involved in the process of labeling. A *gunia* in the area is godly a person who is never accused of instigating the murder nor is he ever accused by the locals. As happened in the case of murder of Mirza Baske's wife in Rasgobindapur PS Case No. 83 dt. 17.06.14, once a woman (or a man) has been identified as responsible for any particular undesirable event, a series of other allegations may be made which may be further 'proven' on the basis of claims about the suspicious conduct of the victim. At times such conduct itself (such as extreme religiosity, removal of objects from a ritual site, any novel ritual practice, etc.) are themselves read as signs of witch-craft and may be treated as evidence to support the labeling. Table 9.6 presents the gender of the victim of witch hunting.

Table 9.6: Gender of the Victim

Victim	*No.*	*%*
Male	18	46.15
Female	21	53.85
Total	**39**	**100.00**

Source: Field Survey Data.

In majority number of cases, victim's behaviour was judged suspicious by local people and have led to the targeting. It cannot be ruled out that there were other factors which aided in the process of victimization in these cases as well. Our data shows that women victims outnumber the men victims of witch hunting. In one case the man who was targeted and murdered along with wife was a secondary victim, who suffered collateral violence. Majority of the victims murdered were middle-aged adults, married women along with widows and single who were most vulnerable to witch-hunting. In fact witch-hunting appeared to be a prevalent form of violence used to target middle aged women fully ensconced in their marital homes. Witch hunts in our case studies testify the examples of extreme brutality and violence including forcible stripping, being paraded naked in public, cutting or tonsuring of the hair, blackening of the face, cutting of the nose, pulling of the teeth to 'defang', gouging out the eye, whipping, gang rape, forcible consumption of human excreta, cow dung or other noxious substances, sexual assault, and killing by hanging, hacking, lynching or burying alive. Subsequent to the branding and the accompanying physical violence leading to death of the breadearner, there may be several other negative fall-outs, social stigma, psychological torture, social and economic boycott, loss of livelihood and violence for the survivors of witch-hunting which can go on for years and sometimes can last a lifetime. The police records indicate the gendered nature of witch hunting, reflecting particular forms of sexual and gender based violence. Public humiliating is common, with instances of forced entry into the victim's house only to drag her outdoors to a public place, tonsure the hair, blacken face, forcibly disrobe and parade the victim and abuses in combination with threat to life are some visible trends. Name calling is rarely limited to being called 'witch'; it is almost always accompanied by a range of sexual slurs and local abuse. Madhu Mehra (2013) argues that witch hunting primarily targets women and the primary victims are women.

Table 9.7: Status of Registered Cases as on April 2015

Sl.No.	*Status*	*No. of Cases*	*%*
1.	Subjudice	26	66.67
2.	Acquitted	7	17.95
3.	Convicted	2	5.13
4.	Under-investigation	4	10.26
	Total	**39**	**100.00**

Source: Field Survey Data.

Large number of cases is either subjudice (67%) in the court of law or under investigation (10%) at the police station level amounting to a total of 77 per cent of the cases as pending. Seven Cases were found where the accused were acquitted. The state had not appealed against acquittal in a single case of witch hunting in the appellate court that has been reported. Two of the cases ended in conviction out of which one was a child offender and has now been released after completion of the term at observation home under juvenile law.

One case was found to be the case finally reported as 'fact true and no clue' as no adequate evidence material or circumstantial could be available to nab the accused for further prosecution. Police authorities went on to suggest that in these sensitive cases, the community sentiment in favour of witch hunting is so strong that matter of physical torture, name-calling, abuses in combination with threat to life and other forms of human right violations are not reported to the police. The police records (FIRs/charge-sheets) as well as related case documents provide some insights into the point at which the criminal justice system begins to interact with victimization connected with grave crime of murder in the name of witch hunting. The non-murder cases are compromised and sorted out at the village level and even are guarded in such a manner so that they are not reported to police. In three of the cases, the accused straight ran to the police station with cut head of the victim after committing the murder. More so police sometimes is not allowed to enter the village to take *suo mutto* cognizance of the cases. Police force enters the place of occurrence where grave crime of gruesome murder takes place. In case of victim lady Pano Hansdah, the police was allowed to enter and could rescue her on assuring the public that they were arresting her as the accused of witch practices causing harm, fever and death of the relations of the perpetrators. None of the perpetrators could be arrested. Police has other difficulties as well. Sometimes witnesses are unavailable, if available they are unwilling to depose, if deposing, they later turn to be hostile. The accused persons claim themselves to be ex-victims of witchcraft. In fact, abettors persuade the vulnerable to enter into commission of witch hunting offenses for their own gain.

VIII

Overview of Findings

This study establishes that the world of spirits and witches is not a dead or insular domain. There has been dispersion in the nature of witch hunts. All accusations appear to follow a series of illnesses. Accusations of occult mal-practice tend to become a way of coping with the uncertainties of human existence and attributing agency to local actors in a context where, in practice, people have little power. Land and property disputes, notions of power, spurning of sexual advances, domestic squabbles, and family feuds have become very common factors. The witch hunts continue to become village affairs especially in tribal regions where people rely on their own internal informal justice system and take law to their own hands. There is some truth in the statement when Schnoebelen says "Witchcraft is real for those who believe in it" (2009:2). It has been so deeply ingrained for generations, socially and culturally, that it can't just be undone. Our case studies indicate a lack of state protection, law and order machinery is sometimes undone at the instance of mass uproar, the village council is instrumental in the persecution of several *dains*, police are ineffectual in providing protection, and murderers go scot free.

A belief in witchcraft is not necessarily problematic but the actions taken in consequence of belief and suspicion create devastations. Such actions violate human rights standards such as the right to non-discrimination, the right to life, the right to be free from cruel and inhuman treatment, the right to security, the right to dispose of wealth and the right to be provided with adequate living conditions. Feelings of envy, hatred, jealousy and fear frequently accompany witchcraft accusations, which have been interpreted as a "conscious or unconscious displacement of responsibility for a rupture in an interpersonal relationship" (Behringer, 2004:26). The bulk of available cases indicate that women are more often subjected to witchcraft accusations, although exceptions do exist. The witch and even her family could be banished from the village and killed. Witch-hunting is found to be an internal matter, an intra-tribe matter. Those making the accusations and those being accused belonged to the same tribe. More than just being members of the same tribe, the accuser and accused were usually closely related to one another, members of the same kin group or even lineage.

There is a range of physical and non-physical violations which accompanies the process of witch-hunting. Table 9.8 summarizes the nature and the nuances of the different types of abuse, humiliation and violence in witch-hunting as disaggregated from literature and our case studies.

Table 9.8: Types of Abuse, Humiliation and Violence in Witch-hunting

Victim Domain	*Accused Domain/Criminal Perpetration*			
Verbal Abuse/ Labelling	*Victim Precipitation*	*Public Humiliation*	*Attempted/ Physical Violence*	*Grave Physical/ Property Violence*
Witch are called as *Dahani, Chirguni, Dayan, Bhootani, Beta Khauki* (Son-Eater), *Bhoot Rakhti Hai* (You Keep Demons), *Bisahin* (Poisonous Woman), *Nagin, Chinal, Jaaduwali, Tanane wali, Kokh Ujadane Wali* (Destroy Wombs), *Kulachhini, Maradmuhi* (Woman in Male Face); *Naanjat, Najarheen, Nakti, Tohni*, and *Tonchah*. Male labelled as *Bhoot, tohna Saitan* and term witch also applicable to men.	Causing Fever, Diarrhoea, other physical and mental illness, premature death, damage to property and farm animals, fire, disaster, accident, injury, infertility, other misfortune: Real or Purported	Parading the victim naked, tearing of victims clothes; rubbing of the nose on the ground and being made to lick one's spit; being physically dragged and dragged by hair, forced consumption of Cow dung Solutions and human excreta	Criminal conspiracy, abetment, deception, Coercion, threats, abduction, kidnapping, illegal detainment, illegal confinement, criminal intimidation, hurt, Molestation, servitude, commercial exploitation, Ousting from the community	Murder, attacked with arms and weapons beheaded sprinkling of red chilli powder on injuries after beating, burn the victim, strangled and blinded teeth being broken/ Set house and property ablaze, Eviction from and grabbing of land, Robbing ornaments, household items.

Source: Field Survey Data.

Thus, the questioning of beliefs that support witch-hunting relate to some aspects of the culture of indigenous people. It is often argued that such cultures and their practices are not to be questioned, leave alone opposed. There is even a claim to a right 'not to be offended' by criticism. But when cultural beliefs and their resulting practices violate currently accepted notions of human rights, then it is human rights that are superior to cultural practices. This study can reasonably establish that witch-hunting is community and region-specific based on the culture of it is own being handed down from generation to generation.

Witch-hunting invariably begins with the labelling of a person as a witch. There are immediate triggering factors and long-term material factors which contribute to labelling of a person as a witch. While the immediate triggers of witch-hunting are clustered around common misfortunes such as illness, death and a bad crop, the long term factors that can be clearly identified in a number of cases include disputes over land, jealousy and personal animosity due to a variety of factors. In a good number of cases the local sorcerers were also found to be involved in labelling and identification of victims. This process may in a small number of cases be leading to "unintended" victims. However, even though the real causes of witch-hunting are difficult to identify in particular instances, strong belief, suspicion and mass hysteria seem to be present in quite a number of cases. In this sense, our case studies support the basic tenets of labelling theory.

Our case studies suffer a greater limitation that they relate to most extreme consequences of witch-hunting terminating in murder and physical assault attempting to murder. In a large number of unreported or unregistered cases the victims face threats of violence, public humiliation and verbal abuse. Again witch-hunting often leads to other less spectacular, but nevertheless serious consequences such as social isolation and ostracization on the one hand and economic deprivation and loss of property on the other which are not easy to overcome and may seriously undermine the life chances of the victims and their families. The neighbours, the community and the State are not always behind the victim and often can be seen as abettors of the violence and ostracism faced by the victim. This provides a grim picture of the role of the larger community in the perpetuation of witch-hunting as a form of violence. The locals tend to argue that such victimization are precipitated by the ex-victims who have suffered some damage caused by the witches. This victimization or criminal perpetration is victim-facilitated. Had the harm not been caused to them, their property or their relations due to witch effect such murder of the victim would not have occurred. Accordingly, our case studies tend to support the victim precipitation theory. One can also reiterate and indicate the links that the issue has with lack of basic educational and health infrastructure, in other words, issues central to governance and development.

Actual instances of witch-hunting may be a result of either of the two scenarios or a combination of the two. In practice it is very hard to distinguish the two as the justification of witch-hunting almost always derives from the first, i.e. from the attribution of malevolent supernatural powers and intentions. It is also possible that the two processes work in tandem. Witch suspected murder is a fact and justification of witch-hunting is a matter of empirical curiosity to be verified on case to case basis. There are both material and imaginary factors behind justification of witch hunting resulting in murder. One lesson can be drawn from the study of witch-hunting is that this form of persecution is no longer bound to a specific historic time. It has taken a life of its own, so that, the same mechanisms can be applied to different societies whenever there are people in them that have to be ostracized and dehumanized. Witch-craft accusations, in fact, are the ultimate mechanism of alienation and estrangement as they turn the accused — mostly women — into monstrous beings, dedicated to the destruction of their communities therefore making them undeserving of any compassion and solidarity.

Here we will return to the questions raised at the beginning of the paper by the binary tension found between actualizing the reality and intellectualizing the occurrence. The binary between real or purported and factual or assumed go unmediated to which each finicky case can approximate. The heuristic signaled through this usage is that a person may be identified as a witch in order to explain an event (such as an illness, etc.), or an event may be singled out as a sign in order to label a person as a witch. This appears to be subtle, but it is a very critical distinction. While the former may be a manifestation of the existence of a belief system which holds the possibility that persons vested with supernatural powers and evil intentions can cause all kinds of harms to others, the latter can be simply a mechanism of targeting a particular person for a variety of reasons ranging from personal animosity, jealousy, revenge and property disputes. One cannot simply run away calling witch hunting as the result of superstition. Blanket uncritical acceptance of witchcraft and witch hunting as superstitious or actions thereto with utter disregard to ground reality may terminate in intellectualizing the occurrence. Empirically grounded acceptance of criminal perpetration due to victim precipitation or undue suspicion or past hostility including envy and revengeful/avenging attitude may amount to actualizing the reality and veracity of the heuristics.

IX

Suggestion of Remedial Measures

The problem is so deep rooted that there cannot be any straight jacket solution. The idea is to begin the process. When the evil practices of witch-hunting pose a serious threat to a nation building in the scientifically progressive twentyfirst century, all our tall claims of development may shamelessly go for a toss. It is time to make sure that occurrences of witchcraft and wizardry merely remain matter of dead past and not gross realities of life. It is not possible for us to provide statistical information on this at this stage, but it appears that the most extreme cases of witch-hunting are those in which the perpetrators were able to convince a lot of other people about the labelled victim being a witch. Where such conviction was not widespread, the consequences were also likely to be less severe for the victim.

The most effective solution to the problem would be to educate the people and also to frame and implement effective laws for the protection of women and people belonging to the 'lower' classes who also constitute another target group of such witch hunts. Laws need to be accompanied by efficient social welfare delivery mechanism as well. As we are aware, witch-hunting cases are on the raise because of a combination of factors, including poor health delivery and schooling, lack of drinking water, sanitation and transport facilities, as well as a general lack of information in remote areas.

Again, the sentences prescribed and the paltry amount of fine recommended in the law (wherever enacted) has proved to be ineffective in dealing with this social menace. Such taboos and dogmas are required to be dealt with firmly by making the penal provisions more stringent. Until and unless there are strict laws devised that aim directly at the crime of witch-hunting, situation would remain the same. Accordingly, anti-witchcraft laws should be amended to enhance the period of sentence to a minimum of three years. No anticipatory bail should be provided under law to the accused.

Therefore, the strategy to combat this social evil has to be multi-pronged. As a matter of fact, the best strategies that the Government through inter agency coordination can adopt are:

- The areas where witch-hunting is most prevalent and the people vulnerable to witch hunting including the witch doctors must be identified.
- Strict enforcement of the Anti-witchcraft law for effective prevention of witch-hunting practices.
- Sensitization of police and other stakeholders, and NGOs working for prevention of witch related atrocities to be more proactive.
- Launching of campaigns against superstition and witch-hunting practices and organizing street plays.
- Organizing Women's Self Help Groups at village level and drawing up creative plans for self-protection and enhancing their self-confidence in such areas.
- Community Policing scheme must include this aspect for intervention.
- District Legal Services Authority may be geared up towards follow-up of awareness generation regarding legal rights of women and monitoring of witch evidences/cases lodged regarding witch related violence.
- Identification and rehabilitation of women survivors and other victims of violence especially those who have no family/ community support.
- It must also provide for a minimum mandatory punishment, so that, the judiciary gets lesser scope to reduce the sentence owing out of mitigating factors. There should be provisions for rehabilitation of the victims, which could lessen down their vulnerability and trauma, post the incident.
- Since, it is an offence against the State (being a criminal offence), the State should initiate investigation on its own, rather than reacting after the king and pawns have gone back into the same box.

Nathan, Kelkar and Satija (2013) go on to suggest that no law can be efficient until the masses, upon whom it shall be binding, are aware of it. The State must ensure that people know that an actionable law is in place, that the victims can fearlessly seek protection under it, and that it can effortlessly bring the culprits behind bars. The areas where witch-hunting is most prevalent must be identified and extensively sensitized in respect of the plight of the victims. Similarly, the vulnerable groups must be educated about their legal rights and the protections that they are entitled to, under the moral and legal fabric of the society.

REFERENCES

Adinkrah, M. (2004): "Witchcraft Accusations and Female Homicide Victimization in Contemporary Ghana", *Violence Against Women*, Vol. 10, pp. 325-56.

Adinkrah, M. and P. Adhikari (2014): "Gendered Injustice: A Comparative Analysis of Witchcraft Beliefs and Witchcraft-related Violence in Ghana and Nepal", *International Journal of Sociology and Anthropology*, Vol. 6, No. 10, pp. 314-21.

Archer, W.G. (1974): *The Hill of Flutes Life, Love and Poetry in Tribal India: A Portrait of the Santal*, London: George Allen & Unwin.

Bailey, F.G. (1997): *A Witch-Hunt in an Indian Village Or, The Triumph of Morality*, Delhi: Oxford University Press.

Bamberger, Joan (1974): "Myths of Matriarchy" in Michelle Zimbalist Rosaldo and Louise Lamphere (eds.), *Woman, Culture and Society*, Stanford: Stanford University Press.

Barman, M. (2002): *Persecution of Women: Widows and Witches*, Kolkata: Indian Anthropological Society.

Barstow, A.L. (1995): *Witchcraze: A New History of the European Witch Hunts*, London: Harper Collins.

Becker, H.S. (1963): *Outsiders: Studies in the Sociology of Deviance*, New York: Free Press.

Behringer, Wolfgang (2004): "Witches and Witch-Hunts: A Global History", *Polity Press*.

Bhaumik, Subir (2008): "Witch Family Killed in India", *BBC NEWS*, June 12, 2008, available at http://news. bbc.co. uk/z/hi/so uth_ asia17449825.html.

Bodding, Paul Olaf (1979): "Some Remarks on the Position of Women among the Santals", in J. Troisi, (ed.), *The Santals*, Vol. 6, New Delhi: Indian Social Institute.

Bosu-Mullick, S. (2000): "Gender Relations and Witches Among the Indigenous Communities of Jharkhand, India", *Gender Technology and Development*, Vol. 4, pp. 333-58.

Carstairs, G.M. (1983): *The Death of a Witch: A Village in North India 1950-1981*, London: Hutchinson.

Chakravarty, Anuradha and Soma Chaudhuri (2012): "Strategic Framing Work(S): How Microcredit Loans Facilitate Anti-Witch-Hunt Movements", *Mobilization: An International Journal*, Vol. 17, No. 2, pp. 175-94.

Chaudhuri, A.B. (1981): *Witch Killings Amongst Santals*, New Delhi: Ashish Publishing House.

Chaudhuri, Soma (2013): "Extending the Logic of Functional Explanations: A Theoretical, Model to Explain the Victimization Process during an Indian Witch Hunt" in *Global Criminology: Crime and Victimization in a Globalized Era*, Edited by K. Jaishankar and Natti Ronel, New York: CRC Press, pp. 315-33.

Chaudhuri, Soma (2013): *Witches, Tea Plantations, and Lives of Migrant Laborers in India: Tempest in a Teapot*, Lanham: Lexington Books, and Delhi: Cambridge University Press.

Chaudhuri, Soma (2014): "Unusual Expressions of Social Protest: Witchcraft Accusations in Jalpaiguri, India", *CAS Working Paper Series (CAS/WP/14-5)*, New Delhi, Jawaharlal Nehru University, CSSS/SSS.

Comaroff, J., and Comaroff J. (1993): *Modernity and Its Malcontents: Ritual and Power in Postcolonial Africa*, Chicago: University of Chicago Press.

Davies, Owen and Willem de Blécourt (ed.) (2004): *Beyond the Witch Trials: Witchcraft and Magic in Enlightenment Europe*, Manchester: Manchester University Press.

Desai, A. (2008): "Subaltern Vegetarianism: Witchcraft, Embodiment, and Sociality in Central India. South Asia", *Journal of South Asian Studies*, Vol. 31, pp. 96-117.

Dixit, Rakesh (2015): "Witch-hunting on the Rise in Maoist-hit Odisha as Tribal Districts Cling to Superstition", *Mail Online India*, 16 March.

Elwin, Verrier (1977): *Maria, Murder and Suicide*, Mumbai: Oxford University Press.

Erickson, K.T. (1962): "Notes on the Sociology of Deviance", *Social Problems*, Vol. 9, pp. 307-14.

Evans-Pritchard, E.E. (1937): *Witchcraft, Oracles and Magic Among the Azande*, Oxford: Oxford University Press.

Farrington, Karen (1996): *Dark Justice: A History of Punishment and Torture*, New York: Smithmark.

Federici, Silvia (2008): *Witch-Hunting, Globalization, and Feminist Solidarity in Africa Today*, New York: The Commoner.

Federici, Silvia (2010): *Women, Witch Hunting and Enclosures in Africa Today*, Sozial Geschichte Online, 3, 10-27.

Frances Dolan (1977): *Dangerous Familiars: Representations of Domestic Crime in England*, London: Cornell University Press.

Frankfurter, D. (2006): *Evil Incarnate: Rumors of Demonic Conspiracy and Satanic Abuse in History*, Princeton: Princeton University Press.

Gaskill, Malcolm, (2010): *Witchcraft: A Very Short Introduction*, Oxford: Oxford University Press.

Geschiere, Peter (1997): *The Modernity of Witchcraft: Politics and the Occult in Postcolonial Africa*, London: University of Virginia Press.

Golooba-Mutebi, Frederick (2005): "Witchcraft, Social Cohesion and Participation in a South African Village", *Development and Change*, Vol. 36, No. 5, pp. 937-58.

Govenment of Odisha (2013): *Odisha Prevention of Witch-hunting Act, 2013*, Cuttack: Government Press Odisha.

Hutton, R. (2002): "The global context of the Scottish witch hunt", in Goodare, J. (ed.), *The Scottish Witch Hunt in Context*, Manchester: Manchester University Press, pp. 16-32.

INSEC (2012): *A Study on Violence due to Witchcraft Allegation and Sexual Violence*, Kathmandu: Informal Sector Service Center (INSEC).

Jensen, G.F. (2007): *The Path of the Devil: Early Modern Witch Hunts*, New York: Rowman and Littlefield.

Kakar, Sudhir (1982): *Shamans, Mystics and Doctors*, Delhi: Oxford University Press.

Kapur, Medha (2015): "Witch Hunting on the Rise Across Several Indian States", *Indiatimes*.

Karlsen, C.F. (1998): *The Devil in the Shape of a Woman: Witchcraft in Colonial New England*, New York: W.W. Norton.

Kaur, R. (2013): "Subtler form of Crime Against Women: Witch Hunting — with Special Emphasis on Cases Reported in Assam", *Criminology Report*, 66 RR, SVNPA, Hyderabad.

Kelkar, G., and Nathan, D. (1991): "Women, Witches and Land Rights", in Kelkar, G. and Nathan, D. (eds.), *Gender and Tribe: Women, Land and Forest*, New Delhi: Kali for Women, pp. 88-109.

Kelkar, G., and Warrier, M. (1997): "Indigenous Asia: Knowledge, Technology and Gender Relations", *Gender Technology and Development*, Vol. 3, pp. 313-19.

Kelkar, Govind, (2000): "Witches: Asia", in Cheris Kramarae and Dale Spender (eds.), *Encyclopedia of Women*, Vol. 4, pp. 2040-43.

Klaits, J. (1985): *Servants of Satan: The Age of the Witch-hunts*, Bloomington: Indiana University Press.

Konar, Arup Kanti (2010): "Tribal Communities and Their Age-Old Sacred Groves: A Fair Fieldwork in the Purulia District of West Bengal, India", *Studies in Tribes and Tribals*, Vol. 8, No. 1, pp. 1-12.

Kosambi, D.D. (1975): *An Introduction to the Study of Indian History*, Mumbai: Popular Prakashan.

Levack, Brian P. (2004): *The Witchcraft Sourcebook*, London: Routledge.

Lindsay, Vicki (2014): "How was Witchcraft Ever a Crime?", *Journal of International Criminal Justice Research*, Vol. 1, pp. 1-11.

Madhu Mehra (2012): *Targeting of Women as Witches Trends, Prevalence and the Law in Northern, Western, Eastern and North-eastern Regions of India*, New Delhi: Partners of Law in Development (PLD).

Madhu Mehra (2013): *Contemporary Practices of Witch-Hunting: A Report on Social Trends and The Interface with Law*, New Delhi: Partners of Law in Development (PLD).

Madhu Mehra (2013a): *Piecing Together Perspectives on Witch Hunting: A Review of Literature*, New Delhi: Partners of Law in Development (PLD).

Marwah, Sonal (2013): "Mapping Murder: Homicide Patterns and Trends in India an Analysis from 2000-2010", *Journal of South Asian Studies*, Vol. 2, No. 2, pp. 145-63.

Miguel, Edward, (2005): "Poverty and Witch Killing", *The Review of Economic Studies*, Vol. 72, No. 4, pp. 1153-72.

Mishra, Archana (2003): *Casting the Evil Eye: Witch Trials in Tribal India*, New Delhi: Roli Books.

Mishra, Arima and Sumita Sarma (2011): "Understanding Health and Illness among Tribal Communities in Odisha", *Indian Anthropologist*, Vol. 41, No. 1, pp. 1-16.

Mukherjee, Anusua (2014): "The Prevalence of Witches", *The Telegraph*, 4 February.

Mullick, Samar Bosu (1998): *Changes in Gender Relations and Questions of Witches Among the Hos and Mundas*, Thailand: AIT.

Nathan Dev, Govind Kelkar and Shivani Satija (2013): *Witches through Changing Contexts: Women Remain the Target*, Working paper No. 004, New Delhi: Institute for Human Development.

Nathan Dev, Govind Kelkar and Yu Xiaogang (1998): "Women as Witches and Keepers of Demons: Cross-Cultural Analysis of Struggles to Change", *Economic and Political Weekly*, Vol. 33, No. 44, pp. WS58-WS69.

NCRB (2009-13): *Motives of Murder and Culpable Homicide Not Amounting to Murder (C.H.)*, New Delhi: National Crime Records Bureau, 2009, 2010, 2011, 2012, 2013 (TABLE 3.2).

Oldridge, Darren (ed.) (2002): *The Witchcraft Reader*, London: Routledge.

Prasad, Pandit Raghubeer (1908): "Monograph on Magic", *Bastar State Compilation No. XXXVIII*, Jagdalpur: Jagdalpur Record Room, Government of Chhattisgarh.

Russell, Jeffrey B. (1980): *A History of Witchcraft: Sorcerers, Heretics and Pagans*, London: Thames and Hudson.

Sah, K.B. (2007): *A Study of the Problem of Witch Accusation in Nepal*, Retrieved on 4/21/2015 from http://www.socialinclusion.org.np/new/files/9749_1khar_Bhusan_133 6478467dGX.pdf

Sau, Ranjit (2003): "Recognition to Witchcraft: Illegal and Ill-Founded", *Economic and Political Weekly*, Vol. 38, No. 51-52, December 27, pp. 5325-26.

Saxena, Swati (2009): "Recourse Rare for Witch Hunt Victims in India", *Women's E-News*, September 17, retrieved from http://www.womensenews.org/article.cfm/dyn/aid/3241/context/archive.

Schnoebelen, Jill (2009): *Witchcraft Allegations, Refugee Protection and Human Rights: A Review of the Evidence*, Research Paper No. 169, Geneva: United Nations High Commissioner for Refugees.

Sen, P.K (1932): *From Punishment to Prevention*, London: Humphrey Milford and Oxford University Press.

Sherratt, Lesley Rowena (2012): *Ethics of Micro-Finance (e-thesis)*, London: Kings College.

Shrestha, Rachana (2004): *Witch-hunting: A Study of Cultural Violence against Women with Reference to Nepal and India*, Master's Thesis, Netherlands: Graduate School of Development Studies, Institute of Social Studies.

Singh, Rakesh K. (2011): "Witch-Hunting: Alive and Kicking", *Women's Link*, Vol. 17, No. 1, pp. 16-21.

Sinha, Shashank, (2007): "Witch-hunts, Tribals and the Uprising in Chotanagpur" in *Economic and Political Weekly*, May 12, pp. 1672-76.

Skaria, A. (1999): *Hybrid Histories: Forests, Frontiers and Wildness in Western India*, New Delhi: Oxford University Press.

Sundar, Nandini (2001): "Divining Evil: The State and Witchcraft in Bastar", *Gender, Technology and Development*, Vol. 5, No. 3, pp. 425-48.

Wardhaugh, Julia (2005): "The Jungle and The Village: Discourses on Crime and Deviance in Rural North India", *South Asia Research*, Vol. 25, No. 2, pp. 129-40.

Wolfgang, M.E. (1958): *Patterns in Criminal Homicide*, Philadelphia: University of Pennsylvania.

APPENDIX I

Summary of Witch Hunting Cases in Mayurbhanj (2010-2014)

Sl. No.	*Police Station Case Reference with Date*	*Place of Occurrence*	*Victim*	*Charges/Framed against*	*Status in Court*
(1)	*(2)*	*(3)*	*(4)*	*(5)*	*(6)*
			2010		
1.	Rairangpur Rural PS Case No.6 dt. 8.2.10 (SR 58-10)	Gopaipur Tulusahi 15 Kms. South West corner to PS	Sita Beshra	Case u/s 302/506/34 IPC against accused (1) Gane *vs.* Anpa *vs.* Ganesh Besra, (2) Denka *vs.* Arjun Besra, (3) Jagu *vs.* Jugal Kesore Besra, (4) Sundar *vs.* Arjun Besra, (5) Raisen *vs.* Ganesh Besra	Subjudice
2.	Rairangour — Rural PS Case No.31 dt.23.7.10 (SR-250/10)	Arbrabhandha 27 kms. West South to PS	Naghu Singh	Case u/s 302 IPC against accused Ratha Singh	Acquitted
3.	Bisoi PS Case No.5 dt. 17.1.10 (SR12/10)	Hijili, Runda Sahi 9 kms. from PS	Gouri Tudu	Case u/s 302/201/34 IPC against accused persons (1) Rama Chandra Tudu, (2) Mara Tudu	Acquitted
4.	Bisoi PS Case No.5 dt.17.1.10 (SR101/10)	Nuadihi, 10 kms South West to PS	Deola Hansdah	Case u/s 302/201/34 IPC against accused persons 1. Rameswar Hansdah, 2. Majhiram Hansdah, 3. Dhanu *vs.* Dhanunjaya Hansdah	Acquitted
5.	Jamda PS Case No.6 dt.4.3.10, (SR81/10)	Matiali, 10 kms. East to PS	Dukhu Tudu	Case u/s 457/324/326/307/ 302/34 IPC against accused persons Laxman Murmu Samara Soren	Acquitted
6.	Tiring PS Case No.15 dt.4.4.10 (SR 103/10)	Janghia, 13 kms. South West to PS	Mecha Bari	Case u/s 449/302 IPC against accused persons Jateya *vs.* Sudarshan Bari	Acquitted
7.	Tiring PS Case No.31 dt. 2.7.10 (SR 220/10)	Dubulabed, 30 kms. South to PS	Gama Gamuda	Case u/s 460/320/34 IPC against accused persons (1) Sunaram Deogam, (2) Dibru Deogam	Subjudice
8.	Tiring PS Case No.34 dt.24.7.10 IPC(SR251/10)	Chudia Hill, 15 kms West south to PS	Lachhu Hansdah	Case u/s 302/201./34 IPC against' accused (1) Durga Hansdah, (2) Jujnar Hansdah, (3) Sida Hansdah, (4) Bhawnra Hansdah	Subjudice

(*Contd.*)

Appendix (*Contd.*)

(1)	*(2)*	*(3)*	*(4)*	*(5)*	*(6)*
9.	Karanjia PS Case No.32 dt. 4.3.10 (SR 200/10)	Kurudia, 35 kms. East to PS	Narandra Gagrai	Case u/s 447/302/506/34 IPC against accused 1. Duburi *vs.* Nageswar Gagrai, 2. Rama Singh Munda	Subjudice
10.	Karanjia PS Case No.48 dt. 19.6.10 (SR 200/10)	Nangaksuka, 17 kms. South to PS	Tumari Besra	Case u/s CS 447/302 IPC against accused Kama Hansdah	Subjudice
			2011		
11.	Bangriposi PS Case No.07 dt.01.02.11 (SR 36/11)	Baunsapahadi, 25 kms. South West to PS	Muniram Tudu	Case u/s 362/34 IPC IPC against accused persons (1) Andru *vs.* Bharat Tudu, (2) Balta *vs.* Lalmani Hansda	Acquitted
12.	Jharpokharia Case No.02 dt.13.01.11 (SR 12/11)	Bazargoda, 35 kms. West to PS	Fulamani Hansdah	Case u/s 302/201 IPC against accused Chandu Hansda *vs.* Kanduru	Acquitted
13.	Rairangpur Rural PS Case No.16 dt.27.03.11(SR 110/11)	In the house of Makra Hembram, 5 kms. East South corner to PS	Kapura Murmu	Case u/s 302 IPC against accused Sana *vs.* Sanmohan *vs.* Fauir Murmu	Convicted
14.	Bisoi PS Case No.33 dt.10.5.11 (SR 187/11)	Rangaibeda Primary School, 17 kms. South West corner to PS	Ratani Marandi	Case u/s 302 IPC against accused Kumari Gourangi Murmu	Convicted
15.	Bisoi PS Case No.38 dt.01.6.11 u/s 302/109/34 IPC (SR 215/11)	Hijili, 13 kms. West to PS	Gurubari Naik	Case u/s 302/109/34 IPC against accused persons 1. Duryodhan Naik, 2. Smt. Bharati Naik	Subjudice
16.	Badampahad PS Case No.07 dt.05.02.11 u/s 302 IPC	Rahindhipa, 28 kms. from PS	Putuni Mohanty	Case u/s 302IPC against accused Dumu Mahanty	Subjudice
17.	Gorumahisani Case No.08 dt.12.02.11 u/s 302 IPC (SR54/ 11)	Dangapani, 14 kms. North West to PS	Chipri Naik	Case u/s 302IPC against accused Manas Naik	Subjudice

(*Contd.*)

Appendix (*Contd.*)

(1)	*(2)*	*(3)*	*(4)*	*(5)*	*(6)*
			2012		
18.	Badasahi PS Case No.7 dt. 23.01.12 (SR No. 30/12)	Baiganbadia, 97 kms. North West to PS	Sarathi Singh	Case u/s 302/201/34 IPC 1. Mangal Singh, 2. Suaram Singh, 3. Shyam *vs.* Soma Singh, 4. Bauda *vs.* Badal Singh, 5. Kanda Singh Vill. Lalganj all PS-Baripada Sadar (Neighbourers)	Subjudice
19.	Kaptipada PS Case No.74 dt. 21.08.12 (SR 374/12)	Khanda Chirabila, 14 kms. West to PS	Sumi Singh	Case u/s 302 IPC Baju Singh of Jambani PS-Kaptipada (Neighbour)	Subjudice
20.	Jashipur PS Case No.61 dt.01.7.12 (SR 302/12)	Nahana, 70 kms. East to PS	Lambra Barja	Case u/s 302/201 IPC Biswamohan Purty s/o Nahiram Purty, Vill. Nawana, PS-Jashipur, Dist. MBJ	Subjudice
21.	Tiring PS Case No.21 dt.21.3.12 u/s 302/34 IPC (SR170/12)	San Kumrum (Raidisahi), 7 kms. North to PS	Sitaram Sundhi	1. Ghana Sundhi, 2. Gulga Bangsing, 3. Retang *vs.* Rengta Bangsingh all of Vill. San Kumrum PS-Tiring	Subjudice
22.	Betnoti PS Case No.42 dt.22.3.12 (SR 174/12)	Sankaraganga canal, 20 kms. North to PS	Jasoda Mohanta	Case u/s 302 IPC Parbana Singh, Vill. Budhikhamari PS-Betnoti	Subjudice
23.	Jashipur PS Case No.104 dt.17.10.12 (SR 472/12)	Ambajari Jungal, 40 kms. East to PS	Ranga Purty	Case u/s 302/201/34 IPC 1. Driver Purty s/o Bijay Purty, 2. Dumbi *vs.* Chalu Bari, 3. Tapi Purti, 4. Kanko *vs.* Rengo Bari, 5. Siba Tiria, 6. Kaka *vs.* Sahu Bari, 7. Tanguru *vs.* Sadam Purty, 8. Bhasala *vs.* Rasika Purty all of Vill. Chandikhaman, PS-Jashipur	Subjudice
24	Bangiriposi PS Case No.104 dt.10.10.12 (SR 454/12)	Sana Nadam, 26 kms. South West to PS	Sauna Murmu	Case u/s 302/201/34 IPC 1. Deepak Hansdah 2. Mangal *vs.* Durga Chandra both of Vill. Sana Nedam PS-Bangiriposi	Subjudice
25.	Tiring PS Case No.60 dt.18.12.12 u/s 365 IPC turned to 302/201/34 IPC(SR170/12)	Bhaludada, 30 kms. South East to PS	Mani Murmu	1. Champai Tudu *vs.* Rento, 2. Bham Soren, 3. Dangi Baske, 4. Sankar Murmu, 5. Tarini Kumar Mohanty, 7. Smt Raimani Murmu w/o Sankar Murmu of Bhalugoda, 8. Renga hembram	Subjudice

(*Contd.*)

Appendix (*Contd.*)

(1)	(2)	(3)	(4)	(5)	(6)
			2013		
26.	Udala PS Case No.70 dt.18.6.13 (SR 309/13)	Tanoka Sahi, 3 kms. North to PS	Manko Soren	Case u/s 302IPC Dibakar Soren s/o Baidyanath Soren Vill. Tanakasahi, Patapur, Udala	Subjudice
27.	Thakurmunda PS Case No.40 dt.22.8.13 (SR 456/13)	Saleibeda, 18 kms. North to PS	Basanta Lohar	Case u/s 376/302 IPC 1. Bisu Lohar 2. Sambhu Lohar, 3. Jangi Hembram	Subjudice
28.	Baripada Sadar PS Case No.98 dt.03.09.13 (SR 519/13)	Saradachand Rapur, 20 kms. West to PS	Sita Majhi	Case u/s 341/307/506 turned to 302 IPC Chandrai Majhi	Subjudice
29.	Jashipur PS Case No.94 dt.11.10.13 (SR 430/13)	Nawana, 9 kms. West to PS	Santoshi Mahakud	Case u/s 364(A)/365/ 34 IPC 1. Satish Ch. Naik, 2. Karana Parida, 3. Pinnada Vankato Krishan	Subjudice
30.	Badasahi PS Case No.136 Dt.15.11.13 (SR 605/13)	Bhimda, 19 kms. South to PS	Chhatia *vs.* Jagat Singh	Case u/s 452/307/506/ 34 IPC turned to 302 IPC 1. Basu Singh, 2. Mantu Singh	Subjudice
			2014		
31.	Jashipur PS Case No.1 dt.10.01.14 (SR 10/14)	Kunarabil, 45 kms. towards PS	Janaki Hembram	Case u/s 302/34 IPC 1. Krushana Alda, 2. Jagana Tiriya	Subjudice
32.	Baisingha PS Case No. 27 dt.15.02.14 (SR 74/14)	Rapitashai, 15 kms. East to PS	Srimati Marandi	Case u/s 302/34 IPC Kandha Majhi	Subjudice
33.	Karanjia PS Case No.52 dt.23.4.14 (SR 212/14)	Rangamatia, 35 kms. to North East to PS	Bhima Birua	Case u/s 458/302/201 IPC 1. Samnath Soy, 2. Manoj Soy, 3. Bharat Birua, 4. Ganeswar Soy	Subjudice
34.	Rairangpur Rural PS Case No. 47 dt.27.07.14 (Non SR)	Jodapokhari, 22 kms. South to PS	Smt Pana Hansdah 60 yrs. wife of Kashrai Hansdah	Case u/s 341/143/147/ 148/307/353/109/ 505(B)/149 IPC 1. Bini Hansdah, 2. Manmohan Hansdh, 3. Dhana Hansdah, 4. Binu Hansdah, 5. Sauna Murmu and others	Subjudice

(*Contd.*)

Appendix (*Contd.*)

(1)	*(2)*	*(3)*	*(4)*	*(5)*	*(6)*
35.	Rasgobindapur PS Case No. 83 dt.17.06.14 (SR 412/14)	Dahisahi, 4 kms. West to PS	Mirza Baske	Case u/s 302/201 IPC Hampa Murmu, Premlal Hembram and Udhab Mahalik	Under Investi-gation
36.	Sarat PS Case No. 19 dt.1.08.14 (SR No. 421/14)	Rajat Nagar, 12 kms. East to PS	Mukta Purty	Case u/s 302 IPC Birsingh Bari	Subjudice
37.	Raruan PS Case No. 65 dt.13.10.14 (SR No. 550/14)	Khaparasahi, 10 kms. towards South of PS	Sing Chatar	Case u/s 302 IPC Ujala Gagrai	Under Investi-gation
38.	Kaptipada PS Case No. 96 dt.19.10.14 (SR No. 564/14)	Dumburjharana, 17 kms. towards West PS	Basu Singh and Ranga Singh	Case u/s 302/506 IPC Sukadev Singh	Under Investi-gation
39.	Jashipur PS Case No. 119 dt.20.10.14 (SR No. 567/14)	Khandbandha paddy field 10 kms. to West from PS	Surya Chattar	Case u/s 302 IPC Budhiram Chater	Under Investi-gation

Source: Compiled from District Police Office, Baripada, Mayurbhanj.

10

Primitive Tribes of Madhya Pradesh and Chhattisgarh: Development Status

V.K. Srivastava

While discussing the Primitive Tribal Groups (PTGs), it is inevitable to ascertain the conceptual framework laid down behind naming the tribal communities as 'Primitive'. The word 'Primitive Tribe' was first used in the country during the Indian Census, 1931, classifying tribes under the most backward classes. It has been reiterated that these tribes are in the state of extreme poverty, many of them are exposed to hostile external situations which forced them to exploitation of a different nature. But the analysis and the data made available have revealed that the scientific criteria or categorical attempt was made to see that which tribal group/ part group needed special treatment in the pre-Independence period while enlisting them in 1931 Census as 'Primitive Tribes', or 'Backward Tribes' specially in the province of C.P. and Berar, as well as in the post-Independence era in 1950,1951 (Part 'C' States), 1956 (amendment order and modification order). Singh (2002) opined that, "For not very long ago, most of these "Primitive Tribal Groups" could neither have been considered "Primitive" in terms of the norms and notion than prevalent, nor could they have treated disdainfully. They lived in their own nature rich encysted world, engaged in evolving their own systems of social and political organization, culture, language, ethos, infact a whole way of life in harmony with the environment in which they were placed".

There are different views about a definition of tribe associated with the thesis propounded by Max Weber, Robert Rodfield, F.G. Baily, G.S. Ghurye and Surjeet Sinha. But as a synthesis, the tribals, who are still resisting acculturation or absorption, possess certain features, once possessed by the tribal groups. The concept of Scheduled Tribe, "A remarkable phrase and social category" has seen inherited from the 1935 Constitution and chosen, in the wisdom to incorporate in the Constitution of India. So, Article 342, of the Constitution of India lays down that President of India "may with respect of any State or Union Territory, and where it is a State after consultation with the Governor of the State thereby public notification specify the tribe or the tribal communities or part of the groups with in Tribes to Tribal Communities which shall for the purpose of the Constitution, be deemed to be Scheduled Tribes in relation to the State or Union Territory as the case may be. But once the notification is issued under Article, it is only the Parliament which can vary or amend the list by enacting a law.

But, who are the "Primitive Tribes"? After Independence, the recent chronicles trace appellation to Dhebar Commission Report (1961). (A Commission known as "Scheduled Areas and Scheduled Tribes was constituted under the chairmanship of U.N. Dhebar on 28th April, 1960). U.N. Dhebar in a forwarding letter to the President of India wrote that amongst the tribals the Commission was "able to notice four different layers. . . . We feel that at the base of these four layers is the class of tribals which is in an extremely under-developed stage and at the top most level amongst the tribals is a layer that can well afford to forego any further help. We feel that this lowest layer needs the utmost consideration at the hands of the Government. . . ." Further, in this context, various Commissions/Committees were set-up to assess the actual condition of the tribal communities. For that purpose mention may be made of various reports, viz. Annual Reports of the Commission of Scheduled Castes and Scheduled Tribes, Reports of many study Teams and some other like Shillu, A.O. (1966) and Renuka Roy (1959) are very noteworthy. It needs here special mention of the Second Scheduled Area of Scheduled Tribes Commission constituted after the gap of forty two years by GoI under the chairmanship of Dilip Singh Bhuria on 18th July, 2002, known as Bhuria Commission, has also found that today, "it is not difficult to recognize further layering the tribal communities (in the context of Dhebar Commission). The top enlist layer and the bottom "Primitive Tribe" Groups' layer are distinct. So, in the present tribal scenario the "lowest layer", i.e. the Primitive Tribes needs the utmost consideration at the hand of Government".

Conceptualization of Primitive Tribal Groups

As per Dhebar Commission Report (1961) 72 Scheduled Tribe Communities have been identified by the then ministry of Home Affairs,

GoI on the basis of low growth rate criterion mentioned and the following two additional criteria:

(i) Pre-agricultural level of technology; and
(ii) Extremely low level of literacy.

From First Five Year Plan to Fourth Five Year Plan, nothing specific efforts could be made to identify the extreme backward class of tribal communities and formulated special development programmes for them. On the eve of Fifth Five Year Plan formulation the entire range of programmes under tribal development was reviewed and ultimately the new strategy of Tribal sub-plan was evolved with the following two long term objectives:

(i) To narrow the gaps between the level of development of tribals and the other areas; and
(ii) To improve the life of tribal communities, under the second objective, the problem of the more backward tribal communities was discussed in considerable details. While considering their problems, it was noted that backward itself needed a closer scrutiny. Amongst the backward, was those groups, who are at distinctly earlier stage of economic evolution like hunters, food gatherers and shifting cultivators. These groups have to be distinguished from those backward communities which are economically worse off, compared to the general tribal communities. It is seen that the tribal groups which are at pre-agricultural level of technology are not necessarily poor. The food gatherer, who may entirely persist on the forest, is not poor because his State of economic development is different, where poverty in the conventional sense has no meaning. Those may be deprivation and consequent 'want' if his natural resources are being encroached upon. This 'want' has to be differentiated from 'poverty' in the modern context.

The tribal development under the new strategy of Tribal Sub-Plan therefore, the two concepts, viz. a prior stage of economic development and lower level in the economic structure have to be distinguished as described above. Those groups which fall in the former category, have been categorized under Primitive Tribal Communities, while those in the later category are termed as the most backward communities. Sinha (1977) had opinioned, "our diagnostic starting point would be the basic persistence technology". We all agree that the groups which live primarily or substainly on hunting and gathering should be regarded as 'Primitive'.

However, agriculture economy has been taken to be the watershed for identification of primitive tribal communities. The pre-agricultural economic groups generally have been included in the primitive communities. The highest form of technology in case of these groups can be said to be practiced by the shifting cultivators. "Shifting cultivation is a stage of graduation from food gathering and hunting to settled agriculture". Even here there are no clear boundaries. There are groups who have been entirely dependent on shifting cultivation, while those are groups who are only nominally or partially dependent on this form of cultivation. It is observed that in defining Primitive Tribal Groups, some more features have to be identified. It is found that literacy being an important criterion may reasonably indicate the general level of social development of a community. Therefore, besides the stage of economic criterion, level of literacy has also been taken as a characteristic to identify the groups which need special attention and could be properly categorized as a primitive tribes.

According to Sinha (1977), the primitive tribal group may be classified into three categories:

(i) Archaic or original primitive groups,
(ii) Primary Primitive Groups, and
(iii) Secondary Primitive Groups.

According to him, "the 'archaic' or 'original primitives' like the hunters of Andaman & Nicobar Island who are accustomed to live, until recently, as completely self-sufficient antonomous entities and the secondary 'primitive tribes' living in the mainland under symbiotic pressure of Indian civilization. These latter groups are 'archaic' in their productive technology, but have long standing dependent symbiotic socio-economic articulation with the persuading dominant peasantry. Unlike the 'archaic primitive', the secondary primitive tribes have learned to accommodate the pressure of encroaching civilization, and, at the same time, carve out an area of relative autonomy in 'ecological riches' outside the adaptive reaches of the larger society.

Problem of Identification of Primitive Groups

In the context of above situation, the task before the planners, administrators, sociologists and anthropologists associated with the job of identifying the primitive tribal groups was to how and in what manner each primitive tribal group is to be identified as it is an 'intensive human problem'. The following approach has been suggested/adopted:

(i) These small communities should be viewed in a broader perspective than has been done so far (*T.A. Srinivasan, GoI*);
(ii) These groups should be identified in such a way that their problem of transitions are attended. So, each tribe should be studied in the context of micro-situation, so that, specific solutions for its specific problems can be found (*Surjeet Sinha*);
(iii) Each group should be identified with reference to their stage of economic development (*B.K. Roy Burman*);
(iv) All small groups should be classified according to their size, rate of growth, plate of ecological equilibrium, isolation and confrontation with other groups (*B.D. Sharma*);
(v) It would be necessary to identify the differences in the 'social dynamics' of a small group and of a larger group so that the process are clearly understood and valid policy conclusions can be derived (*B.D. Sharma*);
(vi) Small tribal groups can be classified on the basis of four characteristics: (a) Size, (b) isolation, (c) Confrontation, and (d) ecological distribution; and
(vii) Among the small groups, there are also 'diminutive groups'. The groups below the size of a few hundred may be identify as a 'diminutive group' (*B.D. Sharma*).

On the theoretical level academic exercises were done by the administrators. Planners and social scientists, attempted to define primitive tribal groups, ascertain their problems and outlined the approaches to identify them. But no survey was done at the field level to identify and focus the real problem of each tribal group on lines of approaches outlined in the above para. However, to categorize the primitive tribal group at last the following criteria have been taken into consideration:

(a) Pre-agriculture level of technology;
(b) Extremely low level of literacy, i.e. below 2 per cent; and
(c) Near stagnant or diminishing population.

Considering the above criteria however, under the Fifth Five Year Plan, the then Ministry of Home Affairs, Government of India identified 52 Scheduled Tribes as Primitive Groups (PTGs). In the then (old) State of Madhya Pradesh five Scheduled Tribe Groups were identified as 'Primitive Tribal Groups' (PTGs), namely, *Abujhmaria* (Hill Marias) of Abujhmarh region of Bastar district, *Saharias* of Gwalior Revenue Division, *Bharias* of Patalkot of Chhindwara district, *Baigas* of Baiga Chak region of Mandla district and *Pahari Korwas* (Hill Korwas) spread over in then Jashpur Tehsils of Raigarh district and in Korba Tribal Development Block of Katghora Tehsil of Bilaspur district. During the Sixth Five Year Plan Period 02 more Scheduled Tribe groups were added (*Kamars* of south-eastern part of Raipur district and *Birhors* of Jashpur Tehsil of Rajgarh district of the then (old) State of Madhya Pradesh. Later, 3 more groups have been added. Though as per the circular of the Government of India, the total number of such 'Primitive Tribal Groups is 75 in TSP States, but in reality it will be 60, as some of groups of these primitive tribal groups live in two or more States. For example, considering the case of *Birhors*, they have also been designated as Primitive Tribal Group in Bihar, West Bengal and Odisha. *Dongaria Khonds* live in Andhra Pradesh, as well as in Odisha. The *Kathods/ Katkarias* live in Gujarat, Maharashtra and Andhra Pradesh, the *Korages* live in Karnataka and Kerala, the *Kurumbhas* live in Kerala and Tamil Nadu, the *Kutia Khonds* in Andhra Pradesh and Odisha, the *Kuttu Naikau* in Kerala and Tamilnadu, the *Lodhas* live in Odisha and West Bengal. Similarly, *Kalam* live in Andhra Pradesh and Maharashtra.

These 75 PTGs are found in 17 States and one Union Territory (Andaman & Nicobar). Out of the 75 PTGs, 45 PTGs (33.3%) are found in 7 States (1.19%), viz. Andhra Pradesh, Bihar, Jharkhand, Madhya Pradesh, Chhattisgarh, Odisha and West Bengal. Out of these 7 States of Central India, 7 PTGs (5.8%) are found in the States of Madhya Pradesh (3) and Chhattisgarh (7) respectively.

Demographic Structure

As a matter of fact the demographic structure of a primitive tribe region must be one of the most important points on which conscious policy decision at a high level must be taken. Therefore, demographic structure must be taken as one of the most important constraints while planning development of small primitive communities.

The population size of small primitive groups may vary say, less than one thousand and more than fifteen thousand. Albeit these figures are conjectural, it may be classified accordingly to the size as given below:

Table 10.1: Classification of Primitive Tribal Group by Size

Sl.No.	*Group*	*Size*
1.	Diminitive Groups	Less than 1,000
2.	Small Groups	1,000-15,000
3.	Normal Groups	More than 15,000

Source: V.K. Srivastava (2007).

On the basis of the criteria mentioned above and guidelines given by Government of India and the Planning Commission, the respective Tribal Sub Plan (TSP) States/Union Territories identified the 'Primitive Tribal Groups' (PTGs) in their States and nodal Ministry, GoI State/UT-wise notified total 75 PTGs. The overall State/UT-wise analysis of decadal population data of each PTG has revealed that:

1. The comparative population data of 12 PTGs falling in 6 TSP States/UT have shown that at the time of identification under PTG all these 12 PTGs were in the category of "Diminitive Group" as per 1961 census. But as per 1991 census, 4 PTG groups, namely, *Thoti* (Andhra Pradesh), *Birhor* (Madhya Pradesh and Odisha of Central India) and *Toda* (Tamilnadu) have come under the category of "small Groups" and have also shown remarkable growth rate during the period of four decades.

Table 10.2: State of Primitive Tribal Diminitive Group and Transformation into Small Group

Sl. No.	*Name of States*	*Names of PTG*	*Population (1961)*	*State of Diminitive Group*	*Population (1991)*	*Growth Rate*	*State of Diminitive/ Small Group*
1.	A.P.	*Thoti*	546	Diminitive Group	3,654	14.94	Small Group
2.	Kerala	*Cholanai-kayan*	306	-do-	234	–0.72	Diminitive Group
3.	M.P. (old)	*Birhor*	738	-do-	2,206	76.0	Small Group
4.	Odisha	1. *Birhor,*	248	-do-	825	100.0	Diminitive Group
		2. *Mankirda*	138	-do-	1,491	100.0	Small Group
5.	Tamilnadu	1. *Kota*	833	-do-	752	–10.7	Diminitive Group
		2. *Toda*	714	-do-	1,100	35.0	Small Group
6.	Andaman & Nicobar	1. *Sonipee*	71	-do-	131	45.0	Diminitive Group
		2. *Jawara*	42 (1971)	-do-	32	—	
		3. *Onge*	31 (1971)	-do-	89	—	-do-
		4. *Sentielest*	97 (1971)	-do-	101	—	-do-
		5. Great Andamanese	24 (1981)	-do-	—	—	-do-

Source: V.K. Srivastava (2007).

2. There is decadal growth variation in each PTG population at all India level; the population growth during the decade 1961-71, 71-81 and 81-91 has been 44.86 per cent, 31.3 per cent and 15.33 per cent, respectively. The overall growth for the four decades (1961-91) has been 67.93 per cent.
3. Some of the PTGs have registered negative growth during the decade 1971-81 and some during the decade 1981-91, but overall they have registered positive growth.
4. As per 1991census the total population of these PTGs is 24,12,664 in Indian TSP States/UT, which is 3.56 per cent of total Scheduled Tribe population of India (The population of 16 PTGs is not included in this because of non-availability). In 7 TSP states of Central India, the total population of PTGs is 1,45,6,959 which is 3.93 per cent of total population of Scheduled Tribes of these states. It is clear from Table 10.3.

Table 10.3: Population of Scheduled Tribes and Primitive Tribal Groups in the States of Central India (1991)

Sl. No.	*Name of States*	*ST Population*	*PTG Population*	*%age of PTG Population*
1.	Andhra Pradesh	42,00,000	2,86,078	6.81
2.	Bihar including Jharkhand	66,17,000	3,70,638	5.80
3.	Madhya Pradesh including Chhattisgarh	1,53,99,000	6,73,068	4.37
4.	Odisha	70,32,000	58,225	0.82
5.	West Bengal	38,09,000	68,950	1.81
	Total	**3,70,57,000**	**14,56,959**	**3.93**

Source: V.K. Srivastava (2007).

PTGs of Madhya Pradesh and Chhattisgarh

Before bifurcation of Chhattisgarh State from Madhya Pradesh, on the advent of Fifth Five Year Plan, under the new strategy of Tribal Sub-Plan, as per the recommendations made by Working Group constituted by the then Ministry of Home Affairs, GoI and also guideline issued by the Ministry, efforts were made to identify the PTGs. Apart from economic criteria, some more distinguishing features like (i) pre-agricultural level of technology, (ii) low level of literacy, and (iii) stagnation of diminishing population, were taken into consideration. Accordingly, the following five tribal groups were identified as a Primitive Tribal Communities in the State of Madhya Pradesh during the Fifth Five Year Plan:

1. Abhujmaria (of Abhujmarh),
2. Baiga (of Baiga Chak),
3. Saharias (of Gwalior Division),
4. Bharias (of Patalkot), and
5. Pahari Korwas.

During the period of Sixth Five Year Plan, '*Kamar*' and '*Birhor*' communities were further identified in Madhya Pradesh and included in the list of Primitive Tribal Groups. Thus, the total number of identified Primitive Tribal Groups in the State became seven. Out of these *Abhujmarias*, *Baiga* and *Bharias* are location specific, and rest PTGs have been found in a number of districts. At the time of inclusion of these 7 PTGs during the period of Fifth and Sixth Five Year Plans, their total population was 2,38,755.

A reconnoitral survey was done in 1992 for population enumeration and to collect relevant details of these PTGs. As per survey the total population of these seven PTGs, has been 6,11,710, which is 3.96 per cent of the then scheduled Tribe population in the State. The details are given in Table 10.4.

Table 10.4: Primitive-wise Population and their Habitation in the State of Madhya Pradesh — 1992

Sl. No.	*Name of PTG*	*Total Population of PTG*	*Total No. of Families*	*% of Literacy*	*District*	*Blocks*	*Number of Village*
(1)	*(2)*	*(3)*	*(4)*	*(5)*	*(6)*	*(7)*	*(8)*
1.	*Abhuj-maria*	17,016	4,327	4.20	Bastar	1. Narainpur 2. Orcha 3. Dantewada 4. Bijapur	235
2.	*Baiga*	1,34,357	27,531	7.77	Mandala	30 Blocks Shahdol Balaghat Bilaspur Rajnandgaon	1,197
3.	*Bharia*	2,021	238	15.50	Chhinwada	Tamia	12
4.	*Birhor*	935	281	5.21	Rajgarh	Lalunga Dhamjaigarh Tamnor Pathalgaon Begicha Kuukuri Kansable	249

(Contd.)

Table 10.4 (*Contd.*)

(1)	*(2)*	*(3)*	*(4)*	*(5)*	*(6)*	*(7)*	*(8)*
5.	*Pahari Korwa*	27,019	6,142	4.26	1. Rajgarh 2. Surguja 3. Bilaspur	16 Blocks	320
6.	*Kamar*	13,310	2,867	6.72	Raipur	1. Gariaband 2. Manipur 3. Chhura 4. Nagri 5. Sihowa	249
7	*Saharia*	41,7171	60,997	4.33	1. Gwalior 2. Morena 3. Bhind 4. Datia 5. Guna 6. Shivpuri 7. Sheopur	26 Blocks	1159
	Total	**6,11,710**	**1,02,383**		**18**	**89**	**3,421**

Source: State Government of Madhya Pradesh.

The State of Chhattisgarh was constituted on 1st November, 2001, covering the entire eastern part of the old Madhya Pradesh. Out of total 7 PTGs, *Baiga*, *Saharias* and *Bharias* have been notified PTGs for Madhya Pradesh and *Abhujmarias*, *Pahari Korwas*, *Kamars*, *Birhors* and *Baigas* living in Bilaspur, Korba, Kawardha and Rajnandgaon districts of the Chhattisgarh state. *Baigas* are PTG for both States. After bifurcation of Chhattisgarh State from the State of Madhya Pradesh the position of PTGs in both the states are as shown in Table 10.5.

Table 10.5: Details of PTGs of Madhya Pradesh and Chhattisgarh and their Population, Literacy and Sex Ratio Figures as per Latest Survey Done by Respective States

Sl. No.	*Name of PTG*	*Population*			*Literacy (%)*	*Sex Ratio*
		Male	*Female*	*Total*		
(1)	*(2)*	*(3)*	*(4)*	*(5)*	*(6)*	*(7)*
Madhya Pradesh						
1.	*Bharia*	1,060	1,075	2,135	56.24	1,075
2.	*Saharia*	1,63,196	1,48,526	3,11,722	29.78	1,048
3.	*Baiga*	88,347	85,146	1,73,493	35.80	1,037
Chhattisgarh						
1.	*Kamar*	11,474 (49.02%)	11,559 (50.18%)	33,033	37.65	1,007
2.	*Baiga*	34,250 (50.49%)	3,299 (49.05%)	67,241	39.20	963

(*Contd.*)

Table 10.5 (*Contd.*)

(1)	(2)	(3)	(4)	(5)	(6)	(7)
3.	*Pahari Korwa*	17,394 (50.98%)	16,728	34,122	22.02	962
4.	*Abhujmaria* (2002)	9,602 (49.49%)	9,709	19,401	19.25	1,021
5.	*Birhor*	1,277 (48.63)	13,492 (51.37%)	626	20.83	1,056

Note: Total Literacy rate of Scheduled Tribe in Chhattisgarh is 42.71 (2001).
Total Literacy rate of Scheduled Tribe in Madhya Pradesh is 41.44 (2001).
Source: Madhya Pradesh Directorate of Tribal Area Development and Planning, 2007.
Chhattisgarh State Tribal Research Institute's Publication 2008.

As per the above table the population and literacy of all the PTGs have increased almost within a decade according to survey done by both the States during the years 2004-05 and 2005-06. The sex ratio is also in the favour of female population. The growth rate of population and literacy during the period 1992 — 2004-05 can be seen in the given Table 10.6.

Table 10.6: The Growth Rate of PTG Population and Literacy during the Period 1992 to 2004-05 in Both the States

Sl. No.	*Name of PTG*	*Population Growth (%)*			*Literacy (%)*		*Growth (%)*
		1992	*2005*		*1992*	*2005*	
1.	*Baiga*	1,34,357	2,40,734	+79.17	7.77	39.20	+31.43
2.	*Bharia*	2,021	2,135	+5.61	15.5	56.40	+40.90
3.	*Abhujmaria*	17,016	19,401	+14.01	4.2	19.25	+15.05
4.	*Birhor*	935	2,626	+180.85	5.21	20.83	+15.62
5.	*Pahari Korwa*	27,018	34,122	+26.28	4.26	22.83	+18.67
6.	*Kamar*	13,310	23,033	+73.05	6.72	37.25	+30.53
7.	*Saharia*	4,17,171	3,11,722	–33.82	4.33	29.78	+25.45

Source: V.K. Srivastava (2007).

It is clear from the above table that *Saharia* is only PTG whose population has gone down by 33.82 per cent and *Birhor* has the highest population growth, i.e. 180.85 per cent. *Bharia* has minimum population growth, i.e. 5.61 per cent. The literacy rate of all the PTGs has increased, the highest is of *Baiga* (31.43%) and lowest is of *Abhujmaria* (15.05%). Here, it is remarkable to note that as per 2001 Census the literacy rate of Scheduled Tribes in Madhya Pradesh and Chhattisgarh has been 41.16 per cent and 42.71 per cent respectively, while growth of literacy rate in some of the PTGs in between the period 1992-2004 has been 39.20 per cent (*Baiga*), 56.4 per cent (*Bharia*), and 37.25 per cent (*Kamar*), which is quite remarkable.

Brief Description of Primitive Tribal Groups

1. *Abhujmaria*

Abhujmarias are a part of the larger *Gond* tribe inhabiting the territory of Abhujmarh in the tehsils of Narainpur, Bijapur of Bastar and Dantewara districts (now these tehsils are districts of Chhattisgarh state). About the origin of *Abhujmarias*, it is said that a couple *Gond* tribe were in love and they ran away to this inaccessible area with the fear of their community and settled there. The offerings of this couple latter called *Abhujmarias*. The Abhujmarh area has been kept outside the ambit of normal administration since (about) 1930. Even before 1930 inaccessibility had kept this area almost untouched. After Independence, the programme of tribal development block was started in the area in 1965. Thus, extension agency can be considered to have been given access to this region as a matter of State policy.

These *Abhujmarias* are settled at the bottom area of the hills of Abhujmarh, live in small huts and do shifting cultivation. In beginning their economy depended on shifting cultivation, hunting, gathering forest produce, but now, they are doing settled cultivation and grow corn, '*kopra*', *Mung*, '*urad*' dals and seasonal vegetables and earn wages.

The *Abhujmarias* are patrilineal/patriarchal and divided in so many lineages in their social life. These lineages are divided in so many clans, known as '*Goti*'. The marriage of male is done at the age of 18-19 years and of female 16-17 years. There are various ways of acquiring mates, viz. marriage by elopement, intrusion and offering 'Bangles' by the boy to the girl. Remarriage is permissible.

As regards the political organization, traditional caste *panchayat* is in operation. The area *panchayat* is headed by 'Manghi' followed by 'Patel' and 'Gaita'. These *panchayats* settle all types of disputes.

The main deity are 'Buradev', 'Thakurdev', 'Lingopen' and 'Buridokori'. They offer the birds and certain animals to their 'Delies' at the time of worship. Main festivals are 'Pola', 'Kaksar' and 'Pandum'. 'Gaita' is the religious priest. They are highly superstitious and believe in magic (*Jadu-tona*) oriented rituals. Dance and music is their passion. Their folk dances (*Kaksar* and *Garidance*), folk songs (*Dadaria*, *Rilo*) and folk drums are famous. They speak 'Madi' dialect, which is part of Dravin/Gondi language.

Gradually, socio-economic changes are coming in their material culture and day to day social life due to implementation of development programmes. Their main problems are poverty, lands are unirrigated, malnutrition, poor health and limited source of income. The natural resources in this area is plentiful and population is sparse.

2. *Pahari Korwa*

The PTG *Pahari Korwa* is a branch of *Mundas* of Chotanagpur which forms one of the principal centres in India of aboriginal tribes. In other words, they are Munda branch of Astro-Asiatic sub-family of Austric family. Colonol Dalton in his descriptive ethnology of Bengal has written that *Pahari Korwas* are the drop links of colorian chain. It is said *Pahari Korwas* moved westward into 'Khudia Reigion' of erstwhile Jashpur state (at present Jashpur is district of Chhattisgarh state) from Chotanagpur at a date which cannot be fixed and are the original settlers in 'Khudia region' of Jashpur, when it consisted virgin forests. The tradition as well as philogical and cultural evidences have shown that *Korwas* of Khudia region were divided in the social life into two groups long ago and were called "*Dehori Korwas*" and *Pahari Korwas*, of what was since a single tribe. *Korwas* settled and living on plains were called '*Dehari*' and those lived on to hills, called '*Pahari*'. From Jashpur in due course of time they further migrated to the adjoining region of erstwhile Surguja state (at present Surguja is a district in Chhattisgarh) and settled in Surguja at place namely, Ratanpur Betkuli. From Surguja, a group of them migrated to the Palamau highlands (Jharkhand state) and further in the hills of Vindhyachal near Dudhi, Mirzapur district of Uttar Pradesh.

Regarding the origin of the tribe, one mythological story is prominent, which reflects a dim light on the etymological derivation of the name of tribe. The story is that once upon a time, lord Mahadev and Devi Parvati sown the paddy after burning a patch of forest land, called '*Daahi*', in the *Korwai* dilect. To protect the paddy from wild animals lord Mahadev made a image of man (Statue) with mudy soil and put bow and arrow in the hands and placed him in the middle of the cultivated land. At the time of harvesting lord Mahadev found the paddy crop intact, so on the request of Devi Parvati gave life to the 'mud man' saying that you have protected the paddy crop producing the sound, 'Ko-rava-ko-rava' (who is)". So, you would be called "Korwa".

Right from the beginning isolated by extensive forests and difficult terrains, the *Pahari Korwas* inhabiting the region have preserved their traditions, customs and material cultures which are in all respect different from the life of those communities who are leading a settled life.

The natural setting of the tribe has made them peculiar in day to day life. They are slothful, aberrant, extremely furious, short tempered and stubborn in nature. They can live on starvation, but would not go out to earn the meal.

The social organization by the tribe is based on the totemistic clan exogamy. Marriages by service and intrusion (*Dhuku*) are common among them. Divorce and polygamy are common. Widow remarriage is allowed. Livorate and seroate are found and they are socially sanctioned.

Their economy runs around the gathering, hunting and a little cultivation. At present some of them have settled in the plain areas and have started cultivating '*Kodo-Kutki*', '*Godali*', corn, pulses like '*Mung*', '*Kulthi*', etc. Their land is stony, unirrigated and 80 per cent are landless. Wage earning is in practice. The earning is less and expenditure more. The deficit is compensated by taking debts. In this way, indebtedness is increasing day-by-day.

The tribe is animist. They worship their ancestral spirits. They do not have organized traditional *panchayat* of their own community, the disputes are settled within themselves.

Due to developmental schemes being implemented for last four decades, changes are coming among them. Their main problem is poor economy, land alienation, health and lack of basic amenities.

3. *Baiga*

Baigas are a part of larger *Gond* tribe. As mentioned earlier the *Baigas* of '*Baiga chak*' region falling in Mandla district of Madhya Pradesh spread over in 27 forest villages had been identified a a Primitive Tribe in the Fifth Five Year Plan. At that time about 3,000 *Baigas* were living in the region. Gradually, the *Baigas* inhabiting the regions of Dindori, Mandla, Sahdol, Umaria and Balaghat districts of Madhya Pradesh and Bilaspur, Korea, Kawardha and Rajnandgaon of Chhattisgarh states have been enlisted in the category of PTG.

As far as origin of *Baiga* is concerned, it is said that God Brahma, gave '*Hal*' to the tribe called *Gond* and '*Tagia*' (Axe) to another called '*Nanga Baiga*' as he remained without cloth and his discent called *Baiga*.

Right from beginning *Baigas* have been living amidst forests, making small huts for shelter. Their items of material culture are made of soil, forest timbers/bushes to use in daily life. Bow and arrows, axe and fishing traps have been used for hunting. In earlier days they used to do shifting cultivation, now a days they do cultivation on hill slopes. Producing *Koda*, Corn, *Madia*, *bati* paddy, *urd* and *Mung* pulses.

Collection of Minor Forest Produces (MFP), and hunting small animals. In rainy season fishing is done. Their economy is very poor.

In their social life, they are divided in many sub-groups, *viz.* Biujhwar, Bharotia, Narotia, Kodwan (Kundi), Kurka Baiga and Sawat Baiga. Their clan is exogamous. These clans are totemistic.

Mostly marriage are settled by the elders of the family. Besides, marriages are done through — marriage by service (Lamsena), elopement and intrusion (Dhukoo). Divorce and remarriage are also permissible.

Caste *panchayat* is in operation, 'Mukaddam' is head, and 'Diwan', 'Samrath' are recognized officials. All the disputes are settled by the *panchayat.*

Their religion is magico-religious. Main deities are Buradeo, Bhimsen, Dharti Mata, Dulhadeo, Baghdeo, etc. They offer birds and wine while worshipping their deities. 'Bhumika is the main priest. 'Karma' is the main dance form danced on all the ceremonial occasions.

Changes are visible. Shifting cultivation has been minimized. Living pattern is also changing. They are being nearer to education. Some Baiga youth are also employed in Government services. Their problem is economic. Unirrigated and fellow land are the main hurdle in cultivation. Malnutrition, poor health, superstition and restricted source of income are their main problem.

4. *Birhor*

Birhors are small community. Their habitation in the Chhattisgarh State is less, spread over the regions of Bilaspur, Jashpur and Korba districts. They are mainly located in Ranchi, Hazaribagh and in Purnia falling in the State of Jharkhand/Bihar State. They are interspersed with communities and generally live in groups of 3 to 4 families. They live on the fringe of forests and outskirts of larger villages.

Birhors are offshoot of Kolarian group of tribals. In Birhore dialect 'Bir' means forest and 'Hore' means man, Man living in the forest.

They live in small huts. Their main diet is rice, '*koda-pej*' (Bear of *koda*), *kulthi* and forest produces.

Their economy is poor. They cultivate millets, make ropes and collect minor forest produces. Land holding is very poor.

In their social life, the Birhore who are nomadic are known as '*uthalu*' and who are settled at a place called '*Jhadis*'. Their clan is exogamous and totemistic. Marriages are done by settlement, *Dhukoo*, elopement, exchange (Golat). Divorce and remarriages are permissible.

Birhors practice magico-religious rituals. They have strong belief in '*Jadu-Tona*'. They are worshiper of Sun, besides, worship ancestral spirits. In worship, they offer wine, hen, goat, etc.

Due to implementation of general development programmes and family oriented programmes, certain changes are being observed, specially living pattern, settled life and cultivation. Their main socio-economic problems are to earn for livelihood, health and hygiene, malnutrition, illiteracy and superstitions.

5. *Kamar*

Kamars are located in 11 Blocks of Raipur, Dhamtri, Mahasamunda and Kankare districts of Chhattisgarh State. The tribes believes that they have their origin from 'Devgongarh Village' of Raipur Development Block. Still they maintain their old material culture. They live in soil-mud made huts having roof made of straw and bamboo. They consume everything which they find easily. In their social life, they are divided into two groups — 'Pharpatia and 'Bunderjeeva'. The former group resides on hills and later on plains. They have totemistic exogamous clan. Marriage by elopement, service and intrusion are prevalent. The custom of '*Ghar jamai*' is also prevalent. Divorce and remarriage of widow is permissible.

They have their own caste *panchayat* to settle all the community disputes. Due to implementation of development and family oriented programmes, changes in their living pattern and attraction towards education have come. They have started sending their children to schools.

The main problem of Kamars is poor economy. There is lack of resources of earning.

6. *Saharias*

Saharias are spread over in whole of Madhya Pradesh, specially their concentration is on the border of Madhya Pradesh and Rajasthan. They are known in shifting their villages in no time whenever they experience any pressure from any other group. This is one of the communities which are said to have lost their nerve.

The name Saharia probably means inhabitants of the '*jungle*' (forest), from the Persian word '*sehr*' meaning a jungle.

Saharias living alongside of roads are not much different in the language and the dress from other people in the region, but in the interior the conditions are quite different. Their usual food mainly consists of lesser millets and inferior cereals.

In their social life, they move from one place to another for livelihood. Clans are totemistic and exogamous. Marriage among them is generally performed at an early age, but there is no hard and fast rule about the marriageable age. Biogamy is also practiced. Divorce and remarriage of widows are permitted.

The economic condition is appalling. With the opening of the area of their habitation, there has been large scale of land alienation of land by the stronger communities. So, they have hardly any land of their own, and earn wages as an agricultural labour. They are virtually purchased by a nominal price (bonded labour) by land owners and creditors. There are two systems of employing the Saharias as an agricultural labour, viz. '*Hali baholi*' or '*Mohinder*' and '*Hali bauta*'. Under the first system they are paid lumpsum at a time and some food according to need and high rate of interest is charged; and in the other system Saharia is employed as '*Hali Bauta*', where no cash is given to him, but food to eat.

They worship Hindu God and Goddesses. Their main problem is indebtedness, illiteracy, land alienation, poor health and nutrition and earning the livelihood.

7. *Bharias*

Bharias are one of the smaller tribal groups of Madhya Pradesh. They are also found in Seoni and Mandla districts. A small section of this community is in Ptalkot region of Chhindwara district. The Patalkot region is a deep depression in the hilly region, the approach being extremely difficult, as the vertical walls locally known as 'Kanat', the total depth being about 3,000 feet. There are twelve villages in Patalkot region in which these *Bharias* are spread over. So far as communication is concerned, steps are constructed in the year 1950. The communication between one village and another located at different heights is also very difficult and there is almost vertical slopes. Thus, the region is inaccessible and the vertical slope paths are not easily negotiable. This small group *Bharia* is a classic case of a primitive group caught in a difficult terrain subsists totally on the local resources. Here the ecological equilibrium appears to have been disturbed because of institutional factors. The command of the local *Bharia* community over the forest resource has been lost to the State forest department with the result they leave to eke out a living superstitiously.

It is said that *Bharias* were its sole occupants. They practiced shifting cultivation and subsited on forest produce. There were food grazing grounds and they reared cattles. In due course of time, Gond families from the near surroundings came down to graze their cattles and got settled in some villages. Earlier these *Bharias* lived isolated, but after incoming of Gonds the social intercourse increased among these communities. The material culture of *Bharias* considerably changed and now *Bharias* cannot be distinguished from the *Gond* of the upcountry.

Social exclusiveness has now given away, but there is sharp distinction between the economic life of *Bharias* of patalkot and in the surrounding areas. The economy of *Bharias* is still continues to be almost self-sufficient except for the purchase of cloth and edible commodities like salt. Bulk of their food requirement is drawn either from meagre produce of shifting cultivation or from minor forest produce. Food gathering is done as there is well defined cycle for their subsistence. Their subsidiary occupation is also animal husbandry. The tribe is used to keep milch animals and sell milk products.

The problem of indebtedness is there. There has been no appreciable efforts on the public health. There is no protected water supply.

The Bharia society is extremely equalitarian. There are no rich person or destitute. They meet mostly their requirements by mutual borrowings.

Efforts for Development of Primitive Vulnerable Tribal Groups

After adoption of tribal sub-plan strategy for over all development of the Scheduled Tribes and the tribal areas, under the strategy as discussed above the PTGs were identified in the State of Madhya Pradesh during the Fifth Five Year Plans. So, the development strategy/plan involved differently for the seven identified PTGs for their overall development. These identified PTGs were at different stages of socio-economic development.

In the beginning the following instructions have been issued by the Government of India during the year 1977 to the State Governments to prepare project for each PTG:

(a) An exhaustive programme for them has to be formulated. Primitive groups are to be impoverished as the very concept of the poverty may be unknown to them. Hence, special programmes will have to be taken up as a part of general development in the area;

(b) The organization of society under SFDA/TDA model will be beneficial in the programming for primitive tribes. The society should have specific perspective plans for each of the communities, so that, continuity of the work to be conducted can be provided;

(c) The development can only succeed when a group of sensitive personnel is appointed to the task. The appointment of the officer cannot be made on functional basis, as programmes relate to a small group numbering about 50 to 100 or 200 families;

(d) The project should give protection for the economic activities of PTGs. External predatory forces sniping at their produce and leaving them bare should be warded off, so that, members of PTGs are in a position to fully enjoy the fruits of their labour;

(e) The project prepared for each group must cover the entire gestation period, so that, the project should come to an end only when the PTG has become a viable one;

(f) In settlement programmes generally some subsistence allowance is given without any labour input which can be demoralizing and misused. A mechanism has to be found where by the community should be given the feeling that they are earning their subsistence and nothing is paid to them extra;

(g) A programme providing working opportunity for a period of 300 days in a year on minimum wages should be formulated. The principle of converting the manpower of the group into the capital assets has to be followed. Thus, the entire land reclamation works can be taken up by the beneficiary group itself;

(h) Irrigation programmes can be taken up provided bulk of the land belongs to the PTG. In the plantation programmes the approach has to be to give the ownership of the tree to the PTGs while land may continue to belong to the state;

(i) Health is the biggest problem to the PTGs. The entire PTGs should be medically checked up;

(j) The PTGs under consideration have to be equipped mentally and psychologically, so that, they are able to withstand the depradation among them by external agencies. This can be done by educating them in a way which does not erode their distinct personality and cultural individuality; and

(k) A substantial adult education effort should be made amongst PTGs. In the first instance reading material should be prepared keeping in view their own local situation and their problems.

The Government of Madhya Pradesh did not prepare a separate plan for each PTG, but launched four groups of schemes, viz. family oriented, economic, community infrastructure and human resource development programmes on the subsidy and loan basis. The loan component was kept only 20 per cent and subsidy upto 80 per cent.

The economic development programmes included Integrated Rural Development (IRD), the development of agriculture and allied activities, self-employment and family oriented income generating schemes based on subsidy and loan basis.

The Community Development Programmes (CDP) included distribution of uniform, text books, provision of health facilities, establishing agriculture farms, provision of *Ashrams*, Contour building, sericulture, bamboo plantation, distribution of iodized salt, provision of soap, employment training programmes. The infrastructure programmes included approach road, bridges and culverts, stop dams, nistari tanks, construction of school buildings. Under Human Resource Development Programmes all the educational and training programme are included to help in equipping a person for getting suitable employment.

In order to implement these four groups of schemes for the development of PTGs, six development agencies have been registered under Registrar, Firms and Societies. Details of agencies are as Table 10.7.

Table 10.7: PTGs Development Agencies Registered under Registrar, Firms and Socieites

Sl.No.	*Name of PTG*	*Name Agency and Headquarters*
1.	*Abhujmaria*	Abhujmarh Development Agency, Naracupar, Bastar district
2.	*Baiga*	Baiga Development Agency, Dindori, Mandla district
3.	*Bharia*	Bharia Development Agency, Tamia, Chhindwara district
4.	*Birhore*	Jashpur Sarvotomukh: Vikas Pradhikaran, Jashpur Nagar, Raigarh district
5.	*Kamar*	Kamar Development Agency, Gariaband, Raipur district
6.	*Pahari Korwa*	Pahari Korwa Development Agency, Jashpur Nagar, Raigarh district
7.	*Saharia*	Saharia Development Agency, Gwalior district, under the control and supervision of Saharia Development Agency, a cell has been created in all the five districts, viz. Morena, Datia, Gwalior, Guna and Shivpuri to assist the agency.

Source: V.K. Srivastava (2007).

Looking to the poor performance of the State Government, during the year 1992, however, a new approach was adopted wherein Five Year Development Plan based on actual socio-economic surveys of these PTG were prepared taking into account their aspirations.

With a view to providing very dynamic and effective administrative and financial structure separate district wise agencies were registered for each PTG. While *Kamar*, *Bharia*, *Abhujmaria* and *Birhor* have been located in all area/region of a single district, the *Baiga*, *Saharia*, *Pahari Korwa* have been located in more than one district — the *Baiga* in five district and *Saharia* in all the six districts of Gwalior and Chambal Revenue Divisions. It was found difficult to ensure effective implementation of schemes from one place (where the headquarter of agency located) to all the districts. Even the distribution of funds was disproportionate in all the districts — giving more funds of the district in which the agency was situated.

It was decided to establish an agency in a district in which the population of PTG was 2,000 or more. In 16 districts such agencies were established. Besides, a post of Director, PTGs has also been created to administer the functions of these agencies. It was also decided to nominate a member of the primitive community concerned, as the Chairman of the agencies and person as a members. One another important measure has been taken to issue family identity cards to each primitive tribal group family, so that, they can get advantage of development work easily. A sizeable amount has been spent in last two decades (1975: 1994-95) on PTGs. A comprehensive picture of the amount received from Government of India and expenditure incurred on programme since Fifth Five Year Plan to till year 1994-95 is given in Table 10.8.

Table 10.8: The Amount Received from GoI and Expenditure Incurred on Different Programmes on PTG during Fifth Five Year Plan (1975-80) till Year 1994-95

(*₹ in lakh*)

Sl. No.	*Name of PTG*	*Amount Received*	*Expenditure on Programmes*				
			Family oriented Eco. Development	*Community Development*	*Infrastructure Development*	*Establishment*	*Total*
1.	*Kamar*	250.56	42.87	165.87	19.38	—	228.12
2.	*Bharia*	120.95	20.87	27.47	34.12	25.22	107.68
3.	*Abhujmaria*	313.45	49.36	110.15	129.22	—	288.73
4.	*Baiga*	1,274.42	238.60	718.11	175.28	—	1,131.99
5.	*Pahari Korwa*	300.00	78.33	61.35	117.38	—	257.06
6.	*Birhor*	68.00	19.34	17.14	21.36	—	57.84
7.	*Saharia*	533.41	84.45	239.88	133.38	—	457.71
	Total	**2,860.88**	**533.82**		**630.12**	**25.22**	**2,529.13**

Source: Development of Primitive Tribal Groups in India by P.K. Mohanty, Kalpaz Publication, Delhi, p. 252.

It is clear from the analysis of data of above table that out of total amount of ₹ 2,860.88, lakh ₹ 2,529.13 lakh (88.40%) could be utilized and out of this, ₹ 533.82 (21.68%) could be spent to benefit, 63,935 (62.44%) PTG families out of total 1,02,383, families. Besides, 52.98 per cent and 24.9 per cent amounts have been spent on community and infrastructure development programmes.

As regards providing employment in the Government service, special employment opportunities, the requisite qualifications for the recruitment to the certain posts was relaxed as per State Government's General Administration Department (GAD) order no. F.NOC-3-17/86/3/1 dated 26th August, 1986. As such 17 teachers and 44 peons got recruited from Pahari Korwa community, 3 teachers and 8 peons from Birhor community, in Baiga agency area 210 Assistant teachers from Baiga community and 2 Assistant teachers got recruited from the Bharia community.

After the reorganization of the State of Madhya Pradesh out of total fund available ₹ 800.00 lakh from GoI, ₹ 569.00 lakh has been made available to the PTG agencies in Madhya Pradesh and ₹ 231.00 lakh to 6 PTG Agencies of Chhattisgarh state.

During the Ninth Five Year Plan Period (1997-2002), against total ₹ 4,091.00 lakh ₹ 3517.54 (85.98%) lakh has been spent on PTGs.

Besides the implementation of routine programmes/schemes for PTGs from the funds given by GoI under Special Central Assistance (SCA) and Article 275(1), the Ministry of Tribal Affairs, GoI, also launched a Central Sector Scheme during the year 1998-99 for PTGs for their Special Protection and development which have not been covered under any existing schemes. During the year 2004-05 the Ministry of Tribal Affairs (Government of India) started providing insurance cover to the earning member of PTG family. Under the Janshree Bima Yojana of Life Insurance Corporation of India within the remaining years of Tenth Five Year Plan. Under the scheme the amount released for the years 2004-05 to 2007-08 to Madhya Pradesh and Chhattisgarh states is given in Table 10.9.

No amount has been released during the years 2009-10 and 2010-11 under the scheme.

Problems Being Faced by Ministry of Tribal Affairs, GoI with Regard to the Development of PTGs

It has been found that the Central Government have not been getting proper feedback and response timely from both the State Governments

Table 10.9: Statement Showing Amount Released to States/UT and PTG Heads Covered since 2004-05 under Janshree Bima Yojana under the Scheme of Development of Particularly Vulnerable Tribal Groups (erstwhile Primitive Tribal Groups)

(₹ *in lakh*)

Sl. No.	*Name of the States*	*Estimated Number of Families*	*Targeted No. of Families*				*Amount Released during*			
			2004-05	2005-06	2006-07	2007-08	2004-05	2005-06	2006-07	2007-08
1.	Chhattis-garh	45,500	8,000	18,000	0	0	40	90	0	0
2.	Madhya Pradesh	90,000	20,000	40,000	30,000	0	100	200	150	0

Source: Annual Administrative Report 2008-09, Ministry of Tribal Affairs, GoI, New Delhi.

regarding the status, aspirations and implementation of the specific scheme, etc. Such problems have been summarized as under:

(a) Since, the Fifth, Sixth, Seventh and onward Five Year Plans, after the identification of PTGs, funds have been provided to the States for the development of PTGs almost residing in Integrated Tribal Development Project (ITDPs), the erstwhile Ministry of Welfare/Social Justice and Empowerment had requested and now the present Ministry of Tribal Affairs, GoI is continuously requesting the State Governments to take up development of PTGs on a project basis. It has, however, been found and experienced by the concerned Ministry, GoI, that projects even specific schemes for the development of PTGs have not been forthcoming from the States. Further, though a part of Special Central Assistance (SCA) is being utilized by the States, specifically for PTGs, the feedback on results achieved is inadequate. The exact amount utilized for the development of PTGs out of SCA as well as State plan funds has not been reported by the State Governments;

(b) The State Governments are not monitoring properly the socio-economic progress, educational and other fields as well as the demographic features on continuing basis for different purposes, including for the purpose of assessing the need for continuation of a particular PTG in the list and communicating the Ministry, GoI, Review and revision of the criteria also should be kept under scrutiny;

(c) PTG-wise approach for protection and development is required at the State Government level, which is not taken care of. As a matter of fact before embarking on ideas concerning approach, policy paths of development and other conceptual matters, it is necessary to have look at the situation as it prevails on the ground. The reports of the various working groups constituted by the planning commission on each plan have also not embodied the States and profile of each of the PTGs as it existed then. In fact the informations made available to the Central Ministry are scanty, sketchy and inadequate. It generally indicates funds received and expenditure done therefrom by the State Governments. Thus, according to the Ministry of Tribal Affairs sources, they do not possess adequate materials on the demographic, economic, educational, health and other sectors of individual PTG on account of non-receipt of data, information, statistics from the concerned State Governments;

(d) In the Sixth Five Year Plan and Seventh Five Year Plan period, it had been the guideline of GoI, that a separate Project Report should be prepared for each tribal group, taking into account its unique features, particularly cultural, environmental and socio-economic. It was prescribed that the first phase of development should aim at conservation and re-organization of the traditional skills of the groups, while the second phase should spell out the development programmes. Rehabilitation of the eco-system was given a high priority. Above all, it was emphasized that each blue print should be prepared based on the groups own proclivity expressed by the group's representatives in consultative assemblies. It is found that this pivotal function of preparation of one project Report for each tribal group has fallen into arrears, betokening a State of neglect. So, it is felt that the first and foremost need is preparation of Project Reports for these communities in dialogue with them, reflecting their ideas of needs, aspirations, development, etc. For the purpose, it is necessary to strike a rapport with them; and

(e) The Planning Commission had observed that adequate attention has not so far been made by the State Governments for the development of PTGs funded out of SCA, State Plan Resources, Schemes for NGOs, Vocational Training for tribals, educational complexes for the low literacy pockets, etc.

Issues Need Immediate Attention

The objectives are to achieve total development of the entire population of PTGs. There are some burning issues relating to these groups: (i) The cause of decline in the population of certain PTGs should be investigated and causes removed; (ii) While maternity and child health facilities are extremely important for them, family planning measures for limiting the family size are not relevant in their case; and (iii) the areas specific or tribe specific multi-sectoral projects should be taken up for development of PTGs.

Priority should be given to:

(a) Primary education and Adult education;
(b) Health Services;
(c) Schemes for economic development of families;
(d) Provision of the minimum needs already identified under MNP to the extent these have not been or not be provided under state's TSP or other Central Sponsored Schemes;
(e) Provision of social services should not be delayed;
(f) Dedicated personnel is required to implement the programmes as PTGs are very sensitive in nature;
(g) To provide protection for the existing economic activities of PTGs;
(h) The programmes should be prepared on the basis of providing opportunity for a period of 300 days in a year; and
(i) Health care is very much required in case of the PTGs, specially *Baiga, Abhujmaria, Bharias* child care and rapid treatment is very much required for Saharia children and concurrent monitoring and evaluation of each schemes/programmes is to be taken on continuous basis, so that, the vulnerability of each PTG can be assessed and accordingly proper steps could be taken.

Conclusion

1. The objective of this chapter has been two fold: understanding the concept of 'primitive' and tribal communities identified and listed as Primitive Tribal Group, even today, after four decades are primitive, to whom GoI have been forced to give a new nomenclature 'Vulnerable Tribe Groups' why? How long they would be primitive/vulnerable? Because even after passing Six Five Year Plans (Fifth to Eleven) to call or indicate the listed PTGs still 'primitive' is like : "Laughing Buddha". It is shame on the part of Government Planners, administrators and so-called academician, who coined the word 'primitive' and could not transform this into the category of normal Scheduled Tribes. Even

the working group constituted by the Planning Commission GoI, on the eve of Ninth Five Year Plan has also observed that the word 'primitive' is now not relevant to use for these communities. The observation of working group is as under:

> "Before proceeding further, one question which might be regarded as minor in one context, but which has significant implications in understanding of these groups, having also psychological bearing on these groups themselves, pertains to their nomenclature. The repeated use of the term 'primitive tribal groups' has given wide currency to it. But we are not happy over its usage. The phrase 'primitive' have evidently pejorative overtones. It seeks to elevate the non-tribal sections of the society and depressing these groups to base cultural levels. Do the relevant groups merit the description?"

The above observation of the working group is meaningful and echoes the same feeling and emotions which has been expressed for 'primitive' by Bhupender Singh. The State of primitiveness is to be carefully examined in case of each primitive tribe. But the State-wise study has revealed that the respective States are implementing the development schemes in routine manner and not keen to bring these notified primitive tribes in the category of other Scheduled Tribes.

2. Under Tribal Sub-Plan strategy and approach, the concept of primitive Tribal Group was evolved, but the criteria adopted to identify them could not be honestly followed, actually those archival, diminutive and small tribal groups were listed under PTG, which had been categorized 'extremely underdeveloped stage by the Dhebar Commission (1961) and supported by other committees and Bhuria Commission (2004).
3. All the seven PTGs is identified and listed for Madhya Pradesh and Chhattisgarh states falling in Central India have been studied in terms of demographic structure, socio-economic conditions, health and in other areas and in brief it is found that:

   (a) On the eve of Fifth Five Year Plan and further Sixth and Seventh Five Year Plans, *Bharia*, *Pahari Korwa*, *Kamar*, *Birhor* and *Saharia* have been location specific, but with the span of time they all have been acknowledged for whole of the State. This approach enhanced the area of PTGs and have impact in the implementation of development programmes;

(b) The analysis of demographic data has revealed that according to the 1991 Census the population of PTGs in Central India is 4.15 per cent of total population of all five States of Central India, and out of them 4.32 per cent PTGs reside in Madhya Pradesh and Chhattisgarh. All the PTGs of Madhya Pradesh and Chhattisgarh have projected positive population growth almost in a decade, even more than normal growth of other Scheduled Tribes. *Saharia* is the only PTG which has registered negative population growth. Similarly, on education part decadal growth of literacy of these PTGs has increased remarkably as compared to general tribal communities. As regards the growth of PTGs families, it was 1,02,383 according to survey done in the year 1992 and in the survey of 2004, it has increased to 1,35,500, i.e. registered 32.34 per cent growth. The Ministry of Tribal Affairs, while allocating the funds under central sector scheme and to give coverage to the PTG families under *Janshree Bima Yojana* of Life Insurance Corporation of India, has given enough funds during the 2004 — 2009-10 to both the States.

(c) As per the survey done by the Tribal Research Institute (TRI), Bhopal, Madhya Pradesh and TRI Chhattisgarh (2002), about 40 per cent *Kamar*, 26 per cent *Baiga*, 38.30 per cent *Pahari Korwa*, 23.37 per cent Birhor, 19.32 per cent *Abhujmaria*, 60 per cent *Saharia* and 40 per cent *Bharias* are landless. And all these PTGs do cultivation; *Kamar* (80%), *Baiga* (20%), *Pahari Korwa* (53.19%), *Birhor* (59.36%) and *Bharias* (55.2%). Correct data about *Abhujmarias* is not known. The rest of PTGs working population is engaged in earning daily wages, agriculture labour and work as marginal worker.

(d) Health problem and malnutrition is common to all; and

(e) The common problems among these PTGs are shortage of basic amenities, viz. drinking water, availability of various diseases, limited source of income, unirrigated land, superstitions, less availability of food grains, forest produces and protective facilities during the rainy season, land alienation and indebtedness.

4. The above findings based on foregoing analysis of facts and discussion clearly reveals that:

   (a) It would be inhuman to place them in the category of PTG, in other words vulnerable, because their demographic, health and economic indicators clearly show that they are now at par with their other breathren tribal communities. Yes, in certain areas of development they need immediate attention. Here, it is necessary to mention that their material culture and livelihood pattern are also at par with other non-PTG tribal communities.

   (b) While evaluating and assessing the development aspects of these PTGs the facts discussed in the foregoing photographs related to development of PTGs should be kept in mind. In brief, the efforts have so far made for the protection and development of these PTGs, could be summarized as under:

      (i) Under Tribal Sub-Plan approach the development of infrastructure in the PTGs area has to be done from the funds of State plan of the respective States. And for the family benefit oriented programme, the funds is provided by the concerned Ministry of Government of India from Special Central Assistance (SCA) and from Article 275(1) for community oriented and creation of basic amenities. To get the funds from the Article 275(1), the concern State Government has to prepare project and send it to the Ministry, GoI, for approval, sanction and get the fund. As mentioned earlier, the lack of communication, feed back and persuasion, the development project, made and sent to GoI to get the required funds could not be materialized in many cases;

      (ii) For last four decades State Governments have been getting maximum funds from GoI, so a tendency has been developed that let these PTGs continue as PTG so that, funds could be made available from GoI. This is the main reason that State Governments did not bother to do benchmark survey of each PTG on five year basis;

      (iii) The working group has been constituted by the Planning Commission, GoI, on the eve of every Five Year Plan, has given so many recommendations to the Central and State Governments each time. But no attention has been paid, only keeping them for academic purposes; and

(iv) The Government of India has always been handicapped in appreciation of position of each PTG. In the absence of evaluation of programmes/schemes, the Central Ministry has been unable to built up suitable plan and programmes for each PTG.

Author of this article conducted ethnographic study of the *Pahari Korwa* forty years ago when the tribe was identified as PTG. His study covers the tribe from cradle to graveyard. Today the scenario is altogether different.

At last it can be said that as regards the developmental aspect of PTGs to arrest their various socio-economic and psychological problems, from time to time, during the plan era, various development approach/ programmes have been introduced for their overall development and transformations. Even after Eleventh Five Year Plan, i.e. after more than four decades, it looks that unless radically different, the predominantly bureaucratic process would continue to do reverence merely to the established rituals and thus the PTGs, who have been renamed 'Vulnerable Tribal Groups' during the Tenth Five Year Plan would remain always most backward for the tribal administration for another coming decades.

REFERENCES

Government of India Report (2004): *Scheduled Area and Scheduled Tribes Commission Report*, New Delhi: Ministry of Tribal Affairs, p. 2.

Jashpur Estate Final Settlement Report, 1942.

Mohanti, P.K. (2002): *Development of Primitive Tribal Groups in India*, Delhi: Kalpaz Publication, p. 9.

Sinha, Surjeet, (1977): "Primitive Tribes? The First Step" (ed.) by Surjeet Sinha and B.D. Sharma, New Delhi: Ministry of Home Affairs, Government of India, pp. 2, 18.

Srivastava, V.K. (2003): *Tribal Scenario of Madhya Pradesh and Chhattisgarh*, Bhopal: Sharan Publication, p. 10.

Srivastava, V.K. (2007): *The Pahari Korwas Socio-economic Conditions and their Development*, New Delhi: Sonali Publication, pp. 4, 164.

11

Livelihood Securities and Community Forest Management with Particular Reference to Primitive Tribes of Madhya Pradesh

Debashis Debnath

Introduction

India is a country, which is famous for its indigenous people living in the natural habitat constituted by forests, hills and water bodies. The Indian indigenous peoples, known as 'tribals' or 'Scheduled tribes' (Constitutional or political category), are found to be living in the hilly and forested areas of rich bio-diversity. Since, the British regime the Government policies of nationalization of the forest lands and products brought out a good amount in State exchequer and generated man-days for tribal collectors. But the deprivations of their rights and alienation from their ancestral lands have developed various issues in their cultures and life. In the historical context, the transformation of community-owned village commons to the State owned forests during the British rule and after the attainment of Independence, two polices and several acts were framed to marginalize the tribal groups. But 1960s onwards, community regime was found strengthened by the self-initiated forest protection by the indigenous peoples in different parts of the indigenous land, resulting into the National Forest Policy 1988 as pro-tribal or pro-poor policy and thereby resolution for initiating participatory forest management. Adopting 1988 National Forest Policy various community-based forest Management systems have been initiated, which are known as Joint Forest Management (JFM) and Community Forest Management (CFM). Forest Management is now a decision-making process for the conservation, management, development and sustainable harvesting of the bio-resources in Forest Lands. From the inception of the Participatory

Forest Management various actions have been taken up to provide livelihood securities to the fringe forest dwellers of the State forest by developing small and micro-enterprises. To develop common property resource management situation, the management system emphasizes people-centred, people responsive and pro-democratic process with social arrangements of community-based social grouping in promotion of traditional livelihoods with preservation and conservation of bio-resources and bio-diversities.

Thus, the Forest Department commenced the partnership with the villagers in forest management involving the tribals and women in protection, management and development of the forest resources of the reserved and protected forests. They view their forest management as an integrated and holistic system of forest land management rather than individual species. Thus, long-term management strategies actually increase biological diversity developing their own cultural system for protection, preservation and conservation of forest resources, which establish following links between culture and bio-diversity:

(a) Species conservation, and
(b) Habitat preservation.

The preservation is not simply the mechanism, but is governed by the knowledge, conservation ethos and cultural practices. The latter are bounded by the community institutions, which are adapted to the changing socio-economy and, policies and programmes. Biodiversity conservation appears to be an integral part to many traditional management systems from tropical forests to coastal fisheries. Thus, self-interest of traditional peoples has been the key to bio-diversity maintenance. As traditional peoples are integrated into the global economy and come under various pressures, they often lose their resource base, and in the long run, their knowledge systems, social institutions, and their worldview which shape their relations with the environment. The process of decoupling of traditional peoples from their resource base is likely to reduce the resilience of their social systems, as well as their local ecosystems through bio-diversity loss.

From that point of view, forest management systems are referred to as indigenous, when they are primarily based on local experience of the specific society and have evolved over time and transmitted from generation to generation by word of mouth or by practice. In the participatory forestry their decision-making rights and responsibilities starting from planning, implementation to evaluation were given due importance. In this, two more institutions like civil societies or NGOs and market, which have also been added to catalyze the developmental activities. In the implementation of participatory forestry, building of community institutions on the basis of institutional mechanism and utilization of forest resources in a sustainable way. In the institutional mechanism at the grass roots level the decentralized governance was also set-up into decision-making processes as well as in actions. But participation has not been to that extent as expected and the community institutions has not been found strengthened due to lack of belongingness, various intra- or inter-conflicts of different world-views of multi-stakeholders and lack of mutual-trust. The indigenous peoples applied the indigenous knowledge for conservation and utilization of various non-timber species for their survival and livelihoods. But in the implementation of participatory forestry, the basic objectives of conservation of the bio-resources and species diversities, viz. collection and conservation of the non-timber forest products including medicinal plants, participatory silvi-culture, processing, value addition and local market development were not given due importance to that extent as required.

Objectives of the Study

Attempts have been made in this chapter to show on empirical data the community mobilization of these PVTGs in the Community Forest Management, which shows the transmission of their own knowledge conservation practices, traditional techniques, conservation ethos, innovation for conserving and restoring the ecological sites.

Background

Madhya Pradesh is the second largest Indian state in size and better known as 'Tribal' and 'Tiger' state. The State is divided into 11 agro-climatic zones. The forests are distributed over all the agro-climatic zones. Out of total 3,08,245 sq.km. geographical area, which is 9.4 per cent of the country's geographical area, 30.82 per cent comes under forest cover, which equals 2.33 per cent of total forest cover of India. At present, as per 2011 census, out of the total populations of the State, that is 7,26,26,809 the population of tribals in the State is 1,53,16,784 constituting 21.09 per cent of the total population of Madhya Pradesh. There were 46 identified Scheduled Tribes and three of them have been identified as "Primitive Tribal Groups" (PTGs) in the State, presently also known as 'Particularly Vulnerable Tribal Group (PVTG). They are distributed as follows:

1. *Baiga* — Mandla, Dindori, Shahdol, Anupur, and Balaghat districts;
2. *Sahariya* — Guna, Sheopur, Shivpuri, Morena, Gwalior, Vidisha, Rajgarh districts; and
3. *Bhariya* — Patalkot in the Tamia block of Chhindwara district.

The study was conducted in six villages of the Baiga-Dindori district:

1. *Sahariya* — Sheopur district; and
2. *Bhariya* — Patalkot of Chhindwara district.

Methodology

Stage 1: The first stage of research consisted of the following activities: Literature review was undertaken

(i) On empirical studies of Indigenous knowledge, and
(ii) From the ethnographies of all the tribal communities selected for this study.

Stage 2: *Coverage:* Looking into the objectives of the project the three tribal groups were selected on the basis of pre-agricultural economy and strong indigenous knowledge. In this regard, three Primitive Tribal Groups — *Baiga* of *Baiga chak* of Dindori district, *Bhariya* at Patalkot of Chhindwara district and *Sahariya* in Sheopur district — were purposively selected. Six villages for each tribal group were sampled on the basis of the criterion as follows:

(a) Uni-ethnic tribal village.
(b) Bio-diversity rich areas.
(c) Less accultured group/area.
(d) Good forest areas.
(e) Village institution and forestry activities.

Stage 3: The following tools and techniques were adopted:

(a) *Questionnaire technique:* Semi-structured Questionnaire for inventorying land and identification of problems at the local level;
(b) Schedule for household scale livelihood analyses in which livelihood constraints and opportunities are identified;

(c) Participatory Rural Appraisal (PRA) and Participant Observation;
(d) Semi-structured interviews for key informant or opinion leader to examine social, financial, physical, human and natural capital assets used by households to ensure livelihood security;
(e) Focus group discussion; and
(f) Village workshop.

Stage 4: Data Analysis and Preparation of the Final Report in the following manner:

(a) Descriptive under different titles and subtitles;
(b) Tabular form: Both qualitative and quantitative;
(c) Discussion of the qualitative and quantitative data; and
(d) Results and analysis, and Report preparation.

Stage 5: Socio-demography and socio-economy of the studied Villages:

Table 11.1 shows the socio-demography and socio-economy of the six tribal communities.

Table 11.1: Socio-demography of the Sampled Villages

Sl. No.	*Socio-Demography Data*	*Baiga of Dindori*	*Sahariya of Sheopur*	*Bhariyas of Chhindwara*
1.	Total sampled villages	6	6	6
2.	Name of the villages	Talwar Tola, Kapoti, Kharideeh, Bangladadar of Karanjia Block and Kandavani & Sara of Bajag Block in Dindori distrcit	Upri Khoree, Nichli Khoree, Parond, Chak Bilari, Sonipura of Karhal Block and Sironi of Vijaypur Block in Sheopur district	Chimptipur, Gal Dubba, Rather, Kariyam, Gurhi Chetri, Ghat Linga of Tamia Block in Chhindwara district
3.	Total HH in sampled villages	360	344	218
4.	Total ST Population in 6 sampled villages	1,711 (100%)	1,506 (100%)	1,469 (100%)
5.	Total ST Male in sampled villages	923	804	748
6.	Total ST Female in sampled villages	788	702	721
7.	Sex Ratio in sampled villages	854	873	964

Source: Primary Data from the Survey of the Gram Panchayat Office of the 18 Villages and the Office of Divisional Forest Officer, M.P. Forest Department of the districts.

In the socio-economic condition the *Baigas* highly depend upon forestry activities, though they eke out their existence in labour and non-agricultural labour activities. Similarly, the *Sahariyas* and the *Bhariyas* also depend upon forestry activities, labour and non-agricultural labour activities. In their agricultural occupations the *Bhariya* population is mostly engaged in agricultural livelihoods, followed by *Baiga* and *Sahariya*. Of the total *Sahariya* working force 25 per cent of them are involved in agriculture labour activities, followed by 19.4 per cent *Baiga* and only 8.01 per cent *Bhariyas* are engaged in agriculture labour. Cent-per-cent *Sahariyas* work as non-agricultural labour, half of the *Baiga* community is involved in non-agricultural labour, less than one-fourths (15.2%) is involved in non-agricultural labour. Whereas 100 per cent population is involved in forest produce collection in all the three PVTGs communities in the six sampled villages. All the sampled eighteen villages representing the three PVTGs are situated in close proximity with the forests. The villagers depend on forests for their survival. They have developed a symbiotic relationship with the forests. The *Baigas*, the *Sahariyas* and the *Bhariyas* are dependent on forests for fuel, fodder collection of forest produce, medicinal herbs and plants for self-consumption and sales in the local markets. In their land holding pattern 19.4 per cent the *Baigas* are landless and 80.6 per cent marginal farmers having the land area below 2.5 acres. Among the *Sahariyas* 25 per cent are landless, 68.9 per cent marginal, 4.7 per cent small (between 2.5 and 5 acres) and 1.6 per cent medium farmers (between 5 and 10 acres). Similarly in the *Bhariyas* 8.02 per cent are landless, 70.5 per cent marginal, 6.3 per cent small and 15.2 per cent medium farmers. In consequence, most of the *Baigas* are found below the poverty line. A large number of *Baiga* families (above 80% of the total families) have income less than ₹ 10,000. Similarly a large no. of *Sahariya* families has average income in a year less than ₹ 10,000. All the *Bhariya* families have average income annually less than ₹ 10,000. In their educational status among the *Baigas* 54.41 per cent, among the *Sahariyas* 82.6 per cent and among the *Bhariyas* 60.45 per cent are illiterates. Of the literates in the *Baigas* above the three-fourths of them have passed out the primary standard and only 6.96 per cent have crossed the secondary standard. The educational status of females of the *Baigas* is declining. Very negligible population has crossed high school and higher education. On the contrary, among the *Sahariyas* 15.80 per cent of them have crossed the primary levels and very negligible population has passed out secondary standard, high school and higher education. In the *Bhariyas*

22.47 per cent and 8.78 per cent of the literates have crossed primary and secondary standard and of the rest very negligible population has crossed high school and higher education. As these three tribal communities have their own system of healing their diseases in the traditional practices, mostly they depend on that. Now, various schemes of the Government have been implemented in the tribal villages for developing their health status. But the tribes have not benefitted to that extent due to unawareness, inaccessibility to their habitation, negligence of the administration and inefficiencies of the implementer.

Major Findings of the Research

From the analysis of the above primary and secondary data, as given and other information collected during studies, the objectives-wise research discussion is given below:

(1) *Study on the role of indigenous knowledge in conserving bio-diversity in the Particularly Vulnerable Tribal Groups of Madhya Pradesh.*

All the primitive tribal groups (PTG) conserve the bio-diversities through diverse uses of various species, religion-cultural practices and socio-cultural traditions and in health purposes. The *Baigas* are found to utilize various parts, viz. roots, seeds, rhizomes, tubes, seeds, etc. or products, viz. fruits, flowers of the species under commercial or local level trading, traditional use and health use. Some of the species have the multiple uses signifying the bio-diversity conservation. Sometimes the whole plant or extracted part is used. The *Sahariyas* are also found to utilize various parts, viz. roots, seeds, rhizomes, tubes, seeds, etc. or products, viz. fruits, flowers of the species under commercial or local level trading, traditional use and health use similarly. Some of the species have the multiple uses signifying the bio-diversity conservation. Sometimes the whole plant or extracted part is used. Similarly, the *Bhariyas* are found to utilize various parts, viz. roots, seeds, rhizomes, tubes, seeds, etc. or products, viz. fruits, flowers of the species under commercial or local level trading, traditional use and health use. Some of the species have the multiple uses signifying the bio-diversity conservation. Sometimes the whole plant or extracted part is used. Thus, these PTGs of M.P. have developed the symbiotic relationship with the forests and they have evolved various strategies to conserve the bio-diversity of the forests. One method of forest conservation by the PVTGs is through traditions. Various parts of their bio-diversities are used in their life-cycle rituals. The sacred groves are found in all the three PTGs, which have the areas protected, preserved and conserved with religious affiliation and having varied species conserved for different utility and purposes. There are some temples which have the trees protected, preserved and conserved with religious affiliation for conservation of various species. In three PVTGs a number of taboos observed in the trees like *Sal* among the *Baigas*, *Shaitu* among the *Sahariyas* and *Mahua* among the *Bhariyas*. A number of sacred water resources are observed in three PVTGs. All the PVTGs describe the different places of their habitation in various ways with the significance of IK; it describes the individual or community ownership. These may be open space, farm lands, and ritual spaces for worship or funeral, natural resources and so on. The Indigenous people have centuries old heritage of medicinal plants and herbal medicines for curing human illness in tribal world. Some medicinal plants are used by the Baigas to cure ailments, which they collect, use and sell it in their local market. Similarly, for medicinal purposes the *Sahariyas* use various herbs, plants and roots. These tribes rely on forest products from natural ecosystems to sustain their livelihoods.

(2) *Study on effectiveness of traditional bio-diversity conservation management and livelihood practices in the forest management in tribal communities under study.*

Forest management is now-a-days a decision-making process with people's participation, popular democracy and people's responsiveness under decentralized governance and institutional mechanism with significant stakeholder's roles, rights and responsibilities for conservation of bio-diversities and livelihood securities of the main primary beneficiaries. Such beginning of the community forest management in India took place in the pro-tribal 1988 national forest policy, which was followed by the declaration of the resolution of Joint Forest Management (JFM) by the Ministry of Environment and Forests, Government of India. Then, it commenced the community mobilization by the Forest Department (FD), the local NGOs or CSOs for involvement in protection and forestry activities.

In this context the sustainable livelihoods approach comprising the food security, sustainable employment generation, increasing crop productivity, soil and water conservation, value addition and marketing of NTFPs, *in situ* conservation and *ex-situ* cultivation of medicinal plants, infrastructure development, community asset building and capitals development, etc. were adopted. Thus, indigenous knowledge system is inextricably mixed up with the participatory forestry starting from plantation, silvicultural operations, inventorization of collection or gathering the daily requirement for living, its protection, preservation and conservation for local solutions or pathways towards global development, Hence, in the present day participatory forestry activities are treated as the cumulative effort of livelihoods, ethos and community regime management These three PVTGs are basically forest-dwelling tribes. Their prime economy is based on the collections, utilization, processing and selling of the numerous NTFPs, which support their livelihoods. On the basis of the availability of the amount of the products, they collect and process before selling the market. They use their indigenous knowledge (IK) and customary practices in collection of number of NTFPs including medicinal herbs for their self-consumption and nominal income by selling some amount in local market. Due to regional economic system they have been pulled towards peasnatization of having plow-drawn agricultural livelihoods in the modern farming system. Earlier they had traditional practices of shifting cultivation, in which they produces different varieties of crops and vegetables in different soils. Now, these PVTGs are largely agriculture dependent communities. In the development process, after getting pulled to the agriculture of plough cultivation due to crops diversification they are shifted to traditional bio-diversity based livelihoods to the cultivation of cash crops like paddy, wheat, maize, barley, etc. except *Baigas*, who still grow rice, *kodo* and *kutki* in traditional system of cultivation. The rice is their staple diet. The traditional methods of crop sowing are practiced and thus the yield is just sufficient to meet their daily requirements. As they have not the sufficient income, employment, savings or investments, so, the overall population below poverty line is estimated to be 44 per cent whereas the fringe villagers are 80 per cent below Poverty line and they have the meager land and they are not so much capable to invest in labours, fertilizer or seeds, they remain in poverty due to lack of opportunity to earn money from their agricultural livelihoods. The *Baigas* are hardworking people whereas the *Sahariyas* were found as lazy and dependent on Government to fulfill their requirements. The cultivation is done by them. The *Bhariyas* living in Patalkot valley do not have proper agricultural fields, the land is uneven and their staple diet is maize. There is no irrigation facility available in these eighteen villages, they are dependent on rainfall to fulfill the water demand, and the rainfall is always inadequate. The *Baiga*, the *Sahariya* and the *Bhariya* live hard life every day. They earn every day, they have no bank balances, they do not believe in hoardings. They are searching out alternative livelihood options, with the initiative of the Government initiative in the field of live-stock management, horticulture and fishery. But huge number of indigenous species in livestock, fruits and vegetables (horticulture), as mentioned above, are found. The livelihood options would be cost-effective as these suits to the favourable inputs and local climatic conditions.

(3) *Study on the role of indigenous knowledge system for policy implication in the present forest systems.*

There are ample scopes to enhance their income sources from the forest products as they are living in the fringe forest villages and are depending to the large extent on collection of fuel wood, fodder, NTFPs including medicinal plants, cattle grazing and marketing of the raw products at the nominal price in the local market. Moving away from the income or consumption criteria the poverty has been equated with help of livelihood security. In the three PVTGs the people have attempted to livelihood security by producing some products. For instance, in the *Baigas* they produce broom of *chhind*, rope of *mova* grass, honey, *mahua* liquor and *mahua* oil; in the *Sahariyas* they produce *bael* pulp and basket of *Harsingher* and the *Bhariyas* ropes and broom. All of them they produce in their traditional skills with locally available raw materials.

The main attempts are the community mobilization of the people in the participatory or decision making process in the forest management by which beneficiaries or key stakeholders who influence the direction and make the community input in implementation of a development or natural resource management with a view of enhancing their well-being. It is required to get people interested in a community-based natural resources management initiative. The process may be commenced from motivation and confidence building. Effective participation is one in which all the relevant stakeholders take part in decision-making processes and are also able to influence the decisions in the sense (Agarwal, 2001). Community Forest Management allows a community's problems, needs and solutions to be addressed while incorporating scientific and technical knowledge and skills. Well specified institutional systems in an empowered community would provide process information necessary for management of decision-making and would minimize transaction costs which allow a community forest to be managed similarly to private property with regard to ownership and responsibilities (Padgee *et al.*, 2006). The need for involving community in developing forest/ environmental management plans with people's democracy and responsiveness has been advocated. It attempts for enhancement of the resource stock through plantation, conservation and rehabilitation. Then, to achieve the livelihood goals the institutional mechanism of stakeholder's roles and responsibilities of both formal and informal institutions has significance and importance. These goals attempted to achieve both the economic and non-economic factors, viz. sustainable income and employment, community well-being, educating the people through transmission of their own knowledge system, cultural practices, conservation ethos, innovation, assessment of essential requirement and its fulfilment. To achieve these goals the strategies could be chalked out on the basis of micro-plan, assessment of community assets, micro-finance, infrastructural development and human capacity building. The projects could be implemented on the basis of strategies, which provide the benefits which are shared on equitable basis through robust institutional norms. The sharing also builds up the livelihood strategies and leads to personal or community empowerment comprising of social, economic and political. Participation is a vital component of self-help and empowerment process. So, besides in planning and decision making there is an urgent need for involving the community to develop indicators and to measure progress towards sustainability (Fraser *et al.*, 2006). People must be involved in those decisions that effect on their lives, thus gaining confidence, self-esteem and knowledge and development of new skills. The process is cumulative; the more skills, the more the person is able to participate and the more he can gain. Participation must facilitate learning action and the achievement of goals (Onyx and Benton, 1995). This empowerment process will culminate to the direct impact on community mobilization and institutional mechanism in cyclic order. The framework (Figure 11.1) for various steps from community participation to empowerment through livelihood securities with the bio-diversity management.

Conclusion

The Indigenous Knowledge system of the tribal populations is found in their cultural practices, ecological knowledge, institutional arrangements, etc. But under the influence of the modernization their traditional knowledge are dying out. Sometimes these are fossilized in nature. Now-a-days due to the participatory forest management attempts has been found appropriate to bring these communities into the age-old common property resource management in which such communal ownership and their knowledge or wisdom would be strengthened,

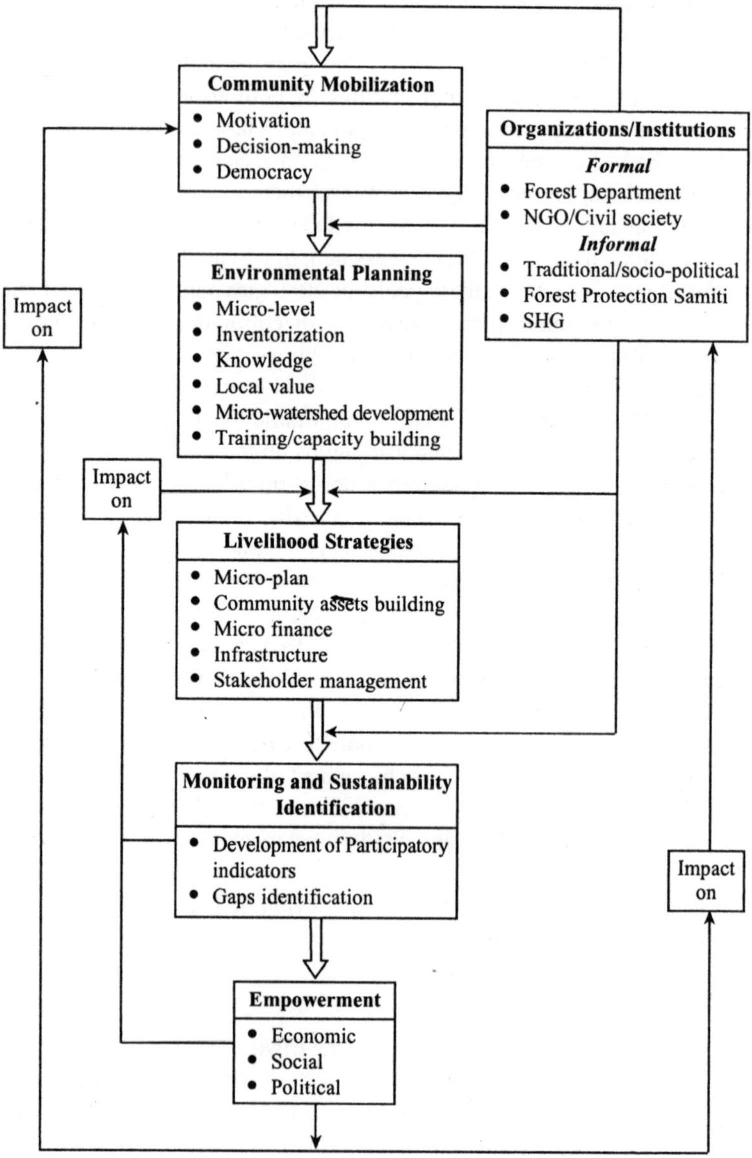

Figure 11.1: Framework for Development through Integrated Conservation and Development

resulting into a better situation of pro-democratic and decentralized governance in favour of community forest management in a sustainable manner.

REFERENCES

Agarwal, B. (2001): "Participatory Exclusions, Community Forestry, and Gender: An analysis for South Asia and a Conceptual Framework", *World Development*, 29 (10): 1623-48.

Debnath, D. (2013): *Indigenous Knowledge, Biodiversity Conservation and Livelihoods Development*, New Delhi: Serials Publication.

Fraser *et al.* (2006): "Bottom Up and Top Down: Analysis of Participatory Processes for Sustainability Indicator Identification as a Pathway to Community Empowerment and Sustainable Environmental Management", *Journal of Environmental Management*, 78: 114-27.

Onyx, J. and Benton, P. (1995): "Empowerment and Ageing: Toward Honoured Places for Crones and Sages", in Craig, G. and Mayo, M. (eds.), *Community Empowerment: A Reader in Participation and Development*, London: Zed Books, pp. 34-33.

Pagdee, A., Y.S. Kim and P.J. Daugherty (2006): "What Makes Community Forest Management Successful? A Meta-study from Community Forests Throughout the World", *Society and Natural Resource*, 19(1): 33-52.

12

Asuras and Birjias on the "Pat" and Ghat Below Netarhat: Study on Vulneration

S.P. Sinha

Introduction

Available enumeration of PVTG's population in the State of Jharkhand as per-2004 official report has been a little more than one lakh ninety two thousand. Wherever they are, they have been in a larger village or villages forming their habitat within the habitat of the larger tribal communities. As if, they have been a functional part of the larger whole to eke out their livelihood and *vice-versa*.

Pat region of Netarhat has been at a height of more than 3,600 feet having extension of Jobhipat and Dumarpat upto Rajandera area of Gumla District cut off from all the three sides having triangular shape forming a table land intersected by small or big gorges in succession and gullies in all the slops down to the valley meeting rivers below. These slops are steep scarps called ghats. In pockets there are few top scarp vallies like "Tahir".

Mostly, *Asuras* and *Birjias* have been living in this physiographical condition which is ultimate reach of mankind. Their folk lore, folk song, folk story are still reflective of the fact as to how they reached and settled in this part of the world. Earlier work of Shaileshwar Prasad (1968) has been a record of work in his book entitled "*Where the three Tribes meet*". Thus, circumstantial evidences and author's long experience of research in this area along with their folk lore, folk stories, folk tale and folk songs reflect the vulneration of *Asuras* and *Birjia*'s meted out by the larger tribal groups *Mundas* in the East and South-East and *Oraons* on the North, North-West and North of the final present settlements. In fact from time immemorial they were pushed and forced to go in the high hills, *pats* and *ghats* mostly inaccessible areas from all the sides.

Traditional Economy

Looking at the traditional economy *Asuras* and *Birjias* have been traditionally forest dweller, iron smelters, shifting cultivators, Basket makers, food gatherers and occasional hunters.

The entire area has been rich in minerals, mines, Jungles full of wild life. Step by step this area got populated by the *Asuras*, *Birjias*, *Mundas*, *Oraons*, *Kishans* and *Birhors*, etc. They have altered the earth accordingly for their survival in such a remotest part of the earth in the long past. Thus, they had developed their economic pursuits and style of life. Folk tale, folk stories and world view have been proof of their expertise in Iron smelting and "*Beonra*" (shifting cultivation) to which they had a demand of their product including basketry and leaf plate making. It had fitted well in the larger network of socio-cultural interaction and co-habitation in a larger area even to a longer distance. They used to get all the raw materials in the nearby hills and forests. During the lean period they earlier used to depend on the M.F.P. abundant in the forest nearby and also on occasional hunting called famously "*Dhantijhumka*". It is important to mention here that age old saying goes like — "*Naina ka Loha, Bashkareha Ka Ghee* and *Aygu Ka Chawal*" famous and in larger demand as branded one in the whole of the region. Name "Netarhat" stands for the two terms: "*Netar*" means bamboo and *hat* means market. In fact Netarhat had been earlier market of Bamboos for Paper mills in Assam and elsewhere. As if Netarhat region is the final abode of these two PVTG — *Asuras* and *Brijias*.

Vulneration in the Past

Before the arrival of *Mundas* and *Oronas* on the Ranchi plateau and further to the pat region of Netarhat area the whole of Ranchi plateau was the land of *Asuras* and *Birjias*. Smaller in population, but since, the past to them displacement and deprivation had been the rule in various ways adversely affecting these two tribal smaller communities. *Mundas* and *Oraons* are not at all the Iron smelters. "*Umedanda*" has been the place wherefrom *Mundas* and *Oraons* one by one tracked up from the Hazaribagh plateau to Ranchi plateau more than 2000 years ago (S.C. Roy, 1912) displacing the *Asuras* who had their *Asuras Bandh*, Pond and running Iron smelting furnaces besides shifting cultivation of their style called famously "*Beonra*". Thus, the *Asuras* were deprived of their all those pursuits they had those days.

Circumstantial evidence can be seen in the form of iron slag spread in a larger area on the earth where the *Asuras* had their smelting and smithy work besides the famous "*Bandh*" even popularly called today as *Asura Bandh*, followed by the pond which *Asuras* had dug long ago in the past.

Another evidence lies with the abandoned big sized charcoal making furnaces plenty in number before Khunti at a distance of 40 kms. right South of Umedananda and then "Psycho" a famous place where from Asuras's township have been unearthed by the Archaeological Survey of India — a positive proof of Asura kingdom there in the past (A.S.I., 2002).

As regards *Oraons* they also in the past by way of coming from the Southern India *via* Rohtash Garh tracked up to the Ranchi Plateau 1,000 feet above Hazaribagh plateau just after the *Mundas* and went West ward-South. They had to fight with the *Mundas* and with the help of *Lohars* (Smiths) in the area Oraons could settle in the Western part of Ranchi District famously called "*Bhuinhars*" (settled agriculturists). They were so clever that they took over all the good plots prepared by the *Asuras* and *Birjias* for their shifting cultivation. Thus, further South and South-West the *Asuras* and *Birjias* were pushed further and further by the *Mundas* and *Oraons* by dint of their populous strength and wisdom. Still they recall as to how they were displaced by the "*Bhuinhars*" *Oraons* and deprived of their good quality of "*Beonra*" land. This way circumstantial evidences also enough to prove as to how these two PVTGs had been vulnerated in the past by the *Mundas* and the *Oraons*.

But now the *Asuras* and *Birjia*'s are only found living in the hills, *Pat* and *ghat* region of Netarhat far away from "*Umedanda*" and "*Khunti*" not less than 100 kms in the West and South-West respectively. Even today they remember their fight with the Mundas and the Oraons. They recall all those as to how *Mundas* famously known as "Khunt cut" means who at first cleared the forest and started settled agriculture, i.e. plough cultivation by pushing out *Asuras* by hook or by crook further and further in the forest and hills. Thus, finally *Asuras* and *Birjias* reached at *Pat* and *Ghat* below besides the neighbouring hill tops and slops. Even today they are surrounded by the *Mundas*, *Oraons* and few other tribes like *kishans* and few non-tribals like *Sahukars*, *Gwalas* and *Halwai*, etc.

Thus, all above facts prove firstly that these two PVTG *Asuras* and *Birjias* had been vulnerated by the *Mundas* and the *Oraons*, major tribal groups long long ago.

Also, it proves secondly that the present abode of *Asuras* and *Birjias* are not their choice, but they had been forced ultimate to settle in the *Pat*, *ghat* and the top-scrap valley of Netarhat region.

Again looking at the passing scene that they were vulnerated to get displaced from at first Umedand at a height of 1,000 feet above Hazaribagh plateau to Khunti area then to Netarhat areas further 1,000's feet above the Ranchi plateau inaccessible area full of wild life and dense forest. This way, they were deprived of their hearth and homesteads by uprooting them from every now and then.

Present State of Affairs

Last, but not the least, as if the most important to look at the present State of affairs of governance since British era. Its impact has been as follows:

(a) Both *Asuras* and *Birjias* are now no more traditional iron smelter. Some of them are iron smith.

(b) Both of the PVTGs are now no more shifting cultivator. They are doing terrace cultivation, i.e. fallow plough cultivation in the scarps of the ghat and a little or very little regular paddy cultivation in the foot of the Pat scarp or in the top-scarp valley like "*Tahir*" or on the pat below the Netarhat dam.

(c) Earlier they were absolute forest dweller of gree lust forest full of wild life doing food gathering, occasional hunting called "*Dharti Jhumka*", but they are not so affluent. Hardly they get to meet their daily need.

(d) Their basket making was commercial as well as to serve the local need. Now, their Basketry is rare. Leaf plate making is now vanished.

(ϵ) They have been forest labourer, Agricultural labourer and earth cutter (*Chauka Katai*).

(f) Earlier they had farmstead now they in their homestead as others are in villages and hamlets fully settled.

(g) They were affluent in growing "*Arhor*" pulse and Maize, but now, it is a matter of dream.

(h) They were traditionally skilled in smelting, smithy, forestry, wild boar and goat trapping, but now no more they are.

(i) Earlier, they were master of fertile land using their land in their style of land use. Now in larger area simply they are land owner to say, but more expectator because top fertile soil cover has undergone stony intermixture leading the earth cover infertile.

No doubt change is the unchanging nature of "Nature" and "Culture" both (S.P. Sinha, 1981, 2006). Change has been inevitable so the above mentioned drastic change led them to adopt the change and then adapt only to survive in such an inhospitable condition. Reasons behind are as follows.

Forest Policy

Tribal economy is simple, but complex and forest have been the ultimate survival source. *Asuras* and *Birjias* way of life have been well translated with the forest in the Centre. But since British era of 1870 till Elwin's suggestion of isolation to keep all those tribal groups at a distance from the non-tribals having minimum contacts led to the enforcement of several Acts.

Worth of timber was considered so important for the Britous, as if, a dream house and have they at first in 1865 passed Indian Forest Act and declared it as Government Reserved forest. By forfitting tribal authority over the forest overall only a little collection rights were given. Though that led to resentment but of no use. Later on Britishers passed (amended) forest acts in 1894, 1925 and in 1935 and thus tried any how to administer the forested areas which undergone serious repercussion. At last when India became Independent the Forest National Policy in 1952 come to regulate in Reserve/National Forest, Protected Forest and village forests in a check and balance mood, but failed to a larger extent.

That way the hill and pat dwellers were brought from fire to the frying pan. *Asuras* and *Brijia*'s "*Beonra*" (shifting cultivation) was thus at first banned by the Government drastically affecting these two tribal communities. This challenged their survival and thus led to migration and starvation death bringing a decline in their population by 9 per cent in 1971 census report. It was emphasized severally. Again in 1959 a National Policy came to allow people to develop as per their genins and nothing should be imposed on them by respecting tribal right on land and forest and no over administration and encouraging their institution to work. Quality of humanity was kept uppermost not the money. By way of reformulation National Forest Policy in 1988 as well kept at bay the interest of *Asuras* and *Brijias* in the then Bihar when J.F.M. came into existence. That too did not help and correct their fate with the share given by forest regulation to those tribals in that areas.

Shifting Cultivation

The best proof as to who at first tracked up about more than 1,000 feet above the Ranchi Plateau and reached this remotest part in the plateau region of Netarhat lies with the shifting cultivation of *Asuras* and *Birjias* called "Because" best suited to the area and the people to sustain with. They used to grow surplus of coarse grains and pulse along with vegetables not only for their consumption, but sufficiently to earn through Barter exchange or latter on in cash. During "Beonra" days they could get sufficient fuel wood, timber logs for construction and repair. Thus, it was also source of survival for the *Asuras* and the *Birjias*. That has been another setback to them when today there has been dirth of all these forest produce used by the PVTG.

Basketry

Earlier below valley the area was rich in bamboo being cut and marketed at Netarhat wherefrom transported to the paper Industries outside. Thus, *Asuras* and *Birjias* also were busy in making varieties of baskets for self and also for commercial purpose.

But, now the bamboo cover in the valley disappeared due to indiscriminate cutting by all the neighbouring communities for the self-use restricting basketry of the two PVTG.

Follow Cultivation

Earlier the two PVTG were master of the total area of hills and forest in this region, but were befooled by their neighbour "*Bhinhars*" *Oraon* in the nearby when they entered their name in the record of right having ulterior motives and means and took possession of most of the good quality of land declared and cultivated by the PVTG for "Beonra" or for doing fallow plough cultivation. That cheating amounted to frustration in many a ways of their house roof repair and fence repair of their Bari land. They started their style of life in farm house in their prehistoric past to which one aspires to achieve even today by the advanced society/ commercial farm houses phenomenal in Kerals, Meerut (U.P.) and Gujarat.

Their style of shifting cultivation starting in April-May for selection of a patch of land and slashing small timber logs, under woods, bushes, creepers, etc. They used to let it to dry in the scorching sun of April, May and June upto the onset of monsoon. By the time they used to collect all the required timber logs for the self and also for sale or exchange.

But, the Promulgation of Forest Act 1952 made them bewildered by banning "Beonra" in the then South Bihar including Palamau having *Pat* region of Netarhat as well. Thus, the two PVTGs were thrown from fire to the frying pan without taking any alternative and welfare measure on this account to the affected one.

Even then the cutting of forest continued in connivance of the local people by the nefarious game of the contractors, forest officials, etc. Green lust forest vanished day by day wherefrom the two PVTG used to collect MFPs throughout the year, as if, an ultimate source.

Kothi Dhukai

Earlier the two PVTG *Asuras* and *Birjias* were doing iron smelting known as "*Kothi Dhukai*". They had good demand of their manufactured iron implements in the neighbouring areas and also outside the region. Earlier mentioned folk tale is a positive proof of their make — iron implements for hunting, harvesting, earth cutting and axing logs and underwards, etc. were very famous.

Surprise to know that near the hill stops of *Asuras*'s Ramjharia village and *Birjias*' "Naina" village inclusive of "Karmkhand" and in between all the hills are full of iron ore. The two PVTG used to mine iron ore for their smelting and smithy work. It is said that their manufactured implement last long without any rust.

They could get good quantity and quality of charcoal while clearing a patch land for their "Beonra", twin gain — one Beonra field and other coal for smelting iron as well. If more coal was required then only they could cut a thick trunk tree and burn for charcoal.

But ban on Beonra in 1952 led automatically to the stoppage of the famous cottage industry of "*Kothi Dhukai*" (Iron smelting). In due course the famous cottage industry of *Asuras* and *Birjias* vanished one by one. The author could see only in 1979 the last "*Kothi Dhukai*" by Mr. Olde Birjia of Karamkhand at the age of 80 years along with three others in the forested hills of Naina village towards Karamkhand. It was only because they could not get good quantity and quality of charcoal for their little furnace to run. Again mining iron-ore required licensing next to impossible those days.

Again Tata made iron implements floated in the market from outside giant factories who also captured the demand gradually due to easy availability.

Hence, all abandoned the *Kothi Dhubin* and only a few took over to the smithy work to cater the need of the local people.

Bauxite Mining

Pat region including hills of the area are rich in Bauxite reserve for the last 100 years right from the British era industrialists have been mining Bauxite-ore for alluminium and Hindalium indiscriminately. Bauxite is dug from 7' to 10' under the earth. Mines are open castes. Very interesting that monetization attracted the two PVTG *Asuras* and *Birjias* in majority to give their land for mining and loose cultivation through generations. Now, their top cover of land is inter mixed with broken bauxite ruble, coable and pebbles as well powdery dust leading to the stage of infertile soil solomen for years together to go long in future. It has made them disgusted to go through generations. Decades per decade passed but their land even till date does not retain fertility in spite of their several tillage and broad casting of F.Y.M.

Observation

Knowingly or unknowingly enactment of forest laws from time to time through centuries even from the British era till date above narration of facts reveals as to how vulneration to these PVTG — *Asuras* and *Birjias* has been going on every now and then. This gets reflected in their cultural dynamics to adjust and adopt to system in times to come in untired manner.

Surprising to mention that Heavy Engineering Corporation (H.E.C.), Tata Industrial Group and several other industries are wonders in invention and in many a way to benefit the people and the Nation at large but, blunder committed to keep at bay these traditional skilled iron smelter two PVTG and others like wise *Korwas*, *Agarias*, etc. This has been a Himaliyan blunder by the planner and the Government as well who did not care to consider the genius of the PVTG — *Asuras* and *Birjias* to utilize and solve their bewildered frustration at least to employee one from each family and bring them in the mainstream of the nation to march successfully along with others and prosper hand in hand (S.P. Sinha, 2006).

Several MOUs are signed but without considering the fate of the most deserving one PVTG called today. Also forest regulation earlier, drastic step of vulneration, needs to relook largely to consider the future of PVTG for their survival specially — *Asuras* and *Birjias*. Forest is, as if, their life support natural system (S.P. Sinha, 2006) developed through centuries eco-system. Now, any step taken in their case ought to be vulneration free in future to come.

REFERENCES

Prasad, Shaileshwar (1968): *Where the Three Tribes Meet.*

Roy, S.C. (1912): *Munda and their Country*, Ranchi.

Sinha, S.P. (1981): *Birjia : A Scientific Study in Cultural Ecology* (Ph.D. Thesis).

Sinha, S.P. (2006): "Asuras and Birjias A Top Pat and Below Ghat Netarhat: Study on Rights and Social Justice", *J.S.R.*, Vol. 34, No. 182 to 200.

13

Impact of Forest Based Livelihood Intervention for the Development of Sahariya Tribe

Prodyut Bhattacharya and *Swapan Kumar Kolay*

Introduction

In India, 300 million people are poor and still dependent on nature or natural resources for livelihood and income generation. Of these an estimated 100 million are forest dwellers who are primarily dependent on forest not only for meeting their multiple household needs but also for their food security. Out of 68 million tribal population of the country, 50 per cent are directly dependent on forest for their livelihood requirements like food, fodder, medicinal plants, small timber and a variety of non-timber forest produces (NTFPs) which they collect from forest.

At national level it is estimated that the value of NTFPs is nearly US $ 1 billion annually (Poffenburger, 1990). This huge and over increasing pressure resulted to initiate the present forestry sector to emphasize towards poverty alleviation and livelihood improvements. Various forest programmes have been initiated like social forestry, community forest management, joint forest management, non-timber forest produce (NTFP) development and a range of Integrated Conservation Development Projects (ICDP) including bio-diversity and livelihoods, medicinal plant conservation and cultivation, etc. — NTFPs contribute significantly in tribal and rural economy as apart from own consumption (60%) it is also sold in local market (Rao and Singh, 1996). Other estimates suggest that up to 35 per cent of income of tribal household in India comes from the collection and sale of unprocessed NTFPs (Giri, Bhattacharya and Santra, 2001).

Forest Profile of Madhya Pradesh

Madhya Pradesh has the largest forest cover amongst all the States with 95,221 sq.km. of forest cover or 31 per cent of its geographical area. This is around 12.44 per cent of the total forest cover of India. Most of the forests are under dry deciduous type that is ecologically fragile and in most cases are under extreme pressure of increase population and incidence of forest fire. Most of the north-western region of the State falls under this forest type. The population in the region is tribal dominated who is almost entirely dependent on forest for their livelihood. There is an alarming decline in the forest cover of the area due to the incidence of very high poverty and intense biotic pressure on forest resources. The dry deciduous forest of Sheopur district is rich in floral and faunal diversity. The mixed forest patches are rich in variety of trees and plant species bearing large variety of NTFPs including the medicinal and aromatic plants. It was observed that over three fourth (80%) of forest species yield commercially valuable NTFPs are traded in local market.

Undivided Madhya Pradesh is the abode of 7 Primitive Tribal Groups (PTGs) and Sahariyas is one of them who are mainly living in the districts of Morena, Sheopur, Shivpuri and Guna. There are over 300 villages in the Sheopur Forest Division. Almost all of these villages are vulnerable from the point of view of ecological stability and long term survival of threatened species.

The forests of the region are under intense biotic pressure mainly arising from cattle grazing, Illegal lopping, felling and unsustainable collection of Non-Timber Forest Products (NTFPs). Due to scanty rainfall and intense grazing by cattle herds of Gujjars the ground flora is almost absent in most of the patches.

As the resource base has diminished and the demands of the resource has increased, the environmental services, recreation and NTFP have come to be appreciated as being equal to or more important industry than industrial timber and fiber, particularly in India. Many new stakeholders, from local forest user group through to powerful international Non-Governmental Organizations (NGOs), have gained a voice in the debate. Forest management has to take stakeholders into account for political and for instrumental reasons. Indeed a main driving force in the development of community forestry has been recognition that people living in forest areas have a major influence on the ecology and that they need to be involved if management is to succeed.

In income and consumption terms, there are three main components to overall role of forests and forestry in poverty alleviation:

1. Resources are used to meet current consumption needs, as a regular part of subsistence-level livelihoods.
2. Forests are used as 'safety nets', where people draw on available resources to meet emergency shortfalls and to keep from getting worse off in times of need.
3. Forest for 'poverty reduction' in the sense number of households below the poverty line is reduced (Belcher, 2005).

In the dry tropical forests of Sheopur there is rampant destruction of NTFP bearing tree/plant species. Apart from illegal lopping and cutting of the trees, there is widespread damage to the trees/plants due to unsustainable collection/harvesting. There are two broad categories of unsustainable harvesting/collection practices of NTFPs. In first case the tree species, as in case of *Emblica officinalis*, whose fruits are collected, is damaged due large-scale lopping and felling of trees. Further the fruits collected are immature, seeds of which are not viable for further propagation. Such practices have resulted into very poor regeneration status of species in the natural forest and pose threat to their long-term survival (Bhattacharya *et al.*, 2000). The spurt in the demand for NTFPs and market forces generated by this has contributed to this to large extent. The local traders of NTFPs in the small towns have traditionally instigated the tribal collectors of NTFPs into destruction of NTFPs trees in the unhealthy competition for making the most of the resource in short-term. At present, most the NTFPs like fruits of certain trees are harvested completely from the natural forest, leaving nothing for further regeneration. Lack of awareness and training to the collectors is also a major cause. In the second category of unsustainable practices, the collection/harvesting technique adopted by the collectors is putting the species under threat. One major concern is the technique adopted for the collection of gums and resins from trees like, *Boswellia serrata, Sterculia urens* and *Anogessius latifolia* that are found in large patch in the forest of this region. Due to faulty tapping technique employed, there are large number of deaths of such trees in the natural forest due to permanent damage to tree trunks. Since regeneration of such species takes a long time in natural forest, there is alarming reduction in the tree cover of these species.

High anthropogenic pressure due to over-grazing is another pressing concern in this area. Nearly 95 per cent of the nearly 0.4 million cattle of Sheopur graze in open forest. There is almost complete absence of stall-feeding and grazing lots are also non-existent. Hence, for the Gujjar community the forest is open access resource where they can leave their cattle for forage without any outside control. An estimated 1.5 times cattle graze in Sheopur forest compared to its carrying capacity (Pant, 2000). Ecologically, this has been a disaster. Rampant incidents of lopping, pruning and illegal felling are common place. Major species like *Ghot, Kardhai, Ber* and *Khair* are worst hit by unrestricted lopping. Degradation of local forest has dealt a body blow to the livelihood and income generation of tribals. For gathering common forest products they have to work harder and travel farther. Seasonal time span for the availability of common NTFPs like *Anola* has shrunk from month availability in forest a decade back to a week in recent times.

In recent times inter-community resource use conflict has also resulted into large-scale destruction of forest. The local cattle rearing community of Gujjars allegedly are responsible for much of the illegal lopping and cutting of forest for collection of fodder. The cutting of *Mahua* trees, which is venerable to the tribals, by the Gujjars has further strained the social relations between Sahariya and Gujjars. To deprive the Gujjars from fodder, the Sahariya put local forest on fire, resulting in large area of forest destroyed in fire every year. To overcome these problems, International Centre for Community Forestry (ICCF) implemented some developmental activity which was supported by Ministry of tribal Affairs, Government of India. The following objectives of these developmental activities are given below:

1. To explore and promote participatory village level NTFP based income-generating activities.
2. To promote and develop community initiated sustainable management of NTFPs with key emphasis on sustainable collection/harvesting regime through awareness generation.
3. To promote skill and capacity development through imparting training to NTFPs collectors.
4. To develop local level institutions for effective marketing of NTFPs so those optimums benefits are accrued to the collectors with the use of techniques like Management Information System.
5. To explore the scope of linking Joint Forest Management (JFM) activities for better NTFP management.
6. To study the impact assessment of various activities.

Methodology

Basic information on occupation structures, caste, and income, asset ownership was collected through census survey that covered all households in Sheopur district. A total of 310 household were chosen for more intensive study. Sample sizes for the villagers varied from 40-80 households, depending on the size of the villages and were selected through stratified random sampling. In addition to this, qualitative data were also collected from Sheopur Forest Division and various Forest Range offices, key informants at the village level and poor households across all locations. Focus Group Discussion (FGDs) was used as a tool to understand structures of power and patronage as well as exclusionary process and how these impacted on beneficiary selection.

Three quantitative surveys were conducted. The first was a census where every household was covered. The questionnaire was pre-tested, revised and translated. It was designed to collect basic information on demographic, occupation structure, income, assets and access to pro-poor programmes.

Next, a seasonal survey was conducted on for NTFP availability. The size of the sample was 40-80 households depending on the size and variability of the population and the sample was selected by stratifying the population based on the census data. Proportionately more households were selected from the category of the landless poor to ensure that diversity within poor groups was captured.

Study Area

The project was implemented in the Sheopur Forest Division of Madhya Pradesh. This area is bound by river Chambal and district Morena in north and Rajasthan in south, river Chambal and Parvati form the western boundary and block Pohri, which is 35 km. from Shivpuri forms its eastern boundary. The topography of the area is flat with slight undulations. The project site is located at 25°20' and 26°15' north latitude and 76°30' and 77°39' E longitude in the Sheopur district which is situated in the north-western part of the State of Madhya Pradesh bordering states of Rajasthan and Uttar Pradesh. It is located at a height of 238-498 m above sea level. The average annual temperature on the region is 24.73 °C and average annual rainfall is 764 mm.

The field work carried out in 5 villages namely — (i) Goras, (ii) Sesaipura, (iii) Richi, (iv) Ameth, and (v) Panwara of Sheopur district, Madhya Pradesh (Table 13.1).

Socio-economic Profile

As per 2001 census the total tribal population of the state is 1,22,33,474 which is 20.27 per cent population of the state. India has 74 primitive tribal groups and 7 of them live in undivided Madhya Pradesh. The District of Sheopur, on the north-western border of M.P. is one such area where primitive tribal group "Sahariyas" forms the major population. The Sahariyas are mainly found in the Morena, Sheopur, Shivpuri and Guna district of Madhya Pradesh. Their usual food mainly consists of lesser millets and coarse cereals. Their economic condition is appalling. They have hardly any land of their own. They are virtually purchased as agricultural laborers at very nominal prices by landowners.

Table 13.1: Study Villages with Surveyed Household

State	*District*	*Block*	*Village*	*Surveyed Household*
Madhya Pradesh	Sheopur	Karhal	Goras	80
			Sesaipura	55
			Richi	70
			Ameth	40
			Panwara	65
			Total	**310**

Source: Field Data.

Another important element in the local demographic composition is the Gujjars, the cattle rearing community, which migrated to this district 4-5 decades ago from Rajasthan. Total population of the District is 5,59,715 with the growth rate of population from 2001 baseline being 3.33 per cent. For the whole district the tribal population is 21.53 per cent of the total, scheduled castes are 16.16 per cent and rest 62.31 per cent are others. Interesting aspect to note here is the significantly high population of tribal in villages adjoining forest area. Survey done by the local Forest Department indicates over 40 per cent of population in the radius of 5 km from forest is those of tribals reinforcing the traditional belief of tribals being closer to the forest. In fact Sahariyas are found mostly in villages within the forest or those very close to it. An estimated 3 out of 10 person in Sheopur subsists on annual income less than ₹ 5,000-6,000 and only 14 per cent have income level above ₹ 2,000. Villages deep inside the forest are deprived of basic facilities like health care, education, roads and potable water.

Tribal Community in Sheopur is heavily dependent on NTFP generated income as they lack agricultural land and other traditional means of livelihood. In many cases the benefits from the NTFPs are accrued not only to the collectors, but also to the primary processors who often live in the adjoining rural areas. NTFPs also serve as the source of food security to vast population who is squeezed out of forest and have little land for cultivation.

However, at the local level the NTFPs play a crucial role in providing livelihood support to the forest dependent people mainly the tribals. Fuel wood, small timber, medicine, fodder, etc. are traditionally extracted from the forest. Apart from this, NTFP collection/harvesting is also a source of income to the local community. An estimated 80 per cent of the tree/plant species in the forest bear NTFPs of commercial importance. Approximately 90 different types of NTFPs are traded in the local market. Some of the important and highly valued NTFPs with their seasonal collection pattern are listed in Table 13.2.

Table 13.2: Important NTFPs of Sheopur and their Parts Used

Sl. No.	*NTFP (Local Name)*	*Botanical Name*	*Part(s) Used*
1.	*Aonla*	*Embellica officinalis*	Fruit
2.	*Shatawar*	*Asparagus racemosus*	Root/tuber
3.	*Bel Guda*	*Aegle marmelos*	Fruit pulp
4.	*Baheda Sabut*	*Teminallia bellerica*	Fruit
5.	*Baheda Bakli*	*Teminallia bellerica*	Bark
6.	*Shankhpushpi*	*Convoluvlose pluricolis*	Whole part, Leaves
7.	*Hansraj*	*Adiatum lunulatum*	Whole plant
8.	*Patol Patra*	*Trichosanthes cucumerina*	Whole plant, leaves and root
9.	*Kankol Mirch*	*Piper cubeba*	Fruits
10.	*Shivlingi*	*Diplocyclos palmatus*	Leaves, roots and seed
11.	*Malkangani*	*Celestus peniculata*	Seed
12.	*Amaltash Phali & Guda*	*Casia fistula*	Fruits and Fruit pulp respectively
13.	*Mugdha Parni*	*Centella asiatica*	Whole plant and leaves
14.	*Balaa Khareta*	*Sida cordifolia*	Whole plant, roots, seeds and leaves
15.	*Kamal Phul*	*Mallotus phillppinensis*	Fruits, flowers
16.	*Gurmar*	*Gymnema sylvestre*	Roots and leaves
17.	*Ber*	*Zizyphus mauritiana*	Fruit and leaves
18.	*Nagarmotha*	*Cyperus rotundus*	Tuber
19.	*Chitraka Mul*	*Plumbago zeylanica*	Root and Bark
20.	*Indirajau*	*Wrightia tinctoria*	Root, leaves, bark and seeds
21.	*Palash Phul*	*Butea monosperma*	Flower
22.	*Varahikand*	*Takka asperarox*	Tuber
23.	*Mahua Phul and Gulli*	*Madhuca indica*	Flower and Fruits respectively
24.	*Samhalu*	*Vaitex nigandu*	Seed
25.	*Neem Gilo*	*Azadirachta indica*	Fruits
26.	*Anantmul Kaladeshi*	*Hemidesmus indicum*	Root
27.	*Harsinghar*	*Nyctanthes arbotristis*	Seed
28.	*Khair*	*Acacia catechu*	Seed and Gum
29.	*Kullu*	*Steculia urens*	Gum
30.	*Dhawra*	*Anogessius latifolia*	Gum
31.	*Salai Chid and Dana*	*Boswellia serrata*	Oleo-resin and Seed
32.	*Tendu Patta*	*Dyosporus melanoxylon*	Leaves

Source: Field Survey, Primary Data.

Sheopur is a veritable showcase of large number of NTFPs, and an estimated 150-165 tons of which is collected annually from the forest. For almost whole the year round, over 300 villages in the district are vibrant with activities related to collection/harvesting and processing of NTFPs or making preparatory survey of the forest in advance of collection season. The scale of activities may vary in intensity and spread over the year depending on availability of NTFPs. NTFPs like *Salai Gum, Aonla, Baheda, Satawar* and *Tendu Patta* are most important from commercial point of view. *Salai* gum collection contributes maximum to the local economy. Over the year the importance of *Salai* gum in the household economy has prompted local tribals to evolve indigenous system of tenure right on *Salai* tree to prevent any chances of conflict. In this system, the tribals have distributed the *Boswellia* trees in the forest among themselves on permanent basis for collection of gum. In the local forest *Nyctanthes arbor-tristis*, a weed grows extensively. The stem of this weed is utilized for manufacturing baskets on a large-scale, which is then sold in the local market. In overall terms the NTFPs provides exclusive source of employment to the tribals for at least 8 months of the year and only about 1-2 month time the tribals are engaged in agriculture related activities. In terms of economic contribution, average estimated household income from NTFPs is about ₹ 15,000 (about US $300) for a year. In comparison average annual income from agriculture-related activities and other economic activities for a household is only ₹ 6,400 (Bhattacharya and Hayat, 2003). Destruction of NTFPs species is mostly due to unsustainable harvesting of NTFPs prompted by unbridled commercialization of NTFPs. The key issues are thus awareness generation among the stakeholders and developing an institutional support to address issues/problems related to sustainable management and utilization NTFPs.

Looking the whole picture of the tribal dependency on NTFPs for their livelihood it is crucial to establish NTFP based micro-enterprise at village level to get better return from the NTFPs being collected in the area. To develop micro-enterprise, necessary input like capacity building, local level institutional infrastructure, development of marketing linkages and mechanization of processing of NTFPs are required to be introduced which will play key role in the development of the Sahariya community of the Project area.

Different Developmental Activities Conducted for Sahariyas

A series of activities were adopted beginning from selection of site, resource identification, training, assessment of available non-timber forest products in the local forest area, the possibility of value addition for their marketability and also the potential marketing channel for the end products.

Socio-economic Survey

For the project implementation site selection was made based on socio-economic survey in consultation with local forest department, villagers and traders. Several parameters were kept in the mind such as Sahariya population, quantity of NTFPs being collected, accessibility to the villages and networking among the adjoining villages for the huge collection and processing of NTFPs. Based on above parameters and base line socio-economic survey six villages namely Goras, Sesaipura, Ameth, Panwada and Richi were found suitable for the implementation of the project. The general information of the villages is shown in Table 13.3.

Table 13.3: Village-wise General Information

Name	*Name of the Village*				
	Goras	*Sesaipura*	*Richi*	*Ameth*	*Panwara*
Panchayat	Goras	Sesaipura	Richi	Ameth	Panwara
Sarpanch	Hari Singh	Kashi Ram	Soram adi	Mannu Adi	Usha Adi
President of Van Samiti	Bodi Ram Gurjar	Rajendra Gupta (Trader of NTFPs)	Mahendra Pratap Singh Chouhan	Gobind Singh Yadav	Pahalwan Singh Yadav
Forest Range	Goras	Sesaipura	Karhal	Moravan	Karhal
Forest Sub-range	Goras	Sesaipura	Goras	Sesaipura	Karhal
Forest Beat	Goras	Sesaipura	Richi East	Ameth	Panwara
No. of Hemlets	10	3	4	2	3
No. of Tribal Household	321	143	318	136	150
Tribal Population	1,605	695	1,520	680	612
Source of Water	Hand Pump–5, Sheep river and 1 bore	Hand Pump–4, Bore–1	Hand Pump–2, Well–1, Pond–1, Kalari river and 1 bore	Hand Pump–4, Bore–1	Hand Pump–8, Pond–1, Well–1
School	Primary and Middle School	Primary, Middle and H.S. School	Primary School	Primary, Middle and H.S. School	Primary, Middle and H.S. School
Hospital	PHC	PHC	PHC, Goras	PHC	PHC
Electricity	Yes	Yes	Yes	Yes	Yes

Source: Field Survey Data, ICCF, IIFM, Bhopal.

Identification of Potential Resources

After Selection of villages on the above criteria the village resources were identified in order to develop NTFP based micro-enterprises. The resource available were skilled manpower, availability of electricity, suitable cottage/working place, continuous availability of the sufficient quantity of NTFPs at the village and knowledge of local folk medicine system is desirable for the purpose. Based on the analysis of various sources of income (Table 13.4) at Sesaipura and Goras villages have been installation of mini-pulveriser.

Table 13.4: Various Source of Income (%) in the Selected Villages

Sl.No.	*Name of Villages*	*Source of Income*		
		Agriculture	*Labour*	*NTFP*
1.	Goras	14	32	54
2.	Sesaipura	9	30	61
3.	Ameth	16	38	46
4.	Richi	7	42	51
5.	Panwada	13	38	49

Source: Field Survey Data, ICCF, IIFM, Bhopal.

Assessment/Quantification of Available NTFPs

For assessment of the NTFPs of the project site primary data was derived from regular visit and meetings with the cross-section of local communities by conducting village PRA exercise, questionnaire and vegetation survey method (Table 13.5). It is estimated that nearly 10-15 tone of NTFPs (*Bel*, *Anola*, *Satawar*, etc.) is being collected by the villagers. Also secondary data was generated through literature review visit to local forest department offices, revenue department, Sahariya Vikas Pradhikaran office to assess the quantum of NTFP production of the area.

This can be utilized for the processing in the pulveriser and for further value addition. The networking with the near by villages can be established for the collection of greater quantities if needed.

Provisions for Income Generation Activities

Value addition and processing of NTFP play a vital role in ensuring higher returns to the collectors. The process of value addition can be applied from the stage of collection by adopting appropriate timings for individual NTFP, which will yield higher returns. After collection, grading of products based on size, quality, colour and stage of maturity also influences the product price. These products can be sold raw or after primary level processing like grinding, drying, de-seeding or de-pulping which can yield further higher returns.

Table 13.5: Estimated Production of NTFP in Sheopur: Quantity and Economic Contribution

Sl. No.	*NTFP*	*Estimated Production (Quintals)/ No.*	*Estimated Value (₹ lakh/ US $)*	*Estimated Household Income (₹/US $)*	*Average Collection/ Manufacturing Period (Days)*
1.	*Aonla*	500	10.00/2000	2200/44	20
2.	*Baheda*	450	0.90/1800	600/12	10
3.	*Bael*	200	1.20/2400	960/19.2	30
4.	*Marodphali*	35	0.14/280	500/10	45
5.	*Malkangani*	25	1.00/2000	450/9	60
6.	*Satavar*	50	0.75/1500	1200/24	35
7.	*Mahua* Flower	250	2.25/45000	800/16	30
8.	*Mahua* Fruits	220	0.55/1100	600/12	45
9.	Honey*	225	5.60/11200	500/10	30
10.	*Salai* Gum	5302	159.06/319200	4500/90	120
11.	*Tendu Patta*	18340.83	167.71	1200/24	14
12.	Basket Making* (No.)	12000	0.36	1100	50

*Collected in select areas only

Source: Field Survey Data from traders of Karhal Town, ICCF, IIFM, Bhopal.

Capacity Building

Since it is well accepted that capacity building operates as catalyst of change at various scales, number of training programmes, exposure visits and mass awareness campaign were conducted under the project for the local communities. Some of the activities were envisaged to enable the local community to envision, plan and implement actions in forest management relevant to generating and sharing benefits from forests:

(a) Training of Stakeholders on Business Skill

For sustainable and smooth functioning of pulveriser machine, processing and selling of materials, training were imparted to the villager from time to time. In order to institutionalize the whole process, one village level committee was formed for the maintenance of pulveriser and monitoring purchasing and sale of raw and processed materials by keeping record in the register.

(b) Training of Stakeholders on Sustainable Harvesting of NTFPs

(i) *Scientific Satawar Harvesting*

Satawar is one of the important and prized plants for Sahariya community. The tuberous roots of *Satawar* is collected from the forest and sold in the local market. The local community practices unsustainable harvesting of tuberous roots of *Asparagus*, which is the chief cause of depletion of the plant population in the forest. To check this, unsustainable and destructive harvesting of *Asparagus* few training were imparted to the community members. Traditional collectors were trained on the scientific aspect of its collection. The main focus on the training was on the fact that care should be taken to replace the dug out soil on the rhizome and at least 5 per cent of the tubers should be left with the rhizome for fast recovery of the plants and for renewed yield.

(ii) *Sustainable Kullu Gum Harvesting*

Kullu gum is harvested from the *Sterculia urense* (*Kullu*) tree. It is the second major source of income of *Sahariya* community. This is a very slow growing species, which takes nearly 20-25 years to maturity and for gum oozing. The gum collection practice adopted for by the *Sahariya* severely damages the tree due to uncontrolled harvest by deep incisions made on the trunk. As a consequence within a few years the tree dies of severe cut and wounds. To check the population of fast dying trees, villagers were trained of scientific harvesting method of *kullu* gum for sustainable yield.

(iii) *Scientific Harvesting of Forest Honey*

Nearly 100-150 quintals of honey is harvested from the forests of Sheopur. Mainly rock bee (*Apis dorsata*) is found in this region. Although honey harvesting/collection is a very old practice of *Sahariya*, but the technique used by them is very unsafe and destructive in nature which not only affects the quality of honey but also the bee and hive population. *Sahariya* tribal people used to squeeze honeycomb for separation of honey, which also contains eggs, pollens, wax and other impurities in it. Therefore the villagers were trained for safe and scientific method of honey collection along with the existing honey hunter group. In this method only the honey-containing portion of the beehive is cut apart instead of removing the entire hive thus minimizing the chances of impurities and loss of the bee population. Thereafter, the honey is extracted by using centrifugal machine. They were also provided with special kits and equipment including sting-proof dresses.

(iv) *Training on Sustainable Harvesting of Aonla and Bel*

Series of training were imparted to the villagers on sustainable harvesting of various NTFPs like *bel*, *anola*, etc. Earlier the villagers used very crude and destructive method of collection whereby they were causing severe lopping and trimming of the fruit bearing branches of the tree. In some cases even entire tree was felled to grab the harvest. All these resulted into reduced harvest next year and so on. Hence, they were trained for sustainable harvest of the crop and made to understand the need of preserving the tree for their future progeny. Also some street plays and cultural activities were performed to make them understand the need of conservation of forest and forest produce.

(c) Training on Processing of NTFP at CSV, Wardha

In order to set-up village level NTFP based micro-enterprise for the processing and value addition of various NTFPs 10 villagers were trained at Centre for Science of Villages, Wardha. They were trained for processing of *Aonla, Bel, Harra, Bahera* and *Satavar* during the training for its primary processing as well as value added products like *Aonla Murabba, Aonla Pachak, Bel Murabba, Triphala Churna, Satavari Kalp*.

(d) Mass Awareness Campaign

For sensitizing the NTFP collectors to stop destructive harvesting of NTFPs and overcome from the exploitative marketing a mass awareness campaign through *Kala-Jatha* (art performing group) was organized in the selected village. In this context 10 days workshop was conducted at the Karhal range for presenting *Kala-Jatha's* activities covering folk songs and plays related to the campaign. This *kala-Jatha* was used for organizing the whole campaign. Two plays and five songs related to conserving forest based produce and their values towards the livelihood of dependent population were highlighted. Posters and pamphlets were also distributed amongst the villages. Apart from the mass campaign time to time focus group discussion and meeting were also conducted at the villages to maintain sensitization towards the harmful and destructive practices.

(e) Development of Marketing Network

Processed material can be sold to local as well as distant market. Marketing linkages are to be developed by contacting traders, medicine man, pharmaceutical companies, Government departments (MPMFP Federation, Khadi Gram Udyog Kendra), etc. To develop marketing skills amongst salesman, training on marketing strategies may be organized at the villages.

One NTFP based outlet is also proposed to be opened at the Forest range office, Karhal to publicize and sale the product in collaboration with local forest department. In order to sale the processed NTFPs generated by village institutions, distant marketing linkages have been identified and established. In this connection a tour was made to the Nursingpur forest division for having an exposure on processing of NTFPs for development of micro-enterprise. A tour was also conducted to MFP Federation for tying up marketing linkages between the rural institutions formed at village to the federation's outlet for selling the processed NTFPs. The Federation promoted the proposed marketing system against the 10 per cent commission over the total sale.

(f) Formation of Self-Help Group (SHG)

The community being a an under privileged and backward one has hardly any organized effort to collect and utilize its available means of resources. Therefore, few self-help groups were formed to promote them for various types of income generating activities and developmental activities (Table 13.6). This would also be helpful for them to obtain institutional status as well as financial support in the form of help or loan for further strengthening.

Table 13.6: List of SHGs Formed at Village for NTFPs Related Activities

Sl. No.	*Name of Village*	*Name of SHG*	*Name of President*	*Amount Per Month Deposit*
1.	Goras	Shri Savai Bhoj	Mr. Nanda	120
2.	Sesaipura	Shri Ganesh	Mr. Murarilal	140
3.	Ameth	Shri Ram	Mr. Hari Ram	120
4.	Richi	Jay Durga	Mrs. Banti Bai	110
5.	Panwada	Mahila Shakti	Mrs. Kanya Bai	150

Source: Field Survey Data, ICCF, IIFM, Bhopal.

(g) Micro-credit Disbursement

To start the NTFPs based micro-enterprise, disbursement of micro-credit as seed money for the purchasing raw materials and for further processing was considered to be crucial at the beginning. This credit may be taken back or given to other village to replicate after Independent, stable and profitable running of pulveriser in previous village. The details of micro-credits are given in the Tables 13.7 and 13.8.

Table 13.7: List of Samiti Formed in the Village for the Micro-enterprise Development

Sl.No.	*Name of Village*	*Name of Samiti*	*Name of President*
1.	Goras	Lagu Van Upaj Prasanskran Samiti	Chunnilal Patel
2.	Sesaipura	Lagu Van Upaj Prasanskran Samiti	Ramji Lal

Source: Field Survey Data, ICCF, IIFM, Bhopal.

Table 13.8: Details of Micro Credit Disbursed

Sl. No.	*Name of Village*	*Micro-Credit Received*	*Time of Receiving Micro-Credit*	*Forms of Returning Micro-Credit (in %)*		
				Labour	*NTFP*	*Agriculture*
1.	Goras	₹ 800	Rainy season	10	60	30
2.	Sesaipura	₹ 1000	-do-	8	64	28

Source: Field Survey Data, ICCF, IIFM, Bhopal.

Establishment of Community Boiler

The traditional practice of boiling of NTFPs like *bel* and *anola* in the age old home made *chulhas* was not only time consuming and hazardous to the health and hygiene of the local tribals, but it also resulted into huge loss of forest biomass being used as fuel by individual at their houses. Considering the loss of time, energy and resources it was decided to install a community boiler for boiling of NTFPs. It required less energy, fuel and effort of the person operating it and at the same time allowed quicker and safer mode of processing of NTFP saving their time and energy. Thus, the villagers were allowed with more time to be utilized in other income generating activities or protection of forest resources.

Establishment of Mini-pulveriser

Through detailed discussion to the stakeholder three-phase electric operated mini-pulveriser with the capacity of grinding 7-10 kg. NTFP per hour in two villages namely — (1) Sesaipura, and (2) Goras. Along with this pulveriser one electrically operated packaging machine was also provided for the packaging of powdered materials. The pulvilizer was used for grinding of NTFPs, viz. 1. *Asparagus*, 2. *Bel*-pulp, 3. *Trifhala (Anola, Harra* and *Behera)*, 4. *Arjun*-bark and several other medicinal leaves like *kalmegh,* vitex negundo, etc.

The pulverizer has contributed in the enhancement of the rate of same product in raw form they used to sell at throughaway price to tradetrs. This has increased the income generation about 200-300 as compared to raw selling which was prevailing in the whole area.

Two full time trained workers were provided for operating this pulveriser and packaging machine. Efforts are also made to orient selected youths from intervention village to market their products at the local as well as distant markets. Opportunities were provided to attend with their product at *Van mela* during last 7 years; through this exercise they got first hand exposure of direct marketing of their finish product in urban market. This is a common facility created from the project which could be of use for the local people of the village as well as other adjoining communities.

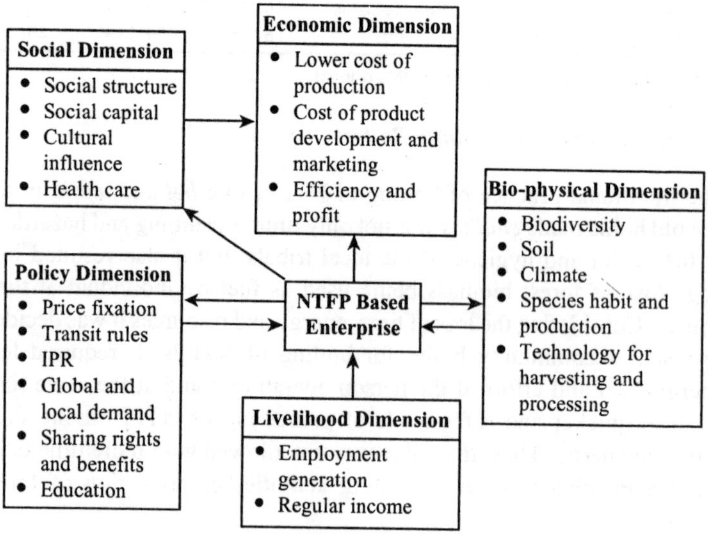

Figure 13.1: Model for Integrated NTFP based Enterprise Development

Development of Marketing Network

The strengthening of stakeholders' capability to produce bulk of NTFPs processed or semi-processed with the help of community boiler and pulveriser created the need for marketing network outside the village. Earlier the community people were selling the raw materials as a distress

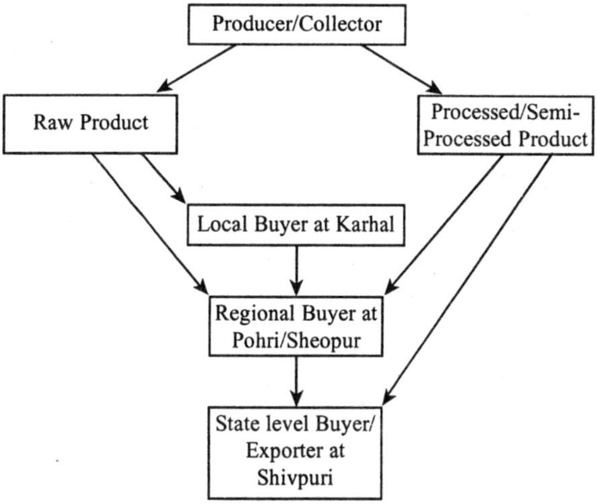

Figure 13.2: Possible Marketing Network of Local NTFPs to Generate More Income at Collector Level

selling in the grip of handful of middlemen. But with introduction of micro-credit concept from the project activity it was possible to make them look for outside market. Therefore, a chain of seller-buyer link was made with grassroots level collector to processor and then buyer.

Impact Analysis

Positive Impact

It must be emphasized that one reason for the success of this project was its participatory nature. Discussions and interactions were always held to find out what are the people's priorities they were encouraged to make their own decisions. Further, no free dole was given; instead, the people were motivated to work towards their chosen alternatives and pursue livelihood opportunities on their own steam for which assistance was provided. This helped them become stakeholders in their chosen alternate livelihood. Impacts of the projects are many folds, which are narrated in the following section.

Livelihood Generation

A list of alternative income generation activities taken up by the villagers which has brought changes in the project villages. Some specific instances of the changes that have come into the villagers' lives are outlined below:

- *Building Trust and Confidence* — The project has secured the trust of the local people and built their confidence, so that, they are able to take charge of the creation, planning, development and implementation of their villages' micro-plans.
- *Creation of a Bond* — A collaborative social bond has been forged between the Forest Department, and participating villages to sustainable scientific harvesting of NTFPs and improve the grassroots economy.

The following are examples of how the project has benefited the villagers which in turn has make their understanding on Forest resources positively. The attitudes to reduce/abandon their erstwhile exploitation and degradation activities:

(a) There has been a direct resource dependency in more than 6 forests-dependents in the villages. The unsustainable NTFPs collectors who were dependent on the forest for livelihood have adapted to scientific harvesting technique unsustainable harvesting in general reduced by 50 per cent in the project villages through protection and strict vigil by Forest Protection Committee (FPC).

(b) Villagers have taken up plantation rising in some areas resulting in NTFPs production for sale.

(c) Grazing incidence within project intervention and adjoining villages has been reduced by more than 50 per cent mainly in the plantation areas due to awareness and vigil of protection by FPC.

In other instances, owners of cattle sold them and purchased NTFPs through SHGs loans. In Goras and Sesaipura villages, after the formation of a FPC, fire incidence in the adjoining forest has been reduced by 80 per cent, grazing incidence reduced by 55 per cent, fuel wood collection reduced by 40 per cent which has appeared in the questionnaire survey asked to the local villagers in project area.

Table 13.9 shows the success of the project in achieving its ultimate goal of sustainable management and cultivation of valuable plants increased. Before the formation of FPC, no. of NTFP collectors followed traditional methods of collections in different villages in the entire target area was 267. This was increased to 933 after the project was implemented; recording a total percentage drop of 50 per cent a very high increased indicating a high success rate.

Table 13.9: Village-wise Data Among the Sahariya Households on Scientific Harvesting Efforts of NTFPs Before and After FPC Formation and Project Implementation

Sl. No.	*Name of the Village*	*No. of NTFP Collectors followed Traditional Methods of Collections in Different Village*	*No. of NTFP Collector followed Improved Technique after FPC in Different Villages*
1.	Goras	70	258
2.	Sesaipura	66	129
3.	Ameth	46	145
4.	Richi	38	185
5.	Panwada	47	216
	Total	**267**	**933**

Source: Primary Survey Data.

(d) In Goras and Sesaipura, a NTFP processing-*cum*-Herbal Clinic was built with the help of an initial investment from the project as well as peoples' contribution for different activities help the all villagers.

(e) Out of the assistance of some amount will be allotted for alternative income generation activities through the SHGs, after successful recovery of loan would be enabled the FPCs to provide assistance, setting in motion a different Village Level Committee (VLC) revolving fund mechanism.

(f) Greater awareness has been created among all the target villages on the need. It has contributed sustainable harvesting of NTFPs, value addition, processing, nursery raising marketing and other income generating activity.

(g) Mass awareness generation campaign *Kalla Jatha-rally* was organized jointly by the team and the villagers. This brought harmony and understanding in the minds of the local people thereby effectively propagating the conservation message. Due to the tremendous awareness generation capacity of the rally, Forest Department officials feel inclined to continue the programme every year so that the message will spread in a continuous on-going process.

Developing a Positive Attitude and Awareness

The sustainable harvesting and management of NTFP, approaches firmly established, the villagers now identify and dedicate themselves to the cause of conservation and have formed a positive bond with the different range official at Sheopur Forest Division.

By providing the villagers with more efficient cooking equipment, alternate sources of, income and biomass production as well as the capacity to access such alternatives (through the SHG loan scheme), the project has weaned the villagers away from the forest. Cattle have been disposed of, timely harvesting of NTFP have been greatly increased and as a result of which, the forest has begun to regenerate and recuperate. It is clear, therefore, the ultimate goal of the project-intervention villages is slowly but surely becoming an attainable reality.

It is also noteworthy that these villagers (members of FPCs), have come to realize the importance of the forest and are, in consequence, protecting it by preventing others from grazing/felling as well as informing the Forest Department about instances of gave violation, a clear case of the establishment of 'social fences'. The result of the project gives an opportunity to test a new tool and means for forest protection. It gives a lot of satisfaction.

The activity has been able to bring to an end the hostilities of traditional adversaries for the Forest Department and the local people.

The following are the outline of impacts of the intervention:

(a) It helped in reducing the present exploitative marketing of NTFPs prevailing in area by providing them marketing linkages and marketing them self-sufficient through introduction of the concept of micro-credit.

(b) Community has checked or stopped the present destructive harvesting of NTFPs by adopting scientific method of harvesting.

(c) Forest Protection Committee is now able to manage the whole activities related to micro-enterprise starting from collection to selling.

(d) Economic return from the NTFPs collected have increased by two ways:

- Direct marketing from village to distant market by avoiding middlemen.
- Processing of raw NTFPs items before selling to the traders.

(e) Using the institutional infrastructure for controlling destructive harvesting has reduced NTFPs depletion from the forest due to unscientific and burgeoning exploitation.

(f) It may control the minimum price of NTFPs at the local market by developing networking amongst the village to village committees.

Conclusion and Recommendations

Hundreds of villages in the remote and backward areas of Madhya Pradesh depend on the forest as a resource for livelihood and income generation. However, the NTFPs resources in the forest are affected by several means. Commercialization of many NTFP species which were hitherto collected for household and subsistance purpose led to unsustainable harvesting regime which is threatening the long term availability of many products. The commercialization of several medicinal, dye and industrial gum products have severely impacted the production quality and the overall rural economy in tribal area. Still in Sheopur district there is lot of potential to strengthen tribal economy by small interventions in these tribal pockets. These interventions should be with local resources. In this regard following aspects has to be incorporated for forest based livelihood intervention:

- Village level procurement centre need to be developed which should have linkages with MFP primary cooperative society.
- At village level NTFP collectors group, SHG may be developed which need to be linked with nationalized/cooperative bank for providing micro-credit support to establish village/cluster level processing units/micro-enterprise.
- There is an urgent need for district level coordination with FD, revenue department, agriculture, *panchayat*, financial institution to develop a district level plan, with the leadership of *Sahariya Vikash Pradhikaran* (Sahariya Development Authority) for forest based income generation activities.
- Large scale village level/household level nursery development activities need to be promoted for NTFP species for sustainable supply of these products for future generation.
- There are several important products which are collected by the tribal in bulk need to be harvested sustainable, various training programme, skill development programme needs to be organized throughout the year in these tribal pocket.

To integrate the tribals alienated from traditional practices of forest conservation, it is essential to strengthen the tribal institutions which are many instances. Market reform is key to ensuring remunerative return to collectors and making them empowered for forest conservation. The recent changes made by the policy-makers related to transit pass and its relation to sustainable harvesting of NTFPs also had limited impact due to extreme poverty of the Sahariya and very low literacy level and the fact that it failed to address entire chain of issues, mainly the market reforms. Recently, the Forest department and Indian Institute of Forest Management (IIFM), Bhopal has initiated several programmes for management of NTFPs which has yielded positive results even these efforts could be further linked with Prime Ministers proposal of 100 days employment in rural areas. It can certainly contribute to India's commitments to Millennium Development Goals (MDG) which is still a long way to go. The potential of NTFPs in poverty alleviation is enormous and can assist in all the 8 MDGs (Kaushal and Melkani, 2005). Through this project, IIFM was able to convince the policy-makers, forest department, traders, communities, NGOs and academic institutions at local, national and international level that sustainable harvesting of NTFP with value addition and micro-credit are the effective means to meet the livelihoods objective as well as conservation objectives.

So, from the above discussion it is clear that the effort of IIFM needs to be strengthened through continuous campaigning, capacity building training, micro-credit support and micro-enterprise to achieve the 100 per cent poverty reduction in terms of number of household above poverty line and a healthy and productive forest.

Acknowledgement: We extend our thanks to Ministry of Tribal Affairs, Government of India, New Delhi for the financial assistance of this research project.

REFERENCES

Anon (1998): *Plan Sheopur Forest Division*, Forest Department, Madhya Pradesh.

Bahuguna, V.K. (2000): "Forests in the Economy of the Rural Poor: An Estimation of the Dependency Level", *Ambio*, 29(3): 126-129.

Bechler, B.M. (2005): "Forest Product Markets, Forest and Poverty Reduction", *International Forestry Review*, Vol. 7 (2).

Bhattacharya, P. and S.F. Hayat (2003): "Issues in Sustainable Management of NTFPs for Livelihood Generation of Tribals: A Case from Sheopur District of Madhya Pradesh, India", paper presented at the National Workshop on *Non-wood Forest Products — New Mechanisms and Strategies*, held by Government of India in New Delhi between 29-30 May, 2003.

Bhattacharya, P., S.K. Kolay and N.K. Bhagat (2006): *Science and Technology Application for Enhancement of Rural Livelihood: Community Based Sustainable Management and Cultivation of Shatawar (Asparagus racemosus) in Chambal Ravine of Sheopur District of Madhya Pradesh*, DST-Final Report (Unpublished).

Champion and Seth (1969): *Forest Types of India*, Government of India.

Giri, T.K., P. Bhattacharya and S.C. Santra (2001): "Ecology and Economy of Non-Timber Forest Product in Village Life — A Case from Bankura District in West Bengal", *Annals of Forestry*, Vol. 9, No. 1, pp. 2.

Gutman, P. (2001): *Forest Conservation and the Rural Poor: A Call to Broden the Conservation Agenda*, WWF Macroeconomics for Sustainable Development Programme Office, Washington, D.C.

Kaushal, K.K. and V.K. Melkani (2005): "India: Achieving Millennium Development Goals through Non-timber Forest Products", *International Forestry Review*, Vol. 7 (92).

Proffenberge, M. (1990): *Wasteland News*, Aug.-Oct. (1997), pp. 46-55.

Roa, A.R. and B.P. Singh (1996): "Non-wood Forest Products Contribution in Tribal Economy", *Indian Forester* (April).

Shrivastav, V.K. (2003): *Tribal Scenario of Madhya Pradesh and Chhattisgarh*, Bhopal: Sharon Publications.

Working Plan (2000): Sheopur Forest Department, Madhya Pradesh.

14

Toto, the Born of the Mountain in Jalpaiguri District: Some Problems Highlighted as PVTG

Sajal Samadder

Introduction

An isolated village, located in the western part of *Dooars* (70 kilometer from Siliguri), tucked away in a far corner of Madarihat block of Jalpaiguri district of West Bengal in India is known as Totopara. The village, right at the foot-hills of the Bhutan Himalayan range, is once the sole habitat of the Totos, the Particularly Vulnerable Tribal Groups (PVTGs) of West Bengal. The Totos came to reside at this particular geographical location at least 10 generations ago, though there is no historical record available as to exactly when their ancestors came to this *mouza*. But every Toto share a peculiar belief, that if they leave Totopara, and venture to settle somewhere down in the plains, they won't survive a single month. They are strictly orthodox as far as faith and ritualistic gestures are concerned, and not inclined to go out of their village and seek for a better living elsewhere. The nearest railway station, Hashimara, is some 16 kms. away. Madarihat, the nearest police station and an important trading centre is 32 kms. off, while the nearest market place, Lankapara, is situated at a distance of 11 odd kms. During the first settlement survey conducted by D. Sanders in 1889-1994, the area of Totopara mouza was recorded as restricted and reserved for the "Toto"s only. Subsequently, the land was given on lease to the Totos.

As per their natural taboo Totos do not cause destroy or harm to the bio-recourse of Totopara and nearby rivers, hills and forests. Because their belief in Supernature stands in favour of saving the natural resource. They believe that they are born of the mountains, as their abode of love-faith-hope and despair is built in the lap of these mountains. But in this era of global market economy Totopara could not remain free from outside enchrochers.

Identity

According to Grierson they are similar to that of Rai, Limbu or Subba, Lepcha or Rong, Dhimal and Bhutia and such others residing in the Tibeto-Himalayas to sub-Himalayas (Grierson, 1909:250-251; Sanyal, 1973:45). They are Mangoloid stock with a darker skin. According to a survey conducted by the Cultural Research Institute of West Bengal in September 2003, Toto tribe have a population of 1,227 (presently 1,346) the sex ratio being 653:574. Some researchers opine that Totos have migrated from Bhutan. There are proofs that this particular *mouza* was a transit point in the orange trading route from Bhutan to Madarihat. It is believed that the Totos used to work as orange carriers. Now-a-days orange and cane vegetation have been vanished from Jaldapara. The ancient routes through Duars have been lost, but Totos are still maintaining their folk life. However, orange plants are still at irregular intervals there in Totopara. But, the exact anthropomorphic origin of the Totos still remains a mystery.

Totopara Mouza

The Totopara mouza is divided into 6 segments, *Panchayat Gaon, Subba Gaon, Mondal Gaon, Mitrang Gaon, Puja Gaon and Dhumchi Gaon*. They have a very strong *Panchayat* — like institution, which governs almost every social activity, from selecting the time of crop cultivation to marriage festivities and even death rites. Individual land ownership was introduced in Totopara in 1969 and the District Collector possessed more than 1,600 acres of the total area leaving only 347.43 acres of land to then 89 Toto families. However, the Totos still continued to cultivate in around 400 acres of the residual land at the south-eastern course of the Totopara village; that place on the bank of Torsa River was a fertile extend, but within 1981-82 the forest department tookover its possession in the territory of the Forest Conservation Act.

·Their huts are to be found in the centre of the village, arranged rather asymmetrically along the lanes and bye-lanes, mainly due to undulations of land form. A closer scrutiny would, however, show a clustered formation of the huts.

Hut along with the homestead is important component of their socio-economy. The houses are built on thick wooden and bamboo poles, 5/6 feet above the ground level. The floor is also built with bamboo and wooden platforms. There is an uncovered protection of bamboo/wooden platform in front of the house known as Dui. Each of the huts generally have a single room, which is divided into 3 or 4 parts, viz.

1. sleeping place for the family or **siri**;
2. sleeping place for guests or **dai chilka-siri**;
3. a place for the household deities or **jeri**; and
4. a cooking place, usually between **siri and dai chilka siri.**

The average family size in the population is observed with 4-5 members. Small size families consisting of 2-3 members and these are 26 families who have more than 8 persons who are classified under 'very large' type.

Clan

Totos are divided in 13 clans. Names are, Donkobei, Dankobei, Badubei, Bandhbei, Prongabei, Narenchankobei, Lenkaijibei, Nubebei, Diring Chaugobei, Mankobei, Mantrobei, Manchigbei, and also Chaugobei. Each of these 13 clans have different ancestral deities, different taboos.

There is a general council at the top of the village. This community council is the supreme decision making authority of the Totos. The *Kazi* or *Subha*, chief justice. The *Kazi* holds the office of religious head as well. In this hierarchy, the Gapu is the second most important person. Till date, Totos have been keeping shy of the State judiciary and police. They know how to solve their own matters themselves. No Toto has hitherto visited Madarihat P.S. for settling their disputes.

The Totos are fond of their tradition. There are several Paw who organize community function and rites under the supervision of Subha. Such a Paw is entitled to perform a name giving ritual.

These days, the statutory *gram panchayat* have become the most powerful body. It appears that the traditional seat of the Subha is gradually losing many of its executive powers to the *gram panchayat.* Khagen Toto (30 years) and Smt. Rama Toto (38 years) are elected as *panchayat samiti* members (as observed in the year 2006).

Love Nature and Society

Love, to Totos is a passion pure and fragrant of mountain's own breath. Their way of love making searches for, and finds tranquil spaces, out in the bosom of mountains, terrains, rivulets and springs. As they patrol their *Marua* fields, Toto men and women exchange their hearts to the other sex. Thus, the seeds of love seeks fertile land, and finds it. And, the love tree takes root and, the fruit of love, will now be blossomed in the lap of the mountains. The maid leaves her family, with her betrothed. Toto couples who steals away from the society before marriage, Subha convenes a meeting to take them back, and the pregnant maid is sent to her parental home. Now, the communion is "socialized" into a wedlock.

Their marriage rituals form an important component of their ethnographic entity. As mentioned before, the sex ratio is well loaded in favour of the male sex (only 468 female per thousand male). The married couples are generally separated off the main family branches, to inspire their regenerative prowess. For a Toto, a marriage ceremony is a costly affair, even by their standards. They are forced to lend money, or even mortgage lands in order to pay the requisite "fee" to the Subha and his associates, and feed the entire village to their capacity for as many as four days! The invites are served rice, roasted pork and/or beef and home made liquor.

Witch Doctor

The poor soul is found cursing the Totos for their strict adherence to traditional medicines, and lamenting his own sorry plight as direct resultant. One Homaeopathic practitioner was posted by the Government, albeit the amount of awareness and confidence he has been able to generate among the Totos, as heard from his own mouth, are pitifully small. Till now, the Totos, much to the annoyance of the previously mentioned medic almost always resort to the Baidangi, their own witch doctor. He makes both the diagnosis and prognosis of the disease by invoking/threatening away of the spirits and advice the patient party accordingly. At times, Totos have to spend big sums, chiefly acquired as loans, to pay the community Baidangi's fees!

Occupation

Almost every Toto household owns some livestock — cattle, pigs and a few fowl birds. There is no shortage of grazing grounds for the animals, either. Since, they do originally belong to a nomadic race, the Totos were not too interested in cultivation not so many years ago. Close contact with Nepalis generated interests among them to cultivate. At those times of the year when they have no other occupations available, they have began to till their lands of late. A primitive kind of step (*jhoom*) cultivation is practised by them. They do have enough lands to grow crops, although there is a scarcity of irrigation water in their lands. Agriculture, however is the main occupation of 260-odd Toto families. A 66.2 per cent of them are small land holders, the remaining ones do not own any land. the Totos continued to cultivate in around 400 acres of the fertile land at the south-eastern direction of the Totopara village on the bank of Torsa River.

Every Toto family likes to grow a smallish kitchen garden in the homestead. They grow beetel nut, jack fruit and bamboo. In fact, beetel nut and bamboo trees are the two chief sources of earning cash.

Economy

The economic scenario tells a sorry tale. Out of 260, only 19 families depend on service and partially on agriculture. As many as 144 families stay still below the poverty line. Among these 144, there are 27 families who live in real distress, with a miserable economic status. In the crop yielding months, many of the Totos work as agriculture labourers in the fields. But, during the lean months, they could manage to earn paltry sums, working as orange carriers from Bhutan to Madarihat. Scars of pauperization are distressingly evident in the Toto socio-economic fabric.

23 members of their tribe have found jobs in some Government and private offices (as per my observation in the year 2006). The first one among them to pass the Higher Secondary level in Science stream is Bhakto Toto — who has been rewarded with Branch Manager's post in *Uttarbanga Ksetriya Gramin Bank.* Recently the Government of West Bengal announced establishing a separate department for tribals in north Bengal that will look into the interests of endangered communities in the region like the Totos, Labhas and Boros. The only woman a 25-year-old Ms. Rita Toto completed her graduation from Prasanna Deb Women's College under North Bengal University in Jalpaiguri district in 2010. Recently she appointment in the Backward Classes Welfare Department as a social worker.

Health

They themselves have very little or no concern regarding their unclean, unhealthy surroundings and habits. Mal nutrition, coupled with unhygienic lifestyle makes them fall prey to tropical diseases like diarrhoea, hookworm infections, scabies, dermatitis, etc. The malaria parasite, of course, takes its due share of lives in this region.

Most of their male folks are lazy enough not to get involved in strenuous physical activities. A sizeable portion of the Toto families are over head and ears in debt, mainly owing to their drunken habits. They brew a liquor from *Marua* and other lower millets at home. Most of them live on a steady diet of maize and *Marua*. They have an unwholesome habit of eating half, at times unboiled food. This is why they frequently suffer from gastro-intestinal and a few other illnesses. The general health, as a consequence, is very poor. Lack or absence of public health infrastructure aggravates the situation.

Though the State Health Service institution has not yet any birth control campaigns, keeping their slim population in consideration — but some awareness have filtered through mass media like radio and television. Such exposure has inspired a few Totos undergoing vasectomy operations beyond Totopara. Queerly enough, they tend to conceal their ethnic identity, and introduce themselves as Nepalis before the surgeon's forceps.

The public health scenario has been showing improvements than earlier, but not sufficient. NGOs like *Toto-Kalyan Samiti* are working there.

Education

Way back in 1951, the Backward Classes Welfare Department, Government of West Bengal built a primary school in Totopara. A post of teacher-*cum*-welfare organizer was created in 1964.

The school got recognition from the District School Board, Jalpaiguri. Another primary school was established in Ponwar Gaon, a village close to Totopara.

The head teacher of *Bharat Mahajati Mandali* school. *Bharat Mahajati Mandali*, voluntary organization, aided by the Government has been devoting themselves for imparting education among the Totos. They have established a hostel which makes room for 299 students. At present, there are 171 Toto students, which include 69 girls as well. The Toto student admits that they feel at ease with Bengali as the medium of instruction.

In general, the school going percentage in the primary level is satisfactory. But, number of drop-outs increase from Class III onwards. A scarcity of Toto girl students observed.

Totos do not inherit any written tradition. The literate section of them tend to prefer Bengali scripts. The linguists have been divided over whether the *Devanagri* (Hindi) script should be ideal for them to documentise their language.

The only poet in Toto tribe, Dhaniram Toto has published a book of Toto poems. It is written in Bengali scripts. Their language and scripts which could favour their expressions have been an interesting issue for the Linguist.

Only 6 Totos have so far completed their conventional education. Sanjit Toto and Rita Toto have graduated and while the others have completed their basic schooling.

Conclusion

This strong Mangoloid tribe is clinging on to its roots struck in the mountains. But, an air of sagacious aloofness, which at times, derogates into ignorance is very evident among them. Their troubles are manifold, viz.

Problem I: Encroachment of foreign elements, non-tribals into their ancestral land. The Nepalis have stripped hundred odd acres of fertile land from lands lawfully reserved for them, close to the Poner Gaon.

Problem II: One of their major worries have been a scarcity of irrigation water. Calamities like deforestation, soil erosion and flood have only worsened the scenario. Developmental efforts for horticulture and floriculture is badly needed.

Problem III: Poor sanitary and drinking water is another worry for Totos. Most of them are patients of water-borne diseases, as a consequence. Excessive consumption of local brews, eating of half cooked beef and pork flesh, chewing beetel nuts have increased their health hazards. They do not want to get shifted to Pucca, airy and lighted houses made by Indira Avas Yojana, as the believe in ancestral spirit Chinea who "lives" in the dark corners of their generation old huts. The spirits wont stay there with them in those houses.

Problem IV: The political tension of border area now being a problem for Toto. Keeping their socio-economic scenario in mind, it can be concluded that if various Governmental/Non-Governmental Agencies lend their helping hands, a positive effect on their economy may well be imparted through beneficial schemes. A successful campaign should, and must include knowledge and experience sharing would surely help to generate healthy impacts on the Toto livelihood.

The West Bengal Government has announced establishing a separate department for tribals in north Bengal that will look into the interests of primitive communities in the region like the Totos, Labhas and Boros.

At the same time Government has started providing free food grains to members of the community. For last decades Government has constantly giving input for their betterment of life. But still Toto males are in the hangover of laziness. So, it is a big question whether these administrative advantages really develop their perspective towards self-development, or encouraging sustainable economic progress in this context of changing global market. Keeping in view of the socio-economic condition of Toto community it can be said that the development programme for this community to be designed and to be implemented as per their social needs. It should be really effective, meaningful and easily acceptable for the Totos.

Mountains are their best friends, philosophers and guides; and that is all they seek to know, and do know. It is observed that besides the soil of the lands, there are members of six other communities, namely — Kagatey, Yulomo, Sherpa, Dukpa, Bhutia and Tibetans. These people, it is believed, have encroached into the lands reserved for Totos. Gradually, these encroachers have become the major chunk of the population. As a matter of fact, the Totos form only a paltry 25.08 per cent of the total population of the Totopara mouza!

Mountains, it is said, make hearts nobler. Far off the dazzles and glitters of our society, this primordial tribe has struck to their roots. Greed is a foreign word to them, they do not, and want not to know that even their marginal existences are challenged by cultures of consumerism every day. Yet, till date, they have stayed away from all the lures of outer world. Ask any of them, if they are anxious about encroachments of "civilization and sanskritization" — all they would do is broaden their smiles, smile overpouring onto wrinkles of their foreheads: "We Are born of the mountains!"

REFERENCES

Chaudhuri, S.K. (2004): *Constraints of Tribal Development*, New Delhi: Mittal Publications.

Das, A.K. (1967): *The Toto*, Kolkata: Cultural Research Institute, Special Series No. 11.

Grierson, G.A. (1926): *Linguistic Survey of India, Vol. III: Tibeto-Burman Family, Part-I*. Kolkata: Central Publication Branch, Government of India.

Majumder, B. (1991): *A Sociological Study of the Toto Folk Tales*, Kolkata: The Asiatic Society.

Majumdar, B. (1998): *The Totos: Cultural and Economic Transformation of a Small Tribe in the Sub-Himalayan Bengal*, Kolkata: Academic Enterprise.

Moitra, M. (2004): "Uttarbanger biluptoprai janojati: Dhimal", in R. Biswas (ed.), *Uttarbanger Jati-O-Upojati* (in Bengali). Kolkata: Punascho.

O'Malley L.S.S. (1907): *Bengal District Gazetteers: Darjeeling*, New Delhi: Logos Press (reprint 1999).

Risley, H.H. (1891): *The Tribes and Castes of Bengal* (Vol. 1), Kolkata: Firma KLM Pvt. Ltd. (Reprint 1998).

Sanyal, C.C. (1973): *The Meches and the Totos: Two Sub-Himalayan Tribes of North Bengal*, Siliguri: North Bengal University Press.

Sarkar, A. (1993): *Toto: Society and Change (A Sub-Himalayan Tribe of West Bengal)*, Kolkata: Firma KLM Pvt. Ltd.

Sunder, D. (1895): *Survey and Settlement of Western Duars: A Comprehensive Five Year Plan for the Development of Toto Tribes*, Jalpaiguri: District Welfare Committee for Scheduled Castes and Scheduled tribes, Government of Bengal.

15

Role of Traditional Healers in Improving Health Status of Baiga: An Analysis

Manish Mishra and *D. Debnath*

Introduction

Tribal people are the ecosystem people who live in harmony with the nature and maintain a close link between man and environment. Plants are the basis of life on earth and are central to people's livelihoods. The life, tradition, culture of tribal's have remained almost static since last several hundreds of years. The knowledge accumulated by them through a long series of observations from one generation to another is transmitted oral communication for power possessed by medicinal plants in cure of various diseases and ailments. The need for the integration of local indigenous knowledge for a sustainable management and conservation of natural resources receives more and more recognition (Posey, 1992).

The earlier study on the ethnobotany in Madhya Pradesh on traditional health care by numerous ethno-botanists such as (Bhalla *et al.*, 1992; Jain, 1963, 1991, 1992; Jain and Tarafdar, 1963; Maheshwari, 1989 and 1996; Maheshwari and Dwivedi, 1988; Prasad *et al.*, 1990; Rai *et al.*, 1996, 2002, 2003, 2004; Rai *et. al.*, 2001; Rai and Nath, 2005a and 2005b; Rai and Nath, 2000 and 2005; Saxena and Shukla, 1971; Saxena, 1988; Saxena and Kushwaha, 2004; and Tewari, 1984). A large number of traditional herbal healers in tahsil Multai district Betul, exist belonging to the tribal community and are utilizing local plants in ethno-medicinal practices prevalent in the area and resulted in the documentation of 47 medicinal plant species belonging to 29 families and 45 genera (Dahare and Jain, 2010). However, Baiga chak area of Dindori is relatively unexplored and little work has been done in context of ethno-botany because of low population of tribe's. So, the present study was undertaken. Information on ethno-medicinal plants used by Baigas, for the various ailments and disorders recorded during field trips has been documented in this study.

Study Area — Baigachak, Dindori

The Dindori district is situated at the eastern part of Madhya Pradesh touching Chhattisgarh state. The district touches Shahdol in east, Mandla in west, Umaria in north, and Bilaspur district of Chhattisgarh state in south. It is located at 81°34' longitude and 21°16' latitude. The holy river Narmada passes through the district. It is situated at a height of 1,100 m. above sea level amongst herbal-rich, Maikal mountain ranges. Dindori has many historical as well as spiritual places. The district is covered in seven block namely Dindori, Shahpura, Mehandwani, Amarpur, Bajag, Karanjiya and Samnapur.

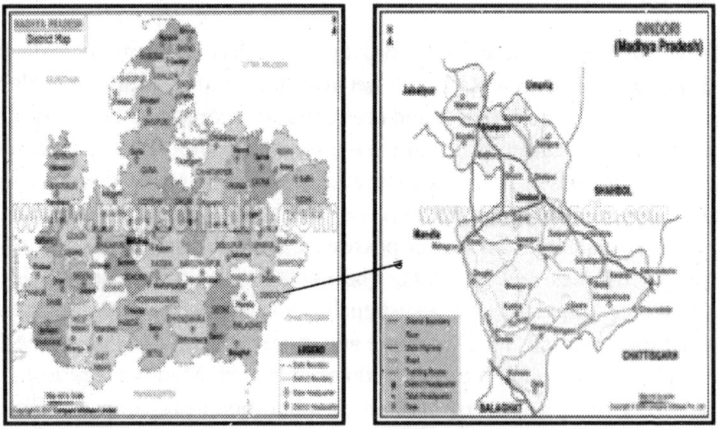

Figure 15.1: Map Showing Study Area — Dindori District

Being primarily rural-population dominated district, Dindori district carries a high percentage of Scheduled Tribe categories in its population. The major tribes of the district are the *Baigas*, *Koal*, *Pradhan*, *Dhulia*, *Bhoomia* and *Agaria*. The *Baiga* are very primitive tribes which can be found only in this district. This tribe is inhabitated in around 52 villages of Block Bajag and the area is known as *Baiga chak*. The most backward community is that of the *Baigas*. The socio-economic status of the Baigas is very poor. They are traditionally addicted to alcohol. These communities cultivate the fields merely for their self-subsistence. The feeding habits of these tribes are not healthier. Whatever additional income is there they never try to save it or engage in enterprising activities. Rather they spend it on alcohol. The other tribes are also poor and posses similar characteristics (Tiwari, 1997).

About Baiga Community

The Baigas are very particularly vulnerable tribal groups (PVTGs) which can be found only in this district. The *Baigas* are also known as the "National Human". The *Baiga* tribals of Madhya Pradesh are the indigenous people who have lived in the forested areas of districts Dindori, Mandla Balaghat since time immemorial. It is said that the very first Baiga was born from the womb of Mother on the Hill of Elephants and he was named Nanga Baiga. Since then, they have always been referred to as 'Sons and Daughters of Mother Earth' (Varrier Elwin, 1939).

The *Baigas* are the most primitive and interesting forest tribal of the district. Their few implements of agriculture or the chase are supplied by the local smith, and their food, supplemented by countless roots and fruits they obtain by their own slight exceptions. The Baiga takes coarse food and shows no extravagance in this aspect. They eat coarse grain, *kodo*, and *kutki*, drink *pej*, eat little flour and are normally content with what little that they get. One of the prime foods is *pej* that can be made from grounding *macca* or from the water left from boiling rice. Local people gave testimony that this food is much better and healthier than many other food that they eat. Also, beyond doubt they eat several items from the forest that includes primarily *Chirota Bhaji*, *Gular* leaves such as *chirota*, *chinch*, *chakora*, *sarroota*, *peepal*, etc. They also eat Birar Kand, Kadukand and other rhizomes. Mushroom is also a delicacy. Numerous fruits such as mango, *char*, *jamun*, *tendu* are also eaten (Sharma, 2007).

The great majority of the *Baigas* have now taken to plough cultivation, as perforce they must, seeing that *bewar* (shifting cultivation) cultivation has been put a stop to everywhere both in *malguzari* and in Government forest, except the *Baiga chak* area. This is a block of some 36 square miles of rugged and inaccessible jungle in the heart of the heart of the Maikal Range, containing six (at present only four) villages, which was set apart for the Baigas about 35 years ago. Here they were allowed to pursue unfettered their ancestral methods of hunting and agriculture at the rate of one rupee per axe; but side by side with this concession attempts were made to wean them to plough cultivation (Tiwari, 1997).

Material and Methods

The temperate climate and the equitable distribution of rain make forest of Dindori an ideal plateau for dense vegetation cover. The forest of Dindori district is home to various invaluable medicinal plants like *brahmi, gulbakawali, safedmusli, kalimusli, tejraj, bhojraj, patalkumda, kali haldi, devraj, hatahjodi, jatashankari*, and *ashva gandha*. At present the local vaids use them to make herbal remedies, some of which are well known for their potency.

Table 15.1: List of Surveyed Forest Ranges, Villages of Baigachak Region, Dindori District, Madhya Pradesh

Name of Block	*Name of Village*	*Average % of Baiga*
Samnapur	Dhaba, Paudi, Ajgar, Kandavani, Dhurkutta, Jeelang	70-80
Karanjia	Do muhani, Kandatola, Ladradadar, Kharidih, Padripani, Kindrabehra	80-90
Bajag	Jalda Bauna, Khamera, Chadha, Tatar, Silpidi,Tarach	80-90

Source: Primary Data.

The information's about the uses of various locally available yams and tubers in the natural forests was obtained from the local inhabitants (*Baigas*), local medicine men, Vaidyas and forest officials. *Baiga chak* area of Dindori district is mostly dominated by tribal population. The area is highly affected by several diseases as this part of the Bajag block of the district is maintaining very high API (>30 per thousand) since last several years. The area is a hilly terrain and inaccessible during rainy season with poor communication facilities, so control of diseases is logistically difficult in the area. Livelihood of the local inhabitants mainly depends on forest produce, agriculture and other casual and poverty alleviation programmes run by Government agencies. People mostly believe in traditional practices of healing and their myths and superstitious beliefs forbid them to utilize the modern treatment facilities/ services. The study was carried out in the three forest ranges (Bajag, Karanjiya, Samnapur) in five villages each in *Baiga chak* area of Dindori district (M.P.). A Total of 75 respondents including females were randomly interviewed using structured and open ended questionnaire. Average age of the male and female respondents was 38.5±13.0. About 59 per cent of the respondents was illiterate in the study area. Most of them were involved in occupations such as agriculture and other casual labours, collection of forest produce, etc.

While collecting information on ethno-medicinal plants special attention was paid to record information from local *Vaidya*, *Ojha* and traditional herbal healers. The information was documented involving field study by contacting and interviewing traditional healers, *ojhas*, *gunias*, etc. for plants used to cure various types of diseases.

Results and Discussion

Table 15.2: Habit-wise Number of Rare Plants Used as Medicine in the Study Area

Trees	*Herbs*	*Shrubs*	*Climber*	*Total No.*
2	15	3	10	30

Source: Primary Data.

Around 30 rare species (including wild yams, medicinal plants) being used by the 12 traditional healers/Baiga's have been documented from Baigachak area of Dindori district (Table 15.2). The study recorded a total of 30 medicinal plants belonging to 10 families including 15 herbs, 3 shrubs, 2 trees and 10 climber species are climbers which are used as medicine.

Table 15.3: Different Categories of Traditional Healers Enumerated in the Study Area

Gunias/Baiga's/Traditional Healers	*Male*
Generalists	5
Specialists for poisonous bites	1
Traditional bone setters	1
Fever/Asthma/Skin	4
Individual organ related/specific diseases	1
Total	**12**

Source: Primary Data.

The major plant families are Fabaceae, Liliaceae, Euphorbiaceae, Cucurbitaceae, Malvaceae and Asteraceae recorded. The plant parts used are roots, leaves, fruits, barks, seeds and sometime whole plants against weakness, jaundice, asthma, toothache and mouth ulcer. The method of preparation fall into categories like plant parts applied as paste, juice extracted from the fresh plant parts, decoction and external and internal consumption are involved in the treatment of all diseases. The habit of the plant, plant parts used against the diseases has been presented in the Tables 15.4, 15.5 and 15.6.

Table 15.4: Wild Yams, Tubers Utilized by the Traditional Healers/*Baiga* Tribes of Dindori District, Madhya Pradesh

Local Name of Yams/ Tuber Species	*Medicinal Uses by Traditional Healers/Baigas*
Kanihakanda, Khus or *Donchikanda* (*Dioscorea bulbifera*)	After burning and powdering used for disinfecting and cutting of newly born child Baby *Nal* (umbilical cord).
Kadugeethkanda (*Dioscorea pentaphylla*)	Paste of the leaves made with mustard oil is rubbed into affected areas for the treatment of rheumatism.
Baichandi kanda (*Dioscorea hispida*)	Jaundice, Stomach ache, Malaria, Fever, etc. Leaf paste made with oil is rubbed into affected areas for the treatment of swellings.
Vidarikand or *Birarkanda* or *Bhui kumhda* (*Prureria tuberosa*)	Diarrhea, bleeding, swelling in body, potency, etc.
Tikhur kanda (*Curcuma angustifolia*)	Maste of rhizome given to patients facing Heat stroke, Decoctio also given for Weakness, Sexual strength, etc.
Rabikanda/Dhursi kanda (*Dioscorea bulbifera)*	Paste of wet tuber given for Scorpion bite, poisonous insect bite.
Jangli Suran (*Amorphophallus sylvaticus*)	Paste of wet tubers given for Wound healing, Also given during Asthma attack and for liver disorders.

Source: Primary Data.

The information depicted in table shows various species of yams and tubers used in curing various ailments by the traditional healers (Table 15.4). Yams and tubers are very important source of food for survival in the *Baigachak* region. Most of the Yams like *Kanihakanda* (*D. bulbifera*), *Baichandi kanda* (*D. hispida*), were used as vegetable after thorough washing, boiling and skin removal. The tubers are eaten baked, boiled, or fried much like potatoes. Similarly, these yams were also used for curing various diseases after some modification and processing, i.e. *D. bulbifera* is used for cutting umbilical cord, *D. hispida* is used in curing Jaundice, Stomach ache, Malaria, Fever, etc.

The tubers like *Vidarikand* (*P. tuberosa*) which is used as raw for making vegetable is also used medicinally for curing diarrhea, bleeding, swelling in body, potency, etc. *Tikhur kanda* (*C. angustifolia*) is an economically important tuberous herb. Its tubers were also used as general health tonic and helpful in heat stroke, general weakness, sexual strength, etc.

The plants and its parts being used by the traditional herbal healers against the diseases prevailing among tribal/local people of the area have been documented and given as Table 15.5.

Table 15.5: Wild Tubers Used by the Traditional Healers/Baigas of Dindori District

Name of Tuber Species	*Medicinal Uses by Gunias/Baiga Tribals*
Kanihakanda or *Donchikanda* (*Dioscorea bulbifera*)	For disinfecting and cutting of Umbilical cord of newly born child.
Kadugeethkanda (*Dioscorea pentaphylla*)	General weakness worms, leprosy.
Baichandi kanda (*Dioscorea daemona*)	Jaundice, Stomach ache, Malaria, Fever, etc.
Lodangikanda (*Disocorea spp.*)	Used in Stones in the urinary tract, bladder, kidney.
Saidukanda (*Disocorea spp.*)	Used in curing wounds, tumors, boils, sunburn, cut
Badainkanda (*Disocorea spp.*)	Used in injury and carbuncle.
Vidarikand Birarkanda or *Bhui kumhra* (*Prureria superba*)	Diarrhea, bleeding, Swelling in body, potency, etc.
Tikhurkanda (*Curcuma angustifolia*)	Heat stroke, Weakness, Sexual strength.
Ravikanda (*Disocorea bulbifera*)	Scorpion bite, poisonous insect bite, etc.

Some critically endangered and rare medicinal plants utilized by traditional healers in curing different human ailments are listed Table 15.6.

Table 15.6: List of Critically Endangered and Rare Medicinal Plants Used by the Traditional Healers of Baigachak, Dindori

Name of Species	*Plant Part Used*	*Name of Disease/Part Affected*	*Method of Application*
(1)	*(2)*	*(3)*	*(4)*
Gulbakawli (*Hedychium coronarium*)	Flower	Eye related diseases, Cataract	Flowers were kept in water until decomposed, extract is separated and few drops were poured in eyes to treat cataract and improving eye sight and vision.
Bhanvarmal (*Hymenodactylon excelsum*)	Roots	Tooth ache, snake bite	Dried roots kept beneath teeth. Chirchita is mixed with this species equally and paste were applied to infected part, some time decoction is given.
Paras peepal (*Thespesia populnea*)	Seeds, Bark	Whooping cough, Asthma, Skin, Burn	Seeds were roasted in fire and eaten with Pan leaf. Ground up bark is used to treat skin diseases.
White Bach (*Acorus calamus*)	Rhizome	Children's growth	Fresh roots were rubbed on surface and paste given with Honey.

(*Contd.*)

Table 15.6 (*Contd.*)

(1)	*(2)*	*(3)*	*(4)*
Van haldi (*Curcuma amada*)	Flower, Rhizome	Jaundice	Dry flowers were powdered, also in liquid form with water.
Rohila (*Bauhinia varigata*)	Bark	Scar, boil	Dried bark powdered and spread on boil, scars, etc.
Hadjudi (*Cissus quadrangularis*)	Stem	Broken bone, abscess	Stem pasted with hot oil and tighten around broken bone. Paste of stem pasted in abscess part.
Banjhita (*Rubia cordifolia*)	Seed, Leaf	Malaria, Fever	Crushed, powdered seeds along with Jaggery and 2 leaf were crushed and sieved and given.
Baibidanga (*Embelia ribes*)	Fruit	Fever, worm	Fruits were powdered and given for de-worming. Powder also boiled and liquid given to cure fever.
Bajoor Ganth (*Lea indica*)	Roots	Arthritis gastric, heart pain	Equal quantity of *satawar*, *rohila*, *bajorganth* in boiled water given as liquid paste. Imbibe cloth in paste rubbed to chest for heart pain.
Safed musli (*Chlorophytum spp.*)	Roots	In Fertility, Health tonic	Dried root power with milk. Chewing wet roots. For weak patients given as *laddus*, for women after delivery. It is also often fried in ghee (clarified butter) and one wed to relieve sore throats and mouth ulcers.
Tejraj (*Peucedanum nagpurense*)	Roots	General weakness	Chewing directly.
Bhojraj (*Peucedanum dhana*)	Roots	General weakness	Chewing directly.
Kali haldi (*Curcuma caesia*)	Rhizome	Cough, Cold, headache	Rubbing fresh roots on stone plate, paste given to patients. Chewed directly. Dry powder with milk given to cold affect patients.
Kalihari (*Gloriosa superba*)	Rhizome	Stomach ache, snake bite	Cut pieces were used after drying. Powdered roots are chewed mixing with Jaggery (making tablets). Crushed and sieved extract drink mixing with water for snake bite.
Bidari kanda (*Dioscorea bulbifera*)	Rhizome	Scabies, Stomach ache, White liquid	Dried and Powdered roots with water. Immature root chewed for stomach ache.

Discussion

In the present study, data collected through ethno-botanical survey included rare and critically endangered plant species with their vernacular names, use and mode of preparation. The tribal people of *Baigachak*, Dindori district are using 38 rare plant species belonging to 12 families respectively. Among them 2 are trees, 3 are shrubs, 10 are climbers, 15 are herbs. The most commonly represented families in all the study sites are Fabaceae, Liliaceae, Euphorbiaceae, Caesalpiniaceae and Cucurbitaceae. Traditional medicine had minimal adverse effects with exception of vomiting and inflammations, since, the dosages are not fixed (in most cases unknown) (Gidey, 2009).

Therefore, there is need for traditional healers to undergo training in basic health care delivery. Traditional healers should be encouraged to transfer their knowledge to interested persons in their communities. As most of the medicinal plants are wild and harvested for their roots to prepare remedies, the healers in consultation with Government officials should take care not to eradicate the medicinal plant species altogether. Awareness creation among the traditional healers and community at large is important in order to preserve the indigenous medicinal plant species. Conservation measures such area closure whereby a ban is placed on farming, grazing, tree felling will help minimize environmental degradation and the attendant global warming (Endashaw, 2007).

Unfortunately, there has been a rapid decline in the traditional practice of individual healers identifying plants and preparing various formulations for direct distribution to patients. With the increased availability and acceptance of conventional Western medicine and many of those who are familiar with the tenets and benefits of Ayurveda are not receiving the full respect. By documenting the herbal formulations prepared by traditional *vaidyas*, it may be possible to prevent unfortunate scenarios like the recent attempt by commercial interests in the United States to patent the traditional Ayurvedic medicinal plant and culinary spice turmeric (*Curcuma domestica* — Zingiberaceae) (Johnston and Webb, 1997).

Before the 1980s, the reputation of the respective traditional healers and the formulations developed by him were sufficient criteria for people to believe in its value. Today, the reduced number of knowledgeable and recognized traditional healers clearly reveals a major disruption in the ancient custom of carrying forward this traditional knowledge. Although the study on which this article reports succeeded in capturing substantial information about the traditional healers and their use and preparation of herbal formulations, additional studies are needed to complete the work. Moreover, the documented properties of the medicinal plants utilized by various traditional healers should be clinically evaluated to further strengthen their validity and to encourage the preparation of new formulations. The various formulations provided by traditional healers must be preserved to ensure the integrity of this time-honored knowledge of traditional healing (Kala, 1998; Kala, 2005; Kala, 2006).

Conclusion

Traditional healers or Baigas, are basically tribal practitioners using specific plant parts and specific dosages for the treatment of different diseases. Medicinal plants are consumed raw or in the form of a decoction, as infusion for oral treatment, or raw paste when applied externally. The parts of the plant most used for medicinal purposes are rhizomes, roots, stem, bark, leaves, flowers and whole plant. Juice and paste are the main methods of preparation. They mix several plants as ingredients to cure diseases instantaneously. By and large, fresh part of the plant is used for the preparation of medicine. Mostly raw, dried medicinal plants are used as simple drugs and some plants are used with some other plant parts. This practice is going since time immemorial by the local healers traditionally, from their ancestors. The local people's faith on traditional medicines and inaccessibility to modern medicines has helped local healers to continue their treatments. Moreover, treating with locally available medicines, will also helpful in improving their health status of *Baiga* tribes.

The information generated from the present study regarding the medicinal plant used by *Baiga* tribes need pharmaceutical investigation including alkaloid extraction and isolation along with few clinical trials. This could help in creating mass awareness regarding the need for conservation of such plants and also in the promotion of traditional medico knowledge within the region besides contributing to the preservation and enrichment of the gene bank of such economically important species before they are lost forever. People of *Baiga chak* region realize on medicinal plants and in most problems they gone to *ojhas*, *gunias* or *bhumkas* because of the bad health condition. There are a lot to be done in this promising field with the active support of village people, so that, importance of these economically important plants could be rejuvenated for the benefit of our future generations and also need to improve health care condition.

Investigation of traditional medicine is very important for the welfare of rural and tribal communities for the treatment of conventional illness. This may add to the expensive and inadequate health care facilities in rural areas. There are a lot to be done in this promising field with the active support of village people, so that, importance of these economically important plants could be rejuvenated for the benefit of our future generations and also need to improve health care condition. In developing countries, traditional healers or *Vaidyas* are a significant health care resource and efforts have been made to incorporate them into primary health care programmes.

Acknowledgements

The authors are thankful to the Divisional Forest Officers (DFOs) of Dindori district and field forest staff of Bajag, Karanjiya range for providing field facilities, survey and valuable suggestions. We are also thankful to the Director, Dr. G.A. Kinhal for his kind cooperation and guidance.

REFERENCES

Bajpai A.K. and P. Bhattacharya (1991): "Some Unique Folk Medicines of *Baiga* Tribes of Mandla District", *M.P. Indian Journal of Forestry Science*, 7(1): 203-204.

Bhalla, S., J.R. Patel, N.P. Bhalla (1992): "Ethnomedicinal Studies of Genus Indigiofera from Bundelkhand Region of M.P.", *Journal of Economic and Taxonomic Botany*, Addl. Series 10: 221-332.

Dahare, Dinesh K. and Jain, Aruna (2010): "Ethnobotanical Studies on Plant Resources of Tahsil Multai, District Betul, Madhya Pradesh, India", *Ethnobotanical Leaflets*, 14:694-705.

Endashaw, B. (2007): "Study on Actual Situation of Medicinal Plants in Ethiopia". Opted from http://www.endashaw.com dated:...

Gidey, A. (2009): *A Study on Traditional Medicinal Plants of Central Tigray*, (Mimeo), Ethiopia: Mekelle University.

Jain, A.K. (1992). "Ethno-botanical Studies on Sahariya Tribals of Madhya Pradesh with Special Reference to Medicinal Plants", *Journal of Economic and Taxonomic Botany*, Addl. Ser. 10: 227-32.

Jain, S.K. (1963): "Observation on Ethno-botany of Tribals of Madhya Pradesh", *Vanyajati*, 11(4):177-83.

Jain, S.K. (1965): "Medicinal Plant Lore of Tribals of Bastar", *Economic Botany*, 19:236-50.

Jain, S.K. (1991): *Dictionary of Indian Folk Medicine and Ethnobotany*, New Delhi: Deep & Deep Publications, p. 311.

Jain, S.K. and C.R. Tarafdar, (1963): "Studies in Indian Ethnobotany: Native Plant Remedies for Snake Bites Among *Adivasis* of Central India", *Indian Medicinal Journal*, Vol. 57: 307-09.

Johnston, B.A. and G. Webb, (1997): "Turmeric Patent Overturned in Legal Victor", *Herbal Gram*, No. 41:11.

Kala, C.P. (1998): *Ethnobotanical Survey and Propagation of Rare Medicinal Herbs for Small Farmers in the Buffer Zone of the Valley of Flowers National Park, Garhwal Himalaya*, Kathmandu, Nepal: ICIMOD.

Kala, C.P. (2005): "Indigenous Uses, Population Density, and Conservation of Threatened Medicinal Plants in Protected Areas of the Indian Himalayas", *Conservation Biology*, 19:368-78.

Kala, C.P. (2006): "Preserving Ayurvedic Herbal Formulations by Vaidyas: The Traditional Healers of the Uttaranchal Himalaya Region in India", *Herbal Gram*, 70:42-50.

Maheshwari, J.K. (1989): "Case Study of Three Primitive Tribes of M.P. (*Abhujmarias*, *Baigas* and *Bharias*) of Central India, in Methods and Approaches in Central India", *Society of Ethnobotanists*, pp. 187-88.

Maheshwari, J.K. (1996): "Ethnobotanical Documentation of Primitive Tribes of Madhya Pradesh", *Journal of Economic and Taxonomic Botany*, Additional series No. 12:206-13.

Oomachan, M. and J.L. Srivastava (1996): *Flora of Jabalpur*, Jodhpur: Scientific Publisher, p. 354.

Posey, D. (1992): "Traditional Knowledge, Conservation and the Rain Forest Harvest", in *Sustainable Harbest and Marketing of Rain Forest Products* (eds.). Plotkin, M. and L. Famolare, Washington DC.: Island Press, pp: 46-50.

Prasad, R., R.K. Pandey and P. Bhattacharya (1990): "Socio-economic Ethno-medico-botanical Studies at Patalkot: A Case Study of *Bhariya* Tribe", *Proceedings of National Seminar on Medicinal and Aromatic Plants*, Jabalpur: SFRI, pp. 46-59.

Rai, R. and V. Nath (2000): "A Case Study of Baigas and Rajbeda Van Samiti — Chilpi Buffer Zone of Kanha National Park", *Proceedings of National Seminar on Sustainable Forest Management through People Participation*, Jabalpur: TFRI, pp. 179-83.

Rai, R. and V. Nath (2005): "Some Lesser Known Oral Herbal Contraceptives in Folk Claims as Anti-fertility and Fertility Induced Plants in Bastar Region of Chhattisgarh", *Journal of Natural Remedies*, 5(2):152-159.

Rai, R. and V. Nath (2005): "Uses of Medicinal Plants by Traditional Herbal Healers in Central India", *Indian Forester*, 13(2):463-68.

Rai, R., V. Nath and P.K. Shukla (2001): "Characteristics and Ethno-botanical Studies on Primitive Tribe of Madhya Pradesh: Ethnomedicine and Pharmacology", *Recent Progress in Medicinal Plant*, (ed.), New Delhi: Research Book Centre, pp. 543-52.

Saxena, H.O. and C.S. Shukla (1971): "Medicinal Plants of Patalkot (Chhindwara) Madhya Pradesh", *Technical Bulletin No. 13*, Jabalpur: State Forest Research Institute.

Saxena, K.K. and T.S. Kuswaha (2004): "Adoption of Organic Farming Practices", *Indian Research Journal on Extension Education*, 4(1-2): 30-33.

Saxena, O.H. (1988): "Observation on Ethnobotany of Madhya Pradesh", *Bulletin Botanical Survey of India*, 28:149-156.

Sharma, Kunal (2007): *The Baiga (the Medicine Man)*, Keystone Foundation, The Nilgiris. www.livingforest.blogspot.com. Website viewed on 15/12/2014.

Tewari, D.N. (1984): *Primitive Tribes of Madhya Pradesh: Strategy for Development*. New Delhi: GoI.

Tiwari, S.K. (1997): *Baigas of Central India*, New Delhi: Anmol Publication Pvt. Ltd.

Verrier Elwin (1939): *The Baiga*, pp. 53-55.

16

Livelihood of Baiga Women: Issues and Prospects

Neelu Rawat

Introduction

Tribal economy is historically non-monetized and revolved around the basic requirements of food and shelter. They depend upon the local ecology for their survival and forest plays an important role in earning livelihood. They earned their livelihood from shifting cultivation and collection of edible forest produce. But, with the passage of time several direct or indirect interventions have abrupted their economy and today tribal economy revolves around agricultural activity, wage work within and outside village through migration, marketing of firewood and other forest related activities (Chaudhary, 2010). When we look at the livelihood of *Baiga*, we found that their life revolves around the forest whether for cultivation or for food gathering and hunting. Vidyarthi in his work (1981) found the *Baiga* engaged in hill cultivation in northern belt of Central India. Khera, in the study of *Baiga* found how they collect herbal roots, shrubs from forest, and women also engaged in collection of several forest produce. Rai and Nath (2000) found *Baiga* excellent in wood cutting, and women involvement in collection of forest produce. Ban on shifting cultivation and forest policy have affected the tribal livelihood. After 1991 globalization came as a new factor to threat the tribal economic and cultural heritage. Multi-national companies started expanding their reach to remote tribal area to establish their companies. Many scholars believe that globalization is anti-tribal because of formation and expansion of consumer culture, expansion of market force, etc. tribes are going to loose their economic and cultural identity. Rehabilitation and displacement are attacking the natural resource heritage and indigenous economic activities, even with promise to maintain sustainable development, there is a gap between promise and implementation because it is difficult to displace or rehabilitate in same economic and cultural terms. Tribal women are historically involved in economic activities by collecting forest wood and earn to meet day to day needs or in other forms like agricultural activities. But in contemporary India it can be seen that many factors in name of development are affecting the economic and cultural identity of tribes.

In this era of globalization where we talk about 'Global village' we should keep in mind the socio-cultural and economic heritage of tribe and should maintain their natural characteristics because in Constitution of India there is a right to maintain culture, so tribal economic and cultural identity should not be attacked in name of development. Exclusive growth and sustainable development do not say development of one in cost of other. This study focuses on economic activities of tribal women. This chapter is an attempt to assess the problems faced by Baiga women of Baigachak due to shrinking forest and increasing necessity.

Baiga

Baiga tribe was first explained by Captain Thomson, then Deputy Collector of Balaghat-Bilaspur zone sent report to Christain missionary on *Baiga* tribe during 1868 to 1885. Russel and Hiralal had picturized the history of *Baiga* in 'Tribes and Caste of Central India Provinces' in 1931. The landmark study of *Baiga* tribe was Elwin's exclusive work '*The Baiga*'. Elwin focused almost all the aspect of their life. The tribe mainly depend on forest produce for their livelihood. Madhya Pradesh tribal museum presented and outline on *Baiga* tribe — "The *Baigas* mainly live in dense forest and hilly regions of Mandla, Dindori, Shahadol, Umaria, Balaghat and Amarkantak in Madhya Pradesh". They are considered as an offshoot of the *Bhumias* of Chhota Nagpur.

The *Baigas* consider themselves to be servant of the earth and the king of the forests. Systematic Baiga villages came into existence much later. Earlier, they used to practice shifting cultivation without using the plough by clearing forests. After some year, they used to shift to some other nearby area. Even today, the forests are the first love and choice of the *Baigas*.

According to a *Baiga* origin myth, there existed a black hillock amidst surrounded by water on all sides, from which a cluster of bamboo emerged. *Baiga* was born on one hollow end of a Bamboo and the

Baigin from the other end of it. The Baigin saw the *Patalwasi Dharti* or the earth in her dream. Next day the *Baiga* sent Kariman crow to locate the earth. The crow brought the earth and the Baiga sprinkled seeds of earth on water. Meanwhile the Baiga couple was blessed with a son and a daughter. They came down from the Bamboo on the earth, but it was shaking. The Baiga couple realized that the earth will not be stable without propitiation with worship. With the intention of sacrificing their children they put them in the Dhuti of Bamboo and moved away. On the way they first came to see a hen and cock, goat and a she goat and then a boar couple. On knowing their intention they all gifted their children to them for sacrifice, for survival of humans on earth. The Baiga couple got made the nails of iron, copper and brass by the Agaria, Tamasur and Kansasur brothers. After invoking the nails, they drove them in *Nau Khand Dharti* (earth). Then Naga Baiga-Nagar Baigin made offerings to the earth and the earth became stable on the water surface.

Even today in Mandla-Dindori area the Baigas perform the soil worship for the Gonds and other tribes before sowing every year. They also prepare seeds for them.

The Baigas have five principal *Gotras* and a fort or a sacred place is attached to every *Gotra*. Each *Gotra* has a sign. Baiga *Gotra* or *Vansh* is called *Jaat*. The social structure of the Baigas is very systematic and functions very smoothly. They have a *Panchayat* comprising *Mukaddam*, *Diwan*, *Samrath*, *Kotwar* and *Dawar* which is authorized to settle all the disputes. *Mukaddam* is the head of the village and *Dawar* is the priest.

The various aspects of Baiga life are associated with forests and they are dependent on them. The articles used in rite of passage are also obtained from the forests. The Baigas are very good hunters, too. They use various types of nooses for catching wild animals and birds.

After ban on shifting cultivation now they have begun to practice normal cultivation, but unwillingly. Earlier, the Baigas used to take many crops at a time including *Kodo*, *Kutki*, *Kangani*, *Madia*, *Sama*, *Ratauni*, *Bajara*, *Kang*, *Silar* and pulses like *Rahar*, *Urada*, *Jhunjharu*, *Jhuraga*, *Barbati*, etc. Now, this diversity is gradually vanishing. They now grow paddy, wheat, Soybean, etc.

They *Baiga* lifestyle is very simple and their houses are also not much adorned. Their houses generally consist of a single room and there is a *Parchhi* adjoining it in the front. There is a courtyard in front of the *Parchhi*, a hedge of sachcher woods is created around the house which they call *Parda*.

Living amidst green *Sal* forests the Baigas wear very simple clothes which are generally white. Their aesthetic sense has a very special profundity, having no room for glamour or refulgence. They Baiga women are so much fond of tattooing they get every part of their body tattooed with large figures in detail. There is a specific tattoo for every part and the tattooing is done by people of Badi-Badanin community.

The Baiga men and women are very much fond of dancing and they dance all night at the *Madai Melas*. Their principal dance forms are *Baigani*, *Karma*, *Saila*, *Bilama*, *Parghauni*, *Fag*, *Jharpat*, *Gendi*, etc."

Objective

The broad purpose of the chapter are —

- To know the role of Baiga women in family livelihood.
- To know the challenges of these women in contemporary India.
- To come with prospects of improvement.

Material and Methods

The study is exploratory in nature and based on studies conducted earlier on Baiga, field observation and informal interaction with Baiga women was utilized as techniques of the study. For a comparative analysis secondary sources data was also used. Conversation with the women coming in weekly market of Dindori, Shahdol, Anuppur, Umariya, Amarkantak (Pendra Road), etc. was helpful to know the challenges they are facing in earning livelihood. Information from the local doctors, shopkeepers and officers engaged in developmental work was also collected. Activities of Baiga women such as wage labour, going to health care centres for treatment of their children, purchasing of essential goods from local shop, etc. cannot be neglected, so these activities were also observed. Gazetteers, census report and reports by Government or Non-Governmental Bodies played an important role in providing relevant information on historical aspects of *Baiga* tribe, their economic activities particularly involvement of women. The Baigachak is the study are which comprises nearly 52 villages.

Findings and Discussion

Historically, tribal women played significant role in family economy and their contribution in earning livelihood is more or less equal to their male counterparts, but when we talk about Baiga it is no doubt to say that their family economy revolves around their women, it means women have more contribution than men. Women had direct participation in shifting cultivation and forest produce collection. These produce were both minor and major for both marketing and domestic use. Edible produce include root, fruit, honey, *mahua*, *achar*, meat of birds, etc., they also catch fish from forestlake. *Sal* and *tendu* leaves, firewood, brrom grass, bones of dead animal, etc. were collected in non-edible forest produce. These forest produce were used as food, medicine, in making liquor, house construction, in chilam, for making marriage pole, etc. Beside domestic purpose forest produce was also sold in nearest market. Ban on shifting cultivation and forest policy affected their traditional economy and limited their access to forest. Their economic activities which revolved around forest then changed which can be categorized as —

(i) Wage work.
(ii) Collection and marketing of forest produce and firewood.
(iii) Migration (Seasonal).

Wage Work

Now, Baiga women do wage work as agriculture labour and in construction work in the surrounding towns. Planting and harvesting of rice is the main agriculture work of these women. The wage rate is not fixed, there is a fluctuation can be seen as per the availability of wage labour. In mathematical term, it can be said that availability of wage worker and wage rate are inversely proportional. Gender based discrimination is also seen, women get low wage rate in comparison to their male counterpart. Although there is no discrimination in wage rate in MNREGA, the ratio of women worker is low. Working hour for men and women are same, but wage rate varied. Such a long time hard work badly affects their health.

Collection and Marketing of Forest Produce

Beside forest produce, Baiga women collect firewood from forest and sell it in the nearest town. Historically, they have skill and enjoy collecting forest produce; they wake up early in the morning and go for forest produce collection in group. They are acquainted with forest and attached with forest historically and culturally, so, feel secure in forest also as they feel at their home. The work they perform is not an easy task. They collect produce and process to make it fit for sale in market which requires time and hard labour. But the price they got of their produce is negligible against their hard work because the price is usually determined by the buyers. Neither they have the knowledge about real cost nor they have any other option except selling to the shopkeeper (*Sahukar*). Government has mechanism to fix the forest produce price, but no such mechanism was found there. The work is also risky because sometime they get injuries while working in forest. Their struggle does not end here, many of the time they are exploited by the forest officers in name of breaching forest laws. They do not have knowledge of laws nor have capacity to protest, so they are afraid of forest officers but fear and risk seems to be little in front of earning bread for family.

Migration

Women of Baigachak seasonally migrate to Chhattisgarh and Odisha to earn wage by working as agricultural labour. They migrate in month of July-August for plantation of rice and again migrate at the time of harvesting in month of November-December. They get both cash and grain as their wage, usually at the time of plantation wage is given in cash and the wage at harvesting time is given in both cash and grain. Some women migrate with their children which affect the children education. They have limited resources at their working place, sometime do not have proper accommodation and live beneath the tree. Sometime they fall ill due to their hard work and poor accommodation and their siblings too.

If we look at the Baiga women daily work then find that they work from sunrise to sunset. They leave home early in the morning to collect forest produce, they return from forest and do domestic work like cooking food and taking care their child then they move for wage work. After wage work, they again perform domestic work. Baiga women contribute from construction of house to earning livelihood, they have more responsibility. The earning of men cannot be neglected, they also earn, but major part of their earning is spent on themselves. Traditionally, men are habitual of drink, *chilam* and chewing tobacco, so they spent their earning on these things. Earlier, they drink self made liquor, but exposure to outer world introduced them with country liquor and English wine. They use these drink and spend their earning, in few cases man spends his wife earning for drink. When man gets over drunk, he fights with his wife which affects the next day wage work. Continuously, absent is wage work is common for men because most of the time they are drunk. In this way the responsibility of child, essential things survive, etc. are took by women. If child become ill, women have to walk on foot for a long distance for treatment. Shortage of money pulls them to borrow money. Today, Baiga women are facing many problems which can be said as:

(i) Labourious lifestyle.
(ii) Health Problem.
(iii) Stressful life.
(iv) Needs and struggle in changed environment.
(v) Indebtedness.

Excess hard labour is problematic itself and responsible for many minor and major illness. Changing environment has raised their desire and necessity; they want to live like non-tribals which has increased their expenditure. They are now facing socio-economic insecurity. Their education, health and livelihood is matter of concern. Government has implemented several developmental programmes and schemes, but these are insignificant for desired change. Although development can be seen among them, but there is a need to better interference for their social security, education security, health security and food security. The most important security that should be provided is livelihood security because it is the base of all security.

REFERENCES

Chaudhary, S.N. (2010): *Tribal Economy at Crossroads*, Jaipur: Rawat.
Khera, P.D. (1991): "The Baiga and Sal Forest", *India of Minor Forest Produce.*
Elwin, V. (1939): *The Baiga*, London: John Murrey.

17

Social and Economic Development among Bharias of Patalkot: A Sociological Exploration

Sunil Kumar Yadav

Introduction

Social change is a multi-dimensional and complex process which occurs in all society irrespective of their structure, rigidity and stage of development. Many scholars have given their theories on social change which are categorized as evolutionary, cyclic, functionalist or dynamic and conflict theories. As per the view of these scholars, the term social change is used to indicate the changes that take place in human interactions and inter-relations. This work is an assessment of social change in context of development so, it can be said that any change can be termed as development when it occurs in a desirable dimension and direction. While change results in modification or alteration or replacement of the old with the new ones, development aims to achieve human well-being. Economic change is a transformation that occurs within an economy that increases, sustains or depletes its vitality. India is a country known for its diversity in terms of language, culture and socio-economic condition, etc. Among these diverse communities tribal is one which are being said to be backward and marginalized from colonial period to till date. The concept of 'Tribe' is a colonial construct concept which is ambiguous itself and further compounded with the term 'Primitive'. The uses and definitions of tribe in sociological and anthropological literature are varied and conflicting; some scholars appear to define it on the basis of common language, other on common culture, some on basis of ancestral lineage and others on common Government rulers. It was called with various names by scholars like backward *hindus*, *adivasi*, *janjati*, *adimjati*, etc. In Constitution of India, it is also not defined but as per the Article 342 of the Constitution of India any tribe listed in the Constitution of India are scheduled tribe (Xaxa, 2008). According to Tribal Annual Report 2014-15 nearly 748 such communities spread over States and UTs of India. Since, these groups were termed as backward and marginalized, developmental measures including programmes and activities meant for the uplift and progress of tribal people were initiated. In due course, various committees were constituted to evaluate the status of development among tribal people. In 1961, The Dhebar Commission, in its report identified four different layers in tribal community and the class of tribal at the base in an extremely under-developed stage (Dhebar Commission Report, 1961). The study team under the chairmanship of P. Shilu Ao reiterated the view of Dhebar Commission showing concern about a marked development imbalance among the tribal communities. They advocated that the lower layer needed the utmost consideration and should be made the special concern of the State Government. The study team also included a list of backward tribal communities (Shilu Ao Report, 1969). On the eve of the Fifth Five Year Plan, it was recognized that special programme should be taken up for the primitive group on the line of Shilu Ao team. In 1975, Ministry of Home Affairs, Government of India organized a workshop to outline criteria to identify primitive tribe. The proceedings of the workshop was later edited by S. Sinha and B.D. Sharma and published by Ministry of Home Affairs in 1977 titled 'Primitive Tribe: The First Step' which is the first official document on primitive tribe. On the basis of debate occurred in the workshop the Government came out with criteria to categorize any tribe as primitive and these criteria are:

1. Prc-agricultural stage,
2. Low or stagnant population growth, and
3. Extremely low level of literacy.

Any group/community fulfils any or more criteria will be termed as 'Primitive Tribe' (now known as Particularly Vulnerable Tribal Group). At present there are 75 such communities reside in 18 States and one UT in India (Annual Report, 2014-15).

Particularly Vulnerable Tribal Group in Madhya Pradesh

There were seven tribal communities were identified as primitive tribe in undivided Madhya Pradesh, after creation of new State Chhattisgarh three tribal communities remain in Madhya Pradesh which are as under:

1. Bharia of Patalkot in Chhindwara;
2. Baiga in Mandla, Dindori, Balaghat, Umaria and Shahdol; and
3. Saharia in Gwalior, Datia, Morena, Bhind, Shivpuri, Guna, Ashoknagar and Sheopur.

The Bharia of Patalkot call themselves "Bharia" distinguishing themselves from the Bharia outside the Patalkot who call themselves "Bhariya Bhumiya", Bhumiya means 'owner, lord or master' of the soil but the meaning of Bhariya is obscure (Kurup, 1985). It is simple meaning can be taken as '*bhar*' or 'weight', the Bharia then so called load carriers or coolies. Bharias have forgotten about their affinity so knowledge about their origin is apparent, one of the stories of origin says that Arjun, when matters were going badly with the Pandavas in their battle against Kauravas, took up a handful of *bharru* grass and, pressing it produced men who fought in the battle and became the ancestors of the Bharias. Russel and Hiralal consider that Bharia is the contemptuous form of *Bhar* and belong to the great *Bhar* tribe who were once dominant in the eastern part of the United Provinces (Russell and Hiralal, 1916). One of the stories says that when the Maratha territories were taken over by the British, Raghuji III hide in the Patalkot and men who carried belongings of Raghuji III settled there and they are now called Bharias.

Baiga is one of the primitive tribe of Madhya Pradesh basically survive on collection of forest produce. The term '*Baiga*' means priest and the tribe is also called *panda*. Catchment of Narmada is their habitat which includes district of Balaghat, Bilaspur, Mandla, Rajnandgaon and Shahdol, but their main concentration is in the Tehsil of Baihar, Bilaspur, Dindori, Mandla, Niwas, Gaurela and Pushprajgarh (Debnath, 2005). It is divided into three sub-groups namely — Bhinjhwar, Bharoti and Narotia.

The Saharias are considered to be member of Kolarian group and a sub-branch of the Bhils. Living in north-western part of Madhya Pradesh the community is placed under the category of primitive tribes. The members of this tribe mainly live in Shivpuri, Guna, Gwalior, Morena, Bhind, Vidisha, Raisen, Sehore and Bundeli Janpad. They also live in Kota, Shahbad and Kishanganj areas of Rajasthan.

As it had been earlier mentioned that developmental initiatives for tribal had began in Colonial period, after Independence various programmes and projects have been implemented and several are going on, but still the tribe are at the bottom of development ladder and PVTGs are more backward. Taking this into account special assistance programmes have been formulated for PVTGs development. The study focused the Bharia community of Patalkot with the objective to outline the socio-economic changes among them.

Schemes for Tribal Development

Under Article 275(1) of the Constitution of India special central assistance is given to States/UTs to supplement their efforts for tribal development in tribal sub-plan area which are basically meant for family oriented income-generating schemes in the sectors of agriculture, horticulture, minor irrigation, soil conservation, animal husbandry, forests, education, cooperatives, fisheries, village and small scale industries.

Fourteen Tribal Research Institute (TRIs) have been set-up by Andhra Pradesh, Assam, Bihar, Gujarat, Kerala, Madhya Pradesh, Maharashtra, Odisha, Rajasthan, Tamil Nadu, West Bengal, Uttar Pradesh, Manipur and Tripura to provide planning inputs to the State Government for tribal development. In the field of education development various schemes are being implemented — Girls and Boys hostels for STs were constructed under Third Five Year Plan to provide residential facility, Asharams Schools were opened in Tribal sub-plan area, vocational training centres were opened in tribal areas, Tribal Cooperative Marketing Development Federation of India Limited (TRIFED) was set up in 1987 by Government of India to provide marketing assistance and remunerative prices to ST communities for their minor forest produce and surplus agriculture produce, various scholarship and fellowships are being provided to ST candidates as economical support for education, coaching classes are being held for ST students, grant-in-aid is given to voluntary organizations working for tribal welfare.

Besides these schemes, a central sector scheme was introduced in 1998-99 for the all-round development of PVTGs covering housing, infrastructure development, social security, insurance, etc. In 2007-08 a comprehensive long-term 'Conservation-*cum*-Development (CCD) Plans' have been formulated for Eleventh Five Year Plan Period which envisages a synergy between efforts of State Government and Non-Governmental Organizations. Development agencies for PVTGs have been established in 1978 to monitor the developmental schemes in tribal sub-plan area, to conduct survey, etc. There are eleven such developmental agencies are set-up in Madhya Pradesh — Bharia Development Agency in Tamia, Chhindwara District, Saharia Development Agency at Gwalior, Sheopur, Shivpuri and Guna; and Baiga Development Agency at Mandla, Dindori, Shahdol, Umaria, Pushprajgarh and Baihar.

Objective

The broad objectives of the study are:

1. To know the socio-economic changes among the Bharia of Patalkot;
2. To find out the leading and impeding factors of development; and
3. To analyze the criterion of their identification as PVTG in comparison to other tribal community residing in Patalkot.

Methodology

The study is based on field observation and a review to the earlier studies, carried to explore the problems and perspective of Bharias development residing in the Patalkot. The infrastructural availability at villages, lifestyle of villagers, resource availability, outcome of institutional input, etc. are also analyzed. Group interview was also carried to pin-point the issues of development. Secondary sources data such as, report by Bharia Development Agency, NGOs report, census report and any Governmental or Non-Governmental data relating to Patalkot were also used in the study.

Study Area

Madhya Pradesh occupying geographical the central position in the country. It was created in 1956 as a result of reorganization of States merging Madhya Bharat, Vindhya Pradesh and Bhopal with Bhopal as its capital. In November 2000, the south-eastern portion of the State was split to form a new State of Chhattisgarh. Thus, the present Madhya Pradesh come into existence, the second largest State in the country after Rajasthan, spread over a geographical area of about 308 lakh hectare. It is a part of peninsular plateau of India lying in north central part, whose boundary can be classified in the north by the plains of Ganga-Yamuna, in the west by the Aravali, east by the Chhattisgarh plain and in the south by the Tapti valley and the plateau of Maharashtra. The topography of the State can be defined by Narmada-Son valley and can be divided into three physiographic regions, i.e. Central highland, Satpura-Maikal ranges and the eastern plateau. It is a medley of ethnic groups and tribes, castes and communities. In term of ethnic groups and tribes the State has the largest tribal population in the country. As per Census 2011, it has 15,316,784 tribal population belongs to 43 tribal groups and sub-groups (Annual Report, 2014-15). The scheduled tribe constitutes 21.1 per cent population of the state which is dominated by *Gond*, *Bhil* and *Korku* tribe.

The State is predominantly rural because nearly 72.4 per of population reside in villages (Census, 2011). As per census 2011 the State has 54,903 villages, 23,012 *gram-panchayats*, 313 developmental blocks, 342 sub-districts, 50 districts and 10 divisions. The sex ratio of the state is 931 per 1,000 male

Chhindwara

Chhindwara is situated at 2,236 feet above sea level on Satpura Plateau (Kalia, 1972). The district spread over 11,815 sq.km. Of area (District Census Handbook, 2011) lying between 21°28' and 22°49' North and 78°10' and 79°24' East (Russel, 1907). It is surrounded, on the north by Hoshangabad and Narsingpur districts, on the east, by Seoni district, on the south by Nagpur and towards the west, by Betul district (Kalia, 1972). Looking at the history of district, it appears to have been ruled by the Nandas, Mauryas, Sungas, Vakatakas, the Kalachuri's and the Gond rulers (Russel, 1907). The early history of the district is vested in obscurity, but the authentic history of the district begins from the sixteen century when parts of the district fell under the domination of the rising Gond dynasty of Deogarh. After the fall of Deogarh dynasty Chhindwara formed part of the Bhonsla kingdom of Nagpur. Then, Marathas had dominancy over the area (Russel, 1907). In British India Chhindwara was formed as the annexation of the Nagpur state in 1854 and at first belonged to the Nagpur Division. After the formation of the Central Provinces in 1861, Chhindwara was transferred to Nerbudda division with headquarter at Betul, only for a year. It formed part of Nagpur Commissionery since 31st October, 1931, immediately after the abolition of Nerbudda Commissionery. The Commissioner system was abolished in old Madhya Bharat on 1st November, 1948. Chhindwara district became a part of Jabalpur division after the creation of new Madhya Pradesh on 1st November, 1956.

As per census 2011, the number of Tehsils in the district is 12, there are 11 Development Blocks and number of villages is 1965. The district occupies 8th place in the State according to population with having 20,90,922 persons in 4,42,366 households (District Census Handbook, 2011). The scheduled tribe population is 7,69,778 constituting 36.82 per cent of district population. The literacy of the district is 71.16 per cent which is higher than the State literacy rate, i.e. 69.32 per cent. Economy of the district is mainly dependent on agriculture and when we look at the figure then find that 29.55 per cent and 44.12 per cent workers are cultivators and agricultural labourers respectively (District Census Handbook, 2011).

Tamia Development Block

It is situated at an altitude between 1,771 feet to 4,200 feet above sea level and is bounded on the north by district Hoshangabad, on the west by Mahadeo hills, on the east by Dulhadeo hills and on the south by Parasia and Chhindwara coal mines (Kalia, 1972). It is completely rural spread over 1,282.68 sq.km. Of area having 191 villages (District Census Handbook, 2011). There are 23,290 households in the block with 1,14,176 persons (Census, 2011). The scheduled tribe population of Tamia is 89,431 from 17,549 households. The main tribes living in the Block are Gond, Bharia, Pardhan and Korku. Gonds are numerically largest and Bharia, who are supposed to be most primitive and one among the three particularly vulnerable tribal groups are mainly concentrated in Patalkot region where they earn their livelihood through collection of minor forest produce and agriculture partially.

Patalkot

Patalkot is a "bowl-shaped valley, the home of the *Bharia* tribe is situated approximately between 22°24' and 22°26' North, and between 78°40' and 79°10' East is about 31 sq. miles in area falls under the Tamia Development Block (Russell, 1907). It is a land locked area and is surrounded by lofty hills of Satpura ranges except a narrow opening from which a stream (Dudhi River) is flowing to the north (Kalia, 1972). The hills around the Patalkot valley rises to about 1,500 ft. below the general elevation and is deeper when it falls to river beds (Russell, 1907). Maikal ranges of Satpuras hemmed in the valley. Motur range in the east of Patalkot, Kabahad in the south-east, on the north-west the range continues beyond Lotia and Batkakhapa and is called Dulhadeo mountain. So far as number of villages under Patalkot is concerned, there are different views among researchers and enumerators. While some say that its number is 12 of which one village is uninhabited today, others (Dixit, 1999) document 29 villages. Hopefully this variation is because of inclusion of small hamlets as an independent village. In the same way there is difference about number of families and size of the population. According to Dixit (*op. cit.*) during 2000 there were total 474 households with having 2,694 persons in all the villages, of which

384 households and 2,060 persons belonged to *Bharia* tribe. On this basis it may be said that more than 90 per cent population of Patalkot is of Bharia.

The inhabitants of these villages are Gonds and Bharias who were practicing shifting cultivation (Kalia, 1972), but they are now has moved as settled cultivators with State interventions. There are 796 households in these twelve villages comprising 3,835 persons in which 1,923 are males and 1,912 are females (Census, 2011). As per census 1981, the total population of Patalkot was 1,664 in which Bharias were 1,589 and the rest was Gond, it means 98.5 per cent population was Bharias. As per the survey conducted by Bharia Development Agency Tamia in 2009-10, the population of Bharia is 2,665 which is nearly 70 per cent of Patalkot population. As documented by Tiwari (1985) 12 villages found in Patalkot are as given in Table 17.1.

Table 17.1: Details of Patalkot Villages

Sl. No.	*Gram Panchayat*	*Village*	*Total HH*	*Total Population*	*Bharia HH*	*Bharia Population*
(1)	(2)	(3)	(4)	(5)	(6)	(7)
1.	Kaream Rated	Chimtipur	49	250	19	85
		Ghogri Gujjadogri	15	80	0	0
		Kaream Rated	110	539	104	556
		Palani Gaildubba	65	361	35	158
		Total	**239**	**1,230**	**148**	**799**
2.	Ghatlinga	Ghana Saldhana Kodia	107	523	57	342
		Ghatlinga	133	486	62	247
		Gudhichhatri	69	300	47	300
		Total	**309**	**1,309**	**166**	**889**
3.	Harrakachhar	Dhurni Malni Domni	41	180	10	56
		Jadmadal Harrakachhar	68	342	41	188
		Jhiran	1	6	0	0
		Khamarpur Sehra Pachgol	104	597	95	472
		Sukhabhand Harmau	34	171	33	157
		Total	**248**	**1,296**	**179**	**873**
		Grand Total	**796**	**3,835**	**503**	**2,561**

Source: For Columns 2, 6 and 7 — *Survey Report 2009-10*, Bharia Development Agency, Tamia, Chhindwara, Madhya Pradesh.
For Column 3 — Tewari, D.N. (1985): *Primitives Tribes of Madhya Pradesh*, New Delhi, Government of India.
For Columns 4 and 5 — *Primary Census Abstract, 2011*, Office of the Registrar General of India, New Delhi.

Findings and Discussion

The theories of social change talks about broadly two factors responsible for any change — 'endogenous' and 'exogenous' or 'internal' and 'external'. Internal forces exist within the society, but external forces refer to influence emanating from the presence of other societies in a given society's environment. Since, the study is an indirectly overlook of impact of institutional intervention in Bharia community so changes occurred in influence of NGOs, civil societies and Government intervention through programmes and schemes were analyzed in the study. A.M. Kurup had studied the socio-economic change in Bharia community in 1985, which picturized the changes occurred in socio-economic life of Bharia people. For him, Bharia had moved from '*lamjhana*' (marriage by service) and '*ghusri*' (marriage by intrusion) to arrange marriage, shifting cultivation which was called '*dahia*' to settled cultivation, traditional cloth to modern cloth (pent-shirt for men and *saree*-blouse for women), etc. Tewari (1985) also noticed improvement in education of Bharia. Kalia (1972) also mentioned the changes occurred due to interventions. These studies were the pioneer of Bharia community studies which unveil the inadequate development among Bharias. Even the studies conducted after the initiation of special assistance programmes for PVTGs development depicts the picture of their development is not satisfactory. Some of the studies of PVTGs in general and Bharia in particular reveals their socio-economic development.

Mahapatra (1978) in the study of Santhal found slow and halting modernization of agriculture. Study of Narayan (1992) reveals the inadequate development of Sauria Paharia due to their strict adherence to old tradition. Lack of awareness among people, inadequate infrastructural development, etc. were found by Duary (2005) among *Lodha*, *Kheria* and *Birhor*. Srivastava (2007) found noticeable condition of indicators of PVTGs. A comparative analysis of two tribes residing in two distinct cultural and political settings was presented by Khera (2008). As per Khera, an active political setting worked in desirable manner of development. Stagnant development was emphasized in Lanjia Saoras by Tripathy (2011). Health status of *Bharia*, *Baiga* and *Saharia* was found poor by Debnath (2012). Sisodia and Dalpati (2012) found ill functioning of developmental scheme. There are several more studies which explore the change and development among particularly vulnerable tribal groups and also highlighted the lagging factor. Similarly, Bharia community is also in the phase of change and there are also lagging and promoting factors with them. Since, Bharia of Patalkot is identified as a particularly vulnerable tribal group on basis of criterion for PVTGs, three major criteria, viz. pre-agricultural technology, extremely low level of literacy, stagnant population growth are going to be discussed with the focus on infrastructural development and resource availability.

Agriculture

Land, manpower and agricultural inputs are the three major basic requirements for cultivation. As far as land is concerned it should be suitable for cultivation, it means fertility, topography, irrigation facility, etc. should be proper, the manpower should have skill of agriculture and agricultural inputs refers to good variety of seed, fertilizer, pesticide, agricultural tools and machines. Patalkot is spread over 31 sq. miles which includes both Government and private land. In private land the agricultural land availability of all the twelve villages is as shown in Table 17.2.

Table 17.2: Agricultural Land in Patalkot (in acre)

Sl. No.	*Village*	*Land (in acre)*	*Irri-gated*	*Non-irri-gated*	*Percent-age of Irrigated Land*	*Fallow Land*	*Fallow for 2-5 Yrs.*	*Fallow for above 5 Yrs.*
1.	Chimtipur	87.9	7.3	80.6	8.3	12.5	0.7	1.4
2.	Ghogri Gujjadogri	40.7	5.7	35.0	14	3.8	1.6	0.2
3.	Kareamrated	294.7	55.7	239.0	18.9	49.8	20.4	9.0
4.	Palani Gaildubba	496.2	123.8	372.4	24.9	89.3	44.8	5.9
5.	Ghana Saldhana Kodia	218.0	34.2	183.8	15.6	8.0	11.8	11.2
6.	Ghatlinga	446.3	32.7	413.6	7.3	28.2	17.2	0.3
7.	Gudichhatri	197.9	28.8	169.1	14.5	4.4	4.4	24.8
8.	Dhurni Malni Domni	33.7	0.8	32.9	2.3	0.6	0	0.1
9.	Jadmadal Harrakachhar	219.8	9.9	209.9	4.5	5.5	0.2	8.5
10.	Jhiran	6.9	1.9	5.0	27.5	0	0.2	0.1
11.	Khamarpur Sehra Pachgol	195.0	41.3	153.7	21.1	3.0	0	15.9
12.	Sukhabhand Harmau	58.6	0.7	57.9	1.1	0.4	0.2	3.2
	Total	**2,295.7**	**342.8**	**1952.9**	**14.9**	**205.5**	**101.5**	**80.6**

Note: The data are converted from hectare to acre and one number after decimal is taken so there may be slightly variation.

Source: http//:www.landrecords.mp.gov.in (date: 09/07/2015)

Only 14.9 per cent of total agricultural land is irrigated in the twelve villages of Patalkot. While field observation very few people were found irrigating their field with motor pump and sprinkler, few irrigating their field with pipe connecting at the bottom of pit made under waterfall, majority of the villagers are unable to irrigate their field due to lack of water sources and equipment of irrigation. This compels them to depend on rainfall so they only cultivate *Kharif* crops in which maize (*Zea mays*), French bean (*balhar*) (*Phaseolus vulgaris*) and *kutki* (*Picrorhiza kurroa*) are the main. A negligible portion of villagers grow wheat. The land of Patalkot is hilly and it becomes very difficult to plough the field. They do not have good breed of bull to plough the field and tractor is neither affordable for them nor do suitable for uneven land.

Settled cultivation is an imposed change and they are not much aware of the modern agriculture due to lack of training and proper knowledge. Although agricultural equipments are distributed and they are trained to use such equipments, but the unfavourable environment make them useless. They are not unwilling to adopt the modern agriculture but the uneven terrain, heap of stones in field, lack of irrigation facilities, etc. pull them back. Government is distributing agricultural equipments, seeds, fertilizers, etc. and providing in subsidized rates through developmental programme for agricultural development, but land quality and irrigation resources has been neglected. An area, which has poor quality of soil, undulating land, absence of irrigation facilities and small land holding per family can hardly acquire subsistence economy. Other potentials of the area should also be focused for development and to provide subsistence economy. Small scale industries should be promoted, since broom making and bamboo work is near to be vanished from Patalkot, since, area is rich in medicinal herbs its plantation should be promoted on commercial basis, wild mango (*Mangifera indica*) trees are found in significant number so improved variety of mango can be promoted for commercial purpose and plantation of economic species trees should be promoted.

Education

The educational status of tribal community is considered to be lagging in comparison to non-tribal community, the situation of tribal of Patalkot in general and Bharia in particular is same. Government has initiated several programmes for education improvement and Ashrams schools have been opened in tribal areas for their development. It has passed several decades of developmental initiations and the condition of Patalkot is still unsatisfactory. The infrastructural development for improvement in education is not as per the requirement. The availability of schools/ colleges in Patalkot is showing in Table 17.3.

Table 17.3: Availability of School/Colleges in Patalkot

Sl. No.	*Village*	*Primary School*	*Middle School*	*High School*	*H. Sec. School*	*Other*
1.	Chimtipur	2	1	—	—	—
2.	Ghogri Gujjadogri	1	—	—	—	—
3.	Kareamrated	2	—	—	—	—
4.	Palani Gaildubba	1	1	—	—	—
5.	Ghana Saldhana Kodia	2	—	—	—	—
6.	Ghatlinga	1	1	1	—	—
7.	Gudichhatri	1	—	—	—	—
8.	Dhurni Malni Domni	—	—	—	—	—
9.	Jadmadal Harrakachhar	2	1	—	—	—
10.	Jhiran	-	—	—	—	—
11.	Khamarpur Sehra Pachgol	1	—	—	—	—
12.	Sukhabhand Harmau	1	—	—	—	—
	Total	**14**	**4**	**1**	**0**	**0**

Source: http://www.educationportal.mp.gov.in (date: 09/07/2015)

There are only fourteen primary schools available in Patalkot, four middle schools, only one high school. There is no higher secondary school and facility for higher education was found. Children have to go out of the village for middle school and higher education. The area is situated in a valley and there is no means of transportation, so, they have to walk several kilometres on foot through hilly slopes and plain, this regular walking make them tired and become factor of severe diseases. In rainy season, it becomes very difficult to go to school which is also a factor of absenteeism. Their economical condition is not so, well that they can afford fare where vehicle is available. All the villages have Ashram schools, but not for upto the higher secondary class, for higher secondary they have to go Ashram schools of Jabalpur and Indore. The conditions of these Asharam schools is not so good as Duary (2005) mentioned in his study of Birhor that hostels made by Government for tribal children were unhygienic for living and did not have proper infrastructure, the distribution of educational equipment like blackboard, chalk, pencil, slates, etc. were inadequate. Although Government has made arrangement of free and compulsory education under developmental policies but there are so many expenditures which are not bearable for the guardian who is struggling to earn livelihood. Their economy majorly depends upon minor forest produce, they collect minor forest produce and sale it to the market in instalment whenever they require money. In condition of produce failure, they struggle for day to day bread. Community, which is struggling day to day to earn bread for family, it is difficult to expend money on education. Livelihood security is the main necessity for them which should be fulfilled first to make them think of other like education and health.

Health

Before going through the health related problems of Bharia of Patalkot, let have a look on infrastructural availability (Table 17.4)

Table 17.4: Health Centres/Hospitals in Patalkot Villages

Sl. No.	*Village*	*SHC*	*PHC*	*CHC Hospital*	*Govt. Clinic*	*Private*
1.	Chimtipur	—	—	—	—	—
2.	Ghogri Gujjadogri	—	—	—	—	—
3.	Kareamrated	—	—	—	—	—
4.	Palani Gaildubba	1	1	—	—	—
5.	Ghana Saldhana Kodia	—	—	—	—	—
6.	Ghatlinga	1	—	—	—	—
7.	Gudichhatri	—	—	—	—	—
8.	Dhurni Malni Domni	—	—	—	—	—
9.	Jadmadal Harrakachhar	1	—	—	—	—
10.	Jhiran	—	—	—	—	—
11.	Khamarpur Sehra Pachgol	—	—	—	—	—
12.	Sukhabhand Harmau	—	—	—	—	—
	Total	**3**	**1**	**—**	**—**	**—**

Note: SHC — Sub Health Centre, PHC — Public Health Centre, CHC — Community Health Centre.

Source: http://www.health.mp.gov.in (date: 09/07/2015)

The infrastructure of health improvement is not upto the mark in the Patalkot. There is one Public Health Centre (PHC) in Gaildubba, Sub-Health Centres are in Gaildubba, Ghatlinga and Harrakachhar. They have to depend on *anganwadi*, ASHAs and their traditional way of healing for any treatment. Community health centre and Government hospital is far away from the village. Transportation facility is very poor in that areas, even few *dhanas* (small section of village) are situated in very remote area which can be reached only through *zig-zag* path of hilly terrain. If any person becomes ill, firstly he is traditionally treated at home, when the situation becomes out of control only then person is carried to the hospital for treatment. This delay in treatment sometime causes death of the person. Bharia are also not much aware about diseases and cause of disease. Their diet is not as per the recommended diet allowance (RDA), their diet mainly consisted of cereals (maize and *kutki*), they rarely consume pulses, bathua (*Chenopodium album*), *poari* and *dobai* are used as green vegetables. French bean is used as both vegetable and pulse. Sugar, jaggery, fat and oil consumption is very low, intake of milk is low and only consume in tea. Their diet is also lacking in nutrients like calorie, minerals, etc. This has resulted into malnutrition of Bharias. Pregnant and lactating mother does not take any supplement food.

The infrastructural development in Patalkot for improvement in their health, education and to provide a subsistence economy is inadequate. Firstly, the Government should develop proper infrastructure then should make them aware about education, good health and modern agriculture. Non-tribal communities are not untouched with the health problems, problems in field of education like drop out, absenteeism, etc., but they have options and facilities because of proper infrastructure and tribal areas should also have such facilities.

Gond is another tribal community resides in the Villages of Patalkot, Gond population constitutes nearly 30 per cent of total population of Patalkot. In some of the villages, more than fifty per cent population is Gond — Jadmadal Harrakachhar, Dhurni Malni Domni and Chimtipur. Their socio-economic status is more or less equivalent to Bharia. They avail the benefits of schemes for tribal development but Bharia population is benefitted with the special packages for PVTGs beside schemes of tribal development. Bharia has been declared as PVTG, but Gond not instead they share the same resource and infrastructure availability. They live in same geographical area, cultivate the same hilly terrain with the available resource, they also collect the forest produce. Their children go to the same school and have to travel a long distance for middle and high school education. As far as health is concerned they too depend on traditional medicinal herb and go to the same health centres for treatment. It is a matter of concern why they are not included in PVTGs list. If Gond of Madhya Pradesh has better socio-economic status in comparison to other tribal communities, it cannot be said that Gond of Patalkot has also better socio-economic status. Even Bharias residing in villages at periphery of Patalkot like Srijhont, Phansidhana, Karrapani, Dongra, etc. do not have better socio-economic and health status.

REFERENCES

Debnath, D. (2012): "Tribal Health and Nutrition (Socio-ecological Issues and Ways Ahead in Contemporary Participatory Process of Natural Resource Management)", in S.N. Chaudhary (ed.), *Tribal Health and Nutrition*, Jaipur: Rawat Publication, pp. 212-24.

Debnath, D. (2005): "Role of Not-timber Forest Products in Traditional Economic System and Cultural Practices of a Primitive Tribal Group — The Baiga Caste of Mandla District in Madhya Pradesh" in Sarit K. Chaudhari and Sucheta Sen Chaudhari (ed.), *Primitive Tribes in Contemporary India*, New Delhi: Mittal Publication, pp. 85-100.

Dhebar, U.N. (1961): *The Scheduled Area and Scheduled Tribes Commission (Dhebar Commission)*, New Delhi: Government of India.

Dixit, D.N. (1993): *Patalkot ki Bharia Janjati mein Striyo ki Sthiti Evam Bhoomika*, Bhopal: Hindi Granth Academy.

Duary, Nabakumar, (2005): "Economy and Education Among The PTGs in West Bengal", in Sarit, K. Chaudhari and Sucheta Sen Chaudhari (ed.), *Primitive Tribes in Contemporary India*, New Delhi: Mittal Publication, pp. 297-313.

Government of India (2014-15): *Annual Report*, New Delhi: Ministry of Tribal Welfare and Development.

Government of India (2011): *Census Report*, Delhi: Office of the Registrar General and Census Commissioner.

Government of Madhya Pradesh (2011): *District Census Handbook — Chhindwara*, Bhopal: Directorate of Census Operations.

Government of Madhya Pradesh (2009-10): *Survey Report*, Tamia: Bharia Development Agency.

http://www.educationportal.mp.gov.in

http://www.health.mp.gov.in

http://www.landrecords.mp.gov.in

http://www.mptribalmuseum.com

Kalia, S.L. (1972): "Survey Report of District Chhindwara", *Bulletin of the Tribal Research Institute*, Vol. X, Nos. 1 and 2, pp. 1-10.

Khera, Reetika, (2008): "Starvation Deaths and Primitive Tribal Groups", *Economic and Political Weekly*, Vol. XLIII No. 52, December 27, pp. 11-14.

Kurup, A.M. (1985): *Continuity and Change in a Little Community: A Study of the Bharias of Patalkot in Madhya Pradesh*, New Delhi: Concept Publishing Company.

Mahapatra, Sitakant, (1978): "Modernization of Tribal Agriculture: Technological and Cultural Constraints", *Economic and Political Weekly*, Vol. XII, No. 13, April 1, pp. 581-85.

Narayan, S. (1992): "Development and Tradition in a Primitive Tribe", in Buddhadeb Chaudhari (ed.), *Tribal Transformation in India, Vol. II Socio-economic and Ecological Development*, Delhi: Mittal Publication, pp. 146-54.

Russel, R.V. (1907): (ed.), *Central Provinces District Gazetteers*, Chhindwara District, Mumbai.

Russel, R.V. and Rai Bahadur Hiralal (1916): *The Tribes and Castes of the Central Provinces of India*, Vol. II, London: Muray.

Shilu Aao, P. (1969): *Shilu Ao Commission Report*, New Delhi: Government of India.

Sisodia, Yatindra Singh and Tapas, Dalpati (2012): "Saharia Primitive Tribal Group in Madhya Pradesh: Critical Evaluation of Welfare Measures Related to Health", in

S.N. Chaudhary (ed.), *Tribal Health and Nutrition*, Jaipur: Rawat Publication, pp. 173-84.

Srivastava, V.K. (2007): *The Pahari Korwa: Socio-economic Condition and Their Development*, New Delhi: Sonali Publications.

Tewari, D.N. (1985): *Primitive Tribes of Madhya Pradesh*, New Delhi: Government of India, Ministry of Home Affairs, Tribal Development Division.

Tripathy, S.N. (2011): "Problems of Marginalization and the Exclusion: A Study of Primitive Tribes In Eastern India (Odisha)", in Rajas Parchure, S.N. Tripathy and J.R. Ambewadikar (ed.), *Excluded People in India: Problems and Prospects*, New Delhi: Manglam Publishers and Distributors, pp. 18-55.

Xaxa, Virginius (2008): *State, Society and Tribes: Issues in Post-colonial India*, New Delhi: Pearson Education India.

INDEX